COMPARATIVE CONTRACT LAW ENGLAND, FRANCE, GERMANY

COMPARATIVE CONTRACT LAW ENGLAND, FRANCE, GERMANY

P. D. V. Marsh

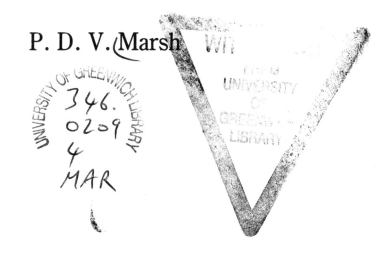
Gower

The text reflects the law as at 30 September 1993.

Published by
Gower Publishing
Gower House
Croft Road
Aldershot
Hampshire GU11 3HR
England

Gower
Old Post Road
Brookfield
Vermont 05036
USA

Reprinted 1996

British Library Cataloguing in Publication Data
Marsh, P. D. V.
  Comparative Contract Law : England, France,
  Germany
  I. Title
  346.02

  ISBN 0–566–09006–6

Library of Congress Cataloging-in-Publication Data
Marsh, P. D. V.
    Comparative contract law : England, France, Germany /
  P. D. V. Marsh.
      p.   cm.
    ISBN 0–568–09006–6
    1. Contracts—Great Britain.   2. Contracts—France.
    3. Contracts—Germany.   I. Title.
  —Germany.   I. Title.
  KJC1720.M37   1994
  348'.02–dc20
  [342.82]   93–37358
                                                                     CIP

Typeset in Century Old Style by
Raven Typesetters, Chester
and printed in Great Britain by Antony Rowe Ltd, Chippenham, Wiltshire

Contents

Preface

The inspiration for this book came from the time I spent establishing and negotiating contracts, primarily under French law, for the fixed equipment for the Channel Tunnel Project. That experience showed the lack of understanding on both sides of the Channel of commercial people and their professional advisers of the legal system and substantive laws prevailing in the other country. For example, French and Germans could not understand that under English law a tender expressed to be binding for a fixed period could be withdrawn at any time before acceptance. Their English counterparts were equally surprised at the scope under both continental systems of pre-contractual obligations and the virtual inability under French law of professional sellers, even in a business contract, to limit their liabilities for latent defects.

It is that gap in understanding which I hope this book will fill so as to give business people and their lawyers an awareness both of the opportunities which the foreign legal system offers them, and the pitfalls which they must seek to avoid. It is not a substitute for specialist legal advice, which should always be sought when negotiating a complex contract subject to a foreign law. However, it should also provide, to business people and lawyers alike, an informed basis and focus for the obtaining of such advice.

To keep the work within manageable bounds its scope has been restricted to the three most significant contracts: those for the sale of goods, for the carrying out of construction and engineering works, and for the provision of services. Further it is limited to contracts between business organizations and does not cover contracts with consumers which is now a specialized area of law in its own right.

The treatment of English law is more extensive than is perhaps necessary for the English reader, but it is my hope that this will make the book equally of interest to our French and German colleagues in showing them the essential differences between their contractual rights and liabilities under English law in comparison with those of their own system.

In writing a book of this nature I inevitably owe a debt to those who have preceded me, and I would like particularly to mention the classic works of Zweigert and Kotz, *An Introduction to Comparative Law*, and of Reinhard Zimmermann, *The Law of Obligations, Roman Foundations of the Civilian Tradition*. I would also like to thank Professor Jacques Ghestin of the University of Paris for the advice which I received from him when consulting him professionally and for his encouragement.

It remains only to thank my friends who have read through the parts dealing with their own legal system and corrected my errors: Guilhem de Löye, Directeur des Affaires Juridiques France Telecom, Direction Régionale Rhône-Alpes for the French text; Dr Gerhard Dannemann, Fellow in German law at the British Institute for Comparative and International Law for the German text; and Herr Klaus Boemke Dipl.-Ing/Architekt of the British VOB Club for the chapter dealing with German construction contracts and advice generally on the VOB conditions. Of course any errors and inaccuracies which remain are my own.

Translations are my own unless otherwise stated.

The law is given as at 30 September 1993.

P.D.V. Marsh

At p. 315 reference is made to the case of *Balfour Beattie Construction (Scotland)* v. *Scottish Power*. When the case came on appeal to the Inner House it was held, following the view expressed in the text, that the defendants must have been aware that an interruption in the pouring of the concrete would have caused a condemnation of the operations. However, on a further appeal to the House of Lords this judgement was reversed on the grounds that the Board, as suppliers of electricity, had no reason to be aware of the consequences which would follow such an interruption (*The Times*, 23 March 1994). The writer still considers this is to place the assumed knowledge of a business organization at too low a level.

List of Works cited by Author only

Abderrahmane, D.B., *Le Droit Allemand des Conditions Générales des Contrats dans les Ventes Commerciales Franco-Allemandes*, Librairie Générale de Droit et de Jurisprudence, Paris 1985.

Abrahamson, Max W., *Engineering Law and the I.C.E. Contracts*, 4th ed., Applied Science Publishers, London 1979.

Atiyah, P.S., *The Sale of Goods*, 8th ed., Pitman 1990.

The Rise and Fall of the Freedom of Contract, Clarendon Press, Oxford 1988.

Brierley, John E.C., *Major Legal Systems in the World Today*, Stevens, London 1985.

Brissaud, *History of French Private Law*, Rothman Reprints, New York 1968.

Brown, L.N., and Bell, John S., *French Administrative Law*, Butterworths 1993.

Buckland, W.W., *A Textbook of Roman Law*, 3rd ed., Cambridge University Press 1966.

Buckland, W.W., and McNair, A.D., *Roman Law and Common Law*, 2nd ed., Cambridge University Press 1974.

Caston, Albert, *La responsabilité des Constructeurs*, Editions du Moniteur, Paris 1989.

Cheshire, Fifoot and Furmstone (cited Cheshire), *Law of Contract*, 12th ed., Butterworths, London 1991.

Cohn, E.J., *Manual of German Law*, British Institute of International and Comparative Law, London 1968.

Cornu, G., *Vocabulaire Juridique*, Presses Universitaires de France 1990.

Dannemann, G., *Introduction to German Civil and Commercial Law*, British Institute of International and Comparative Law, London 1993.

David, R., *French Law*, Louisiana State University Press 1972.

David, R. and Pugsley, D., *Les Contrats en Droit Anglais*, Librairie Générale de Droit et de Jurisprudence, Paris 1985.

Dawson, John P., *The Oracles of the Law*, William S. Hein & Co., Buffalo, New York 1986.

Dufau, Jean, *Le Droit des Travaux Publics*, Editions du Moniteur, vol. 1, Paris 1988.

Fifoot, C.H.S., *History and Sources of the Common Law*, Stevens, London 1949.

Fontaine, Marcel (ed.) *Formation of Contracts and Pre-contractual Liability*, International Chamber of Commerce 1990.

Les Lettres d'Intention dans la Négociation des Contrats Internationaux, D.P.C.I., c/o Masson, Paris 1977.

Gauch, P. et al., *Selected Problems of Construction Law*, University Press, Fribourg 1983.

Ghestin, Jacques, *Traité de droit civil Les Obligations Le Contrat Formation*, 2nd ed., Librairie Générale de Droit et de Jurisprudence, Paris 1988.

Ghestin, Jacques and Bernard Desche, *Traité des Contrats La Vente*, Librairie Générale de Droit et de Jurisprudence, Paris 1990.

Ghestin, Jacques and Martin Billau, *Traité de Droit civil Les Obligations Les Effets du Contrat*, Librairie Générale de Droit et de Jurisprudence, Paris 1992.

Goff and Jones, *The Law of Restitution*, 3rd ed., Sweet and Maxwell, London 1986.

Harris, D., and Tallon, D., *Contract Law Today*, Clarendon Press, Oxford 1989.

Honnold, John, *Uniform Law for International Sales*, 2nd ed., Kluwer 1991.

Horn, Kotz and Lesser, tr. Tony Weir, *German Private and Commercial Law*, Clarendon Press, Oxford 1982.

Houin, R. and Pedamont, M., *Droit commercial*, 9th ed., Dalloz, Paris 1990.

Hudson (by I.N. Duncan Wallace), *Building and Engineering Contracts*, 10th ed., Sweet and Maxwell, London 1970.

Huebner, R., *A History of Germanic Private Law*, Rothman Reprints, Augustus M. Kelley, New York 1968.

Jauernig, Schlechtreim, Sturner, Teichmann Vollkommer, *Bürgerliches Gesetzbuch*, C.H. Beck, Munich 1990.

John, Michael, *Politics and the Law in Late Nineteenth Century Germany*, Clarendon Press, Oxford 1989.

Kahn-Freund, Levy, Rudden, *A Source Book on French Law*, 2nd ed., Clarendon Press, Oxford 1991.

Keating, Donald (by Sir Anthony May), *Building Contracts*, 5th ed., Sweet and Maxwell, London 1991.

Kelley, P. and Attree, R., *European Product Liability*, Butterworths 1992.

Langen, Eugen, *Transnational Commercial Law*, Sijthoff, Leiden 1973.

Levy, Jean-Philippe, *Histoire des Obligations*, Les Cours de Droit, Paris 1978.

Lloyd, Humphrey (ed.), *The Liability of Contractors*, Queen Mary College London, Longmans 1986.

Lorenz, W.W., 'Contracts for Work on Goods and Building Contracts' in Vol. VIII of the *Encyclopedia of Comparative Law*, The International Association of Legal Science.

Malaurie, Ph. and Aynes, L., *Droit civil Les Obligations*, Editions Cujas, Paris 1992. *Les Contrats Speciaux*, Editions Cujas, Paris 1991.

Malinvaud, Ph. and Jestaz, Ph., *Droit de la promotion immobilière*, 4th ed., Dalloz, Paris 1988.

Markesinis, B.S., *The German Law of Tort*, 2nd ed., Clarendon Press, Oxford 1990.

Mazeaud, Henri and Leon, Jean Mazeaud and Francois Chabas, *Leçons de droit civil* Book III, Vol. 2, *Principaux contrats vente et échange*, by Michel de Juglart, 7th ed., Montchrestien, Paris 1987; Book II, Vol. 1, *Obligations théorie générale*, by Francois Chabas, 8th ed., Montchrestien, Paris 1991.

Mousseron, J.M., *Technique Contractuelle*, Lefebvre, Paris 1988.

Nicholas, Barry, *The French Law of Contract*, 2nd ed., Oxford University Press 1992.

Pollock, Sir F. and Maitland, F.W., *The History of English Law*, 2nd ed., by S.F.C. Milson, re-issued Cambridge University Press 1968.

Ranke, F. and Boulin, S., *Guide Juridique et fiscal Republique Federale d'Allemagne*, CFCE, Paris 1990.

Robine, Eric, *La clause de réserve de propriété depuis la loi du 12 mai 1980*, Litec, Paris 1990.

Robinson et al., *An Introduction to European Legal History*, Professional Books Ltd, 1985.

Rodière, René, *Harmonisation du droit des affaires dans les pays du Marché Commun*, Editions A. Pedone, Paris:
Objet, Cause et Lesion du contrat, 1980
Les vices du consentement dans le contrat 1977
Les effets du contrat 1985
La Formation du contrat 1976.

Schlesinger, Rudolf B., Baade, Daaska and Herzog, *Comparative Law*, 5th ed., The Foundation Press, New York 1988.

Silberberg, Harry, *The German Standard Contracts Act*, Fritz Knapp Verlag, Frankfurt/Main 1979.

Simpson, *Legal Theory and Legal History*, Hambledon Press 1987.

Starck, B., Roland, H. and Boyer, L., *Droit civil Obligations*, vol. 2, *Contrat*, 2nd ed., Litec, Paris 1986.
Obligations, vol. 3, *Régime générale*, 4th ed., Litec, Paris 1992.

Szalewski, Joanna Schmidt, *Droit des contrats*, Litec, Paris 1989.

Tallon, Dennis, *La détermination du prix dans les contrats (étude de droit comparé)*, Editions Pedone, Paris 1989.

Treitel, G.H., *The Law of Contract*, 8th ed., Sweet and Maxwell, London 1991.
Remedies for Breach of Contract, Clarendon Press, Oxford 1988.

Viney, G., *Traité de Droit civil Les Obligations*, Librairie Générale de Droit et de Jurisprudence, Paris 1982.

Von Mehren and Gordley, *The Civil Law System*, 2nd ed., Little Brown and Co., Boston 1977.

Watson, Alan, *The Making of the Civil Law*, Harvard University Press 1981.

Weill, A. and Terré, F., *Droit civil Les Obligations*, 4th ed., Dalloz, Paris 1986.

Zimmermann, Reinhard, *The Law of Obligations, Roman Foundations of the Civilian Tradition*, Juta, Cape Town 1990.

Zulueta, F. de, *The Roman Law of Sale*, 1945 reprinted 1949, Clarendon Press, Oxford.

Zweigert, K. and Kotz, H., *An Introduction to Comparative Law*, 2nd ed., tr. Tony Weir, Clarendon Press, Oxford 1987.

List of Cases

FRENCH

Conseil d'Etat

Cour de cassation

Cour d'appel

GERMAN

Reichsgericht

Bundesgerichtshof

Oberlandsgericht and Landgericht

List of Statutes

ENGLISH

FRENCH

Code Civil

Art.

1108	33, 41, 83
1110	98, 121, 124, 174
1116	121, 124, 125
1121	12, 272, 276, 277
1126	33, 83
1129	33, 45, 47, 48
1130	86
1131	95, 97, 98
1133	100
1134	297, 298, 333
1135	70, 333
1137	163
1139	178
1143	321
1144	320, 321
1146	178
1147	43, 157, 163, 279
1149	326
1150	11, 172, 200, 326, 328, 329
1151	326
1152	329, 330
1156	70, 297
1165	272
1184	97, 123, 319, 320, 322, 330, 335
1228	330
1229	330
1231	331
1243	169, 319
1246	84, 168
1376	109
1378	100, 102
1379	100
1380	100
1382	43, 62, 127, 164, 275
1383	43, 123, 275
1384	43, 278
1583	240, 253
1585	241
1586	240
1591	33, 45, 46

Lois

GERMAN

BGB

AGBG (Standard Contract Terms Act)

HGB (the Commercial Code)

List of Abbreviations

ENGLISH

AC	Law Reports Appeal Cases (House of Lords)
All ER	All England Law Reports
BLR	Building Law Reports
Con.LR	Construction Law Reports
IICLQ	Institute of International and Comparative Law Quarterly
KB	Law Reports Kings Bench Division
LQR	Law Quarterly Review
QB	Law Reports Queens Bench Division
QBD	Law Reports Queens Bench Division (1875–1890)
WLR	Weekly Law Reports

FRENCH

AJ	Actualité juridique-Droit administratif
Bull.civ.	Bulletin of the decisions of the *Cour de cassation* civil divisions
Cass.civ.	One of the civil divisions of the *Cour de cassation*
Cass.com.	Commercial division of the *Cour de cassation*
D	Recueil Dalloz
Dr.adm.	Droit administratif (revue mensuelle)
Gaz.Pal.(GP)	Gazette du Palais
JCP	Jurisclasseur périodique (semaine juridique) édition générale
Leb.	Recueil Lebon (des decisions du Conseil d'Etat)
Leb.T	Table du Recueil Lebon
RDP	Revue de droit public et de la science politique
Rec.	Recueil
Req.	*Cour de cassation* Chambre de Requêtes
Rev.trim.dr.civ.	Revue trimestrielle de droit civil
Rev.trim.dr.com.	Revue trimestrielle de droit commercial et économique
RTD civil	Revue trimestrielle de droit civil
RTD com.	Revue trimestrielle de droit commercial et économique
S	Sirey

GERMAN

AGBG	Gesetz zu Regelung des Rechts der Allgemeinen Geschäfts-bedingungen (German Standard Contracts Act)
BGB	Burgliches Gesetzbuch (German civil code)
BGH	Bundesgerichtshof (German supreme court)
BGHZ	Decisions of the German supreme court in civil matters
DB	Der Betrieb (periodical)
EGBG	Einfuhrungsgesetz zum Burgerlichen Gesetzbuch (Introductory Act to the Civil Code)
HGB	Handelsgesetzbuch (Commercial Code)
LG	Landgericht
NJW	Neue Juristiche Wochenschrift
OLG	Oberlandsgerichtshof (Court of Appeal)
RGZ	Entscheidungen des Reichsgerichts in Zivilsachen (decisions of the German Imperial Court in civil matters)
VOB	Verdingsordnung für Bauleistungen (Tend ring Regulations and Contract Conditions for general building and construction works)
VOL	Verdingsordnung für Leistungen (Tendering Regulations and Contract Conditions for public service contracts other than for public works)

ROMAN

Dig.	Digest of Justinian Refs are made using the standard terminology of first the book, then the title, the fragment and the sections. So Dig.XIX,I,3,3 refers to Book 19, Title 1, fragment 3, section 3.
Inst.	The Institutes of Justinian. References are to the book, title and then the paragraph.

1 Historical introduction

GENERAL PURPOSE

The comparative examination of differing legal systems, which nevertheless share a common ideological and sociological base, must start from their historical development.

Not all the differences, and indeed the similarities, between the three systems here under review are due to historical factors. However their histories from even before Roman times have played a significant role in their individual development, and any true understanding of each system as we see it today must be based on at least an awareness of how it has been shaped by its history.

It is the purpose of this chapter to provide a brief outline of that historical development, in so far as it has affected the making of the law of contractual obligations. Those who are interested to read further are referred to the list of works given at the end of the notes to this chapter.

ROMAN LAW ORIGINS

The world's main legal systems have been described as 'families'.[1] We are concerned here with the primary representatives of three such 'families': France the Romanistic family, Germany the Germanic family and England the common law family. But, while being members of different 'families', German and French law share together that which distinguishes them from English law. They belong to the tradition of the civil law, the primary distinguishing feature of which in comparison with English law is that its origins are in Roman law and more specifically in the *Corpus Iuris Civilis*.[2] Indeed it has been said that 'Roman law is the base of all European law at least that of the Continent'.[3] While something of an exaggeration, e.g. Scandinavian law was only weakly influenced by Roman law, and French law in the *Code Civil* relating to the family is derived largely from the *coutumes*,[4] the statement is essentially true for France and Germany and more especially so in the field of contractual obligations.

The rules of Roman law, as they have influenced the development of the civil law, even in instances where they have been discarded finally by the drafters of the civil codes, will be referred to in the text as the subject matter to which they relate is discussed. There are however three general points to be made at this introductory stage.

1

First, Roman law, even at its final stage of evolution under Justinian (see below, p. 4) was not a systemized set of abstract concepts and rules of general application. It was fundamentally a pragmatically developed case-law whether the cases were real or imagined by the jurists for the purpose of exposition. The task of converting the particular rules applicable to the law of individual contracts[5] into a generalized law of contract was undertaken first by the medieval lawyers known as the glossators and the commentators (see below, p. 4), carried on by the natural lawyers and others[6] and completed by the German and French writers whose work was utilized by the draftsmen of the civil codes.

Second, the law that was to be found in the *Corpus Iuris Civilis* was for all practical purposes the law relating to individuals. It excluded virtually all considerations relating to public law and this tradition has been carried on in the French and German civil codes. This, which is a point of great significance in French law, will be discussed in more detail later (see below, pp. 27–30).

It also excluded commercial law, in the sense of the law particular to merchants and to international trade, which developed historically out of the customs and practices of merchants as administered in the commercial courts of the great medieval fairs. Again this division was maintained in both Germany and France so both countries have a commercial code in addition to their civil code.

Third, the Romans were the first people ever to develop formless consensual contracts which required for their validity nothing more than the agreement between the parties.[7] The most significant of these economically was the contract of sale *emptio venditio*. This outstanding achievement has formed the basis of all civil law codes and indeed the particular rules which the Romans established, of which some of the more important were that: the price must be certain; contracts of sale are *bonae fidei*; defects known to the seller must be disclosed; the seller has guaranty obligations in respect of hidden defects which give the buyer particular rights exercisable within a limited period of time independent of the proof of knowledge; otherwise an action for damages for latent defects is dependent on knowledge by the vendor of the defect or the giving of an express affirmation; contracts can be annulled for 'error in substantia'; and the risk in the goods passes when the contract is 'perfected'. All these rules have been largely incorporated into the civil codes. One exception is the passing of ownership which required both agreement and delivery and also either payment or the granting of credit. As we shall see French law only requires the contract of sale to be perfect for the property to pass, while German law still retains the requirement for delivery but without the need for payment (see below, pp. 238 and 241).

In comparison, and despite assertions from time to time that the degree of influence of Roman law on the English common law has been underestimated, there is no evidence to support any direct incorporation of a Roman rule into the English common law of contract and sale of goods.[8] Borrowings there certainly were from France in the last century which made a contribution both to the substance and systemization of the common law of contract and that of sale of goods, some of which clearly had Roman origins.[9] Beyond that the English common law developed in its own particular way and remained almost wholly isolated from civilian juristic influence until the passing of the European Communities Act in 1972.[10]

THE RECEPTION OF ROMAN LAW

The development of Roman law by the Romans lasted some 1000 years from around BC 450 to AD 550. Reshaped by medieval scholars and interwoven with strands of canon and customary law, it became the *ius commune* of continental Europe in the Middle Ages and remained the common law, the *Gemeines Recht*, of a large part of what is now Germany until the codifications of the nineteenth century.[11]

The reception of Roman law in France and Germany occurred however at varying times and therefore at different stages not only of its own development but also of the development of the local customary law. Further, although it is convenient to refer to France and Germany as if they were the unified states of today, at the times when the reception occurred they were widely subdivided and it was the local not any national circumstances which determined the extent of the Roman law influence.

ROMAN LAW IN FRANCE

Roman law entered France with the creation of Gaul as a Roman province in the first century BC and became well established especially in the regions of the south such as Provence. Originally the law only for Roman citizens, it became, through the *ius gentium*, the law which was applicable to dealings between Rome and non-Roman citizens alike. Thus there was extended to non-Roman citizens the availability of most of that part of Roman law which dealt with everyday business affairs even though dealings between the local inhabitants, the *peregrini*, continued to be subject to their own personal law.[12] Later in AD 212 Roman citizenship was extended to almost all inhabitants of the provinces and the distinction between the *cives* and the *peregrini* largely disappeared.

However as Roman power declined the law became increasingly 'vulgarized', that is infiltrated by local customary law. The last truly Roman legislation in the west was the *Theodosian Code* issued in AD 438. There followed a series of Germanic codes written in Latin and drafted almost certainly by Roman lawyers, of which the most influential was known as the *Lex Romana Visigothorum*, or *Alaric's Breviary*, after the King who had it produced. While containing some barbarian customs it was predominantly Roman law, albeit vulgar and simplified, and intended for use by the Romans in France and Spain under Alaric's rule, although in practice its influence became much wider.[13] It was Roman law from this source that remained in use, alongside local customs, by the Gallo-Romans in that part of France south of the Loire, known later as the *pays de droit écrit*, until the twelfth century, though becoming increasingly vulgarized.

In the northern part of France, where customary law had always been stronger, Roman law was largely displaced as a result of the Frankish invasions. The Franks brought with them their own customary law, the Salic law, which, when written down in Latin, became the *Lex Salica*.[14] Other barbarian laws applied to the peoples of different nationalities, such as Bavarians, since at that time each person followed the law of his own tribal nationality so that 'It often happens that five men work or sit together of whom no one has a law in common with another.'[15] Roman law continued to apply only in three instances: first to Roman citizens; second to ecclesiastical bodies such as monasteries; and third where the barbarian law was deficient, as was often the case in private business transactions, a gap which only Roman law could fill.[16] This was always provided that judges could be found who remembered the Roman law. For example, there was a case in the ninth century where it was recognized that since the litigants were two Churches who lived according to Roman law, it was Roman law that ought to be applied, but no judge could be found who remembered it.[17]

However, while the western part of the Roman empire had been collapsing the eastern part had remained secure behind the walls of Constantinople, together with the knowledge and practice of Roman law. But by then it was a law which had many sources and in which opinions were often conflicting. There was the old law found in the writings of the great jurists, the *constitiones* of the emperors, the edicts of the praetors and of the *curule aediles*, and importations from the east and from Greek Stoic philosophy.

In an effort to bring some order into this chaos the emperor Justinian issued instructions in AD 528 for the compilation of a new code and the results published between AD 529 and AD 555 established for ever his place in history. Known collectively as the *Corpus Iuris Civilis* ('the Corpus'), and comprising the Digest, the Institutes, the Code and the Novels, although only the first two were of lasting importance, it has been said to have had more influence on European life than any work other than the Bible.[18]

Yet the Corpus remained relatively unknown in the west and certainly had no influence on law in western Europe until the revival of learning in the universities of northern Italy, especially Bologna, at the end of the eleventh and the beginning of the twelfth century. From there the revival spread to France where for example an important school of law was established at Orleans around 1235.[19]

This was the second stage of the penetration of Roman law into France, now based on the Institutes and Digest, but it was still fragmentary even in the south. While Provence was strongly Roman it was also the home of a wide range of local customs.[20] In general it can be said that in the region roughly south of the Loire Roman law was used as a general customary law to be turned to whenever there was no specific applicable custom, which was usually the case in the field of contractual obligations.

Finally, in the south the efforts of the *parlements* of Aix, Bordeaux and Toulouse with the jurists in the area created a large degree of unification of the law in the fifteenth century based upon the Roman law of the Corpus as it had by then been interpreted and adapted for use by the medieval glossators and commentators.[21] It was only then that one could properly refer to the *pays de droit écrit*. This comprised approximately one-third of France south of a wavy line stretching from the area north of Bordeaux to the outskirts of Geneva.

North of the Loire Roman law never attained the same status as in the south but it was influential in those areas where there were gaps in the customary law and as in the south this largely applied to the law of obligations. Moreover in time many of the customs themselves had become influenced in their form and their interpretation by the application of principles of reasoning derived from Roman law.

By the end of the sixteenth century two events of importance had occurred. The local customs had to a large degree been both recorded and under the direction of the Parlement de Paris rationalized into a kind of *droit commun coutumier* which could be applied to fill in the gaps left by local customs. But although this was important for the preservation of the customary law the scope of that law was restricted to land law, family law, inheritance and so on and did not extend to the law of obligations. Moreover the customs were based on the usages of earlier times. There was therefore a considerable gap still remaining to be filled.

In addition there had developed a well organized, powerful and partially centralized judicial system which was definitely French. It was this system of judges and practising lawyers led by the Parlement de Paris which in the absence of either much academic or legislative assistance had the task of the development and rationalization of the private law. For a time it appeared that they might succeed but in the end they failed, largely because of their own practices and procedures.[22]

The results were twofold. First, there was an enormous amount of law, but it was not uniform even within each of the territories of the *droit coutumier* and the *droit écrit*, let alone across France. There was customary law, borrowings from Roman law and the case-law of the thirteen *parlements* each free to reach its own decision which could include the rules upon which the decision was based. Voltaire's well known comment 'when you travel his Kingdom you change law as often as you change horses' was not unjustified.

Second, however, the strength of the customary element within the law, and of the courts which applied it, meant that France could and did resist the wholesale reception of Roman law which overwhelmed Germany in the late Middle Ages and allowed Roman law in the form of the *usus modernus pandectarum* (see below, p. 8) to take over from the differing laws of each district. It may have been wishful thinking and in advance of its time that Bourjon could write of the 'droit commun de la France et la coutume de Paris' in 1743 but the title is significant.

ROMAN LAW IN GERMANY

No real impact was made by Roman law on Germany in the period preceding the fall of the western empire and in the barbarian era which succeeded it. Following the discovery of the Corpus and the revival of the studies of Roman law in Italy, Roman law was certainly known within the Holy Roman empire during the time of the emperor Frederick Barbarossa in the twelfth century. But the men who knew the 'learned' law were the jurists, administrators and clerks of the empire, not the practising lawyers, and their knowledge and skills had no effect on the settlement of disputes between ordinary people.

5

The empire itself was destroyed as an effective political power by the conflict between the papacy and Emperor Frederick II and in reality by the middle of the fourteenth century such power was in the hands of the electors. There was no proper machinery for imperial legislation or for true judicial control of the numerous local courts staffed by *Schöffen* (local landowners of the knightly class in the country and their equivalents in the towns) each applying the particular oral customs of their own district and dating back to the legislation of Charlemagne.

Questions which raised difficulties could be sent to the *Oberhöfe* which despite the name were not appellate courts but acted in a consultancy capacity and were again staffed by *Schöffen*. They obtained their influence from the perceived quality of the response to the questions referred to them. In some instances this practice became regularized so that there were 'mother' cities to whom 'daughter' cities or country districts referred difficult issues for advice. But in all this there was nothing coherent. The laws that were applied were purely local and decisions were made on a case-by-case basis. Only in Saxony under the influence of the *Sachsenspiegel* (Mirror of the Saxons), written by Eike von Repgow, himself a *Schöffe*, for the guidance of *Schöffen*, was there any real attempt at consistency or the development of a jurisprudence. Otherwise it was all diversity of unwritten custom with no rational framework and no organized body of lawyers.

It was against this background that a number of factors combined to bring about the reception by Germany of Roman law to such an extent that the earlier Germanic law was at one time almost totally eclipsed. The reasons for this, which over the years have been the subject of passionate debate often involving the emotive issue of national pride, are numerous and their relative importance difficult to determine.

Roman law, it has been argued, was not really 'foreign law' and was not seen as such by those then in political power. Despite its practical impotence, the Holy Roman empire could be regarded as possessing a continuity with the empire of Rome itself and to that extent Roman law could be presented as that of the Kaiser. Although this concept was at one time widely regarded as an important factor in creating the reception, in truth it is more in the nature of a myth convenient for the use of those who wished to argue for the true basis of German law being Roman.

Of more significance the Electors, using the law as a means of consolidating and extending their authority, began in the middle of the fifteenth century to establish their own system of Hofgericht (appellate courts) staffed by doctors of law which in practice meant those trained in Roman law. At the same time they obtained from the emperor the privileges of being able to deny the right of their subjects to appeal to any court outside of the Electors' own territory or the obligation to appear before any such court.

Then in 1495 the old, and largely ineffective Imperial Court of Justice, the Kammergericht, was remodelled and entitled the Reichskammergericht. In its new form the court was eventually by 1548 wholly staffed by those 'learned in the law'; from the beginning it was required to apply the 'common law of the Empire' by which was meant Roman law, together with 'such righteous, honest and sufferable ordinances, statutes and customs of the principalities, lordships and courts as shall be brought before it [by litigants]'.[23] As Robinson et al. have pointed out, in practice this meant that Roman law became in effect the common law of Germany and was largely applied to the exclusion of any other, since local laws had to be proved by witnesses whereas Roman law was by definition within the knowledge of the court.[24]

Although the jurisdiction of the remodelled court continued to suffer from privileges of exemption, and had little direct effect on the development of civil law, it was influential in the pattern which it established and which was followed by the superior courts of the territories. This influence became even more marked with the growth in the publication of the court's decisions including the reasoning upon which they were based.

In time some knowledge of Roman law and of Roman-canonist procedure spread. One factor which speeded its wider acceptance was the gradual introduction of formal and elaborate written pleadings and the citation of authorities in place of the older, informal, oral procedures. Confronted with this change, courts still largely staffed by laymen were compelled themselves to turn to lawyers trained in Roman law for what was initially advice but which in time became in effect a decision. With the court now having the ability to use the Roman-canonist procedures and apply the principles of Roman law, which were widely regarded as superior to the older practices, their use inevitably expanded. One fed upon the other.

To the undoubted practical advantages of the new procedures in securing justice there must be added that of the sense of participating in the cultural current of the time – what in modern terminology we would term as 'being with-it'. We may even speculate that the lawyer had a feeling of 'one up-manship' at the successful use for his client of these new techniques. To be a man of the Renaissance was not only to share in the passion for the classical past but to relate its glories to the present and among these was certainly to be numbered the *Corpus Iuris*.

One further factor remains to be mentioned which not only had an effect at the time in the fifteenth and sixteenth centuries but was of lasting influence on the development of German law. That is the practice of *Aktenversendung* – the sending by a court of the papers relating to a case sometimes to an *Oberhof*, more usually as time went by to a university, for an opinion on the matter, which was almost invariably followed. The practice was widespread not just by local courts but at times by appellate courts as well. It reflected the political uncertainties of the times, the fear that local courts would be prejudiced and the lack among the judges of such courts of the degree of legal training now needed as the importance of local custom declined.

In arriving at their opinion the professors relied solely on the papers before them. There was no taking of evidence from witnesses. Often the university to which the matter was referred was in a different territory from the court which had made the referral so as to improve the chances of impartiality. Both these factors in turn reduced the importance of local custom which required strict proof. In the absence of such proof the law that the professors applied was Roman law as it had been developed by the medieval Italian jurists. As collections of their opinions were published so knowledge of and respect for the learned law spread and the importance of the universities to the development of German law grew.

So gradually there was developed the *usus modernus pandectarum* and the Roman law of the Corpus updated by the glossators and the commentators (see above, p. 4 and note 21) combined in varying degrees in the different states of Germany with some elements of the local German law but with no overall harmony and no unified body of professional practising lawyers.

The development of German law was influenced also by two other factors both of which contributed to the drafting of the *BGB*. First there was natural law, the doctrine that law could be derived by reason starting with the most general principles and then deriving from them particular rules in ever increasing detail, of which Grotius was perhaps the most outstanding exponent. But this law of reason as it was taken over by the universities became increasingly abstract and lacking in social reality.

Second, there was the historical school under Savigny which sought to revert to the pure concepts of Roman law without the accretions of the medieval glosses, except in so far as they clarified the Roman texts. The concepts were to be placed in a logical order to create the system which it was believed the Romans could have created but never did. But this was no antiquarian exercise; it was intended to establish a modern law so the concepts had also to be updated to solve the legal problems as they actually existed within contemporary society. But the Pandectist system, as it was known, was still highly conceptual and complete within itself.[25]

The consequences were threefold. First, German law became even more university-oriented and abstract in character. Second, legal rules were formulated not because they were the most apposite to be applied but because they could be derived in a series of logical steps from the initial general concept. Third, the rules, especially in the field of obligations, were based to a very great extent on Roman rules as these were believed to be by the Pandectists.

THE CODIFICATION OF FRENCH LAW

THE MEANING OF CODIFICATION

Codification is the introduction of legislation covering comprehensively the whole of a specific area of law, e.g. private law, the law dealing with persons in their ordinary relations one with another, which sets out the rules applicable to that area of law, either as *lois impératives* or *lois supplétives*. The preferred translation of these terms as suggested by Weston is mandatory or non-mandatory.[26] The intention of the legislator in introducing a code is therefore that there should be nothing left within that field of law not covered by the code, which constitutes therefore a total system complete within itself. Even though a detailed issue which arises may not fall within the precise terms of the code, nevertheless the problem should be capable of being solved by an application of the principles contained within the code.

As we shall see, in practice this intention has not always been capable of being realized but it stands as a basic principle.

THE DEMAND FOR CODIFICATION

In any modern society the task of preparing a code involves very significant effort and there have to be factors present which compel the legislature to undertake the task. In the case of France there were the demands, born of the Revolution, for a law which applied equally to everyone in the whole of France and a law which was sufficiently simple that it could be understood by the layman.

But equally the ground must already have been prepared. In France there had been issued ordinances of civil and criminal procedure in both the sixteenth and seventeenth centuries and a commercial code (1673) together with the *Code de la Marine* in 1681. In the Introduction to the *Droit Commercial* it is said that 'The Ordinance of 1673 known as the Code Savary was the first attempt at overall legislation in the field of private law.'

In addition codification had for over a century been a leading theme of the well-known textbook writers such as Bourjon whose work was referred to earlier (see above, p. 5), Argou who wrote the *Institutions au droit français*, Domat, a leading writer of the natural law school, who wrote *Les Loix civiles dans leur ordre naturel* (1689) and Pothier (*Traité des obligations* 1761 and *Traité du contrat de vente* 1768).

But the ultimate basis upon which the conception of codification rests is that of the systematic treatment to be found in Justinian's Institutes and in the writings of those who reduced the unsystematic mass of the Digest into coherent order. If the Institutes showed that there could be an ordered and comprehensive system it was the great writers from the commentators onwards who paved the way for its achievement within the field of the civil law as opposed to public law (see below, p. 24).

THE PROCESS OF CODIFICATION

Codification in France was relatively swift. Following the sweeping away by the Constituent Assembly of the privileges and servitudes of the feudal system and the wide-ranging changes introduced into the law of marriage and inheritance, attention was turned in 1791 to the unification of the civil law. For practical progress, however, it had to wait until the energies of Napoleon as First Consul were directed to the task. He appointed a four-man drafting committee of eminent practising lawyers to prepare a draft which was completed in only four months. After Napoleon had removed all political opposition to this draft, and it had passed through the scrutiny of the Conseil d'État, often under the direction of Napoleon himself, the *Code Civil* was enacted by 36 laws between March 1803 and March 1804.

That the code could be completed so quickly was owing to the work which had been undertaken earlier, especially that by Pothier in the area of contracts and obligations, and because of the code's largely conservative character.

The *Code Civil* was followed by other codes, the *Code de Commerce*, the *Code Penale* and codes dealing with civil and penal procedure. The only one of interest for our purposes is the *Code de Commerce*. It may seem surprising that there should be a separate code dealing with commercial matters but this is simply an accident of history. Justinian's Institutes did not contain commercial law which was considered a separate subject from that of the civil law and had its origin in the customs of merchants. It had also, as referred to earlier, already been the subject of a code (see above, p. 9) due to Colbert and indeed the original *Code de Commerce* was largely an update of that of 1673.

In any event the distinction was carried forward into the *Code Civil* and as we shall see also into German law and it remains in force today with certain important consequences (see below, p. 31).

STRUCTURE OF THE *CODE CIVIL*

The code is divided into three books and within those 2283 articles. From our viewpoint the significant part of the code is that contained in Book 3 which is entitled 'Des différentes manières dont on requiert la propriété' (The different methods of acquiring ownership). Despite this title the book in fact contains, in addition to some initial articles on succession, the whole of the law of contract, quasi-contracts, delict, the various special forms of contract according to the Roman pattern, of sale, exchange, lease, employment and labour and materials and finally a miscellany of other matters such as partnership, loan deposit and prescription.

Although the grouping together of these unrelated topics may seem strange, what matters from a practical viewpoint is that in general related subjects are dealt with in the various articles in the same section and usually the first article in the section contains the general principle and subsequent articles the particular provisions amplifying that principle. In this way the amount of cross-referencing is reduced to a minimum although some is obviously necessary, e.g. between the general rules on contractual responsibility and the particular rules relating to the sale of goods.

THE CHARACTERISTICS OF THE CODE

It was the combination in the philosophy of the drafting committee and of Napoleon which gave the *Code Civil* its most characteristic features. First the draftsmen did not attempt to make the code totally comprehensive so as to try to deal with all eventualities. A few of the comments on this issue made by Portalis, a member of the drafting committee and government commissioner in the Prize Court, are illuminating:

> We have equally tried to avoid the dangerous ambition to regulate and foresee everything. . . . How can one hold back the action of time? How can one calculate and know in advance what only experience can reveal to us? A code however complete it may appear is no sooner issued than a thousand unexpected questions present themselves to the judge . . . The function of the 'loi' is to fix the general maxims of justice, to establish principles . . . and not to descend into the details of the questions that can arise in each instance.[27]

Second, Napoleon was determined that the text should be clear and straightforward so that it could be read and understood by any intelligent layman such as himself. If he, Napoleon, could not understand it then it had to be rewritten.

This philosophy gave the code its virtues and some would argue its defects. Its drafting is in so many places a masterpiece of both compression and memorable phraseology. As an example consider Art. 1150: 'Le débiteur n'est tenu que des dommages et intérêts qui ont été prévus ou qu'on a pu prévoir lors du contrat, lorsque ce n'est point par son dol que l'obligation n'est point exécutée'. (The debtor is only responsible for the damages which were foreseen or which one could have foreseen at the time of contract, when it was not due to his *dol* that the obligation was not performed.) Other than for the exception for *dol* (which we shall see later is wider in meaning than fraud – see below, p. 124) the article expresses the same rule as that in *Hadley* v. *Baxendale* in terms which it would be difficult to improve.

Of course in this example there are questions still to be answered as to the degree of foreseeability which is required and whether it is the type of loss or the extent of the loss which is to be foreseen. But these are exactly the types of question which the code deliberately leaves to the judge to decide in putting into action the principles established by the code.

Third, despite the revolutionary fervour with which the task of preparing the code was first undertaken the end result was essentially conservative. David has commented that 'in the area of the law of obligations it is hard to cite a single innovation'.[28]

THE EFFECT OF THE CODE

In common with any codification the primary effect is to start again, with the text of the code as the only basis for the field of law which it covers. Past decisions of the courts and the rules of Roman law no longer have any validity. As stated in Art. 7 of the Law of the sixth month of year XII of the Republican calendar which promulgated the Code Napoleon: 'As from the date of the coming into force of these laws, the Roman laws, the ordinances, the general or local customs, statutes and regulations cease to have the effect of general or specific law in matters which are the object of the laws comprising the present Code'.

What went before the code therefore is history – valuable in the understanding of how we arrived at the point from which we start, informative as to the background to the system and rules which we now have and from which we may compare other systems, interesting in terms of academic analysis, but of no help in arriving at a solution to a practical problem. The comparison with the Sale of Goods Act 1979 in English law which has been said to be 'a codifying statute' is instructive. In the first place the Act itself in s.62 makes it clear that the rules of the common law including the law merchant except in so far as they are inconsistent with the Act continue to apply to the sale of goods. Second, in interpreting the Act the courts may still refer back to common law cases which were decided even before the first Sale of Goods Act was passed in 1893.[29] The Act is not therefore a 'code' in the sense that the term is used here to describe the codes of France and Germany, and indeed as it is applied to other civil law countries.

THE DEVELOPMENT OF THE CODE

Since the code was first issued in 1804 it has been developed in broadly three ways:

1. By actual amendment of the text of the code by the passing of new *lois*. We shall see an important example of this when discussing Art. 1792 of the code which was dramatically amended by the Loi Spinetta in 1978 in order to expand the responsibilities of contractors, architects and others who enter into direct contracts with the *maître de l'ouvrage* (building owner) and to introduce new responsibilities for specialist vendors (see below, pp. 187–196).
2. By the addition of new *lois* or *decrets* dealing with particular subjects. There are many of these, some relating to general issues such as contracts of insurance, others to specific matters such as the formalities to be observed in the conclusion of certain leases of property.
3. By decisions of the *Cour de cassation*. (For the French court system see below, p. 36.) Obviously no decision of the courts can ever actually change an article of the code, but the manner in which the courts interpret and apply the code provisions can in practice amend the law whatever may be the theoretical objections (see below, pp. 36–37). One example which we shall examine in more detail later is the reversal in meaning of Art. 1121 on the stipulations for benefit of third parties to a contract (below, p. 276). Another is that of the obligations of the professional seller in relation to the consumer (below, p. 172).

In the introduction of new *lois* and especially in the changes made by the *jurisprudence*, the writings of French legal scholars, 'doctrine' has been of great importance at least throughout this century (see further below, p. 38).

Accordingly although there have been several proposals for a wholesale revision of the code, and indeed initial drafts were prepared in 1954 and 1961 of certain sections, the enterprise has been abandoned and seems unlikely to be resurrected.

The code has not therefore fulfilled the intentions of its originators that it should remain a complete statement of the civil law; nor is it any longer with the accretion of supplementary *lois* and the decisions of the *Cour de cassation*, simple and capable of understanding by any layman. But it has survived and its continued survival seems to remain assured. Moreover it has either been copied wholesale or has provided the basis for laws across Europe, North Africa and Central and South America. Napoleon was certainly correct when he said that it was for his code above all that he would be remembered.

GERMAN LAW AND ITS CODIFICATION

THE MEANING OF CODIFICATION

The meaning of codification given in relation to French law is valid also for German law. The same distinction is drawn between rules which are mandatory and those which are permissive. Even more than the *Code Civil*, the *BGB* seeks to give a detailed answer to any question that may arise, but it has at the same time included 'safety valves' which have allowed the courts to develop the code to take into account problems which its draftsmen had not foreseen and changes in social, technical and economic conditions which even in the second half of the nineteenth century were hardly foreseeable.

THE DEMAND FOR CODIFICATION

In comparison with France the demand for codification among the states which now comprise Germany is a complex story in which many interests were involved. There were the commercial interests which were faced with the practical difficulties of interstate trading given the differences between the legal systems of the main states. Then there was the uncertainty of the law even within the states such as Prussia in which the state law, the *Allgemeines Landrecht* of 1794, was only of subsidiary jurisdiction in certain of the provinces such as Pomerania, Brandenburg and Silesia which affected principally matters of concern to the private citizen but also those responsible for administration, e.g. inheritance and family law. The French civil code was still the law in parts of western and southern Germany, even in certain territories newly under Prussian rule, and provided the basis for the *Badische Landrecht* completed in Baden in 1809. Finally as a subsidiary law there was the *Gemeines Recht* – the old common law of Germany. So a second motive was clearly that of establishing certainty.

But also there were political factors at work. After some hesitation the National Liberal Party strongly supported the concept of national legal unity as a means of furthering national unification and strengthening the national state against particularism of the individual states. There was an identification of the will of the citizen with the 'unified state will'.[30]

THE PROCESS OF CODIFICATION

Again in contrast to France the process was lengthy. The first tentative moves towards codification were made in 1814 by Thibaut but were strongly opposed by the great German jurist Savigny who considered that they were premature and that before any real attempt could be made at codification there had to be a detailed study of the historical sources of law. Only in that way could one avoid the mistake of imposing on the people legislation which was contrary to 'the common convictions of people, the same feeling of inner necessity'.

Thibaut was ahead of his time; the ground had not been sufficiently prepared, and it was not until around 1847 that there began to be general acceptance in principle for the idea of a unified code, although the customs union (*Zollverein*) had been established in the northern states in 1834. In 1848 the Confederation passed the unified law of Bills of Exchange and in 1861 came the German Unified Commercial Code.

February 1874 saw the establishment of a *Vorkommission* which had the task of laying down the guidelines for the future codifying commission. The most important part of their report was that which proposed that the code would only 'correspond to the justified wishes of the German people . . . if it sticks to the proven common law institutions and axioms of the existing civil law system in Germany'. The approach then was to be both technical and formal. The commission itself was appointed in 1874, consisting of members of the judiciary and academic lawyers, but no practising lawyers or representatives of economic or political interest groups. The draft code was published in 1888 and subject immediately to widespread comment and criticism.

The criticism was directed mainly to three issues. First, that led by Gierke against the extent of Roman law contained within the draft and the lack of 'Germanization' which extended to cover the failure of the draft to consider matters of social policy which were thought of as being 'German' as opposed to the individualistic nature of Roman law. Second, the failure, as it was perceived by a wide spectrum of interested parties, of the draft to give protection to their particular interests. Third, the general perception that the code was too markedly capitalistic and in favour of individual freedom which, given the wide disparities in economic power between the parties to a transaction, e.g. employer and workman, industrialist and consumer, was an illusion, so that the draft failed to achieve social justice.

As a result of the criticisms a second commission with theoretically a wider representation was established in 1890 but in practice its work continued to be dominated by professional jurists. The revisions finally made to the draft were not extensive and only introduced what had been described as 'a few drops of socialist oil'. The fundamental basis of the draft was unchanged when it was presented to the Bundesrat in October 1895. On 1 July 1896 the Reichstag accepted the draft code with only very minor amendments and it officially became law on 1 January 1900.

THE STRUCTURE OF THE CODE

The code is divided into five books containing 2385 articles. Although for our purposes we can ignore Books 4 and 5 which deal with family law and the law of succession respectively we have to consider the other three books which comprise:

Book 1   The General Part
Book 2   The Law of Obligations
Book 3   The Law of Property

The most significant characteristic of the *BGB* is the way in which it is constructed so that general rules which may affect more than one type of transaction are 'factored out' and included in Book 1. So in the first section of Book 1 we find the definitions of persons both natural and juristic; in the second section are given the definitions of 'things' (*Sachen*) and the third section describes legal transactions (*Rechtsgeschäfte*). Then follow sections dealing with time periods, prescription, exercise of rights (self-help) and finally the giving of security.

The problem and importance of all this is that if one wants to look up the rules relating to offer and acceptance then instead of going straight to Book 2 – Obligations, second section, first title 'Creation, Content of the Contract', where one could reasonably expect to find them, in fact one has to refer to the third title of the third section of Book 1 entitled 'Contract'.

In the same way if one wants to find out the rules relating to the right to rescind any contract for mistake, references must be made to Book 1, third section, second title, Art. 119.

The justification for this tortuous method of arrangement of the legal rules is that they are logically applicable to any 'legal transaction' (*Rechtsgeschäfte*) and not to a particular transaction set in a specific factual situation. But removing the concept of a legal transaction from its factual setting means that the concept itself is of little practical value.

However the Pandectist doctrines which inspired this method of drafting the code have been admired by jurists in other countries for their orderly and systematic manner of thinking which could be used to reduce a heterogeneous mass of material into a logical form. One can see this at work in England in the first two chapters of Pollock on torts contained in all the editions from 1887 to 1951 which contained first the nature of tort in general and then the principles of liability.

THE CHARACTERISTICS OF THE CODE

The outline of the format and method of drafting of the code have already been indicated sufficiently in the preceding section. So far as the law of contracts is concerned the code, while following closely many of the principles of Roman law which were already included within the *Gemeines Recht*, also departed from Roman law in certain important respects. Thus, following the older German law, the code recognizes a contract for the benefit of third parties, Art. 328 (see below, p. 279); states that an offeror is bound by his offer and cannot withdraw it unless he has provided otherwise, Art. 145 (see below, p. 63); provides that a person who has voluntarily parted with possession of a thing to another loses his right of ownership if the thing is disposed of by that other to a third party who acquires it in good faith, Arts 932 and 935 (see below, p. 264) and states that the risk to the goods passes only on delivery, which is generally also the same time as property passes, Arts 446 and 929 (see below, pp. 247–248).

However the code has remained faithful to the Roman rules when it comes to the remedies of the purchaser in respect of defective goods (see below, p. 209).

Consistent with the principle of freedom of contract (*Vertragsfreiheit*), the code allows the parties the widest opportunity to agree upon the terms of their contract. Only a very few terms of the code relating to contracts are mandatory, e.g. Art. 276(2) which prevents a party from excluding his liability for an intentional fault.

Nevertheless the code does set out as the *ius dispositivum* the rules which will apply to particular types of contract, e.g. contracts for sale and for work unless the parties specify otherwise. The importance of these rules in today's society, dominated as it is by standard forms of contract, is that they constitute a balanced set of legal norms which, according to the requirement of 'good faith' under Art. 242 of the code, cannot be departed from in a standard form contract unless there is substituted an adequate alternative or the variation/exclusion can be justified by the 'general nature' of the transaction. This is now reinforced by Art. 9 of the AGBG. (See further Chapter 20 for the control of standard form contracts.)

THE EFFECT OF THE CODE

The code certainly achieved the objective of unifying German civil law but not that of providing a means for determining the complete answer to all problems. Supposedly the code did not leave any gaps within the field which it covered but three facts soon became clear. First, there were gaps in the code. Second, the coverage by the code of certain topics was grossly inadequate, e.g. the law of employment for which there were only 11 articles while there were 4 on the subject of the ownership of bees. Third, many of the abstract concepts of the code were in fact not based upon a neutral objective validity which was true for all time, but upon the value judgements made by the draftsmen based on the individualistic, bourgeois mentality of the professional academic class of the 1870s.

Not only was there no reformist element in the code but rather a deliberate intent to avoid giving recognition to the economic and social changes which had occurred in Germany in the last quarter of the nineteenth century. By the time it was in force the code was at least 25 years out of date in a period of rapid change.

THE DEVELOPMENT OF THE CODE

That the code has survived, and is the heart of the German civil law, is owing to the way in which the issues referred to in the previous section have been tackled, either by a combination of the courts and academic writers or through legislative action in either amending the code or passing laws separate from the code.

An important gap which was discovered almost immediately after the *BGB* had come into force related to breach of contract. The doctrine as set out in the *BGB* only differentiated between two cases: those of impossibility of performance and those of delayed performance. But it was soon realized that there could be defective performance which did not fall into either of these categories and was not covered by any of the specific remedies for defective goods or work (see below, p. 17). The classic textbook example is that of a purchaser buying a horse which to the seller's knowledge has an infectious disease. The horse infects the purchaser's other horses but itself recovers. The purchaser cannot invoke the rules relating to defects in goods but clearly should be entitled to recover damages.

The courts, following textbook writers, therefore developed by 1902 the doctrine of *positive Vertragsverletzung* (positive breach of contract) to deal with this type of situation although it is not based on any article of the code. It is now of increased importance because of the extent to which German law attaches subsidiary obligations to the performance of a contract in terms of providing information or otherwise fulfilling towards the other party a duty of care (see below, p. 230).

Closely related to the concept of positive breach of contract is the further doctrine of *culpa in contrahendo*, again developed by the courts following a famous article by Ihering (see below, p. 64). Essentially this doctrine holds the debtor liable in a pre-contractual situation where if English law were to grant a remedy it would be in tort. The advantages of the contractual remedy in German law over that of tort are first that it avoids the possibility of the debtor exculpating himself from liability for employees under Art. 831 of the *BGB* and second, it would allow the recovery of pure economic loss which is not recoverable in tort under Art. 823 of the *BGB* other than for damage deliberately inflicted in a manner contrary to public policy, Art. 826 of the *BGB*. (See below, pp. 280 and 284).

Again for the same two reasons textbook writers and the courts have been prepared to find contractual remedies more generally where one would expect the remedy to be in tort, e.g. contracts 'for protective effects for third parties' (see below, p. 281). In contrast, the courts have sometimes been prepared, in relation to goods, to find a remedy in tort, other than for pure economic loss, so as to avoid the damaging effects on the purchaser of the extremely short period of prescription of six months from delivery (see below, p. 280), where under English law the remedy if any could only be in contract.

Most important of all the courts have used the two 'safety valve' provisions of the *BGB*, Arts 157 and 242, that contracts must be both construed in good faith and performed in good faith in order to avoid the debtor being able to avoid liability through the inclusion of clauses avoiding or restricting in standard form contracts the rights which the creditor would otherwise have under the code provisions. The rules established by the courts now form the basis of, and have been incorporated within, the Standard Contract Terms Act 1977 which applies to both business and consumer transactions and is probably the most effective piece of legislation anywhere dealing with contracts in standard form – see further Chapter 20.

In these ways the legislator and the courts with the assistance of academic writers have been able to develop the code so as to avoid the lack of protection which creditors would otherwise have suffered under the trading conditions of the twentieth century. If the constructions used have at times been strained, and the remedies provided in ways which are contrary to strict juristic rules, at least the courts and writers have recognized that juristic concepts cannot be applied other than in factual situations and if that means the concepts have to be stretched in order to do justice, then within the broadest of limits that is what they have done.

So the code has survived with many amendments and a massive judicial commentary without which the interpretation and application of the code provisions cannot now be understood. Because of this there has been a move to amend the code provisions in respect of the law of obligations but although there is a commission working on the matter it is not expected that any reform will actually be effected until at the earliest the beginning of the next century.

THE ENGLISH LAW OF CONTRACT

ORIGINS

The true origins of the English common law of contract do not lie earlier than the sixteenth century and their history is one of the forms of action involved and of the limitations which were peculiar to each. In order to appreciate how it was that an unlikely form of action which originated in tort eventually became the true precursor of the English common law of contract, it is necessary to look first at the forms of action related to contract which then existed but whose own development was stultified by the limitations placed upon them by the courts.

Actions at Common Law

The action in Covenant existed for those cases in which a man had undertaken in a deed to perform some obligation, other than the payment of a specified sum of money, which was actionable only in debt. The problem with the action was that 'it is taken on the deed and without a deed it cannot be maintained'.

The deed was not there as evidence but as an essential prerequisite to the action and the defendant was bound by the deed and nothing but the deed. In consequence the practical scope of the action was very limited and it never played a part in the development of the law of contract.

The action in Debt took one of two forms. First, there was what was known as a debt upon an obligation. The obligation consisted either of a deed or a tally. Second, there was a debt upon a contract. Here the plaintiff relied upon demonstrating that the defendant had received some material benefit. It was the receipt of the benefit, the *quid pro quo*, not any promise to pay which was the basis of the action.

Subsequently, as regards the sale of goods it was held that the action in Debt could lie against the purchaser for non-payment of the goods and in Detinue against the seller for non-delivery, where the bargain had not been performed. The reason for this exception appears to be that once the bargain had been made for a specific chattel then the property passed at once to the purchaser but he could not claim possession until he had paid the purchase price or had been granted credit.[31]

However, the action was heavily circumscribed. In the first place it lay only for a sum certain so if the price had not been agreed then there could be no action. Second, the plaintiff could recover only the exact sum agreed. Third, if the plaintiff relied upon a deed then both parties were bound by the deed so that the action was *stricti juris*. This was so to the extent that if the defendant could not show that the deed had been cancelled and returned to him or discharged by another deed, he would still be liable on the deed no matter what other evidence he could produce that he had discharged the debt.[32] Only if he could establish successfully the plea of *non est factum*, the deed is not mine, could he escape liability. The most common instance of this was where the person executing the deed was illiterate and he was misled as to its contents. The defence of *non est factum* still applies today and is not limited to deeds but its application is restricted (see Treitel *The Law of Contract* p. 291 et seq.).

Finally the trial in an action for debt other than where a deed was involved was usually by wager of law, i.e. the swearing on oath of eleven others to support the oath of the defendant and not by jury. While this may have provided a fair answer in the days when eleven honest citizens could be found in the locality, especially when they were chosen by the court, when it became the practice to allow the defendant to choose them from paid oath swearers, there was little possibility of a proper trial. Of course the defendant might still lose if one of the oath swearers got the ritual wrong by so much as a word since the procedure was one of strict formality but that was hardly a chance that the plaintiff would wish to take.[33] One other unfavourable result of the trial being by wager of law was that if the defendant died an action could not be brought against his personal representatives.

Penal bonds

A generally little known but important part of the medieval law of 'contract' concerned penal bonds. If A wished to be certain that B would perform a certain obligation by a particular date, then he would require B to enter into a bond which was for a sum substantially greater than the value of the obligation, the condition of which was that the bond became void if the obligation was satisfied, but if it was not, the bond was forfeit. Of course in a sale transaction both parties would execute such bonds, the one that he would pay the value of the bond if he did not transfer the property by the agreed date, the other that he would pay the penal amount of the bond if he did not pay the purchase price according to the agreed terms.

It would seem that such bonds were used very much more frequently than actions in covenant since they were more easily enforceable. Their popularity only declined with the rise of a general action in contract and with the actions of equity which granted relief against their penal terms. This, incidentally, was the origin of the distinction we find today in English law between liquidated damages and penalties.[34]

Actions in equity

Because of the inadequacy of the common law remedies many claimants instead of going to the royal courts would petition the Chancellor in Equity. Cases of this happening were particularly common where the claim was one for *quantum meruit*, for which there was no remedy at common law and for the enforcement of parole executory agreements. As we have seen the common law remedy of Covenant required the execution of a deed.

At this time the Canon law had already moved to the point at which it was prepared to enforce any promise made with serious intent in contradiction to the Roman law rule *ex nudo pacto non oritur actio*, to which the civilian jurists still clung if somewhat tenuously.[35] Since the Chancellors of the day were invariably learned ecclesiastics they would appear in general to have applied the same rule as that of the canon law at least when it accorded with good conscience.[36]

Actions other than in the royal courts

There is strong evidence to suggest that many of the cases which involved simple contracts, especially those which were between merchants for the sale of goods, were never brought to the royal courts but were dealt with either in local courts or in the courts specially established at the medieval fairs in order to dispense justice there. Such courts were not bound by the strict formalism of the royal courts and were willing to enforce covenants not made under deed and to adjudicate upon contracts for the sale of goods, for example as to whether or not the goods were of the requisite quality.[37]

However it is clear that such courts could never have developed the basis which was required for a general action for the breach of contract although their activities showed the obvious need for such an action.

THE ACTION OF ASSUMPSIT

The early story of the development of this action lies in the law of trespass. The earliest actions in trespass had to be brought using a writ which alleged that the trespass was against the King's peace but they were limited to instances in which injury had been caused to the plaintiff's goods or to his person. Subsequently the action was extended to situations in which what was alleged was an undertaking to perform some act which had in the event been performed negligently. This was known as trespass *sur le cas* since it relied on the circumstances of the case being described in the writ. However no action in trespass could be brought if the undertaking had not been performed at all. Such an action lay only in covenant since non-feasance was not a tort. As was said in 1503, 'where a carpenter makes a bargain to make me a house and does nothing, no action on the case lies, for it sounds in covenant. But if he makes the house improperly the action on the case well lies'![38]

But this artificial position, if technically correct, could not be maintained. Only a few years later the action on the case was allowed even though what was promised had not been performed. But proof of the express promise was still required as was the fact that the plaintiff had suffered damages.[39]

The next step was the use of the action of assumpsit, i.e. for what was a breach of promise, to replace the action of debt sur contract. This was achieved finally in 1602 in Slade's case when it was accepted that the promise need not be express and therefore something which had to be proved, but could be implied from the debt itself.[40]

So the common law now had a general action for breach of contract. But while there was no problem with actions which had previously been brought in debt sur contract, since clearly if the debt were proven there was an obligation to pay, there were many other types of promise which had previously only been actionable in covenant, i.e. if a deed existed. Which of these simple promises were now to be actionable in assumpsit? The answer was that if the action was not in respect of a debt, then there had to be consideration which consisted of some promise made by the plaintiff to the defendant which was sufficient to support their bargain although it did not have to be adequate. There also needed to be reciprocity so that a past consideration would not be sufficient. As was said in 1587, there must be 'a debt precedent or a present consideration'.[41]

The doctrine of consideration has been the subject of much subsequent refinement and indeed is still being refined today (see below, p. 105) but its basic origins are set in the law as it developed in the sixteenth century.

CLASSICAL CONTRACT LAW – THE NINETEENTH CENTURY

While the roots of the English law lie in the sixteenth century it was in the nineteenth century that a combination of two factors produced many of the general principles which we find in the law today.

First, there was the rise in importance of the executory contract, i.e. a contract formed by mutual promises to be carried out in the future. This seems to have been due to the growth in expanding economic activities which required substantial forward planning and the parties' natural willingness only to commit large resources with the support of legally binding obligations.[42] This is not to say that executory contracts were up to that time unknown – they certainly were known – but the question which such contracts raised was whether or not the promise by the other party constituted valid consideration. If it did then the action on the case would lie since the essentials of the action were 'consideration, promise and breach of promise' but the rules relating to which promises constituted valid consideration were complex.[43]

Second, in the late eighteenth and early nineteenth centuries the practice resumed in England for the first time since Bracton in the thirteenth century, of writing legal treaties which sought to set out in reasoned order the principles upon which the law of contract was based. In so doing, because there was no abstract learning of the older common law, but only the practices of pleadings, the writers turned to the civil law and found there the works of Domat, Pufendorf and especially Pothier all of which had been translated into English. Whether the desire to systemize the English law came first, and then use was made of the great continental treatises, or whether it was the existence of these in English which prompted the English authors to set to work, is an open question. Whatever the answer the impact on English law was considerable.

The doctrines which were derived from the civil law were:

1. That a contract was formed by offer and acceptance. It was not sufficient that there was a promise and consideration; there had to be an acceptance of the promise which contained the offer. *Adams* v. *Lindsell* decided in 1818 appears to be the first case in which this new doctrine was applied by the courts and is important in that the case established for the first time in English law that an acceptance made by post is effective from the time that the acceptance is posted. (See further below, p. 69.)
2. The requirement, independent of consideration, of the need to establish the intention to create legal relations.[44]
3. That the parties should be of one mind – the theory of *consensus ad idem*. Although under English law as it has since developed the intentions of the parties are to be determined objectively by looking at what they did and wrote, the doctrine still retains some influence especially in relation to the doctrine of mistake (see below, p. 115).
4. The 'will' theory that the contract is a product of the intentions of the parties and it is the function of the court simply to determine what the parties have agreed upon. The 'will' theory has been influential and still expresses the basic position at common law that the terms of the contract are those which the parties intended. In practice where the parties have not expressly stated their intentions the court will imply into the contract terms either derived from statute, custom or what they consider reasonable to imply.

   However it is still the position that subject to mandatory statutory rules, e.g. those contained in the Unfair Contract Terms Act, the parties are still free to stipulate by express terms what they intend and even if this freedom for one of the parties may be constrained by economic inequalities, it is that intention to which the courts must give effect (see further below, p. 294).
5. The rules relating to recovery of damages in contract as formulated in *Hadley* v. *Baxendale* were clearly influenced by, if not directly derived from, the work of Pothier which had been incorporated into the *Code Civil*.

Despite these borrowings the English law of contract has retained many of its indigenous concepts on to which the newer doctrines have been grafted. So consideration has remained an essential element for the validity of a contract not executed as a deed. Privity of contract, although not formally established until the middle of the last century, has remained unchanged.

The common law rules requiring a contract to be performed strictly according to its terms, and which give only the most limited effect to mistake, fraud and frustration and none to any duty of disclosure (otherwise than in contracts *uberrimae fidei*), or to the fact of the bargain being unfair or unconscionable, remain intact. Even the doctrine of caveat emptor has only been changed effectively by the passing of the Unfair Contract Terms Act.[45]

NOTES

1. See Zweigert & Kotz, Vol. 1, Ch. 5.

2. Watson, pp. 3 and 4.
3. *Histoire des Obligations*, J. P. Levy, Les Cours de Droit, p. 5.
4. Zweigert & Kotz, Vol. 1, *The Nordic Legal Family* p. 287 et seq.; for the *coutumes* see p. 89.
5. Roman law did not have a generalized law of contracts but a law of individual contracts each with its own particular rules – see Lee, *Elements of Roman Law* p. 345 and Buckland & McNair p. 265 et seq.
6. The Natural Lawyers sought to derive generalized and systematic rules of law from true reason. While they drew upon Roman law when they considered it was in line with reason they were not bound by Roman law. The most celebrated of the Natural Lawyers was Grotius. He refers to contracts as being reciprocal acts distinguishing them from mere acts of kindness and to their being separated into 'I give that you may give; I do that you may do; I do that you may give'. This is taken from the *Digest*, Paul xix.5, but strangely Grotius omits Paul's 'I give that you may do'.

   Grotius notes that from this classification the Romans omitted certain nominate contracts which had their own characteristics because of their common use, but then says that the 'Law of nature ignores these distinctions'.

   De Juri Belli ac Pacis (1646) Translated, Kelsey, Oxford 1925, Vol. 2, Book 1, Ch. XII, p. 343 et seq.

   The famous French Natural Lawyer Domat refers in similar terms to the same division of 'covenants' and to there being no distinction between those with a proper name and those which do not, as regards their binding effects on the parties to carry out that upon which they have agreed. Part I, Title I, Section 1, Arts. 147 to 150, p. 161 et seq. in the translation by William Strahan of *The Civil Law in its Natural Order (1689)*, published in 1850 and reprinted, Rothman & Co, Colorado, 1980.
7. Such consensual contracts were restricted to four: sale, hire, partnership and mandate. The importance of consensualism was that it removed from the criteria for validity any requirements of form, even that of writing and no earnest was required to be given as it was under ancient Greek law. Prior to the existence of the consensual contracts the only general means by which an obligation could be created was through the 'stipulation'. That was originally a formal oral question and answer in which there had to be a complete correspondence between the two and made by the parties at the same time in each other's presence. 'Do you pledge yourself to give me 100 aurei? I pledge myself.' Later the more formal requirements were relaxed and a written record was sufficient, provided it stated that the parties had been present together when the stipulation was made, unless evidence could be adduced that this was clearly false. Inst. III.19.12,17 and for the story generally see the excellent account in Zimmermann, pp. 68 et seq.

   Later stipulations were used to reinforce other contractual obligations much as we would include express undertakings in a contract.
   7(a) Express affirmations *dicta promissave* were prevalent but needed to be distinguished from mere 'sales puffs'. The distinction between the vendor *ignorans* and the vendor *sciens* was drawn clearly by Julian D.19.1.13. The former was liable only for the reduction in price to that which the buyer would have paid had he known the truth. The latter was liable for all losses incurred by the buyer. See further below, Chapter 12, 'The Roman actions'.
8. If ever Roman law were to have had a serious chance of being directly received into English law it must have been in the twelfth century when Vaccarius was teaching Roman law, probably at Oxford, and in the thirteenth century when Bracton wrote his famous *De Legibus et Consuetudinibus Angliae*. At that time the English law of contract was rudimentary and lacked any conceptual framework of the type which Roman law had forged over the centuries. But what Vaccarius taught was the academic Roman law of the early glossators divorced from practical considerations. What Bracton wrote, as regards contracts, was Roman in form only. In substance, and there was not much of it, the law was English. He can do little but recite the Roman names for the consensual contracts. Even when he refers to the sale of goods, the reference is not to a true consensual contract, but to a means of acquiring ownership which seems to require either delivery of the goods, or part payment or possibly even both, in order to be binding. The contract was in fact 'real'. The time was not ripe and the opportunity did not seriously recur.

   For the influence of Vaccarius see the Introduction to the *Liber Pauperum Selden Society*, reprinted, London Professional Books Limited, 1972, Chapter 1 at p. xxiii and Chapter VIII p. cxlviii.

   For Bracton on the law of obligations in relation to Roman law see Guterbock 1866, reprinted, Rothman, Colorado, 1979 at p. 144 et seq., Scrutton *Influence of the Roman law on the law of England*, Cambridge, 1855, reprinted, Rothman, 1985 at pp. 93 and 94, and Pollock and Maitland *History of English Law*, Bk 1 p. 206 et seq. and Bk 2 pp. 194 et seq.

   For general conclusions on the influence of Roman law on English law see Scrutton op. cit., pp. 194 and 195, Pollock and Maitland Bk 1, Chs. v and vii and also Allen *Law in The Making*, 4th ed., Oxford 1946 at pp. 234 et seq. Allen, however, in the author's view, goes much too far particularly in asserting 'that the influence of the *Corpus Juris* has been powerful and continuous from the earliest times' and the cases he quotes do not support him. What can be accepted is that Roman law did influence some parts of English law, more especially in Chancery and in the Court of Admiralty and there rules derived from

Roman law were adapted and became part of English law. But the rules of Roman law were never accepted as binding in themselves only as supportive of the court's conclusions, 'when it was a matter of deciding a case upon principle upon which no direct authority can be cited from our books', per Tindall C.J. in *Acton* v. *Blundell* (1843) 12 M & W 324, 353.

9. For an account of these borrowings see Simpson *Innovations in Nineteenth Century Contract Law in Legal Theory and Legal History*, Hambledon Press, 1987.

10. Both through the directives such as those on Unfair Contract Terms in Consumer Contracts and Commercial Agents, as well as conventions such as that of Rome on the law applicable to contractual obligations, civilian concepts are being introduced into English law and the process seems likely to accelerate. But the process is not one way and it seems likely that the complex German law provisions on damages for breach of contract will be amended in line largely with English law as a result of the incorporation into German law of the Vienna Convention on the International Sale of Goods.

11. See for a brief account of the Ius Commune Robinson et al, *An Introduction to European Legal History*, Professional Books Ltd., 1985, Chapter VII.

12. Buckland, *A Textbook of Roman Law*, Cambridge University Press, 1966 at p. 96.

13. Watson, *The Evolution of Law*, Blackwell, 1985 at p. 81.

14. The *Lex Salica* has been defined as 'that body of Frankish law by which any Frank choosing to acknowledge the kingship of Clovis was bound to live by'. It is predominantly German but compiled in vulgar Roman form. Wallace Hadrill, *The Long Haired Kings*, University of Toronto Press, 1982, p. 179 et seq.

15. Said to have been told by Agobard, Archbishop of Lyons, about 820 and quoted by Lawson in *A Common Lawyer looks at the Civil Law*, Greenwood Press, 1977.

16. See Vinogradoff, *Roman Law*, re-printed 1968, Cambridge, Chapter 1 'The Decay of Roman Law'.

17. J. P. Levy, op. cit., quotes a case in the middle of the ninth century at Chateau Landon (Seine et Marne) 'It was Roman law which ought to be applied because the Church lives by following the Roman law but no Judge could be found who remembers the Roman law'.

18. The main work was the *Digest*, a compilation of the writings of the great jurists of a classical period who had played the leading role in the development of Roman law. Among their duties was that of giving advice to the magistrate or *iudex* charged with hearing a case who were not at that time normally legally qualified. The most eminent of them had the right of *ius respondendi*, that of giving formal advice to the magistrate or the *iudex* chosen to hear a case which if not actually binding was of strong persuasive authority.

    Justinian's intention that this compilation should be a coherent statement of the law as it then existed and eliminate contradictory opinions was however never achieved. The *Digest* is both ill-ordered and full of contradictions. It contains statements both of classical law as well as that of the law of Justinian's time. But it is still a treasure-house of Roman legal learning.

    The Institutes, the other main work, were produced as a first year student's text-book although unusually for such a work it had the force of law. It is a systematic exposition of basic rules with little argument. In practice its influence was wider than planned since it was primarily in this simpler form, rather than through the complexities of the *Digest* that some knowledge of Roman law in its non-vulgar form was transmitted to the west, principally Italy, in the period between 500 and 1100 AD.

19. See for the influence which this school possessed 'Influence de l'enseignement du droit roman a Orleans sur les nations étrangères' and 'L'enseignement du droit a Orleans' in Feenstra *Le droit savant au moyen age et sa vulgarisation*, Variorum Reprints, London, 1986.

20. Levy, op. cit., p. 10.

21. As referred to earlier, the *Digest* was both ill-organized and in parts contradictory. The earliest scholars who worked on the text of the *Digest* were known as the 'Glossators' from their practice of putting marginal notes or 'glosses' against particular paragraphs of the text by way of explanation or cross reference to other paragraphs confirming or contradicting the text being studied. In time these 'glosses' became so extensive that they constituted a complete commentary on the *Digest* of which the best known and most important is the *Gloss of Accursius* completed in around 1250.

    The Commentators who followed the Glossators were more concerned with the use of the *Digest* in conjunction with local laws and customs as an aid to the practical solution of problems in everyday life. No longer was it a matter of understanding the *Digest* but of applying it in contemporary practice alongside other sources of law. The leading figures here were Bartolus who lived in the first half of the fourteenth century and Baldus, a pupil of his, whose work consisted primarily of writing opinions for the benefit either of the parties or of the Court itself. It was in this way that the law of the *Digest* was developed into the *ius commune*.

    See for more detail Robinson et al, op. cit., Chapters III and IV, and for an interesting study of the work of one of the Commentators, Lucas de Penna, *The Medieval Idea of Law* by Ullman, reprinted, Methuen, 1969.

22. See Dawson 'The French Deviation' in *Oracles of the Law*, University of Michigan Law School, 1968.

24

23. Ordinance of 1495 quoted Huebner *History of Germanic Private Law*, Continental Legal History Series, Rothman, Reprints 1968, p. 20.
24. Op. cit., p. 322.
25. See further Robinson et al, op. cit., pp. 472 et seq.
26. Weston, *An English Reader's guide to the French Legal System*, Berg, 1991 at p. 63.
27. Portalis *Discours et Rapports sur le Code Civil*, Centre de Philosophie Politique et Juridique, reprinted 1989, at p. 7 'Discours preliminaire sur le projet de code civil'.
28. David *French Law*, Tr. Michael Kindred, Louisiana State University Press, 1972 at p. 12.
29. See the comments on interpretation of the Act made by Atiyah on pp. 1–4 of his *Sale of Goods*, Pitman, 8th edition, 1990.
30. For a study of the politics of the period relating to legal unity see *Politics and the Law in late 19th century Germany, the Origins of the Civil Code*, Michael John, Clarendon Press, Oxford, 1989, in particular Ch. 3.
31. See Fifoot p. 229 and the case Anon. Y.B. Ed. IV, f.1, pl.2, AD 1478 given on p. 252.
32. See Fifoot p. 231 et seq. and the cases quoted there.
33. See for a description of 'wager of law' or 'compurgation' Pollock and Maitland, Ch. II, p. 634 et seq. and Potter *Historical Introduction to English Law*, 4th ed., 1958, p. 318 et seq. Although long obsolete, the procedure was not formally abolished until the Civil Procedure Act in 1833.
34. For a study on the use of penal bonds and the gradual insistence of the courts that the contracting party was only entitled to recover compensation amounting to the sum required to put him in the position he would have been had the contract been performed, see *The Penal Bond with Conditional Defeasance* in Simpson, op. cit., Ch. 7.
35. The reversal of the Roman rule was originated by canon law which held that failure to keep one's promise even although not on oath was a mortal sin – see Levy, op. cit., p. 134 and *Legacy of the Middle Ages – Canon Law*, Oxford, 1926. It is to be noted, however, that 'nude pacts' in Roman law referred only to those 'contracts' which were innominate and not to nominate contracts such as the consensual contract of sale – see Buckland & McNair, pp. 228 et seq.
36. The question of the influence of the canon law on the English law of contract has been much debated. Fifoot, op. cit., pp. 298 et seq. considers that it was significant and so it appears does Atiyah, although referring to a later period, e.g. at pp. 147 and 148 of *The Rise and Fall of the Freedom of Contract*, Oxford, 1979. Potter, op. cit., also sees the canon law as having been influential in the early development of the law of contract. Pollock and Maitland, Ch. II, p. 202, in contrast refer disparagingly to 'no English canonist having achieved anything for the law of contract' but the weight of evidence is against them.
37. See Fifoot, op. cit., pp. 296 et seq. The matter is clear as regards express warranties for defects not discoverable by the buyer at the time of purchase. But in the absence of an express warranty it seems that the buyer took the risk at least unless he could prove that the seller had knowingly sold defective goods. Fifoot refers to an isolated note by Frowicke, C.J., in 1507 to the seller being liable in deceit if he knowingly sold bad cloth even in the absence of an express warranty. Bewes, in *The Romance of the Law Merchant*, reprinted, Rothman, 1986, refers to the general rule in continental laws and in the Muhammadan law to the seller being liable for hidden defects, whether he knew of them or not, but that this rule did not apply in England which had adopted the principle caveat emptor.
38. Quoted Fifoot, op. cit., p. 337.
39. Fifoot, op. cit., p. 339.
40. In the case Slade had sold standing crops to the defendant for a fixed sum who had failed to pay for them. The jury found there had not been an express promise to pay. After several prolonged hearings it was finally established that 'every contract executory imports in itself an *Assumpsit* for when one agrees to pay money or deliver any thing thereby he assumes to promises to pay or deliver it'. See the report of the case in Fifoot, op. cit., pp. 371 et seq.
41. Fifoot, op. cit., pp. 400 and 401.
42. For an account of this see Atiyah, op. cit., pp. 420 et seq.
43. See Fifoot, op. cit., pp. 402 et seq.
44. See Simpson, op. cit., pp. 187 et seq.
45. It is true that the implied conditions as to merchantable quality and fitness for purpose under the Sale of Goods Act did reverse the caveat emptor rule where they apply; but see Nicholas in *Contract Law Today*, pp. 170 and 171 for the limits of their application. However, until the passing of the Unfair Contract Terms Act these conditions were invariably excluded by express terms both in consumer and business sales. While this is no longer possible in contracts with consumers they will still be excluded under almost any supplier's conditions of contract for business sales with the substitution of some limited warranty which the supplier hopes will pass the test of 'reasonableness' under the Unfair Contract Terms Act – see further Chapter 20.

FURTHER READING

An Introduction to European Legal History, Robinson et al., Professional Books Ltd 1985.

The Civil Law System, Von Mehren, Gordley, 2nd ed., Little Brown and Co., Boston 1977.

An Introduction to Comparative Law, Zweigert and Kotz, 2nd ed., Clarendon Press, Oxford, 1987.

The Law of Obligations, Reinhard Zimmermann, Juta, Cape Town 1990.

Legal Theory and Legal History, Simpson, Hambledon Press 1987.

The Oracles of the Law, Dawson, William S. Hein & Co., New York 1986.

2 English common law and the civil law systems of France and Germany – primary distinctions

It is not the purpose of this chapter to provide a detailed account of the constitutional, legal and judicial systems of France and Germany in comparison with those of England. There are excellent accounts to be found elsewhere.[1] The purpose is rather to identify some of the most important differences which exist between the French and German systems in comparison with those of English law, and also as between themselves, so far as these are helpful in gaining a comparative understanding of contract law in the three countries.

DIVISIONS OF THE LAW

English law is unique in that as regards contracts there are no divisions. A contractual dispute between two business people is heard in the same court as one between two private persons and is judged according to the same rules except where a particular statute differentiates between business and consumer transactions. There is no separate body of law applied to commercial acts and no separate courts established to deal solely with commercial disputes.[2]

Similarly a dispute relating to a contract for construction works between a company and a government department or a local authority is handled by the same courts, in exactly the same way and by application of the same rules, as would be applied to a dispute between a private developer and a contractor.

French law, however, makes two distinctions: first between public law and private law, and second, within private law, between civil law and commercial law.

PUBLIC LAW AND PRIVATE LAW

French law makes the fundamental distinction between public and private law which originated in Roman times, but whose current importance was established in the laws passed during the Revolution. Article 13 of the Law of 16–24 August 1790 provides that

> Judicial functions are distinct and will always remain separate from administrative functions. Judges in the civil courts may not under pain for forfeiture of their office concern themselves in any manner with the operation of the administration, nor shall they call administrators to account before them in respect of the exercise of their official function.

In order, however, to regulate the exercise by the administration of their functions and provide the citizen aggrieved by the act of the administration with some means of recourse Napoleon established the Conseil d'État. In 1806 there was formed within the Conseil what became known later as the 'Section du Contentieux' to deal with judicial matters. Originally its function was only advisory, although the advice was almost invariably followed, but in 1872 it was empowered by the Law of 24 May to reach decisions on its own authority, as any civil court, in the name of the French people.

However it still remained the position that the Conseil only had jurisdiction after a case had been referred to the appropriate minister and the citizen wished to appeal against the minister's decision. Then in the case of Cadot (CE 13 December 1889) the Conseil itself decided that it had jurisdiction both at first instance and on appeal and has been said in the observations on the case, 'Par l'arrêt Cadot le Conseil d'État s'est reconnu le juge de droit commun en premier et dernier resort des recours en annulation des actes administratifs et des recours en indemnité formés contre les collectivités publiques'.[3]

As Brown and Bell have observed, by the end of the nineteenth century the Conseil through its Section du Contentieux manifested all the features which the French associate with a court.[4]

That a court could be established within the administration, staffed by senior civil servants, which has exercised effective control over the acts of the administration may appear strange but all accounts testify to its undoubted success. In fact it has been so successful that two reforms have been needed to try to overcome the backlog of cases. In the first in 1953 the existing conseils de préfecture were turned into tribunaux administratifs and became the *juridiction de droit commun* at first instance. Second, 1987 saw the establishment of five regional cours administratifs d'appel which hear certain appeals from the tribunaux administratifs although other issues continue to go direct to the Conseil d'État.[5]

Apart from its role as the means by which the citizen can protect himself against an illegal act of the administration, the system of administrative courts is the one that must be used by a contractor whose contract is subject to the *droit administratif*. The ordinary civil courts will have no jurisdiction.

Further, the *droit administratif* differs in certain significant respects from that of the *droit civil*. The most important general distinction is that the *droit administratif* is not based upon the provisions of any code but is judge-made law without the strict rules of precedent which apply in England. In theory therefore the judge has the power to change a rule which has applied hitherto, but in practice once a general principle has been established by the Conseil d'État, this will normally be followed in the lower courts.

Such a general principle will not, however, necessarily be the same as the provision in the *Code Civil* even in a like situation to that which is provided for in the code. Although the Conseil d'État has adopted the principles upon which the text of the *Code Civil* relating to the *garantie décennale* in construction contracts are based, it has not adopted the text itself, and there are important differences between the application of the *garantie* under the code and under the administrative law (see further below, pp. 187–195).

It is essential therefore to establish by which of the two legal systems any given contract is governed. Unfortunately this is not always an easy decision to make. There is no single formal criterion by which it can be established which regime applies.

Rules for deciding on the applicable legal system

The only reasonably clear-cut rule which concerns us is that contracts for public works (*marchés de travaux publics*) are always administrative contracts. This was established by the *loi du 28 pluviose an VIII*. Although this rule is easy to state, it is not always easy to apply since it begs the question of what are to be considered as public works. Broadly they are building or civil engineering works, including repairs and demolition, executed for a public body either with the object of serving the general interest, or within the scope of a task of public service.[6]

Outside the rule established by statute, the courts have decided upon the following criteria for defining the administrative contract:

A contract is only administrative if at least one of the parties is a public body and either:

- the *objet* of the contract involves the actual performance itself of a public service, or,
- the contract contains terms which are wholly exceptional in comparison with those which it would be normal to find in such a contract.[7]

Application of the above criteria

1. The only exceptions which have been made to the principle that at least one of the parties must be a public body have been where a concession has been given to a company not publicly owned for the construction and operation of motorways or where it has been decided that the contracting company was acting as 'representative of' the public body in the execution of the construction works.[8]
2. The requirement that the obligation of the contractor must be to execute the obligation itself of the public body means that merely to assist the public body in fulfilling its statutory obligations is not sufficient. So in a well known case a contract merely to supply a town council with cobble stones, so that the town could maintain its pavements, was a contract subject to civil law.[9] Similarly to supply provisions to a public authority would be a contract under civil law while on the other hand a contract

to undertake the actual feeding of Russian refugees which was a responsibility of the state was a contract governed by administrative law.[10]

3. In order for clauses to constitute what are referred to as *clauses exorbitantes* they must not be such as would not normally be found in commercial contracts: as an example, a clause which allows the public body to cancel the contract at any time they wish to do so without the contractor being in default; or a clause which gives the public body authority to 'direct, watch over and verify the performance of the work'.[11]

4. Although the main contract may be governed by the administrative law the sub-contract will be subject to the civil law and the jurisdiction of the civil courts.

Consequences of the choice of system

The choice of which system applies determines which court has jurisdiction – the civil court or the administrative court. Because of the complexity of the rules there are unfortunately many instances in which a case has proceeded as far as the civil *cour d'appel* only for the court to decide that it does not have jurisdiction and for the plaintiff to have to start again in the lower tribunal administratif and vice versa as a result of decisions by the Conseil d'État. Ultimately if the two jurisdictions disagree then the matter has to be referred to the Tribunal des Conflits for a decision.[12]

While at least in theory a civil contract is formed by the two parties freely agreeing to the terms which it contains, both their wills having equal legal validity, an administrative contract is always subject to the inherent superior power of the public body to act in the manner which it considers appropriate in the exercise of its public functions. This will include the right to modify or terminate the contract unilaterally without restriction and if the public body is in default the contractor has no right to exercise *exceptio non adimpleti contractus* (see below, pp. 324–325). Further, the public body may act against the contractor without notice or proof of fault or reference to the administrative court. The public body has not only the power but the obligation to act as it considers fit in the public interest and to require the contractor to perform accordingly.

At the same time the contractor is given the right to require the restoration of the economic equilibrium of the contract if the public body exercises its powers so as to render performance of the contract more onerous, assuming of course that this is not the result of the contractor being in default.

If the contractor is required to continue performance of a long-term contract in totally changed economic circumstances which could not have been foreseen and which are independent of the will of the parties, he has the right to require an amendment of the contract terms/prices under the doctrine known as *imprévision* (see below, pp. 333–334).

Although as stated earlier the rules governing contracts for public works generally follow the principles of the *Code Civil* there are certain important differences especially as regards sub-contractors and suppliers (see below, p. 195).

CIVIL LAW AND COMMERCIAL LAW – FRANCE

Under French law the *Code de Commerce* is the law governing inter alia industrial property rights, companies' commercial partnerships, negotiable instruments and bankruptcy. Traditionally bankruptcy in France was available only to merchants but a procedure for dealing with the over-indebtedness of private individuals was established by the Loi no. 89–1010 of 31 December 1989 and amended by the Loi no. 91–650 of 9 July 1991 which entered into force 1 January 1993. Interestingly the code also contains the legislation relating to consumer protection.

However in practice today the *Code de Commerce* has little relevance in relation to ordinary sales of goods as regards the substantive law which is essentially governed by the *Code Civil*. The only real difference is that in the case of a sale between merchants, *une acte de commerce* as defined in the *Code de Commerce* Art. 632, the court will take into account trade customs and usage, e.g. the presumption of solidarity between co-debtors of a commercial obligation.

In practical terms the main issue is that of the jurisdiction of the court of first instance and the procedure which the court will apply.

If the case is a commercial one then it must be referred to the appropriate *tribunal de commerce*, of which there are some 230 in France, their number and location being related to the level of business activity within the area concerned. The judges, known as *juges consulaires*, are not professional judges but experienced business people elected by an electoral college of the leaders of the local business community and members of the chamber of commerce. Only in Alsace-Lorraine is there an exception to this. There commercial cases are heard by a special division of the normal civil court, the *tribunal de grande instance*, with one professional judge and two lay assessors.[13]

The procedure before the *tribunal de commerce* differs from that of the *tribunal de grande instance* in that it is more informal and essentially oral: oral proof is allowed.

There is of course no equivalent in English law to the *tribunal de commerce* and the suggestion that the term can be translated into the commercial court of the Queen's Bench Division seems inappropriate in view of the use of lay judges and the sheer volume of litigation (nearly 200 000 cases a year) which are heard by the tribunaux, many of them of a minor nature. In fact it is untranslatable. One important consequence of their being staffed by experienced business people and not professional judges is that there is less inclination on the part of litigants in commercial and construction matters to refer cases to arbitration.

CIVIL LAW AND COMMERCIAL LAW – GERMANY

While the concept of public law exists in Germany it does not affect contracts and commercial transactions such as the sale of goods or construction works. These are all governed by the civil code, the *BGB* and the commercial code, the Handelsgesetzbuch (HGB). In addition, as regards public procurement there are regulations which require the authorities to follow the codes of procedure known as the *VOL* for supplies contracts and the *VOB* for public works contracts (see below, p. 222). However there is no separate set of courts to deal with contracts which are subject to these regulations. A public works contract in Germany will be litigated in the ordinary civil courts. The same problems do not exist therefore in Germany as exist in France.

The commercial code

There are not many significant differences in German law between contracts entered into between merchants as defined in Art. 1 of the code and non-merchants. In practice any transaction between registered companies will be considered to be a transaction between merchants.

The only provisions which are of general significance for commercial contracts for sale or for works are:

1. Customs and usages of merchants are to be taken into account in respect of the meaning and effect of the contract – Art. 346, *HGB*.
2. A penalty which is stipulated by a merchant in a contract made in the course of his business cannot be reduced by the court under Art. 343 of the *BGB* (see below, p. 232).
3. If a commercial letter of confirmation, *kaufmannisches Bestätigungsschreiben*, is sent by one party to a transaction to another, then as between merchants, the recipient of the letter must immediately object if he does not agree that the letter sets out the bargain correctly which they have previously discussed say over the telephone. In contrast to the normal rule, silence will be taken to mean agreement, unless the letter has made some major change to what had in fact been agreed to, or introduced some new term which is quite unexpected in the trade concerned (see further below, p. 75).
4. If the sale is a commercial sale between merchants then the buyer must immediately examine the goods to the extent that this is practicable and advise the seller of any defects (Art. 377, *HGB*). Failure to do so will result in the goods being accepted unless it can be established that the defect was not one which was discoverable on such examination. This rule also applies if the goods differ from those ordered unless the difference is so obvious that the seller must have known that they would not be accepted.
5. Some requirements of form do not apply to commercial transactions

Commercial court

At the level of the Landgericht, which is the normal court of first instance for all but the most trivial cases, there is in most Länder a separate division of the court to which the plaintiff can apply if it is a commercial dispute. This court consists of one professional judge who presides and two experienced business people who act as assessors (*ehrenamtliche Richter*). These are the equivalent of the French *juges consulaires* and therefore the position is the same as in Alsace-Lorraine.

CONCEPTUALISM AND PRAGMATISM

It is frequently stated that one of the main distinctions between the common law and the civil law, especially that of Germany, is that the civil law system is highly conceptual whilst that of the common law is pragmatic.

Like most generalizations it contains an element of truth, although today this can be exaggerated, and it is important therefore to understand both the distinction and the factors which are responsible for it.

The primary characteristic of a civil law system is that it possesses a structure made up of logically linked concepts, beginning with general principles and moving on to the more detailed rules, so that the whole fits together as a complete, self-contained entity. Further, this structure extends to the whole of the law covered by the civil code concerned.

So contract forms a part of the wider law of obligations. An obligation, according to the Roman definition still valid today, is 'A tie of law which binds us according to the rule of our civil law to render something'.[14] If one refers to a standard French textbook this definition of an obligation will then be developed and obligations classified according to their source as being 'contractual, quasi-contractual, delictual or quasi-delictual'.[15] Similarly in German law one finds the laws of obligations in Book 2 of the *BGB*. Obligations are created by contract (Art. 305) or by operation of law, e.g. delicts (Art. 823 of the *BGB*). Having defined the general nature of obligations, the details follow as to particular contracts and particular forms of delict.

Since the codes constitute the primary source of law, this type of format leads to a form of reasoning in which, having started with the basic relevant facts, one proceeds by deduction from the general principles relevant to those facts to the particular rule which applies in the case in question. Of course even then the legal rule is unlikely to be framed in such absolute terms that one could do without what Brierley has referred to as 'secondary rules', that is the rules derived from the decisions of the higher courts. Whether such rules are now applicable requires the facts to be examined in more detail.[16]

An example may help to make the matter clear. Suppose that the case concerns the validity of a contract under French law in which the price has not been fixed and no objective mechanism is contained in the contract by which the price can be fixed. The validity of a contract is determined by reference to Art. 1108 of the *Code Civil*. One essential condition for a contract to be valid is that the *objet* (see below, p. 83) is certain. The rules relating to an *objet* are contained in Arts 1126 et seq. and Art. 1129 says that it is necessary for the *objet* to be determined or at least determinable. Finally if the contract is one for sale then under Art. 1591 the price must be determined and designated by the parties.

So the first step is to classify the contract. If it is a contract for sale then under Art. 1591 the contract would be void. To classify the contract it might be necessary to distinguish a contract for sale from one for works or one for distribution (see below, pp. 46–49). This could only be done by applying to the facts the 'secondary rules' derived from the decisions of the *Cour de cassation*.

Even if the contract is not one for sale the *objet* of the contract must still be determined but the 'secondary rules' as to the need for the price to be determined vary according to the contract's classification. Again the court would need to apply such rules to the facts of the contract to decide on the classification and then decide whether or not in the circumstances, and according to the classification, the requirement for a determined *objet* had been satisfied (see below, p. 45).

While therefore the common law lawyer will tend to start by looking for analogous cases – from, it has been said, 'instances to principles', the civil lawyer will start by looking for the applicable rules in descending order of generality – 'from principles to instances'. Even if the common law lawyer is applying a statute his first inclination is to try to discover cases in which the relevant provisions have already been interpreted. By contrast the civil law lawyer will only consider case-law or jurisprudence when he needs to flesh out the principles established by the code through the application of 'secondary rules'.

SOURCES OF LAW

CODES AND STATUTES

As stated already the primary source of law in France and Germany in respect of contracts is the *Code Civil* supported by the commercial code and in France the administrative law applying to administrative contracts. The point was also made earlier (see above, p. 8) that a code differs from an English statute in its comprehensiveness and in its effect of denying any further validity to laws which existed prior to the establishment of the code. In practice there is one exception to this in the survival of long established customs of merchants.

Both the French *Code Civil* and to a lesser extent the *BGB* differ from an English statute also in the way in which they are drafted. An English statute is drafted in great detail and precision in accordance with the wishes of Parliament and with the general attitude towards statutes and their interpretation by the courts.[17] In the past it was also influenced by the idea that the true law was the common judge-made law and that statutes were invaders which had to be kept under strict control. Given the volume of statutory legislation, that is a view which is no longer openly maintained but whose echoes are still to be heard at times.

In contrast certainly the *Code Civil* itself and to a degree the *BGB* are drafted in terms of principles, leaving the courts to decide on the precise meaning of the text. This practice does not however apply to the same extent to the mass of legislation passed more recently in both countries which has tended to follow the English example of detailed drafting.

STATUTORY INTERPRETATION

The general approach of the French and German courts towards statutory interpretation, outside the penal matters, is that it is the function of the court to examine the texts, and if necessary in instance of doubt to refer to analogous texts, with a view to determining the meaning of the statute by reference to its purpose. Preparatory work on the laws as they pass through Parliament may also be consulted. The court will also take into account the need for ensuring the consistency and coherence of the law.

These continental principles of teleological interpretation have been adopted by the European Court of Justice. It has been said of that court that 'difficulties of interpretation are frequently resolved not through a grammatical interpretation but by resorting to an examination of the objects of the provision and its place in the system of the Treaty'.[18]

As regards current practice of the English courts on statutory interpretation the evidence suggests that England is moving closer towards its continental neighbours and looking more towards the design or purpose of the legislation so as to produce the effect intended, rather than, as so often in the past, to stick literally to the words of the text. This is despite rebukes given by the House of Lords to Lord Denning for having dared to suggest that equivalent teleological reasoning to that used on the continent should be applied in England, not just to community law but also to international treaties other than the community treaties and perhaps even wider.[19]

The decision of the House of Lords in 1993 to allow reference to reports of debates or proceedings in Parliament as an aid to construing legislation which is ambiguous or obscure, if such reference could disclose the mischief aimed at, or the legislative intent behind the ambiguous or obscure text, is an indication of this trend.[20]

COURT DECISIONS AND PRECEDENTS

The English doctrine of precedent

The English doctrine of precedent establishes that the *ratio decendi* of a decision by the House of Lords is binding on all other courts and that of a decision of the Court of Appeal is binding on all lower courts and on itself unless overruled by the House of Lords. The House of Lords however has the right, only occasionally exercised, to reverse one of its own decisions.

The *ratio decendi* (the reasons for the decision) become in this way part of English law but not the *obiter dicta*, that is the parts of the judgement which were not necessary for the decision which was reached. The dividing line between the two is of course often not easy to draw. Further, since each member of the court is free to give his own judgement, and while agreeing to the decision may differ in his reasoning from his colleagues, it is difficult on occasions to determine just what was the ratio decendi of the decision which constitutes the precedent.

The differences between this system and that which prevails in France and Germany, while still significant, have become much less so in recent years. However for a proper understanding of the difference it is necessary to say something briefly about the system of the superior courts in both countries.

The French superior court system

There are 30 cours d'appel in France which hear appeals on matters of both fact and law from the tribunaux de Grande Instance and the tribunaux de commerce. The hearing is a complete re-hearing of the case. From the cours d'appel appeal lies only a matter of law to the *Cour de cassation*. As the name implies the *Cour de cassation* does not have the power to issue its own decision on the case but only to uphold or quash the decision of the cour d'appel.

Primarily the function of the *Cour de cassation* is to ensure the uniformity of the application of the law by the lower courts. The court has however extended its control to the reasoning of law by which the lower court reached its decision – see Terré, *Introduction générale au droit*, Dalloz 1991 at page 91.

If the decision is quashed then the case is referred back to another cour d'appel for a re-hearing. From the judgement of the second cour d'appel a further appeal lies to the *Cour de cassation* on a matter of law which will be heard by the court *en assemblée plénière* with a total of 25 judges. If the *Cour de cassation* quashes the second appeal on the same grounds then it refers the matter back to another cour d'appel which this time is obliged to accept the ruling on law of the *Cour de cassation* but is entitled to exercise its own discretion on matters of fact.

A further point is that the *Cour de cassation* has three civil divisions together with a commercial division and it is possible therefore for differences of opinion as between the divisions to arise (see for an example below, p. 273). Again in that event the court will normally sit *en assemblée plénière* in order to resolve the issue.

There is no formal system of precedent in the English sense and indeed until recently it was generally held by legal writers that the decisions even of the *Cour de cassation* were not law in the formal meaning of that term. The decisions were effective only as between the parties.[21] It has however increasingly become recognized that the decisions of the *Cour de cassation* which constitute an *arrêt de principe* (judgement in principle) do in effect constitute 'secondary rules' of law and any opinion obtained from a French lawyer will refer to the relevant decisions of the *Cour de cassation* and even perhaps of a cour d'appel. Decisions of the *Cour de cassation* will be cited by the lawyers to the court and are certainly persuasive. Decisions of the cour d'appel for a particular region are again likely to be persuasive at least within the region for which that court has jurisdiction. Again if one looks at modern French textbooks as many cases will be cited as will be found in an equivalent English textbook and some books have even started to include an index of cases.

The judgements of all the French courts including the *Cour de cassation* are those of the court and no dissenting opinions are expressed. The form of the judgement follows a strict logical pattern and in the *Cour de cassation* is laconic in the extreme, often being only half a page long. In the lower courts judgements are generally longer. However it is possible from the wording of the judgement in the *Cour de cassation* to establish its significance. In particular one should note if the court has set out either at the beginning or during the course of the judgement a statement of principle 'un chapeau' or has affirmed in the judgement that the court below decided the matter *à bon droit* or *légitimement.*[22]

Since formally judgements of any court including that of the *Cour de cassation* do not constitute law, the decisions are never cited in the judgements, indeed any decision of a cour d'appel which purported to be based on a judgement of the *Cour de cassation* would be immediately quashed as having no legal basis. The judgement has to be based formally on an article of the *Code Civil*. The facts of the case, especially in the judgements of the *Cour de cassation*, are usually limited to three or four lines. It follows that there is no room for the English practice of distinguishing one decision from another.

In general case-law in France, without having the binding nature of English superior court judgements, has moved a long way from the position which it once occupied and it must in practice today be regarded as a true source of law. But because of their form the judgements are not easy to interpret and show none of the policy considerations by which they have been influenced. On their own, without extensive comment, their effect on the development of the law would be to that extent restricted but we shall return to this point in the section on doctrine.

The German superior court system

In many respects the German system is similar to the French. There are some 24 regional courts of appeal (Oberlandsgerichte) from which decisions on points of law can be appealed to the Bundesgerichtshof. Essentially the Bundesgerichtshof is a court of *cassation*, that is it either confirms the judgement of the appeal court or refers it back to that court for the case to be finally decided, but if all the facts have been clearly established the BGH can substitute its own decision for that of the OLG. There is no practice of referring the decision back to a different court of appeal.

As regards the judgements themselves, they are much longer than those in the *Cour de cassation* and after having given a brief statement of the facts will frequently proceed to a learned review of the academic literature on the subject. Previous decisions of the court will frequently be cited, sometimes to distinguish them as in English practice, but more often to confirm that the judgement is in line with the court's previous thinking.

Despite its apparent academic approach the Bundesgerichtshof (BGH) has shown considerable courage and skill in developing in conjunction with learned writers what is in essence pure judge-made law, e.g. the doctrines of *culpa in contrahendo* (see below, p. 64) and 'the contract with protective effects' (see below, p. 281) and in certain instances a robust application of commonsense.

DOCTRINE

For a variety of reasons academic writers have had a far greater influence on German and French law than on English law. First, the cradle of the civil law is the university while that of the common law is the courts. Lawyers on the continent have always been trained initially in universities whereas until recently the only training which English lawyers received was through their professional bodies, i.e. the Inns of Court and the Law Society. The prestige of the professors in the main centres of legal learning has been higher than that of their English counterparts and so their opinions have carried greater weight with their one-time students.

Although the picture is changing now, those are the historical circumstances which have encouraged the respect shown by the courts to academic writings and certainly in Germany an interplay between the academics and the courts.

Second, and especially in France, because of the laconic nature of the judgements of the *Cour de cassation*, it has only been through the writers of notes on the cases and learned articles, comments and textbooks that the reasoning behind the judgements has been exposed to review and criticism.

Third, as indicated earlier, there were gaps in the civil codes and a need to modify the codes to deal with economic and social changes not foreseen by their original authors. This is a task for which the courts on their own were not well suited given that there was no scope for the publication of dissenting judgements which could in due course serve to change legal direction. One thinks of the famous judgement by Lord Denning in *Candler* v. *Crane and Christmas Co*. which opened the way fourteen years later to the landmark decision in *Hedley Byrne*.[23]

Finally, judges in France and Germany are professional career judges who after their university education are trained as judges with a status similar to that of civil servants. They are only exceptionally in France drawn from the ranks of the legal profession. Partly because of this, the anonymity of their judgements, and what is today largely a fiction – that they do not make law, only interpret it – their general approach is conservative. They cannot make a name for themselves however eminent they may be considered by their colleagues. If there is to be an advance in thinking it is far more likely to come from the scholar.

INTERPRETATION OF CONTRACTS AND GOOD FAITH

As with the statutes there are distinctions in the way in which a French or German lawyer will interpret a contract as compared with his English counterpart. For instance the English lawyer will tend to interpret the contract literally in accordance with its terms and, for example, draw distinctions between the use of one term rather than another so as to justify the conclusion that the use of different but similar expressions implied that the draftsman intended them to have different meanings. This type of approach is not followed by French and German lawyers who are required not to interpret individual terms literally but to look for the common intention of the parties.[24]

On occasions the literal English interpretation is modified by the use by the court of implied terms, but there is a basic difference here between the approach of the two systems.

In addition, particularly under German law, contracts are both to be interpreted and applied in accordance with good faith. We have noted already (see above p. 22) that there is no general requirement of good faith under English law.

NOTES

1. For France see *The French Legal System*, West et al., Fourmat Publishing, 1992. For Germany reference can be made to the now somewhat elderly but still instructive *Manual of German Law*, E. J. Cohn, British Institute of International and Comparative Law, 1968, and more up to date the summary in the Introduction to *The German Law of Tort*, B. S. Markesinis, 2nd ed., Clarendon Press, 1990 and an *Introduction to German Civil and Commercial Law*, Gerhard Dannemann, BIICL, 1993. For a general overview with interesting examples of civil law systems see *Comparative Law – Cases, Text-Materials*, Schlesinger et al., 5th ed., The Foundation Press, New York, 1988.
2. There is the Commercial Court established formally as part of the Queens Bench Division of the High Court by the Administration of Justice Act 1970 s.3 to allow commercial matters to be dealt with speedily by a simplified procedure and decided by a specialist judge, although regrettably the same delays apply today in this court as elsewhere in the High Court. But it is still part of the High Court and administers the same law as do the other courts of the Queens Bench Division.
3. *Les grandes arrêts de la jurisprudence administrative*, Sirey, Paris, 1990, (Gr.Ar.) at p. 49.
4. *French Administrative Law*, Brown and Bell, 4th ed., Butterworths, 1993 at p. 46.
5. For details see West et al., op. cit., pp. 100 and 101.
6. *Les droits des travaux publics*, Jean Dufau, Éditions du Moniteur, Paris, 1988 s.75.
7. These two criteria are alternatives – see *Droit Administratif*, Rivero, 13th ed., Dalloz, 1990 at p. 148.
8. Decision of the *Tribunal des Conflits*, 8 July 1963, Société Entreprise Peyrot, reported with observations in Gr. Ar. p. 615.
9. C.E. 31 July 1912, Société des granits porphyroides des Vosges, Gr. Ar. p. 154.
10. C.E. 20 April 1956, Époux Bertin, Gr. Ar. p. 536 and for a discussion on this case and that noted above see Rivero, op. cit., pp. 150 and 151.
11. See for example Gr. Ar. pp. 156 and 157.
12. As an example of the problems which can arise a contract had been placed by the local authority for the construction of a new sewage system. An item of construction plant used by the contractor damaged the illuminated sign and glass window of a store. The owner of the store sued the local authority for damages in the Administrative Tribunal and then before the Conseil d'État, only to be told by the latter that jurisdiction belonged to the ordinary courts. The reason for the decision was that according to a law of 31 December 1975 the ordinary courts alone are competent to hear actions in respect of damage resulting from vehicles whether private or belonging to the administration, and the Conseil d'État classified an item of construction plant which moved as a vehicle. C.E. 19 January 1990. This was confirmed again in a recent case in which damage was caused to property adjacent to construction works partially by the vibrations of the construction plant used by the contractor and partially by the method of excavation. The case concerning the damage due to the use of the construction plant could only be heard before the ordinary courts whilst that for the damage due to the way in which the works were being executed had to be brought before the administrative courts. C.E. 16 November 1992.
13. For details relating to the Tribunaux de Commerce see West et al, op. cit., pp. 88 and 89.
14. *Institutes*, Book III, Chapter 13.
15. As an example Weill and Terré, pp. 18 and 20.
16. Brierley, *Major Legal Systems in the World Today*, 3rd ed., Stevens, 1985, pp. 99 and 100.
17. See comments and examples quoted in *British and French Statutory Drafting*, The Proceedings of the Franco-British Conference of 7 and 8 April 1986, Institute of Advanced Legal Studies, the University of London, at pp. 60 and 61.
18. Judge Kutscher in 'Methods of Interpretation as seen by a Judge at the Court of Justice Judicial and Academic Conference 27–28 September 1976', quoted on p. 161 in Lasok and Bridge, *Law and Institutions of the European Community*, 5th ed., Butterworths, 1991.
19. For the story of Lord Denning's efforts and their rebuffs by the House of Lords see Chapter 2 of Lord Denning *The Discipline of the Law*, Butterworths, 1979.
20. *Pepper (Inspector of Taxes)* v. *Hart and others* [1993] 1 All E.R. 42.
21. This is indeed what is stated by Art. 5 of the *Code Civil* 'Judges are forbidden to make general pronouncements and rulings on cases which are submitted to them'. However, most modern French authors would accept that in practice jurisprudence is a source of law, Starck *Introduction au Droit*, 2nd ed., Litec, Paris, 1988 s.827 and see also *Les grandes arrêts de la jurisprudence civile*, 9th ed., Dalloz, Paris, 1991, p. 300.

22. See *Methodes du Droit, Le Commentaire d'Arrêt en Droit Privé*, 3rd ed., Dalloz, Paris, 1989 at s.112.
23. [1941] 2 K.B.64.
24. Under the general heading of 'The interpretation of agreements' Art. 1156 of the *Code Civil* provides that 'In agreements one should seek the common intention of the parties rather than stick to the literal sense of the terms'. This rule is applied if the terms are ambiguous or their meaning uncertain or if, although the meaning of the terms is clear, there is proof that they do not represent the parties' common intentions. However, if the terms are clear and no such proof is given, the court below must not denature the contract in order to do what appears to them to be justice or their decision will be open to be quashed by the *Cour de cassation*. See Mazeaud/Chabas, p. 316 et seq.

Much the same provision is contained in Art. 133 of the BGB which states that 'In the interpretation of a declaration of intent the true intention is to be ascertained without taking account of the literal meaning of the terms'. This is however qualified by Art. 157 BGB which states that 'Agreements must be interpreted according to the requirements of good faith, ordinary usage being taken into account'. The first provision establishes a subjective approach to the interpretation of the contract while the second concentrates on objective considerations taking account of how the one party would have interpreted at the time of entering into the contract what the other had said or written. It is this latter interpretation which is that generally found today in the judgements of the courts.

Despite this it is still the case that the courts have a wider scope for a more liberal and less literal interpretation of contracts than is to be found under English law.

3 Essentials of a valid contract

GENERAL REQUIREMENTS

The essential elements of a valid contract in each system will be briefly identified. The primary common element, agreement, will be the subject of this and the next two chapters. The following chapters will then cover the elements peculiar to each system and their relationship with their nearest English equivalents.

ENGLISH LAW

The requirements for a valid contract under English law are:

- *Agreement* between the parties, usually expressed in terms of offer and acceptance
- *Intention* to create legal relations
- *Capacity* of the parties
- *Consideration*.

FRENCH LAW

Art. 1108 of the *Code Civil* also lays down four conditions as being essential to the validity of an agreement:

- *Consent* of the party who places himself under an obligation[1]
- *Capacity* to contract
- *Un objet* which is certain and which forms the subject matter of the agreement[2]
- *Une cause* which is legal.[2]

GERMAN LAW

- *Consent* of the parties expressed by means of their 'declarations of will' (*Willenserklärung*) which correspond with each other
- *Capacity* of the parties
- *Possibility*. The contract must not have been objectively impossible of performance at the time when it was concluded (s.306, *BGB*).

ELEMENTS COMMON TO ALL THREE SYSTEMS

OFFERS AND ACCEPTANCE – INTRODUCTION

As is to be expected in systems which are consensualist as opposed to formalist (see above, p. 23) there are two primary concepts which are common: the need for agreement and for that agreement to be given by those having the necessary legal capacity. In practice today this latter requirement is only exceptionally of importance in relation to business contracts.[3]

The need for agreement is usually discussed in each of the systems under the related concepts of offer and acceptance which together establish the mutual consent of the parties. This section will deal with offers, Chapter 4 with termination of offers and Chapter 5 with acceptance.

OFFERS AND INVITATIONS TO TREAT

All three systems of law draw a distinction between an offer in a contractual sense, which is capable of being accepted, so forming a contract, and an 'offer' which signifies only the commencement of negotiations: in English terminology an 'invitation to treat' and in French *une offre d'entrer en pourparlers*.

Under each system there are two factors which must be present for an offer to be capable of acceptance. First, there must be an intention on the part of the person making the offer to be contractually bound. Second, the offer must be sufficiently complete to allow of its acceptance.

INTENTION TO BE BOUND – ENGLISH LAW

An offer is an expression of willingness to be bound by its terms once it has been accepted. It is an established rule of English law that no such intention to be legally bound is constituted by the circulation of price lists, catalogues or advertisements for sale or by the display of items in a shop or on the shelves of a supermarket. In all these instances there is only 'an invitation to treat' and the offer is made by the customer – in the example of the shop or supermarket by taking the goods to the cash desk, which the shop-keeper or store manager is then free to accept or reject.[4]

INTENTION TO BE BOUND – FRENCH LAW

In French law on the contrary each of the above activities would be considered as an offer capable of acceptance provided only that the item and price were clearly stated.[5] The issue of the catalogue or the display of the item in the shop is considered as a sign of the continuing will of the seller to sell the item(s) concerned which the buyer accepts by placing his order unless on the facts a contrary intention is established.[6] In the specific case of the supermarket it has been decided with the approval of the *Cour de cassation* that the contract is made when the shopper places the item marked with a fixed price which she accepts in the basket provided by the supermarket for that purpose and which she is bound to use until the check-out. Therefore when injuries were caused to a shopper by the explosion of a bottle of lemonade in her basket, due to improper storage of the bottle close to a source of heat, the store was held to be liable to the shopper in damages for breach of contract under Art. 1147 of the *Code Civil*.[7]

Under English law on the facts as reported the customer would have had an action against the store in negligence but under French law according to the principle *non-cumul* the existence of a contractual responsibility does not permit a claim to be made in delict.[8]

In fact a claim was made under Arts 1382, 1383 and 1384 of the code which cover delictual responsibility but was rejected because the store was held liable for breach of contract.

INTENTION TO BE BOUND – GERMAN LAW

German law on the other hand is closer to English law as regards the distinction between an offer and an invitation to treat. In general the issue of a catalogue or advertisement, or the placing of articles on shop shelves will be considered as an invitation to treat rather than an offer itself. So also will an offer which is qualified as *freibleibend*, an offer which is not binding (see further below, p. 63). There is academic debate on the position regarding items displayed in a supermarket as to whether such display constitutes an offer which is accepted by presenting the item at the check-out, or simply an invitation to treat and the presentation at the check-out constitutes the offer which the cashier accepts by ringing up the till.[9]

COMPARATIVE NOTE

Given modern shopping methods the French solution to the problem appears the more appropriate. Catalogues make it clear that items offered for sale are subject to availability; the normal rule in a shop is that one can only buy at the price shown, and if a shop-keeper does not wish to sell a specific article, because he has already promised it to someone else, then he should not expose it for sale complete with price ticket.[10]

UNIFORM LAW FOR INTERNATIONAL SALES

However, the French solution to the problem did not find favour with the negotiators of the Uniform Law for International Sales under the 1980 United Nations Convention. Article 14 of the Uniform Law draws a distinction between

1. A proposal for concluding a contract addressed to one or more specific persons which will constitute an offer if it is sufficiently definite and indicates the intention of the offeror to be bound in the case of acceptance; and

2. A proposal other than one addressed to one or more specific persons which is to be considered merely as an invitation to make offers unless the contrary is clearly indicated by the person making the proposal.

In his commentary, *Uniform Law for International Sales*, John Honnold (Kluwer, 1991, 2nd ed., p. 136) refers to catalogues describing goods and indicating prices being issued widely and to the difficulties he sees this as creating for sellers if these were considered as offers capable of acceptance, e.g. demand exceeding supply because of production difficulties, which is very much the approach of English and indeed German law. He also suggests that the addressing of offers to 'specific persons' should be defined as 'restricted to the addressees only'.

It is still considered, however, that the preferred commercial solution, even in international sales, is to regard catalogues, certainly those which contain prices and an order form with terms of sale printed on it, however widely issued, as offers capable of acceptance rather than as mere invitations to treat.

COMPLETENESS OF THE OFFER – ENGLISH LAW

The other requirement of all three systems is that the offer must be sufficiently complete to be capable of acceptance. In practice in England the courts may treat this not as a separate requirement but as an indicator of the seriousness of intention to be bound. So, particularly in cases involving large and valuable estates, it has been held that it is legitimate, in deciding the question as to whether there is a contract or not, to consider the probability of the parties having intended to be bound by the use of 'phrases and expressions of doubtful significance'.[11]

A similar approach was taken by Lord Wright in *Scammell* v. *Ouston* where an order issued for the purchase of a van stated that 'it was given on the understanding that the balance of the purchase price can be had on hire purchase terms over a period of two years'. Although the order was accepted no such terms were ever agreed. In describing his second reason for holding that no contract had ever been concluded he said, 'But I think that the other reason which is that the parties never in intention nor even in appearance reached an agreement, is still a sounder reason against enforcing the claim. In truth in my opinion their agreement was inchoate and never got beyond negotiations'.[12]

Certainty of price

English law does not require that the offer should state the price for the goods or services to be supplied since in the absence of any such statement it will be inferred by statute that a reasonable price is to be paid,[13] provided that there is nothing in the offer or 'contract' documents which is inconsistent with this assumption and leaves no room for the application of the statutory inference.

Such inconsistency could be constituted by a statement that 'the price is to be negotiated or agreed between us'.[14] Unless an offer in those terms specifies objective criteria, trade custom or past course of dealing upon which such negotiations are to proceed, or provides a mechanism for settling a failure to agree, then it will be considered that the parties are still really in a state of negotiation and English law does not know a contract to negotiate.[15]

Despite this it would appear that offers which refer to 'price ruling at date of despatch' and so make the price dependent upon the will of the seller, will be held to be valid at least if they refer to the seller's price list or some other standard and perhaps even if they do not.[16]

COMPLETENESS – FRENCH LAW

'The declaration of will only constitutes an offer if it is sufficiently definitive and complete.' The offer should in principle contain all the essential terms of the contract so that a simple 'I agree' by the recipient is sufficient to form the contract. If it is not definitive on price it will be treated only as *une offre d'entrer en pourparlers*.

Certainty of price

The general rule is that for a contract to be valid the price must either be determined or objectively determinable at the time the contract is concluded.[17] This rule is based on Art. 1129 of the *Code Civil* according to which the *objet* of the obligation (under the contract) must be *une chose* determined, or of which the quantity may be uncertain, provided that it can be determined. In the application of this article *une chose* is considered as including the contract price and therefore the requirement should apply to all contracts, although in practice this is not always the case and different rules may be applied according to how the contract is classified (see below, pp. 47 and 48).[18]

In addition to the general rule there are specific rules relating only to contracts for the sale of goods which are set out in Arts 1591 and 1592 of the *Code Civil* and are derived directly from Roman law.[19] Article 1591 of the *Code Civil* states that 'the price must be fixed and settled by the parties' and Art. 1592 states that 'it [the price] may be left to the evaluation of a third party; if the third party does not wish or is unable to make the evaluation there is no sale'.[20]

Consequences of the need for the price to be determined or objectively determinable

Since in order for a proposal to constitute a valid offer, capable of being accepted, it must state the price, it was held by the first chamber of the *Cour de cassation* on 23 May 1979 that a contract of sale of hyacinth bulbs put forward by a producer had not been concluded by a letter from him to a buyer confirming the latter's requirements as to the quantity and quality of the items to be supplied but referring for the first time to the price. It was necessary that this letter, which constituted the only true offer, had received the acceptance of the buyer.[21]

For the price to be objectively determinable under the contract reference must be made to factors which do not depend any more upon the will of either of the parties:[22] 'The sale is void when the price depends upon the mere expression of the will of one of the parties as when the vendor has reserved to himself the right to fix the price . . . the outrageous and one-sided character of this clause puts the buyer in the hands of the manufacturer'.[23]

Nor must the price depend upon a subsequent agreement between the parties. If that is the case the contract is invalid.[24]

Offer referring to vendor's price list

In the same way an offer which simply states that the price will be that ruling at date of despatch according to a price list established by the vendor is not capable of forming a valid contract. If however when informed of the price at the time of delivery the buyer agrees to it then a contract is formed at that time.[25]

Price which is objectively determinable

The offer would be capable of being accepted and forming a valid contract if the elements by which the price was to be determined referred to some objective criterion such as a recorded market price list established by a third party. A mere reference however to 'the price normally payable for goods of the same quality in the market place' would not be sufficient.

The same applies to escalation clauses. The price will be regarded as objectively determinable if reference is made to officially recognized and published indices.

The requirement that the price must be determined or objectively determinable may apply also to such ancillary matters as delivery charges and agents' commissions.[26]

Price determined by third party

While the parties are entitled to leave the price to be settled by a third party agreed between them, the court is not permitted itself to decide to appoint an expert to make such determination. So it has been decided by the *Cour de cassation* that the 'judges were in breach of Art. 1591 of the *Code Civil* in substituting themselves for the parties in deciding upon the appointment of an expert to decide the sale price of cut timber'. It is only if the parties of their own accord request the judge to appoint an expert that he is permitted to do so.[27]

Distribution and framework contracts

The strict application of the rules relating to the requirement that the price must be determined or objectively determinable for a contract to be valid has given rise to a particular problem with contracts for exclusive distribution and franchising.

The terms of such contracts vary but in general there is an overall or 'framework' contract between the manufacturer and the distributor/franchisee under which the latter is bound on an exclusive basis to purchase certain goods for the purpose of resale and the manufacturer provides support in terms of interest-free loans or the supply of equipment. Typically such contracts have covered the distribution of petrol and beer.

The problem which arises is that the actual purchases by the distributor from the manufacturer take place over the period of the agreement at prices which are normally fixed unilaterally by the manufacturer from time to time according to his list price. If however the terms of the exclusive distribution or 'framework' contract relating to the obligation to purchase mean that that contract itself is to be treated as a contract for sale, then it would follow that the prices should be either fixed or determinable under that contract otherwise than at the discretion of the manufacturer.

The *Cour de cassation* has consistently decided that contracts for exclusive distribution which necessarily require for their execution a series of sales are void unless the prices are either determined or objectively determinable, i.e. otherwise than at the sole discretion of the distributor. This has been applied to beer, petrol, lubricants and many other commodities.[28]

In order to side-step the argument as to whether or not these framework contracts are in themselves contracts of sale and so covered by Art. 1592, the *Cour de cassation* has more recently based its decisions primarily on the wider Art. 1129 to which reference was made earlier and which requires that for all contracts whether for sale or otherwise the *objet* of the contract must be determined or determinable objectively (see above, p. 45).

With some hesitation the same reasoning has been applied to franchising contracts containing an obligation on the franchisee to purchase goods exclusively from the company granting the franchise at prices listed by that company in their catalogue, and fixed by them at their sole discretion.[29]

More recently the *Cour de cassation* appears to have withdrawn a little from the rigidity of its previous position in making a distinction first in November 1987 (Com. 9 Nov. 1987) followed in January 1991 (Com. 22 January 1991) and again in July 1991 (Com. 2 July 1991) between contracts of exclusive distribution having as their primary obligation *de faire* and not *de donner*. The first were valid even if the price were not objectively determined whilst the second were void.

However, this distinction was never going to be easy to draw and the later decisions of the *Cour de cassation* have again created uncertainty as to which contracts of distribution will be held valid and which will be declared null. For example a company was affiliated to a grocery distribution chain and was bound to sell only the products of the grocery company which operated the chain with two limited exceptions. When the affiliate terminated the contract prematurely the grocery company brought an action for breach of contract but the affiliate claimed that the contract was void for lack of determination of price. The *Cour de cassation* upheld the judgement of the *cour d'appel* on the grounds that the contract was in effect an exclusive supply contract and that the price was left to 'the free will of the grocery company' so that the contract was void for lack of *objet*. Cass com. 23 June 1992 (Bull civ. IV no. 247).

The uncertainties created by the often conflicting decisions of the *Cour de cassation* relative to contracts for distribution have been heavily criticized by the 'doctrine' since the real objective, to ensure that the prices charged by the supplier to the distributor are reasonable, is not achieved by the blunt weapon of nullity which often allows the distributor to escape from liabilities he now finds inconvenient.[30]

Contracts other than those for the sale of goods

While as indicated earlier the general rule based on Art. 1129 of the *Code Civil*, that the price ought to be determined or objectively determinable in the contract, should in principle apply to the contracts other than those for sale, the matter is not entirely clear.

In contracts for hire or letting either of goods or property, there have been isolated decisions to the contrary of the *Cour de cassation*, but generally the courts have held that the price to be paid and the duration of the hire are essential elements of the contract. Consequently if these were not determined or objectively determinable the contract was void.

Contracts for works

A contract for work (*contrat de louage d'ouvrage ou contrat d'entreprise*) may be valid in the absence of a price which is either determined or objectively determinable. It has been said that in the absence of a price fixed between the parties, 'les juges du fond peuvent apprécier souverainement la rémunération des prestations fournies . . . compte tenu des justifications produits et des circonstances de la cause'.[31]

This is in complete contrast to the position described earlier in relation to contracts for sale (see above, p. 45). What remains the same as for contracts of sale is that the price cannot be fixed unilaterally by one of the parties.

How widely this power may be exercised is unclear. It would certainly seem to apply where there is a generally recognized tariff or scale of fees as for architects. It has also been suggested that it is a convenient way of dealing with lower value contracts made with self-employed tradesmen in which the client often fails to agree a price in advance and relies on the honesty of the tradesman (see the suggestion of M. M. Mazeaud and de Juglart, quoted in Ghestin, p. 585). If however the contract is one of importance, e.g. construction of houses, then the absence of any agreement on price would indicate that the parties were still in a state of negotiation.

Whatever the reason for the distinction between the powers of the judge to fix the prices in the one case but not in the other, the practice seems well established. It does however create the difficulty of classifying contracts as either for sale or for work, e.g. manufacture and installation of equipment.

At one time the distinction was made on the basis of comparing the value of the materials being supplied with that of the work being executed. If the price of the materials supplied exceeded that of the work then the contract was one for sale, but if the respective values were reversed then the contract was one of *entreprise*. But this simple arithmetical comparison was much criticized and the *Cour de cassation* replaced it with the more flexible approach of determining which element of the contract was *l'accessoire* to the other. If the nature and importance of the obligations undertaken by the installer were *accessoire* to the materials being supplied then the contract was one for sale (see Ghestin, *La Vente*, p. 76).

More recently the *Cour de cassation* has adopted as the distinguishing criterion whether the product being supplied was designed strictly according to specifications prepared by the person placing the order so as to satisfy his particular requirement, or was a standard product designed by the manufacturer. In the former case it would be *un contrat d'entreprise* and in the latter *un contrat de vente* (see Malaurie and Aynes, p. 64 and Cass. com. 4 July 1989 B. IV no. 210).[32]

GERMAN LAW

It has been stated as a basic principle of German law that 'an offer must be clear and obvious in all its component parts'.[33] The application of this principle is of great importance in relation to the question of the incorporation into sales and services contracts of standard general conditions of contract which are such a feature of German business practice and have acquired in Germany a particular significance (see below, p. 301).

INCORPORATION OF GENERAL CONDITIONS

In business contracts the incorporation of general conditions may be either express or under certain circumstances by implication. If the incorporation is made expressly then the recipient of the offer has the right to expect that the reference to the general conditions will be made in such a way as to 'stare him in the face'.[34] So a reference made in minute characters perpendicularly in the margin of the document has been held to be ineffective, and a choice of law clause in a set of general conditions which was in such small print that it could hardly be read even with a magnifying glass was also held not to be part of the contract (see BGH II ZR 135/82 30 May 1983 RIW 872). Similarly effect has not been given to references put only on the back of a standard form or below the signature at the foot of the form.[35]

The general rule is that a reference contained only on an invoice is not regarded as effective. This is for two reasons. First, under German law an invoice is considered to be only an accounting document and not one properly to be used for referring to contractual terms. Second, the invoice is issued after the formation of the contract, and to allow terms to which it referred to have contractual effect would be to give one party to the contract the right to modify it unilaterally after its conclusion.[36]

However in certain circumstances express reference to general conditions is not required for them to be incorporated in a business contract, for example where the parties are in a continuing business relationship and their transactions are always carried out on the standard conditions of one of them.

The general principle has been stated by the Federal Court in the following terms:

> when the parties are in a continuing business relationship, when they have always previously submitted their contracts to the General Conditions of one of them and that one has made it absolutely clear without equivocation that he will only contract on his own conditions, then the conclusion without reservation by the other party may be interpreted as a tacit acceptance of such conditions even if they have not been referred to in the course of the new contractual negotiations.[37]

As to what constitutes 'a continuing business relationship', although the concept is important in German law there is no definitive ruling as to when it exists. It is a question of fact in each individual case. The factors which will influence the court in coming to a conclusion are the nature, importance and frequency of the sales and of the economic and legal relationship between them, and whether or not the user has stipulated at least once his intention that the standard conditions should apply to subsequent transactions.

Thus eight transactions in three years was held to be insufficient to create a continuing business relationship when these sales were at irregular intervals, of differing quantities and had no legal relationship between them. However a number of regular sales over a period of five years between a German supplier and a Dutch purchaser was held to be sufficient.[38]

As regards a continuing business relationship permitting the validity of a reference to the general conditions on an invoice, in the face of silence by the recipient, this was allowed when the invoice had been preceded by fourteen others within the period of one year, without the purchaser having made any objection.[39]

The second principal circumstance in which general conditions may be implicitly incorporated is when the use of particular general conditions is standard practice in the trade in question so that any person having regular dealings with a firm in that trade knows or ought to know that all business is conducted on such conditions, e.g. the Uniform German Carriers and Warehousemen's Conditions applying to the carriage of goods and warehousing.

In either of these above circumstances if the other party does not wish to be bound by the standard general conditions then he must say so expressly; silence will be taken to be consent.

Provided that the reference in the offer is clear and obvious, or the general conditions are incorporated implicitly, there is no requirement in a commercial contract for the party making the offer to provide the other with a copy of his general conditions.

It is the responsibility of the recipient of the offer in a commercial contract to find out the obligations which he is being asked to accept and if he fails to take steps to do so by expressly requesting sight of the general conditions he will be regarded as bound by their terms:

> It is established law . . . that in contracts between merchants whether in a continuing business relationship or not, that the General Conditions to which reference is made apply even if they have not been annexed to the written contract and if the recipient did not either have knowledge of their detail by other means . . . it was the responsibility of the recipient to obtain knowledge of the terms of delivery before binding himself contractually.[40]

But this also necessarily means that the party putting forward the general conditions must allow the other a reasonable opportunity (*in zumutbarer Weise*) of examining their text.[41]

References above to a party being bound by the other's general conditions must be read as subject to the general obligation of *Treu und Glauben* under Paras 157 and 242 of the *BGB*, which have been widely used by the courts to deny validity to clauses which they considered did not satisfy the requirements of 'honest dealing in business' or 'reasonable standards of fair dealing in the trade', and to the Standard Contract Terms Act 1977.

In the case of the *Verdingungsordnung für Bauleistungen (VOB)*, the standard tendering and performance stipulations for government construction contracts, which are also widely used in the private sector, it has been decided that in a private sector contract to ensure the *VOB* becomes part of the contract in circumstances where the contractor is not familiar with building practice, it is necessary to provide him with a copy of the text of the *VOB* part B (the standard conditions of contract). It is not sufficient just to offer the text if the contractor requests a copy (BGH 15 October 1991). Again a mere reference to the *VOB* in the enquiry documents will only be sufficient to make it a *VOB* contract if all companies bidding are experienced in the construction field.

Incorporation of standard terms in contracts between German firms and foreign business persons

If the foreign business person has been content to conduct the negotiations in German then an express reference in German to the standard conditions will be sufficient to constitute the necessary notice. It will also be sufficient in that case if, in response to the foreign business person's request for a copy of the standard conditions, they are supplied in German unless a translation is specifically requested.[42]

The language of the negotiations

If the negotiations have been conducted, say, in English, then it appears that the notice of the standard conditions must be given in English. Further, the text of the general conditions should also be provided in the language in which the negotiations have been conducted. Several decisions of the German courts of appeal have ruled that general conditions of sale did not form part of the contract, either because the reference made to them was in a language different from that of the negotiations, or they were written in a language different from that of the negotiations. So when the parties had negotiated in English, the general conditions of the German seller written in German and which were referred to on the front of the letter of confirmation in German, did not form part of the contract (OLG Hambourg 1 June 1979 NJW 1980, 1232). This is the doctrine of the 'language of the negotiations'.[43]

The legal basis for this doctrine appears to be that, having negotiated in one language, both parties have a right to expect that important clauses of the contract will be expressed in that language and that it would be a breach of confidence and good faith for one party to seek to do otherwise.[44] The consequences of that breach of faith would be the exclusion of such clauses from the terms of the contract. From a purely practical viewpoint, however, and to avoid recourse to litigation, a foreign firm faced with a set of general conditions in German should always respond with a demand either for their translation or their elimination from the contract documentation.

The above provisions only apply where the negotiations are conducted at a distance, e.g. by telephone, telex, etc. If an English business person goes to Germany to carry out the negotiations he will be bound by the terms if they are negotiated in German whether he understand them or not. It is up to the foreigner in Germany to look after himself.[45]

Implicit incorporation

The general rule as to the implicit incorporation of general conditions into a contract will apply equally to contracts with foreign business people who have regular dealings with German firms in a particular trade or where they have a continuing business relationship with a German company. So in these cases, where the contract is governed by German law, silence by the English firm following a letter of confirmation would amount to consent.[46]

The Rome Convention

However under Art. 8 of the Rome Convention which is now part of English law under the Contracts (Applicable Law) Act 1990, it is provided that a party may rely upon the law of the country in which he has his habitual place of residence to establish that he did not consent to the inclusion of a term, if it appears from the circumstances that it would not be reasonable to determine the effect of his conduct in accordance with the law of the contract.

This proviso was included inter alia to solve the problem of the implications of silence.[47] Therefore if the transaction was an isolated one, or perhaps the first in which the English business person had been engaged with a German seller, and on the facts of the negotiations it would not be reasonable to expect the English firm to know of the German rule, then he may be able to claim that he was not bound by the letter of confirmation.

REFERENCE IN THE OFFER TO THE CONTRACT PRICE

German law is considerably more relaxed than French on the requirement for the contract price to be determined or objectively determinable at the time of contract.

Although for an offer to be effective either the price must be stated or be determinable German law allows a wide meaning to the term 'determinable'. A contract containing a clause that 'the prices shall be those ruling at the date of delivery' and therefore effectively within the unilateral control of the seller, will be treated as valid, provided at least that it does not offend against Art. 138 of the *BGB* as being 'contrary to good morals' or Art. 242 which requires performance to be effected 'according to good faith' (*Treu und Glauben*). So it was ruled that a contract was valid and binding on the purchaser which stated that 'the billing will be based on the prices in effect on the day of delivery of the articles'.[48] More recently an agreement between business people was held valid which gave the vendor the right to fix his prices unilaterally without giving the purchaser the right to terminate BGH (X ZR 12/84 27.9.1984) [1985] DB 224.

Such rulings reflect two factors: first, the traditional German concept of the freedom to contract (*Vertragsfreiheit*) which permits the parties a wide measure of discretion and under which the validity of the contract may be assessed according to whether or not the parties intended to be bound.[49] The second factor is the turbulent economic conditions that prevailed in Germany between the wars and after World War II which made it extremely difficult for sellers to quote on a firm price basis.

STANDARD CONTRACT TERMS ACT

More recently however the German Standard Contract Terms Act (*AGBG*) 1977 (see below, p. 302), has introduced a rule which makes void in consumer transactions under standard contracts as defined in the Act terms which allow the seller the right to increase the price of goods to be supplied or services performed within four months from the date of contract. This rule applies equally to general clauses referring to goods being sold at the prices stated in the seller's price list at the date of delivery. Even after the four-month period the consumer will be protected under other provisions of the Act against a unilateral right of the seller to increase prices other than for justified cost increases.

As regards business transactions the particular four-month rule does not apply but a 'price ruling at date of despatch clause' in standard conditions which gave rise to a wholly unjustified price increase could be held void under Art. 9, the general provisions clause of the Act, which applies to consumer and business transactions alike (see below, p. 304).

PRICE LEFT TO BE DETERMINED

If the price is not fixed in the contract then provision can be made for it to be determined in one of four ways: first, at the discretion (*nach freiem Ermessen*) of the seller; second, by the seller on an equitable basis (*nach billigem Ermessen*) as is presumed in cases of doubt by Art. 315 of the *BGB*.[50] The distinction in practice between the two is that in the first case if the price is not fixed then the contract will be void, whilst in the second case application can be made to the court to have it fixed.[51] The third method of fixing price is by reference to the 'market price' which under Art. 453 of the *BGB* 'in case of doubt will be taken as the normal market price at the date and place of performance'.

Finally price may be left to the determination of a third party. Under Art. 317 of the *BGB* it is presumed in cases of doubt, i.e. if specific criteria have not been established according to which the third party is to proceed, then the third party is to act in an equitable manner. Failure to do so will result in his decision not being binding and the determination is then a matter for the court. The same applies if the third party fails or refuses to make a decision.

However, if according to the contract the decision is to be made by him 'at his discretion' and he does not act, then the contract is not binding, i.e. the court then has no power to make the decision (Art. 319 of the *BGB*).

UNIFORM LAW FOR INTERNATIONAL SALES

The Uniform Law for International Sale of Goods under the United Nations Convention, Vienna 1980, regrettably does not deal clearly with the issue as to whether or not a price which is either determined or objectively determinable is necessary in order for a contract under the Convention to be valid.

Article 14 certainly requires that for a proposal to constitute an offer it has to be sufficiently definitive and it is so if, inter alia, it 'expressly or implicitly fixes or makes provision for determining the Price'. Does then Art. 14 mean that for a contract to be valid the price must be determined or objectively determinable, assuming that the parties have otherwise indicated their intention to be legally bound, e.g. by signing a sales agreement? The answer appears to be 'no' since under Art. 55 of Part III of the Convention the validity of an agreement in relation to price is a matter of validity to be determined by the applicable domestic law.

NOTES

1. This is the literal translation of the French text. However consent (*consentement*) in the code is to be understood in two senses. It designates first the agreement of the wills of the two parties. Second, it designates the consent of the will of each of the parties to the terms of the proposed contract. In this second sense the text is misleading in implying that in a unilateral contract only the consent of the party under a duty is required. This is not so. Even in a unilateral contract both the parties must consent: the one who is under a duty and the one who possesses a right (Weill and Terré s.75). See Nicholas p. 39 for the distinction between the English and French use of the expression 'unilateral contract'.
2. It is not proposed to translate either of these terms into English. 'There exists no word in English to designate "l'objet du contrat" ' (David and Pugsley s.212) and the same authors in s.185: 'among the conditions for the existence and validity enumerated in the *Code Civil* one finds the concept of "cause" which does not exist in England'.
3. Neither French law nor German law have any doctrine of *ultra vires* and the concept in English law is now only significant in respect of companies incorporated by special statute following the Companies Act 1989.
4. Advertisements were described as 'offers to negotiate . . . offers to chaffer' by Bowen L. J. in *Carlill* v. *Carbolic Smoke Co*. 1893 1 256, 268 CA. In *Fisher* v. *Bell* 1961 1 QB 394 it was stated to be 'the ordinary law of contract that the display of an article with a price ticket on it in a shop window is merely an invitation to treat'. In *Pharmaceutical Society of Great Britain* v. *Boots Cash Chemists (Southern) Ltd* 1952 2 QB 795, confirmed 1953 1 QB 401, the same reasoning was applied to a self-service store: 'the mere fact that a customer picks up a bottle of medicine from the shelves does not amount to an acceptance of an offer to sell. It is an offer by the customer to buy . . . accepted by the acceptance of the price' per Lord Goddard.
5. Weill and Terré s. 134.1: 'The declaration of the will of the offeror may be made under any form . . . either to a certain person or persons as in the case of a merchant writing to his customers with a business proposal . . . or an offer made to the public for example by a display in a shop window with a price ticket attached or by posters, catalogues, newspaper advertisements' . . . 'The declaration of the will only constitutes an offer if it is sufficiently precise and complete . . . so in the case of a sale the item and the price.'

6. Weill and Terré s.142(b): 'in principle when items are exposed in a shop window with a price ticket anyone may require the delivery of the item against payment of the price; the placing of the item in the shop window with a notification of the price constitutes an offer of sale to anyone and the acceptance completes the contract, the essential elements of the contract the item and the price being decided. However the shop-keeper may be considered as having the intention not to sell the item exposed, but only an identical one, as when the item forms part of a window display which requires much time and effort to prepare and cannot be reconstituted several times a day as would be the case if each client were entitled to demand delivery of the items making up the display . . . but the client is entitled to the delivery of one, in this case a dress on a model in a shop window, which is exactly the same as that displayed'.
7. *Source Book*, 3rd ed., p. 311.
8. See the notes in Section II to Art. 1147 of the *Code Civil*, in particular note 53. Dalloz, *Code Civil* 1992–1993, p. 761.
9. Markesinis, p. 436.
10. This latter was one of the examples given by Lord Goddard in the Boots case to justify his decision.
11. 'I think it is legitimate in approaching a document of this kind, containing phrases and expressions of doubtful significance, to bear in mind that the probability of parties entering into so large a transaction and finally binding themselves to a contract of this description couched in such terms, is remote', per Lord Greene in *Clifton* v. *Palumbo* 1944 2 All ER 497.
12. 1941 AC 251 at 268–9.
13. See s.8(2) of the Sale of Goods Act 1979 and s.15(1) of the Supply of Goods and Services Act 1982.
14. *May and Butcher* v. *R* 1934 2 KB 17n. In other circumstances where there is trade usage or a previous course of dealing between the parties the terms used may show a sufficient intention to be bound and the courts will tend to lean this way especially if the contract is executed rather than executory and the parties have acted on the assumption that a bargain did exist – see *Hillas* v. *Arcos* 1932 38 Com.Cas. 23 and *Foley* v. *Classique Coaches Ltd* 1934 2 KB 1. In the Foley case an undertaking by the defendant to buy all his petrol from the plaintiff's filling station as part of a deal for the sale of certain land 'at a price to be agreed by the parties from time to time' and which had been acted upon for a number of years, was held to be valid. In default of agreement a reasonable price had to be paid.
15. An offer to a developer stated 'that the contractors would be prepared to instruct their quantity surveyor to negotiate fair and reasonable contract sums in respect of the . . . projects as they arise . . . based upon agreed estimates of the net cost of the work and general overheads with a margin for profit of 5 per cent'. The developer accepted the offer but was himself not awarded the project. It was held that, as there was no price agreed and no machinery for determining the price otherwise than by negotiation between the parties, there was no contract. In Lord Denning's words: 'a contract to negotiate, like a contract to enter into a contract when a fundamental term is not agreed is not a contract known to the law' (*Courtney & Fairbairn Ltd* v. *Tolaini Brothers (Hotels) Ltd* (1975) 2 BLR 97). See also the recent decision by the Full Court of Victoria in *Australian and New Zealand Banking Group Ltd* v. *Frost Holdings* in which it was said that there was no contract if an essential term such as price was left to be agreed between the parties.
16. This appears to be so but there is also no real authority on the point. The Sale of Goods Act 1979 refers to the alternative that the price 'may be left to be fixed in a manner agreed by the contract' which would imply that if the contract provides for the price to be determined by one of the parties in a particular manner, say by reference to his price list, then the contract would be binding. If however the price were to be fixed by the seller unilaterally without reference to any standard, then it must be doubtful if this is sufficient to create a binding contract. Tallon considers it would do (p. 63 s.2.2.1.17), but the authority which he cites, Lord Dunedin's remarks in *May and Butcher* v. *R* 1934 2 KB at p. 21, 'For instance, with regard to price it is a perfectly good contract to say that the price is to be settled by the buyer' are clearly obiter.
17. Tallon 2.1.0.01–2.1.1.05, Rodière *Objet*, Tableau Comparatif II a). Weill and Terré s.232.
18. Tallon 2.1.1.06 and 2.1.1.09, and Ghestin s.523.
19. 'It is necessary that a price should be agreed upon for there can be no sale without a price. And the price must be fixed and certain . . . when a sale is made for a price to be fixed by a third person the contract shall be binding . . . if this third person does fix a price . . . but if he will not or cannot fix a price the sale is then void. . . . This decision may reasonably be applied to contracts of letting to hire (which included what we would call contracts for work and materials)' Inst. 3.23.1.

20. The *Code Civil* uses the term *l'arbitrage* but as Ghestin points out the task of the third party is quite different from that which is provided for under a normal arbitration clause. The job of the third party is limited to making an evaluation or estimate of the item sold. 'In general terms the task of an arbitrator does not have as its objective the conclusion of a contract under negotiation but only to adjudicate upon the disagreements arising out of its execution'. Ghestin s.522 on p. 582.

21. Ghestin s.202.

22. The classic expression used by the *Cour de cassation* is that the contract is valid 'si le prix est déterminé en vertu des clauses du contrat, par voie de relation avec des éléments qui ne dépendent plus de la volonté l'une ou l'autre partie', Cass. civ. 3e 15 Feb 1984; see Starck s.495.

23. Cass. com. 23 October 1962 Bull. civ. III p. 344 no. 420 – see Ghestin s.527.

24. Cass. com. 24 March 1965 Bull. civ. III p. 208 no. 302 and Ghestin *La Vente* s.386.

25. Mazeaud, Bk III, Vol. 2, s.869.

26. See Ghestin s.522 and decisions quoted there.

27. Cass. civ. 18 July 1979 Bull. civ. no. 220 p. 176 and Ghestin s.522.

28. Ghestin s.526.

29. The Cour de Paris, after prompting from the *Cour de cassation,* and the censuring of an earlier judgement to the opposite effect did this time decide on 19 May 1988 that the prices contained in the catalogue issued by the Société Natalys 'depended solely on the will of Natalys' and accordingly the contracts of franchise were void under Arts 1129 and 1591 of the *Code Civil* – Ghestin, *La Vente* s.388 p. 443. However a subsequent decision of the same court in Paris decided the opposite way on 21 September 1989, in apparent contradiction of the *Cour de cassation.* Yet again however on 8 December 1989 the Cour de Paris did annul a franchise contract for indetermination of price since the price depended on the sole will of the franchisor.

30. See *Indetermination du Prix.* M. A. Frison Roche RTD civ. 1992.269; Malaurie and Aynes, *les Contrats speciaux no 836; Indetermination du prix dans les contrats de distribution: comment sortir de l'impasse?* Aynes Recueil Dalloz Sirey 1993 4th *cahier Chronique* p. 25; RTD com. April–June 1993 pp. 358 and 359.

31. Cass. civ. 3 24 janvier 1978 quoted by Ghestin in note 88 on page 584: 'the trial judges acting within their sovereign power may assess the payment to be made for the work done . . . taking into account the evidence produced and the circumstances of the case'. See also note 11 to Art. 1787 of the *Code Civil,* Dalloz: 'the prior agreement on the cost of the works is not an essential element for a contract for works'.

32. Note by Phillipe Remy, *Rev. trim. dr. civ.* 89 Jan–March 1990 commenting on a decision by the *Cour de cassation* (Comm. 4 July 1989) that it is a contract for work and not a contract for sale when the supplier 'supplies works which are specific to the particular needs specified by the client'. The two requirements of specificity of the work and its being to meet the particular needs of the client are the necessary and sufficient reasons for the contract being classified as one for 'works' and not for 'sale'. There is no need for the judge to evaluate the respective values of the work and materials.

33. Ludwig Raiser, 'Das Recht der Allgemeinen Geschäftsbedingungen' 1935 p. 184.

34. Abderrahmane p. 52 s.59.

35. Abderrahmane pp. 52 and 53 s.60.

36. Abderrahmane pp. 69 and 70 s.97.

37. BGH (WM 1973 1198) 28 May 1973.

38. Quoted Abderrahmane para. 71 p. 58.

39. OLG Zweibrüchen 21 November 1976 OLGZ 1968, 398 and other cases quoted Abderrahmane para. 98 on p. 70.

40. BGH (DB 1976, 116) 30 June 1976.

41. Abderrahmane para. 65 on p. 55.

42. Quoted Abderrahmane para. 71 on p. 58.

43. See Abderrahmane pp. 129–32 for a review of the jurisprudence and also the comments on the 'language of the negotiations' in 'Choice of Law in German Trade Relations' Volker Treinel *ICLQ* October 1988, p. 938. It appears that the doctrine of the 'language of the negotiations' has replaced that which allowed the validity of the incorporation of general conditions into the contract provided they were in an internationally recognized language, e.g. English, French or Spanish although this latter still has its supporters – see Abderrahmane s.203 and Silberberg p. 24.

44. See Langen p. 234 and the cases quoted in note 92.

45. Held by the Bremen Appeal Court that a visiting Iranian businessman who did business when in Germany with a German bank was bound by the German text of their standard conditions of contract although he spoke no German. IPR Spr 1973 no. 25.

46. BGH NJW 1971, 2126 and see generally Silberberg pp. 21–25.

47. See comment on the Convention in the *Official Journal of the European Communities* 31.10.80 p. C 282/28.

48. *R & R* v. *E Reichsgericht* First Civil Senate 22 February 1922 104 ERGZ 98 quoted Von Mehren p. 924.

49. In the case referred to in note 48 above it was stated, 'It corresponds to the principle of freedom to contract (Vertragsfreiheit) a basic tenet of the Civil Code, to permit as a condition any future event including the arbitrary act of one of the parties to the contract', Von Mehren p. 924.

50. See Tallon 2.1.1.18 and the reference to the application of Art. 316 of the *BGB* in cases where there is agreement between the parties that a price ought to be paid but the amount has not been determined.' In cases of doubt the determination is to be made by the party who is entitled to demand the performance of the 'counter-obligation' from which it follows that the price will be regarded as determinable and the contract valid. It follows also that the agreement between the parties will override the presumption of Art. 154 that in the event of doubt as to agreement having been reached on all points the contract has not been validly concluded – see further p. 78.

51. Tallon 3.2.2.04. In practice the German courts exercise wide powers derived from the several articles of the *BGB* dealing with the requirements of the parties behaving in accordance with 'good faith and common usage' (Arts 157 and 242) in order to prevent a contract being void for uncertainty.

4 Termination of offers and withdrawal from negotiations

TERMINATION OF OFFERS UNDER ENGLISH LAW

It has long been an established rule under English law that an offer, even if a promise is made to keep it open for acceptance for a definitive period of time, may always be revoked at any moment prior to its acceptance, unless the promise is supported by consideration or is executed as a deed.[1]

As to what would amount to consideration, apart from the payment of money, there is an argument that an agreement by the purchaser at the bidder's request to supply him with tendering documents and to adjudicate upon his tender, could do so, if in the absence of any such agreement, the firm would have no right to bid. There is suggestive but no definitive supporting authority for this proposition.[2]

The general rule is particularly inconvenient for main contractors obtaining bids from sub-contractors for the purpose of building up their own tender. They may find that, after the purchaser has accepted their tender, the intended sub-contractor either withdraws or modifies his offer. The absence of any consideration for the sub-contractor keeping his offer open would be fatal to any claim by the main contractor against him in contract and English law does not recognize the doctrine of *culpa in contrahendo* (see below, p. 64).

The question then arises as to whether or not in these circumstances the main contractor could have any non-contractual remedy, if the sub-contractor both intended that the main contractor should rely upon his bid in pricing his own tender, and knows that the main contractor has done so. At the moment the answer in England appears to be 'no', although not in America.[3]

However the High Court in Australia has recently extended the doctrine of promissory estoppel in a way which suggests that the English common law may yet in the future also find the means to answer 'yes'.[4] French law, unhampered by the doctrine of consideration, has already done so (see below, p. 60).

EFFECTIVENESS OF WITHDRAWAL

A revocation is not effective until it has actually been received by the person to whom the offer was addressed. In the case of a business, revocation would be effective therefore from the time when the letter containing the notice was opened in the office, or would have been opened in ordinary practice, or a telex or fax was received on the offeree's machine during normal working hours on an ordinary business day. It is not sufficient for the offeror to have formed the intention to revoke; the revocation must have been communicated to the offeree.

It follows also that if there is acceptance of the offer prior to the receipt of the notice of revocation, then there would still under English law be a contract, even though there was no true agreement between the parties.[5]

WITHDRAWAL FROM NEGOTIATIONS

In the same way as English law allows a simple offer unsupported by consideration to be withdrawn at any time prior to acceptance, so it also imposes no obligation on either party to continue negotiations in order to establish a contract:

> It must be right to conclude that, as a general rule a party should be allowed to withdraw from pre-contractual negotiations without incurring any liability; otherwise the process of free bargaining would be serious debilitated.[6]

This principle applies even after the issue of a letter of intent which normally is no more than 'an expression in writing of a party's present intention to enter into a contract at some future date. Save in exceptional circumstances it can have no binding effect.'[7]

It is only if the letter of intent or other instructions from the purchaser require the contractor to perform certain preparatory work in advance of the conclusion of a contract over and above that which a contractor would normally be expected to perform when tendering, and he does so, that the contractor can claim reimbursement of the work so performed.[8]

TERMINATION OF OFFERS UNDER FRENCH LAW

The classical French doctrine was that an offer could be freely revoked at any time up until its acceptance: 'the offer before its acceptance had no binding power'.[9]

However, because as has been suggested of the need to introduce confidence into business relationships, the French courts have now so eroded the classical principle that in practice it is the exceptions which state the rule.[10] The exceptions are as follows. First, if the offeror has fixed a definitive period during which he has undertaken to maintain the offer's validity, then he is obliged to keep it open during this period, unless in the mean time it is rejected.[11]

Second, if the offeror has not fixed a definitive period, but has asked for an immediate reply, then the court will fix a period during which the offer must be maintained, which is adequate to follow for the receipt of a response plus a period sufficient in the circumstances for the offeree to make up his mind.[12]

Third, if the offeror has not fixed a period at all then the offer must be maintained during a reasonable period which will be determined, if necessary, by the *juge de fait* according to the circumstances and trade custom.[13] Generally the period in commercial matters is short; so in an old case at Bordeaux it was decided that on the sale of wine by the growers at the time of the grape harvest, an offer is normally only valid for 24 hours.[14]

It follows from the above that if the person making the offer does in fact withdraw it before the expiry of the period, either express or implied, during which he is obliged to keep it open, then he incurs a liability towards the offeree. This would normally be in damages but if it is still possible to perform the contract which would result from the acceptance of the offer it could be by *exécution en nature* (see below, p. 320).

The difficulty, however, is to find the legal basis upon which such obligation rests and there is disagreement within French doctrine on this point.

One theory is that the obligation results from an *avant-contrat*, either express or implied between the parties. So in a case in 1936 involving the withdrawal by a subcontractor of an offer he had made to the main contractor because of an error in his calculations, the court at Colmar decided that 'an offer may be considered to be binding on the offeror before its acceptance by the offeree from the moment that there is an agreement express or tacit, but unquestionable, that the offer has been expressed to be maintained for a definite period'.[15]

This seems unobjectionable provided that the prior agreement really exists and is not fictitious, but clearly such cases are likely to be in the minority.

The leading alternative theory is that the withdrawal of the offer constitutes a 'fault' which gives rise to a claim in delict. The logical difficulty with this theory, as Ghestin points out, is that the withdrawal of the offer in itself can only constitute a fault if the offeror was already under an obligation to maintain it, yet it was the legal basis for that obligation which we were seeking to discover.[16]

Despite this it is the delictual basis which appears to be that upon which two of the leading French cases have been decided. Both are given in the *Source Book*, second edition pp. 328–33, although omitted in the third edition and both are referred to extensively by Nicholas, pp. 66–69.

In the more recent case, Cass civ. 17.12.1958, the owner of a property offered it for sale to an intending purchaser who wrote stating that he proposed to visit it on 15 or 16 August and the vendor replied agreeing to the visit. The day following the visit the purchaser telegraphed his acceptance of the vendor's offer only to be informed by the vendor that on 14 August, the day before the visit, he had sold it to someone else. On the facts the cour d'appel in Montpellier decided that the evidence produced as to the alleged sale on 14 August was fraudulent, that there had been no manifestation of the will to revoke and therefore the offer was still in force when it was accepted.[17] The *Cour de cassation* concurred with this analysis.

However, in approving the decision of the cour d'appel the *Cour de cassation* also stated that 'although an offer may in principle be revoked before its acceptance it is otherwise where the offeror has expressly or implicitly bound himself not to withdraw it within a certain period.' They then went on to note with approval the judgement of the cour d'appel that 'having authorised the visit of inspection the seller was tacitly obliged to maintain his offer until after the agreed visit'. The vendor was therefore unable to withdraw the offer on 14 August without committing 'a fault engaging his responsibility'. This is clearly the language of delictual liability.

In the earlier case in the cour d'appel in Bordeaux, 17 January 1870, a theatre director sent two telegrams to a well-known singer with whom he was already in negotiation offering her an engagement. The telegrams were delayed and before she issued her acceptance he had already withdrawn his offer and engaged someone else. As a result the *Cour de cassation* held there was no contract since at no time had the wills of the two parties to be bound both existed at the same time. However, as they also held on the facts that the delay in the telegrams reaching the singer were due to the default of the director in the manner in which they had been despatched, which was not consistent with the urgency he required for a reply, they held him responsible for the contract not having been effected and accordingly liable to compensate the singer for the actual loss she had suffered.

No basis for the decision is given other than 'equity and the law require the offeror to remedy the loss'. This can only be delictual or, it can be argued, an *abus de droit*. The director had the right to withdraw the offer but it was an abuse of this right to act as he did by sending the telegrams not by express service and with an incomplete address, especially as these were his final communications intended to lead to the conclusion of the negotiations and for which he wanted an immediate response.

Perhaps indeed the theory of *abus de droit* provides the best solution to the problem. Although the right to withdraw the offer is recognized in principle, the withdrawal would constitute an abuse if the right were exercised in disregard of the legitimate confidence created in the recipient of the offer by the promise to maintain its validity for a definite period[18] or if the circumstances of the withdrawal were in themselves abusive.

EFFECTIVENESS OF REVOCATION

Under the classical French doctrine which required that there should be a point at which the two parties were in agreement, and allowed in principle a person to revoke an offer which had not been accepted, a revocation by the offeror would be effective even if not communicated to the offeree, provided that it was manifest.[19] With the present restrictions on the offeror's right to withdraw the offer the practical significance of this point has largely disappeared.

WITHDRAWAL FROM NEGOTIATIONS AND LETTERS OF INTENT

Unlike English law there can be obligations under French law relating to the actual conduct of the negotiations and also to the continuation of the negotiations at least once they have reached an advanced stage. French law may also give effect to *lettres d'intention* in circumstances in which an English court would treat the letter of intent as having no legal value.

First, as regards the conduct of negotiations there can be a delictual liability under Art. 1382 of the *Code Civil*.[20] This liability arises because there is a fault due to bad faith, or perhaps simply a lack of good faith, of one party in the conduct of the negotiations, without there being any need for it to be shown that he intended to injure the other.[21] It is to be noted that French law has rejected any pre-contractual liability based on an implied *contrat accessoire* as in the doctrine of *culpa in contrahendo* accepted by German and other continental legal systems.[22]

The fault may consist of abruptly breaking off negotiations which are at an advanced stage without good reason, especially if the other party has incurred considerable expense in the expectation of the conclusion of the contract, or of the undue prolongation of negotiations without there being any intention of bringing them to a successful conclusion. It also includes conducting parallel negotiations with two or more firms each being led to believe that they are the only one with whom negotiations are proceeding. The fault here does not lie in the carrying out of parallel negotiations as such, which is quite normal commercial practice, but in the concealment of that fact so that each firm is left to believe that it alone has the virtual certainty of obtaining the contract.[23] Such conduct in England, while it would be regarded by many as unethical, could never give rise to a legal right of action. Even a broken promise is not actionable in English law in tort but only in contract if all the requirements for a valid contract are present.[24]

The practical significance of this pre-contractual liability must not be exaggerated. As between professionals it will often be difficult to prove fault unless the manner of the termination is clearly abusive.

As Joanna Schmidt has written, 'the carrying out of negotiations is part of the professional's work and constitutes a risk of the business of which the effects are foreseen and covered by the general overheads'.[25]

So far as reparation is concerned it is clear that the damages recoverable would include the loss of time and the expenses incurred in the negotiations, and if the negotiations had reached an advanced stage the costs incurred in preparing to execute the contract. It is more debatable whether or not the profits can be recovered which it was anticipated would be earned on the contract. It would seem that this is a matter for the discretion of the *juge de fond* and will depend on his evaluation of the state which the negotiations had reached at the time when they were terminated.[26]

Lettres d'intention

Letters of intent are used at least as extensively in French commercial practice as they are in England. However, there is a marked difference between their legal effect under the two systems. As stated above, French law recognizes a delictual liability if the negotiations are conducted in bad faith or broken off which is absent in English law.

Further, when the negotiations have reached an advanced stage and a letter of intent is issued which sets out a detailed listing of the points agreed to date and establishes a timetable for the conclusion of the negotiations, French law may treat such a document as *un accord de principe*. In that event the obligation to conclude the negotiations in good faith becomes contractual.

The distinction should therefore be noted between the alternative bases of liability. It is delictual if without any pre-contract having been formed the negotiations are conducted or broken off in bad faith. It is contractual if there is a breach of a pre-contract, evidenced say by a detailed letter of intent, which by its terms is sufficiently definitive to establish an *accord de principe*.[27]

Generally the effect of an *accord de principe* is that the parties may not go back on the points which have already been agreed and must continue to negotiate in good faith diligently and in a constructive manner according to the agreed timetable on those points which are still outstanding with the object of concluding the contract. Failure of the negotiations 'without serious discussion, without even formulating a counter-proposal would then justify the judicial termination of the "accord de principe" together with the payment of damages.'[28]

If it is intended that a detailed letter of intent should be contractually binding in the above sense of creating an obligation to pursue the negotiations in good faith, then it is usual to have it endorsed by the other party *bon pour acceptation*. If alternatively it is not intended to be contractually binding then it must be endorsed by some expression such as *bon pour lettre d'intention seulement sans être contractuel* which is broadly equivalent to the English 'subject to contract'.[29]

TERMINATION OF OFFERS UNDER GERMAN LAW

Under ss. 145–148 of the *BGB* an offer is binding on the offeror and cannot be withdrawn by him during the period for which he has undertaken to keep it open or if he has not specified any particular period then until a reasonable time has expired within which he could expect to receive a response. This rule is derived from old Germanic law which defied in this instance the 'Roman reception'.[30] The only exception is when the offeror has qualified his offer as *freibleibend*, meaning 'without engagement' or some similar term when it becomes more the equivalent of an invitation to treat. In practice, during Germany's past periods of severe economic disturbance and raging inflation after the two world wars this exception was widely used and regarded as of great importance. With the current greater economic stability it has become of somewhat less significance.

Unless therefore the offer is qualified as *freibleibend*, any purported withdrawal would be legally ineffective. Even where it is so qualified, and therefore to be considered in the nature of an 'invitation to treat', it is not wholly without legal effect. The German courts have held consistent with the principle of *nach Treu und Glauben* (good faith), that the offeror who receives a prompt but qualified response to his offer must himself answer promptly whether he agrees to the terms of the response or not. If he fails to do so and simply remains silent, then in a business contract he is likely to be regarded as having agreed to what amounts to a counter-offer.[31] This is one example of the legal significance of silence under German law relating to business contracts; another even more significant example is referred to below, p. 75.

WITHDRAWAL FROM NEGOTIATIONS

Unlike under French law there is little practical possibility in German law of a claim arising in delict for the breaking off of negotiations. Article 832 of the *BGB* which establishes the general right to claim damages for negligent acts lists the rights protected as being 'life, body, health, freedom, property or any other right' and this list has consistently been held by the German courts to exclude 'pure' economic loss, i.e. that which is not consequential upon material damage. Article 826 is much wider in terms and would include economic loss but it only applies if the damage has been caused wilfully and *contra bonos mores* which it seems would be improbable to establish in this type of case.[32]

If therefore there is to be any liability in respect of a default by a party in pre-contractual negotiations then it has to be found in contract. The origin of the possibility of such a liability is to be found in the doctrine of *culpa in contrahendo* which began with Ihering's famous article published in 1861.[33]

Initially the doctrine was concerned to provide a remedy for his reliance interest to a party of a proposed contract which had either not been finally concluded or although concluded was void where this was due to an error for which the other party was responsible. Essentially the liability was based on the duty of mutual trust and reliance within what Ihering saw as a special pre-contractual relationship to provide correctly that information which, because of such relationship, ought to be provided.[34]

The question which then arises is the extent to which this doctrine applies to the wider area of failure to exercise good faith in the carrying out of the negotiations themselves.

In principle the mere breaking off of negotiations by one party does not in itself create any liability. That only arises when there is default by that party in respect of the duty of trust which he owes to the other by reason of his having entered into the negotiations. This would be the case for example if by his conduct he had improperly established in the mind of the other party a belief that the negotiations would lead to the conclusion of a contract between them, without this having had any serious intention of that happening.[35] The liability would, however, only be for expenses incurred, i.e. reliance interest.

LETTERS OF INTENT

Article 154 of the *BGB* states:

> So long as the parties have not reached agreement upon all points of the contract which according to declaration of even only one of the parties needed to be agreed, the contract is in case of doubt not concluded. An agreement concerning particular points is not binding even although these have been noted down.

However, this paragraph is only a presumption which can be rebutted. So when the points outstanding are only the general conditions of contract then the behaviour of the parties and in particular the commencement of work may constitute such a rebuttal and indicate an intention to conclude a contract on the essential terms which have been agreed notwithstanding the partial disagreement on the general conditions. It would follow that a letter of intent which specified the essential terms, at least the scope of work, price and delivery period and instructed work to start would be held binding upon the parties.[36]

In any event the existence of a letter of intent of that type, especially one issued late in the negotiations, would strengthen the argument that any subsequent withdrawal from the negotiations by the party which issued the letter would constitute a breach of the obligation under the doctrine of *culpa in contrahendo* to negotiate in good faith.[37]

The remedy under German law for *culpa in contrahendo* is damages for reliance interest (*Vertrauensinteresse*) which are intended to place the party injured in the same position as he would have been had the negotiations not taken place. So clearly he would be entitled to recover for his costs and loss of time arising out of the abortive negotiations but perhaps also for other losses and expenses reasonably incurred as a result of his belief in the conclusion of the contract. He would not, however, be able to recover for loss of his anticipated profits or other benefits.[38]

LETTERS OF INTENT – COMPARATIVE SUMMARY

Of the three systems under review it is English law which is the most restrictive regarding the effect of letters of intent or other pre-contractual 'agreements'. A contract to negotiate is not a contract which is recognized by English law, which also knows of no duty to negotiate in good faith. There is either a contract on the terms agreed by the parties or there is no contract at all, and in the latter event the only liability of the purchaser may be to pay on a quantum meruit basis for any work which he has instructed the supplier to carry out and which the supplier has actually performed.

However, when carrying out negotiations with continental suppliers for contracts which are subject to either German or especially French law, it would be most unwise for the English buyer to assume that he could issue a letter of intent in the same cavalier way and with the same lack of responsibility as he would do in England. While commercial considerations may restrict the supplier's scope for action, the buyer must be aware of the risks he would be taking if he ignored the potential legal liabilities to which he may be subject.

THE VIENNA CONVENTION

As might be expected the Vienna Convention has drawn upon doctrines from both the common and the civil law.

It starts off in Art. 15(1) with the general rule that an offer becomes effective when it reaches the offeree. It continues by stating the position as it is under English law that an offer may be revoked at any time prior to the despatch of an acceptance. However para. (2) of Art. 16 then goes on to provide that an offer cannot be revoked if:

(a) it indicates, whether by stating a fixed time for acceptance or otherwise that it is irrevocable; or
(b) if it was reasonable for the offeree to rely on the offer as being irrevocable and the offeree has acted in reliance on that offer.

This is far closer to the civil law position. Paragraph (b) would clearly cover the situation of the offer from the sub-contractor to the main contractor which is referred to on p. 60 and under the circumstances as stated there would not allow the sub-contractor to revoke his tender. Indeed this example is given by Honnold on p. 144.

However, paragraph (a) is not so clear. Does merely stating a fixed period for acceptance mean that it is irrevocable within that period? It is considered that the use of typical commercial language such as 'Our tender is valid for 60 days', 'The validity period of our Offer is 60 days' or 'Our offer is open for Acceptance for 60 days' would mean that the offer could not be withdrawn within the 60-day period. The English rule to the contrary is based on the doctrine of consideration which is no part of the Convention and the use of such language is surely clear enough indication of an intent to make the offer irrevocable.

Assuming, however, that the party making the offer does in fact withdraw it, what is the remedy of the offeree? Under the Convention it would seem that he can treat the purported withdrawal as a nullity and accept the offer. If the offeror then states that he has no intention of performing, this would constitute a fundamental breach of contract under Art. 25 which would permit the offeree to claim damages under Art. 72 and possibly even under German and French law to require specific performance (see below, pp. 320 and 327).

Because the Convention allows for offers to be irrevocable, and also that offers only become effective when they reach the offeree, it also contains the same rule as in German law (Art. 130, *BGB*) even an irrevocable offer can be withdrawn, provided that the withdrawal reaches the offeree before or at the same time as the offer.

The Convention does not deal at all with the question of letters of intent, nor with possible pre-contractual remedies for the breaking off of contractual negotiations. These matters are all to be referred to the applicable domestic law.

NOTES

1. This was decided as long ago as 1828 in *Routledge* v. *Grant*.
2. This is based on a suggestion by Max Abrahamson in *Engineering Law and the ICE Contracts*, 4th edition, p. 4. However there has been added to his suggestion the proviso that the firm would have no right to bid unless the purchaser agreed, i.e. the bidding was under a restricted or selective procedure. If it was open tendering under the procedure of the EEC Directive 89/440 of 18 July 1989 there would be

no benefit to the bidder since he would be entitled to the documents in any event and it is deemed therefore no consideration for holding his offer open.

3. See the cases quoted by Zweigert and Kotz, vol. 2, p. 38 and the Uniform Commercial Code S.2–205 providing for irrevocability of a written binding offer for a period not exceeding 3 months.

4. *Walton Stores Interstate Ltd* v. *Maher* (1988) 164 CLR 387 reviewed in the LQR, vol. 104, 1988, p. 362 et seq. If the withdrawal is due to the sub-contractor having made an error in his tender negligently, then Cheshire p. 270 makes the interesting suggestion that the main contractor might have a claim in negligence in that because the sub-contractor knew of the main contractor's reliance on the figures quoted, the sub-contractor owed him a duty of care.

5. *Byrne & Co* v. *Leon von Tienhoven* (1880) 5 CPD 344 where the offeror had posted a letter of revocation prior to the posting of the letter of acceptance but which was only received five days later by the offeree. It was held that a contract existed. This contrasts sharply with the classical French position as expressed in the decision of the cour d'appel in Bordeaux (see below, p. 61).

6. Goff and Jones, p. 510. See also *Walford* v. *Miles* (1992) 2 WLR 174 where it was held by the House of Lords there cannot be an agreement to negotiate.

7. Per Judge Fay in *Turiff Construction Ltd and Turiff Ltd* v. *Regalia Knitting Mills* (1871) 9 BLR 20.

8. *William Lacy (Hounslow) Ltd* v. *Davies* [1957] 1 WLR 932 and *British Steel Corporation* v. *Cleveland Bridge and Engineering Co. Ltd* [1984] 1 All ER 504.

9. Ghestin, s.212. To the same effect Weill and Terré, s.136, 'an offer does not bind its originator, a will cannot bind itself'.

10. Weill and Terré, s.137.

10. According to the *Cour de cassation* 'while an offer of sale may in principle be withdrawn so long as it has not been accepted, it is otherwise the case when the person making the offer has expressly or implicitly undertaken not to withdraw it before a certain period of time', Cass. civ. 17 December 1958 D.1959 p. 33. Although in a later judgement the word 'implicitly' was not included this does not appear from other cases to have been deliberate and it is for the *juges de fond* to decide whether or not there was an implicit undertaking. (Ghestin s.216.)

12. Weill and Terré, para. 2(b), p. 146.

13. Weill and Terré, 2 (c), p. 146.

14. Bordeaux 29 January 1892. Other cases have allowed longer periods. Much depends upon the nature of the goods in question.

15. Ghestin, s.213, p. 230. Ghestin emphasizes that this particular decision should not be generalized because the supposed 'agreement' of the parties will in most cases be fictitious.

16. Ghestin, s.217.

17. Note that there was no question raised as to the non-communication of the will to revoke. The cour d'appel was concerned only with the fact that the intention had not been manifested.

18. Ghestin, s.218, in particular note 103. Mousseron, s.186.

19. In the case of the singer, the action by the theatre director in writing to the theatrical agent withdrawing the offer to her and instructing the agent to find another artiste was sufficient to revoke the offer – Source Book, 2nd ed., p. 331.

20. It was confirmed by the *Cour de cassation* on 11 January 1984 that the basis of the liability was delictual and not contractual when the court stated, 'the victim of a fault committed in the period preceding the conclusion of a contract has the right to pursue the reparation of the damage which he considers he has suffered before the court of the place where the damage arose *founded on liability in delict*' Bull, civ. IV no. 16. p. 1. This followed earlier decisions, e.g. Cass. com. 20 March 1972 in which the *Cour de cassation* had confirmed that the cour d'appel had been legally justified in establishing the 'abusive breach of the negotiations' and as a result the 'delictual liability' of the party responsible. See Joanna Schmidt-Szalewski, s.22, for the report of the decision of the *Cour de cassation*, which is also referred to in Nicholas, pp. 70 & 71, and generally the same author in *Formation of Contracts and Pre-contractual Liability*, ICC Publication no. 44019 p. 93.

21. It was decided by the *Cour de cassation* on 3 October 1972 that 'the delictual responsibility foreseen by the Articles of the Code civil may be considered in the absence of any intention to cause harm' Civ. III Bull. no. 491. What however is not clear is whether a simple fault is all that is needed or if it has to be an act of bad faith. There are decisions of the *Cour de cassation* which are difficult to reconcile – see Ghestin, s.228.

22. See Ghestin, s.938 on p. 1084.

23. See Mousseron, s.36, and Ghestin, s.228 on p. 252.
24. *Jordan* v. *Money* (1854) 5 HLC 185 and Salmond and Heuston, *The Law of Torts*, 20th ed., Sweet & Maxwell, 1992, p. 384.
25. Quoted in Mousseron, s.39 on p. 39.
26. Viney, s.198.
27. Cass. civ. 1re 8 October 1963 and Ghestin, s.241, p. 270.
28. See further Harris and Tallon p. 132 et seq.; Mousseron s.79 and Ghestin s.241. Assuming the obligation arising from the *accord de principe* is contractual it is necessary to know whether it is *une obligation de moyens de tenter de conclure* or *une obligation de résultat de conclure*. Generally it is thought that it is only an *obligation de moyens* on the basis that one can only seek to attain success in negotiations – see Starck s.281. Therefore the party prejudiced would have to prove that the breakdown was due to the default of the other.

    However Fontaine (1977) suggests that at a late stage in the negotiations the obligations not to re-open points agreed, to respect the confidentiality of information received and not to engage simultaneously in negotiations with a third party, could become *une obligation de résultat*. In that event the failure itself would entail the fault and the party in default could only escape liability by proving that it was due to *une cause étrangère*. See 'Les lettres d'intention dans la negociation des contrats internationaux', *Droit et Pratique du commerce internationale* t.3 no.2, p. 109, well worth careful study.
29. Fontaine op. cit., examples 5 and 15.
30. See Huebner pp. 414 and 415: 'the binding force of the offer "Antrag" (in older German) . . . was always recognised in Germanic law. . . . The party from whom the offer proceeded was bound by his unilateral word until he received a declaration by the other party. Only after the running of the time expressly set for the acceptance of the offer, or only when according to usages of trade he need no longer await the receipt of the acceptance, was he free'.

    At the time of the preparation of the *BGB* this point became an issue between the pandectists who argued that an offer could always be revoked before it had been accepted, and those, predominantly Otto von Gierke, who argued for the old Germanic rule on the basis of its practicality, especially in commercial matters in which it was well established (it was contained in the original *Commercial Code* of 1861) and the undesirability of having two differing rules one in the civil law and one in the commercial law. The argument was won by those who favoured the Germanic law and the text of the *BGB* is essentially that of the original *Commercial Code*.
31. E.g. decision of the Reichsgericht Third Civil Senate 28 January 1921 50 *Juristiche Wochenschrift* 393 quoted in Von Mehren pp. 878 and 879.
32. In order to be *contra bonos mores* the act must be one which would 'grossly violate the usual standards of those people whose thinking is just and equitable'. The conduct would need to be such that those in business would regard it as 'shocking'.
33. Rudolf von Ihering, *Culpa in Contrahendo, Jahrbücher für die Dogmatik des heutigen romischen unter deutschen Rechts* vol. 4 (1851) pp. 1–112.
34. See further *Essays in Memory of Professor F. H. Lawson* Butterworths, London 1986, p. 95 and Von Mehren p. 837 et seq.
35. See *Définition and Domaine de la Responsabilité Contractuelle*, Institut de Droit Comparé de l'Université de Paris sous la direction de Rene Rodière 1981 p. 119 and the references cited there. Also BGH 12 November 1986. BGHZ vol. 99 (1987) p. 101 and the *Report on German Law in the Formation of Contracts and pre-Contractual Liability*, ICC Publication 1048/9 published December 1990, and 12 December 1980 BGH 34 NLW 1035 (1981).
36. Abderrahmane p. 95. Such a letter of intent may also constitute a *Vorvertrag*, a 'contract to contract' which is contractually enforceable provided that its terms are sufficiently definitive and indicate a genuine intention on the part of both parties to conclude a contract. See *BGH* 13 December 1983 NJW (1984) vol. 37 p. 1665.
37. Fontaine (1977) p. 108.
38. Fontaine (1977) p. 112.

5 Acceptance

The issues relating to acceptance can be conveniently considered under two headings:

- the fact of acceptance, and
- the time when acceptance becomes effective.

THE FACT OF ACCEPTANCE UNDER ENGLISH LAW

Acceptance must be an unqualified expression of assent to the offer. It may be verbal, in writing or by conduct provided in the latter case the terms of the contract can be clearly established and the act was performed with the intention of accepting the offer.

Any alteration in the purported acceptance to a material term of the offer, e.g. price to be fixed and not variable, or the addition of any term to which the purported acceptance is made subject, will constitute a counter-offer which it is then open to the offeror to accept or reject. Any such counter-offer constitutes a rejection of the original offer which is no longer then open for acceptance.

The general rule is that acceptance cannot be inferred from silence alone other than in the most exceptional circumstances. It is only where the silence amounts to 'conduct of inaction' in a situation in which the offeror could reasonably expect the offeree to take positive action if he did not wish to accept, and has acted on that basis, that silence may be considered as acceptance.

THE TIME WHEN ACCEPTANCE BECOMES EFFECTIVE

In order for acceptance to be effective it must be communicated to the offeror, which as a general rule means either actually brought to his notice, as in a conversation face-to-face or on the telephone which the offeror hears,[1] or would have been had the offeror observed normal business practice, e.g. collecting messages from a telex or fax machine during ordinary business hours.

The general rule is not, however, applied when it is reasonable in the circumstances to use the post as a means of communicating the acceptance. Then the acceptance is treated as being effective once a letter, properly stamped and addressed, has been posted provided the parties did not, on the basis of their documentation or negotiations, intend otherwise.[2]

THE FACT OF ACCEPTANCE UNDER FRENCH LAW

In principle, in order for a contract to be formed there must be complete agreement between the offer and acceptance as to all the terms of the contract.

In practice, only agreement as to the essential terms is needed. As regards other terms, those which are *accessoires*, there is an obligation on the parties to seek to reach agreement on these.[3] If however the contract is silent on them, or if the parties cannot ultimately agree, then they will be governed by *les dispositions législatives supplétives* (see above, p. 8) or by general trade customs under Art. 1135 of the *Code Civil*. A term may be essential because it is regarded as such by law for the particular category of contract in question, for example on a contract classified as one of sale, the subject matter of the sale and the price (see above, p. 45, for the necessity of the price being determined or objectively determinable).

As regards the goods themselves the *Cour de cassation* in 1979[4] stated that 'the goods had not been described as a result of which the "objet" of the contract had not been established.' As Ghestin observes (p. 243), in all contracts involving an exchange there will be an *objet* of one of the obligations and the price for its performance. In default of agreement on this *objet* and the price there is no contract. (For the concept of *objet* see below, p. 83.)

Alternatively a term may be made essential by the parties themselves, as when the purchaser requires delivery to be effected on a certain date or at a certain place. In that event, in the absence of agreement between the parties on such a term, the contract will not be formed. It is the responsibility of the *juges de fond* to decide whether or not the common intention of the parties – Art. 1156 of the *Code Civil* – was to make essential a term which is normally regarded as *accessoire*.[5]

The submission of a counter-offer may result in the original offer being regarded as having lapsed but it is not automatic. It depends upon the facts of the case and above all upon the expressed intentions of the offeree. If for example he makes it absolutely clear that he will definitely not under any circumstances enter into a contract upon the price at which the goods have been offered, then the offer will be considered as expired without the need to show that it was actually withdrawn. In this example English law sees the issue as being a matter of law, a counter-offer positively constituting termination of the original offer, while French law sees it as a matter of fact to be decided upon according to the expressed intentions of the party concerned in the particular case.[6]

EFFECT OF SILENCE

As regards silence French law is again similar to English. The general rule in practice is 'he who says nothing does not consent'[7] but it is not a rule of law and a French lower court which based its decisions on the existence of a rule that silence could *never* amount to consent would be certain to have it annulled by the *Cour de cassation*. It is a question of fact to be determined by *les juges de fond* in each individual case, taking into account in particular any trade custom or usage. In practice in business matters a French court appears more likely to find a commercial custom that silence amounts to consent than would an English court. As one author has put it, 'usage confers on silence an objective significance which is in fact a true means of communication analogous to a language'.[8]

POST-CONTRACTUAL DOCUMENTS

The problem of silence has arisen frequently in respect of letters of confirmation, invoices and receipts which may seem surprising from the viewpoint of English law which denies contractual effect to post-contractual documents unless these constitute a modification which is agreed between the parties.

In principle French law adopts the same approach as English; only a formal modification agreed between the parties can vary the initially agreed terms of the contract or introduce terms which modify *les dispositions légales supplétives*.[9] However there are commercial customs relating in particular to letters of confirmation and to invoices which may constitute exceptions to this general rule depending on the facts as found by *les juges de fond*.

LETTERS OF CONFIRMATION

A letter of confirmation is normally used either to record in writing the essential terms of the contract which have already been agreed verbally, say over the telephone, or to complete an agreement by substituting clauses *accessoires* agreed between the parties for those contained in the *dispositions légales supplétives*. Although the letter of confirmation is supposedly only a document interpreting and applying that which has already been agreed, in practice it is only too easy for the draftsman to use it to modify the terms of the initial contract to his own advantage.

The issue then arises as to whether or not the recipient, if he fails to object quickly enough to the terms of the letter, will be held bound by it. Unlike German law, in which it is a *rule of law* in dealings between business people that silence in the face of a letter of confirmation constitutes acceptance, unless there is a 'surprise' clause included (see below, p. 75), in French law it is a *question of fact* to be determined in each individual case by the *juges de fond* according to trade custom, provided that the recipient knew, or ought to have known, of such custom. However the general commercial practice is that unless the recipient objects within a very short period of time, often as little as 24 hours, then silence will be taken as acceptance. It is therefore essential for the terms of a letter of confirmation to be examined both rapidly and carefully.

INVOICES

There is a general commercial practice under which the acceptance of an invoice without protest and even more so its payment may be regarded as acceptance of the essential terms of the contract, i.e. the subject matter of the sale and its price.[10] However mere silence after receipt of an invoice is not of itself sufficient to establish the existence of a contract between the parties in the absence of any other evidence.[11]

As regards other terms, especially those limiting responsibility, silence will not normally constitute acceptance. There must be evidence of positive acceptance by the purchaser.[12] This issue usually arises when the original contract left matters such as guarantees to be governed by *les dispositions légales supplétives* and the seller's terms on the back of the invoice derogate from these.

It is a question of fact to be determined by the *juges de fond* in each particular case as to whether or not silence really does amount to such positive acceptance, taking into account factors such as the nature of the clause and the commonality of its usage in the trade in question, the business relationship between the parties, the professional character of the purchaser, and whether or not the manner in which the clause has been printed was such as to bring it clearly to the purchaser's attention.

In practice today it is likely that silence will be taken as positive acceptance only when the parties already have an established relationship and the evidence that the same clauses have been known to, and accepted by them, on previous contracts. But even this may not be sufficient if the clause is one which limits the responsibility of the party issuing the invoice, unless the recipient, by reason of his profession, must be taken to have known of the general conditions of contract prevailing in their totality within his industry.[13]

OFFERS MADE SOLELY IN INTERESTS OF OFFEREE

There is one further exception to the rule that silence is not consent, which is considered rather strange even by French doctrine, and that is where the offer is made solely in the interests of the other party. This was established finally by an *arrêt de principe* of the *Cour de cassation* 1969 in a case in which a motor cyclist was injured in an accident in which his motor cycle caught fire. A garage mechanic passing by went immediately to his assistance and was badly burnt by an explosion of the petrol tank. The cour d'appel held that there was a contract of assistance and that the motor cyclist was liable to the mechanic in damages. The appeal against the decision of the cour d'appel was based on there having been no contract because there had been no acceptance.

The *Cour de cassation*, in rejecting the appeal, stated that:

> the Cour d'appel did not have to find that there had been an express acceptance since when an offer is made in his exclusive interest the offeree is presumed to have accepted it . . . . and that judges of appeal were legally correct in holding that the person assisted had the obligation to make good the damages suffered by the person who had voluntarily come to his assistance.[14]

More practically, from a commercial viewpoint, the same rule was applied when a landlord told his tenant that he would reduce the rents which were owed to him for a certain period. There was no reply, not even, as Starck comments, 'a thank you'.

Later the landlord sought to claim the rents but the court decided that the tenant's silence amounted to an acceptance of the offer which he had no reason to reject.[15]

TIME WHEN ACCEPTANCE BECOMES EFFECTIVE

For contracts which are formed between people who are present together, which would also include as regards the time at which the contract was concluded those formed by a telephone conversation, French law is the same as English. The acceptance must be communicated. If following a telephone conversation one party confirms to the other in writing the terms of the verbal agreement reached, then the letter will generally be treated as a matter of proof and the contract will be regarded as having been formed at the time of the telephone discussion in which the offer was accepted. But unlike English law the place where the contract is formed by telephone is that from which the call accepting the offer originated.[16]

However with contracts formed by correspondence there has been a dispute for many years between two main rival theories, those of 'réception' and 'expédition'. Under the theory of 'réception' the contract is formed when the acceptance letter is received. Under the theory of 'expédition' the contract is formed when the acceptance letter is sent.

There is no article dealing directly with the point in the *Code Civil* and for a long time the *Cour de cassation* refused to give any ruling other than that the issue was to be determined as a matter of fact by *les juges de fond*.[17]

In practice both theories were utilized although there was a tendency to apply the theory of 'expédition' in answering the question 'where the contract had been formed' and the theory of 'réception' in answering the question of 'when'.[18]

Finally it appears, although this is not accepted by Starck,[19] that the *Cour de cassation* has decided in favour of the theory of 'expédition'. In a decision which seems to be regarded as an *arrêt de principe* of 7 January 1981[20] it was stated by the Chambre Commerciale, in the absence of any stipulation to the contrary the offer was intended to be formed into a contract not by the receipt by its author of the acceptance of the addressee, but by the latter's sending the acceptance'.

As Ghestin comments

> For the Chambre Commerciale once it had been established that the letter of acceptance had been sent within the period stipulated in the offer in which it was open for acceptance, in the absence of any stipulation in the offer to the contrary, there was no need for them to be concerned with the moment at which it reached the offeror.[21]

The decision did not deal specifically with the question of the place where the contract was formed, although it could be interpreted as applying the same rule, namely the place where the acceptance was sent which would be consistent with earlier jurisprudence.[22]

For contracts formed by telex or facsimile the same rules would appear to apply; the contract would be formed by the sending of the telex or fax and the place where the contract was made would be that from which the telex or fax originated. This differs from English law which requires for such contracts the receipt of acceptance and maintains that the place where the contract is formed is that at which the acceptance is received.

THE FACT OF ACCEPTANCE UNDER GERMAN LAW

An acceptance, like any other *Rechtsgeschäft* (juristic transaction), generally only takes effect when it is communicated to the offeror and communication is when the acceptance comes within the 'zone of control' of the recipient, e.g. it is received at his business address during normal working hours.

However under Art. 151 of the *BGB* the contract can be concluded without the offeror being notified of the acceptance 'if such notification is not to be expected according to common usage or if it has been waived by the offeror'. So acceptance can be by conduct, as when goods are despatched following receipt of a customer's order.

According to Art. 150 of the *BGB* the terms of the acceptance must correspond to those of the offer and if the purported acceptance modifies or amplifies the terms of the offer then this is deemed to be a refusal of the offer and the submission of a counter-offer. However, where as is normal in business contracts, the acceptance is not a straightforward agreement to the terms of the offer, but refers to the party's own general conditions, there is an important distinction between what is referred to as a letter of confirmation *Kaufmannische Bestätigungsschreiben* and a confirmation of order – *Auftragsbestätigung* or *Bestellungsannahme*.

The former is a judicially recognized document to which applies the rule relating to the presumed acceptance of its terms by silence (see next section). The latter is simply a counter-offer to which the terms of Art. 150 apply. It is well established that the name given to the document by the parties is not determinative and that the court will decide into which category to place the document according to their view of its true character.[23]

There has to be agreement on all points on which agreement, even according to the declaration of one of the parties, is required and the contract is in case of doubt not concluded (Art. 154 *BGB*). However, as stated earlier (see above, p. 65), this is a presumption which can be rebutted, and where the disagreement is only on the general conditions, and the behaviour of the parties, e.g. in starting performance, shows an intention to be bound by the essential terms, the contract will be considered to have been concluded (see further below p. 77, The Battle of the Forms).

In deciding whether agreement has been reached or not the German courts will today tend to look at the objective interpretation of the words used as they will be understood by the recipient, as indicated in the earlier discussion of Arts 133 and 157 *BGB* (see above, p. 40). This may however as will be seen later (see below, p. 133) lead to rescission of the contract if the objective interpretation differs from what the person making the declaration really intended.[24]

THE EFFECT OF SILENCE

Reference was made earlier (see above, p. 63) to the effective of silence by the offeror on receipt of an acceptance of an offer marked *freibleibend*. Although the general rule is that silence does not constitute a 'declaration of the will', there is one most important exception to this which is in respect of commercial letters of confirmation (*kaufmannische Bestätigungsschreiben*) in contracts between business people.

Such a letter, which as stated previously is well known in German commercial practice as a legal instrument (it is sometimes referred to in judgements as *Bestätigungsschreiben im Rechtssinn* – legal letter of confirmation), has been defined as 'A Letter of Confirmation has as its object to fix for the parties in a definitive and obligatory manner the express and implied content of the negotiations which have preceded the conclusion of the contract.'[25]

In theory it ought to follow from that definition that the letter of confirmation can only be issued after the negotiations have been completed and that it can only record what has actually been agreed. This may be the case, in which event the letter is termed 'declarative', but in practice most letters do not fall into that category.[26]

This is because the Federal Court has not followed a restrictive approach and has allowed validity to be given to letters of confirmation which have been issued prior to the finalization of the contract terms, especially those relating to the general conditions of contract, provided that the oral negotiations or exchange of letters/telexes have reached a sufficiently advanced state. The letter is then termed 'constitutive'.[27]

The importance of all this is that, once such a letter of confirmation has been issued, then, unless it is immediately objected to by the other party, the first party will be held to be bound by its terms. This then constitutes the contract and the court will only refer back to the earlier negotiations if there is a clear and significant inconsistency. Such an inconsistency arose when the terms of a letter of confirmation on the sale of several silos issued by the vendor contained the expression 'bought as seen under exclusion of any warranties' and it was held that this did not override the vendor's prior affirmation that the silos had certain properties which in fact they lacked (BGH VIII ZR 238/83 30 January 1985. [1985] DB 1226).

Moreover the principle of 'consent by silence' when faced with a letter of confirmation will apply, even if for example the letter introduces the other party's standard conditions for the first time, provided that neither document contains any 'surprise clauses' (as the letter clearly did in the case referred to above), and is consistent with the obligation of *Treu und Glauben* including the requirements of the Standard Contracts Act as applicable to business transactions (see below, p. 304).

Thus for example it was decided by the Federal Court on 21 March 1966 that on the commercial sale of a second-hand motorized cement mixer, which had been inspected on the purchaser's behalf by an expert, the purchaser ought to have expected that the supplier's conditions of sale would exclude liability for defects, even though this point had not been discussed in the negotiations. Therefore if the purchaser did not agree with the reference to such an exclusion in the seller's letter of confirmation he should have immediately objected. His silence at that time on this point amounted to consent and therefore the clause was binding upon him.

This case was of course decided before the passing of the Standard Contract Terms Act. While under that Act even in a business transaction the seller cannot in his standard conditions exclude liability for defects, that applies only to *new* goods. As regards second-hand goods it is a matter of whether the court is satisfied that the seller has behaved in good faith. In so far as the court considered that the exclusion was customary in the trade and therefore to be expected and was a 'dictate of common-sense', then it would appear probable that the decision would be the same today (see further on the Act below, p. 304). However where a seller's letter of confirmation in a commercial sale stated that the delivery time was approximate and excluded liability for delay, in contradiction to the terms of the buyer's order, it was held that the seller could not in 'Treu und Glauben', assume the buyer's acceptance by his silence (BGH 26 September 1973 BGHZ 61,282).

There is no equivalent in English law either to the doctrine of judicially recognized letters of confirmation or to that of the possibility of being bound by silence to a point not discussed during the negotiations but included by the other party in his letter of confirmation to which on receipt of the letter one did not make immediate objection. In *Brogden* v. *Metropolitan Railway Co.* which has been suggested as being related to this issue it was not the conduct of the company's agent in putting away the amended draft returned by Brogden marked as 'approved' but without expressing his assent which created the contract (as would have been the case under German law), but the subsequent conduct of the parties in ordering and supplying coal.[28]

THE TIME WHEN ACCEPTANCE BECOMES EFFECTIVE

The basic rule under German law is simple: acceptance is effective as indeed is any other declaration of intention when it comes within the control of the recipient (Art. 130 *BGB*). So it follows the same principles as discussed under Revocation (see above, p. 66). When it is a matter of acceptance by silence, then once it has been proved that the letter of confirmation reached the other party and unless objection is made promptly, which is a matter to be determined according to trade custom and the facts of the particular case, the silence will be considered as the declaration of intention to accept. It would appear that the burden of proof that objection was made rests on the recipient of the letter of confirmation.

The acceptance must be definitive, so when a telex is sent which accepts the offer but contains the words 'letter follows' this will generally mean that the acceptor will finally accept the offer by letter and that in the mean time he reserves the right to make alterations to the contractual conditions. In such a case the contract will only come into being when the letter itself has been received, assuming of course that the letter does amount to an unconditional acceptance (OLG Hamm [2U 86/83] 11 July 1983 DB 2619).

THE BATTLE OF THE FORMS

The expression the 'battle of the forms' is used to describe the situation in which the seller and the purchaser both seek to incorporate their own general conditions into the contract. These can be expected to differ widely in the responsibilities which each is prepared to accept and the obligations they seek to impose upon the other party.

A typical scenario is that the seller submits his offer on his standard conditions printed on the back of his quotation form, and the purchaser issues his order with his standard conditions either printed on the reverse or attached and the seller 'accepts' the order, again referring back to his own conditions. There is agreement on the subject matter of the contract, the price and the delivery period but little or none on the remainder of the terms of contract.

ENGLISH LAW

English law sees this problem in terms of offer and acceptance. The purchaser's order is in reality a counter-offer. If the seller's so-called 'acceptance' simply refers back to his own conditions again, this will be yet another counter-offer and no contract will be formed until the purchaser accepts this, usually by taking delivery of the goods.

However in the leading English case, *Butler Machine Tool Co* v. *Ex-cell-O Corpn*, the seller, on receiving the purchaser's order, sent back the tear-off slip on the bottom which contained the words 'we accept your order on the terms and conditions thereon'. This was sufficient for the court of appeal to find that there had been acceptance and the contract had been formed on the purchaser's conditions, even though the slip had been returned under cover of a letter referring to the order having been entered in accordance with the seller's original quotation. This was because the court interpreted the seller's letter as a reference only to the subject matter of their quotation and not to all its terms. The interpretation is strained because it seems the court wished to avoid having to find an executed contract void for lack of agreement. The majority of the court of appeal, in commenting upon what the position would have been if the seller had not returned the slip, thought that there would have been a contract only when the goods had been delivered and accepted by the purchaser.[29]

It is often said that the winner of the 'battle' will be the one who 'fires the last shot'. While this is not strictly true it is certainly the case that the party who has last put forward his own conditions and has accepted no document from the other side can hardly lose, except in the sense that there may be no contract at all. In this event, if either party at some stage before acceptance of the goods declines to proceed, this could make it difficult for the other to recover his costs incurred.[30] It also creates the unsatisfactory situation that the outcome will in all probability depend not upon genuine intent, but as in the Butler case, on an act of carelessness in either the sales or buying department.

FRENCH LAW

French law approaches the problem quite differently. A distinction is drawn between the essential terms of the contract which express the specific wills of the parties, and upon which there must be agreement in order for the contract to be formed according to its classification, e.g. in a contract for sale the thing being sold and its price, and the general conditions of contract which are *dispositions accessoires*.

If the two sets of general conditions differ, then, in the absence of any express evidence to the contrary, these are taken not to express the 'certain and non-equivocal wills of the parties' so that the contradictory clauses will be deleted and replaced by the appropriate *dispositions supplétives* of the *droit commun*.[31] In this way the existence of the contract is saved. Legally the solution can be justified on the grounds that the *dispositions légales supplétives* apply unless the parties have agreed to the contrary and to the extent that the parties' respective general conditions conflict there has been no such agreement.

GERMAN LAW

German law at one time was much the same as English, utilizing the theory of the 'last word' ('*die Theorie des letzten Wortes*'). So in the classic situation referred to above in which the seller responds to the purchaser's order by referring back to his conditions of sale, and the purchaser makes no further response but in due course accepts delivery of the goods and starts to use them, such acceptance 'renders eloquent his earlier silence' and constitutes acceptance of the seller's conditions (BGH 17 September 1954 BB, 1954, 882).

This constituted an exception to the general rule in German law that, apart from letters of confirmation, silence does not amount to acceptance.

If however the parties remained in disagreement as to whose general conditions applied to the contract, then this did not lead as one might expect from Art. 150.2 of the *BGB*[32] to a declaration that no contract existed. Instead the court was prepared to hold that, relying on the principle of good faith to which the article is subject, and having partially executed the contract, the parties were not able in good faith to allege that no contract existed.[33]

The same result has been reached more recently by applying the principle that Art. 154 of the *BGB* (see above, p. 74) can be rebutted by the actions of the parties. Provided therefore that there is agreement on the essential terms of the contract, the fact that there is disagreement between the parties as to the applicable general conditions of contract, again does not lead to the conclusion that there is no contract between them.

However, in solving the question as to the disagreement between the parties' general conditions German law has now moved away from the doctrine of the 'last word' to that of 'reciprocal annulation'. If the general conditions of the parties are in disagreement one with one another and it cannot be said that one party has accepted the other's terms 'silently', then the terms upon which they disagree will not form part of the contract but will be replaced by the provisions of the general law.[34] Disagreement will be deemed to exist if the terms of one party are additional to, and have no counterpart in, the terms of the other, do not form part of the general law and cannot be said to have been silently accepted.[35] Finally it appears that the replacement by the general law will be limited to those terms disagreed, rather than both sets of general conditions being discarded and replaced in their totality by the general law. However it is thought that this alternative approach could have advantages in practice by avoiding the necessity of making fine distinctions and redrafting clauses in order to obtain coherence.

THE VIENNA CONVENTION

THE FACT OF ACCEPTANCE

Acceptance may be constituted either by a statement or other conduct of the offeree which indicates assent. Silence or inactivity does not in itself constitute acceptance (Art. 18(1)).

The Convention does not deal expressly with the practice of sending letters of confirmation to which, as was referred to earlier under German law and to a lesser extent under French law, the recipient must make immediate objection if he wishes to avoid being bound by the terms contained in the letter, at least if these are not materially inconsistent with the prior negotiations. However Art. 9, which refers to the parties having implicitly made applicable to their contract or its formation a usage of which 'the parties knew or ought to have known and which in international trade is widely known to and regularly observed by parties to contracts of the type involved and in the particular trade concerned', could be wide enough to cover the effect of letters of confirmation, say in the case of an English buyer who dealt regularly with German suppliers in a trade in which the use of such letters was common practice. (See Honnold on this possibility at p. 122.)

At the other end of the spectrum, where an English buyer was dealing with a German seller for the first time, and had no knowledge of the use of such letters, then it would seem that unless the letter came within the scope of Art. 19 of the Convention its terms would not be binding on the buyer if they differed from those of his offer and he stayed silent.

Article 19 is the attempt of the Convention to deal with the question of the 'battle of the forms'.

Having included in paragraph (1) the conventional statement that a reply to an offer which modifies the terms of the offer is a rejection of the offer and constitutes a counter-offer, it goes on in paragraph (2) to provide that if a purported acceptance does not 'materially alter the terms of the offer', then this will constitute an acceptance unless the offeror without undue delay objects to the modifications. In that event the modifications become part of the contract.

Paragraph (3) lists terms which are to be considered 'material', including price, payment, quality, quantity of the goods, place and time of delivery, extent of one party's liability to the other or the settlement of disputes. One might be forgiven for wondering what was left. However there could be matters such as details of the packaging, periods for inspection and the notification of claims which could differ and which, if the buyer wanted to get out of the bargain because the market price of the goods had suddenly fallen, he could try to use as a basis for saying that the seller's acceptance was not in the same terms as the order, and therefore no contract existed.

TIME OF ACCEPTANCE

The basic rule under the Convention, contrary to the English post-box rule, is that an acceptance is only effective when it reaches the offeror (Art. 18(2)) and the acceptance can be withdrawn provided that the withdrawal reaches the offeror before or at the same time as the acceptance (Art. 22). The Convention in Art. 24 applies effectively the same rules as to when an offer or acceptance 'reaches' the other party as apply under German law.

NOTES

1. *Entores Ltd* v. *Miles Far East Corp.* [1955] 2 QB 327: 'acceptance would not be effective if conversation was drowned by the noise of an aircraft flying overhead' and *Brinkibon Ltd* v. *Stahag Stahl und Stahlwarenhandelsgesellschaft mbH* [1983] 2 AC 34 relating to communication by telex.
2. Per Lawton J in *Holywell Securities Ltd* v. *Hughes* [1974] 1 All ER 161 at p. 167.
3. Starck, para. 285.
4. Bull. civ., III no. 4 p. 3.
5. Where a seller had made it clear that it was only after the issue by the buyer of a letter of credit that he would confirm the order, agreement on the *modalités de paiement* was necessary for the formation of the contract of sale. Cass. com. 16 April 1991 Bull. civ. IV no. 148 p. 106 and *Revue Trimestrielle de droit commerciale et droit économique* vol. 1 1992 pp. 214 and 215.
6. The question is extensively examined by Ghestin para. 226–2, pp. 247 and 248 and he concludes with the following extract from a decision of the *Cour de cassation* of 9 December 1987:
   by accepting as a result of the terms of the counter-proposal made by the husband and wife Sautelet that they had made clear *in a manner non-equivocal and definitive* their refusal to conclude the sale at the proposed price, which resulted in the withdrawal of the offer, the court of appeal who did not have to establish a revocation of the offer by Madame Frappa, has by these reasons alone, legally justified its decision.
7. Starck para. 136. This is the opposite of the proverb 'he who says nothing consents'.
8. Ghestin para. 296 p. 309.
9. Ghestin para. 308 quoting a judgement of the chambre commercial of the *Cour de cassation* which had annulled a decision of the cour d'appel on the grounds that the court had not investigated whether the sender of goods 'had knowledge of the clause (limiting the transport company's responsibility) and had accepted it at the moment of the formation of the contract'.
10. Cass. com. 26 May 1987 JCP 1987 IV, p. 266.
11. The *Cour de cassation* 9 March 1988 Bull. civ. III no. 53 p. 30, in a case in which a company refused to pay the cost of some painting works on the grounds that no contract existed, but had received an invoice for them without having issued the slightest reservation or objection, stated that 'this reason alone does not establish the existence of a contract between the parties'.
12. Cass. com. 14 January 1975 Bull. civ. III p. 243 no. 282.

13 Cass. com. referred to above. Cass. com. 12 October 1983 JCP 1983 IV p. 350 in which a clause limitative of responsibility was allowed to be effective since the professional transport agent should have known of the general conditions of the National Federation of Hauliers.

14. Cass. civ. 1 December 1969. See the *Source Book* 3rd ed. p. 314.

15. Starck s.144 p. 49. Req. 29 March 1938 D:1939 1,5. One is reminded immediately of Lord Denning's judgement in the High Trees House case.

16. Starck para. 290 and Weill and Terré p. 141 note 169.2. Contracts by telephone are assimilated to those concluded by people physically present together on the basis that they behave as if they were so and there is no break in time between the offer and acceptance. Interestingly there is an exception when unknowingly a telephone answering machine has been used. However, unlike English law, contracts by telephone will be regarded as having been formed at the place from which the acceptor is telephoning on the basis that once the acceptance has been given from there by telephone the contract is complete, and there can be no subsequent withdrawal by faster means of communication. Weill and Terré p. 163 note 243 and Rodière *La Formation du Contrat* p. 42 note 38 referring to a decision of the Cour d'Appel du Nancy of 20 January 1925 and the note on the case.

17. The respective merits and defects of the two theories are extensively discussed in Ghestin pp. 272–81; Starck pp. 100–109 and Weill and Terré pp. 155–164.

18. Under the old procedural code the place where the contract was formed could under certain circumstances, e.g. in matters of employment, decide which court had jurisdiction. As a matter of social policy the *Cour de cassation* considered that in employment matters it was advantageous for the case to be heard by the court of the district in which the employee lived and it was the employee who normally sent the acceptance. This no longer applies since under Art. 46 of the *New Code of Civil Procedure* the place where the contract is formed is excluded when deciding the question of jurisdiction.

19. Para. 314 p. 108. He believes the lower courts still have freedom to decide between the two theories.

20. Ghestin para. 256–1 p. 281 certainly considers it to be so when he states 'The essential factor however is that the Cour de Cassation has finally chosen, so it seems, to establish a suppletive rule, for which we have waited for so long'. For the concept of 'suppletive rules' and the distinction between imperative and suppletive rules see above, p. 8. This view is supported by Chabas (1981) in *Rev. trim. dr. civ.* p. 849 and in the observations in Henri Capitant *Les Grands Arrêts* p. 338. Strangely Zweigert and Kotz Vol. I, p. 41 do not refer to the decision or the commentaries on it and both regard the matter as still being left by the *Cour de cassation* as one of fact to be determined by the *juges de fond*. Nicholas, 2nd. edn., p. 74, does refer to the decision but seems to doubt its general application.

21. Ghestin para. 256–1.

22. Mousseron refers to the *Cour de cassation* having pronounced in a constant manner to this effect and to the number of judgements adopting this solution as constituting a 'genuine rule of law'. It appears also to be the rule as regards telephone conversations and telex transmissions (Weill and Terré p. 163 note 243.

23. 'The Federal Court has found in favour of giving a functional interpretation of the document (Letter) in dispute taking into account its contents and the circumstances which surrounded its use' Abderrahmane para. 88 p. 65 quoting from the judgement of the court of 9 July 1970 BGHZ 54, 237: 'The delivery conditions of the VDMA (utilised by the seller) became part of the contract because the letter although qualified by the defendant (the seller) as "confirmation of order" is in reality a Letter of Confirmation in a legal sense . . . the designation given by a party to his written confirmation not being essential'.

See also the other dozen cases quoted by Abderrahmane in support of this contention in which letters, and in one case an invoice were requalified by the courts.

24. While German law has moved away from the original concept of the *BGB* that the intentions of the party making the declaration were to be determined subjectively (Art. 133 which refers to 'seeking the true intention without regard to the literal meaning of the words used') to an objective interpretation based on Art. 157, rescission is still allowed if the party was subjectively mistaken as to the content or meaning of their declaration *Geschäftirrtum*, although not if the mistake was in their motive for making it *Motivirrtum* (Art. 119 *BGB* para. 1). Other than in the simplest cases there is an obvious difficulty in drawing the dividing line between the two which is why today attention tends to be concentrated rather on the second paragraph of Art. 119 which assimilates to an error in content one which is in 'the qualities of the person or thing in question which according to normal usage are regarded as essential'. This formula is sufficiently wide to allow the courts a significant measure of discretion in order to arrive at an equitable solution. (For some examples see further below, p. 134.)

25. Abderrahmane para. 78 p. 62 and cases cited there.
26. Abderrahmane paras 82 and 83 p. 63.
27. BGHZ 54, 236, 240. See also Abderrahmane para. 81 and the sources quoted there. It was said in an older case 'it is the creative force of the law inherent in the Letter of Confirmation which is the origin of the contractual bond' RG 5 June 1923, JW 1924, 405.
28. The suggestion was made by Cohn vol. II para. 7.87.
29. 1979 1 WLR 401.
30. The seller would clearly have a right not to proceed. See the judgement of Mr Justice Goff as he then was in the *British Steel Corporation* v. *Cleveland Bridge* case referred to earlier (see above, p. 67) where he recognized the right of Cleveland Bridge to have stopped work at any time prior to the conclusion of a contract. If the buyer declines to proceed then the right of the seller to recover his costs expended may depend upon whether or not he had acted in reliance on a request from the buyer, e.g. some form of letter of intent. The existence of the request establishes the benefit to the buyer which appears still to be the basis of a restitutionary claim. If there has been no such instruction then the seller, on the orthodox view of such a claim, would have to establish a benefit to the buyer which could be difficult if the goods were only in the early state of manufacture. Alternatively it has been suggested that the true basis of the claim is really one for a loss suffered in anticipation based on reliance (see Goff and Jones p. 509). But that is not an action known to English law which has not adopted the German principle of *culpa in contrahendo* (see above, p. 64).
31. Chambre des requêtes, s. 1934. I. 110. Mousseron s.282 p. 117 and cases cited there. Ghestin *La Vente* s.239 p. 280. Paris 19 March 1987; Cass. civ. 11 June 1986.
32. 'An acceptance under amplifications, limitations or other alterations is deemed a refusal combined with a new offer'.
33. BGH 26 September 1973 BGHZ 61, 283. The buyer's order form specified delivery by 15 April 1970 and stated that any deviating terms were not accepted unless confirmed by the buyer in writing. The seller in his confirmation of order stated that delivery would be between the middle and end of April but that the delivery term was approximate and not binding and excluded damages for delay. The goods were not delivered until June. The seller's confirmation was treated as a counter-offer which since it deviated significantly from the buyer's order could not in good faith be treated as having been accepted by silence. The buyer's taking delivery and using the goods did not constitute acceptance since in making delivery the seller did not insist it was on his terms.
34. Köln Oberlandesgericht 19 March 1980, 1980 Betr. 924, and BGH 20 March 1985, 1985 NJW 1838. The court here based its decision in part on the analogy with the Standard Contract Terms Act s.6(2) which states: 'In so far as the (standard) conditions are not incorporated or void, the contents of the contract are determined according to statute law'.
35. So in the above case where the court pointed out that the term in the seller's conditions of sale for reservation of title, which included a provision that the buyer was to assign to the seller all claims which he had against those who purchased the goods from him, had no counterpart in the buyer's conditions of purchase. As there was no agreement, even silently, by the buyer to this term, it was rejected therefore by the buyer's conditions of purchase. Since an extended reservation of title clause of this nature does not form part of the general statutory law the seller's claim to be preferred against the other creditors of the buyer failed. See further Chapter 18.

6 Objet

FRENCH LAW

In the volume on *Objet, Cause et Lésion du Contrat* published by the Institut du droit comparé de l'Université de Paris it is said in the summary table that under English law 'the contract has for its *objet* the exchange and acceptance of promises'. One would however look in vain in an English legal textbook for any reference to the contract having an *objet*, in the sense of the subject matter of the contract. As was stated earlier there is really no way in which the word can be adequately translated into English and the concept simply does not exist under English law.[1] Similarly there is no concept of *objet* under German law.

French law, however, in Art. 1108 of the *Code Civil*, provides that every contract in order to be valid must have an *objet*, and this is amplified by Art. 1126 of the *Code Civil* which states that 'every contract has as its "objet", "une chose" (a thing) which one party is obliged to give (in the sense of the transfer of property), do, or refrain from doing'.[2]

The language of the code in referring to 'l'objet du contrat' is generally recognized among French authors as being misleading,[3], since it is not really the contract which has an *objet*: 'The contract itself only has effects which consist of one or more obligations. It is these obligations created by the contract which have *un objet*: in a contract for sale to deliver something'.[4]

The act of performance of delivery – the *prestation* – again has *un objet* which is whatever item is the subject matter of the sale.[5]

Although the code refers to *choses*, things, this is to be understood widely to include not only material items but also *les prestations d'étude* and what would be included in the 'extensive definition' under English law of 'choses in action', namely debts and all forms of industrial property right such as patents, copyright and trade marks.[6]

The following are the main requirements in respect of *un objet* which must be satisfied in order for the contract to be valid.

DETERMINABILITY

The subject matter of the obligation must be either determined or objectively determinable at the time when the contract is made. The need for the price to be determined or objectively determinable has already been extensively considered (see above, pp. 45–48). Equally at the time when the contract is made the subject matter of the obligation to deliver or do must also be determined or objectively determinable according to its nature.

The *chose* may be a *corps certain,* what would be referred to in English law as 'specified goods'. So in a typical French textbook example this would be 'one or more sacks of wheat carrying a particular marking or number' by which they could be identified. It may also be a *chose de genre,* goods of a particular type which in English terminology would be referred to as 'generic goods'. Again the typical French example is that of '10 sacks of wheat of a particular kind'.[7] The goods sold would then be *individualisées* or in English 'ascertained' at a later date, often only on delivery.

The quantity need not be specified in the contract provided that the contract contains provisions by which they can be determined (second paragraph of Art. 1129 of the *Code Civil*). Generally the French courts in the past have been more relaxed as to the requirement for the determination of the quantity of goods in comparison with their attitude to the contract price. So it was held that the quantity could be specified in terms of a minimum with the maximum left to the agreement of the parties or simply stated as between a minimum and a maximum.[8] However there would appear to be a change of attitude today so that an exclusive supply contract was held to be void for lack of the determination of the quantities involved when the *Cour de cassation* noted that 'the reference to annual turnover did not permit the designation of the successive supplies the "objet" of the agreement'.[9]

As regards the quality of the goods to be supplied, if this has not been specifically stated it may be decided upon by the court according to their interpretation of the contract by reference to such factors as the price, trade custom or previous dealings between the parties. In the absence of any other basis of decision the court would apply the *règle supplétive* contained in Art. 1246 of the *Code Civil* that the seller was obliged to provide goods of a 'medium quality' – neither the best nor the worst.

POSSIBILITY

If the *objet* is impossible at the moment when agreement is reached between the parties then the contract is void. In the old Roman examples one could not sell a hippocentaur or touch the sky with one's finger. The impossibility referred to here is absolute and not one related subjectively to the debtor. The fact that the debtor himself cannot personally carry out the obligation is irrelevant, if he can have it carried out by others or if he has taken on an obligation which he cannot perform for reasons peculiar to himself.

SALE OF GOODS

In practice therefore as regards the sale of goods the rule on possibility is only of real significance in relation to the supply of *un corps certain*. If the contract is for a *chose de genre* then it would be most unlikely that the debtor could not procure the goods from elsewhere if at the time of signature he was unable to supply them himself. It should be noted that we are concerned here with impossibility at the time of contract and not a force majeure event arising post contract (see below, pp. 334–335).

According to para. 1 of Art. 1601 of the *Code Civil*, 'if at the time of the sale, the goods sold have totally perished then the sale is void'. So a sale of beetroot in a silo which, unknown to the parties at the time of contract had become rotten as a result of frost, was held void because of the non-existence of *un objet*.[10] Under para. 2 of Art. 1601 if a part only of the goods has perished then the purchaser has the right to rescind the contract or alternatively to require delivery of the part saved, the price being apportioned accordingly. Both rules are clearly derived from Roman law.[11]

Although in theory when there is a partial loss the purchaser can demand resolution of the contract without the intervention of the court, in practice the court will often intervene so as to prevent the purchaser from exercising the right of resolution in cases where according to the circumstances or commercial custom the proper remedy is judged to be a reduction in the price.[12]

OBLIGATION *DE FACERE* (TO DO)

Again the contract is void for lack of *objet* only if the impossibility is absolute and objective. So if the impossibility is relative to the contractor, as in the case of a small firm taking on a major contract which it does not possess the labour, material or financial resources to accomplish, the firm will nevertheless be held responsible for the consequences of its failure.[13] As has been said, 'the extreme difficulty of carrying out one's duty does not avoid it; it is not contradictory to the essence of an obligation to be heavy and onerous so long as it is not completely impossible'.[14]

But there is an apparent exception to the above rules if the contract is aleatory (see below).

ALEATORY AND COMMUTATIVE CONTRACTS

French law draws a distinction between contracts which are commutative and those which are aleatory. A contract is commutative when each of the parties engages himself to give or do something which is regarded as the equivalent of that which the other party has undertaken.

A contract is aleatory when the equivalent action of one of the parties consists of a chance of a gain or loss for each of the parties according to an uncertain event (Art. 1694 *Code Civil*. A contract of insurance is aleatory and so is that of a *rente viagère*, that is a contract under which an elderly person sells his or her property in return for a life annuity. Although, as the *Cour de cassation* has stated, it is possible to establish statistically with a high degree of certainty the mean life expectancy of a large number of people (and so draw up annuity tables), that does not alter the aleatory character of a contract under the terms of which the importance of the obligations stipulated depends upon the uncertainty about how long a particular person may live. If he or she lives one year the purchaser obtains the property for perhaps a tenth of its value; on the other hand if they live 20 years the purchaser may finish up paying double.[15]

An aleatory contract for sale

A contract for sale may be classified as aleatory if the true subject matter of the contract is not the goods themselves, whether existing or future, but the hope (*spes*) of their existence, the risk of which is assumed by the purchaser. In this event the contract will be valid and the purchaser will be obliged to pay the contract price whether the goods ever existed or not since it was the hope of their existence and not the goods themselves which constituted the *objet* of the contract and this hope existed at the time when the contract was made even if the goods themselves did not.[16]

The principle is taken directly from Roman law under which the favourite example was 'the purchase of the next cast of the net'. The purchaser was obliged to pay the price which he had offered regardless of whatever fish, if any, the net held.[17]

The sale of future goods

In many instances the goods will not have been manufactured or in existence at the time when the contract is signed. This is allowed for in Art. 1130 of the *Code Civil* which provides that future goods may be *l'objet d'une obligation*.

The question then arises as to whether or not the contract has *un objet* in the event that the future goods never come into existence at all. There are three possible answers. First, the contract is commutative; the *objet* is the future goods which it is the vendor's obligation to deliver; the contract accordingly is valid and the vendor will be in breach of his contract unless he can prove force majeure (on which see below, pp. 334–335).[18]

Second, the contract is commutative but subject to a condition suspensive as to the existence of the future goods. If they fail to come into existence, otherwise than due to an act of the vendor, then the contract will be void for lack of *objet*.

The distinction between the two cases is generally related to the subject matter of the contract and in particular the degree of control which the vendor can be expected to exercise. So manufactured goods will fall under the first case while the sale of a crop sown but not harvested (the typical French textbook example is that of a grape harvest sold as a 'standing crop') would be treated as falling under the second. If therefore the crop fails, because for example the grapes are damaged by frost, then the contract is void and while the vendor does not get paid he is also under no liability towards the purchaser in damages.[19]

The practical effect of the distinction is that under the first case the responsibility for proof of *force majeure* rests with the supplier, which may be very difficult for him to establish because of the strictness of the rules (see below, pp. 334–335), while under the second the vendor will only be liable if the non-existence of the goods can be shown by the purchaser to be due to some act on the vendor's part.

Third, the contract is aleatory so that if the purchaser takes the risk that the future goods will exist the contract is valid, since it was the hope of their existence which constituted the *objet* and not the goods themselves. This is only really likely in respect of crops when it may be that the true intent of the purchaser in buying the crop after it had been sown, but before it had grown, was to buy 'whatever crop, if any, comes up on that field even if it is only weeds', with no doubt an appropriate reduction in the price.[20]

OBJET MUST BE LICIT

It is almost self-evident that the *objet* must not be something which is illegal. But it must also not be something which is contrary to *l'ordre publique* or to *les bonnes moeurs* (good morals). In practical terms the importance of these two concepts, which are closely related (*les bonnes moeurs* have been said to be only an illustration of *l'ordre publique*[21]), has been considerably expanded in recent years because of the intervention of the state in economic affairs and in consumer protection.

ENGLISH LAW COMPARISON

In many respects the results arrived at by the two systems of law are similar even though the routes which are followed may differ. The principal areas upon which it is considered worth commenting follow.

DEFINITION OF *CHOSE*

It is tempting and often admissible to translate *chose* as 'goods' within the meaning of the Sale of Goods Act. However it must be remembered that *chose* includes industrial property rights which are specifically excluded from the Act's definition of 'goods'.

DETERMINABILITY

Reference was made earlier to the exclusion under French law of the English rule that where the price is not determined, the buyer must pay a reasonable price and that therefore the failure to express the price or the objective means for its determination within the contract is not an absolute bar to its validity under English law, whereas it is under French law (see above, pp. 45–47).

Equally through the use of the 'implied term' English law to a large degree compensates for the absence of the concepts of the *contrats nommés* and *les règles de droit supplétives* (see above, pp. 33–34).[22] In practice, in the absence of express agreement between the parties upon particular provisions, the use by the English courts of the concepts of the 'implied term', of 'reasonableness' and of 'ascertaining the intentions of the parties',[23] is more likely to lead to the conclusion that the contract is sufficiently determinative to be valid, then would the application by the French court of the *règle impérative* that the contract must have *un objet* which is determined or objectively determinable.

IMPOSSIBILITY

In contrast to the French rule English law does allow albeit exceptionally for the validity of a contract whose performance may be impossible at the time when it was concluded. There is no general provision under English law that for a contract to be valid its performance must be possible. The question is essentially one of the interpretation of the contract[24] and in relation to a contract for the sale of goods the following alternative constructions are possible:

- that the seller guaranteed unconditionally the delivery of the goods;
- that the delivery of the goods was subject to a condition precedent that this was possible;
- that the buyer assumed the risk that the delivery of the goods was possible.

Comparing these possibilities with the rules under French law as to *objet* it is necessary to distinguish between goods which are specific, i.e. 'identified and agreed upon at the time of the contract' (the French *corps certain*), and those which are unascertained, equivalent in meaning to the French *chose de genre*.

Specific goods

The general rule is expressed by s.6 of the Sale of Goods Act which corresponds to the second alternative above, 'Where there is a contract for the sale of specific goods and the goods without the knowledge of the Seller have perished at the time when the contract is made then the contract is void'.

This is almost the rule of French law under Art. 1601 (see above, p. 85). However, unlike the French rule which is a *règle impérative* the better opinion would appear to be that it is only a rule of construction which could be displaced by the clear intention of the parties. A case could therefore fall under either of the other two alternatives although in practice the most likely is the first, under which the vendor is in effect guaranteeing the goods' existence.[25]

So in *McRae* v. *Commonwealth Disposal Commission*, which concerned the sale of the non-existent wreck of an oil tanker on a non-existent reef, it was held by the High Court of Australia that the sellers had by the terms of the contract warranted the existence of the wreck. Accordingly they were found liable in damages for the expenses to which the purchaser had been put in fitting out a salvage expedition.[26]

This is a result which could not have been reached by a French court, which would have been bound to have held the contract void for lack of *objet*. However it is probable that the court would have been prepared in such a case, while not giving effect to the contract which was null, to have declared that the vendor was liable for a quasi-delictual fault[27] in leading the purchaser to believe in the existence of the wreck, and to require him therefore to pay damages.[28]

If however the third alternative applies this is simply the equivalent of the French *contrat aléatoire*. What the buyer has purchased is a *spes* and if the goods do not exist then he is still bound to make payment.

Partial impossibility

As Atiyah has said, English law is 'somewhat obscure' on this issue and he has suggested that it all depends on the construction of the contract as to the respective obligations and responsibilities of the parties. This contrasts sharply with the clearly defined position under French law.[29]

Unascertained goods

Unascertained goods may be in existence at the time when the contract is signed, e.g. when the sale is one of a certain quantity to be taken from bulk or they may be future goods which the vendor will manufacture or acquire, or a crop which he intends to grow.

Where unascertained goods are wholly generic and either already owned by the seller or ones which he intends to acquire, then it is ordinarily no business of the purchaser as to how the seller intends to perform his obligations. The rules in English and French law as to generic goods are essentially the same. The seller is responsible for performing his contract unless under French law he can establish that performance was prevented by *force majeure*, or under English law that the basis of the contract has been destroyed by frustration. In either case the event giving rise to *force majeure* or frustration occurs before the risk in the goods has passed to the purchaser (see further below, pp. 318–319 and 334–335).[30]

Future goods

As regards future goods which are to be manufactured or grown, then as we have seen French law may regard the contract as being subject to a condition precedent that the goods will exist and if that condition is not satisfied for a reason not imputable to an act of the seller, then hold the contract void for lack of *objet*. The same result has been reached in England in respect of crops which were intended to be grown on a certain field by holding that the contract was frustrated because of a general crop failure.[31]

However where goods are to be manufactured by the seller then the normal rule would apply that the seller would be held to guarantee the goods' existence, from which he would only exceptionally be released under the doctrine of frustration.[32] This again parallels quite closely the French rule that the supplier is bound to deliver in the absence of being able to prove that his failure was due to *force majeure* (see further below, pp. 334–335).

GERMAN LAW COMPARISON

DETERMINABILITY

The question of determinability was discussed earlier in relation to the establishment of the contract price (see above, pp. 49–53) and the principles there enumerated apply generally to the terms of the contract. The obligations of the parties must be determined or objectively determinable and they must not offend the requirements of 'good morals' (s.138 p. 1 *BGB*); nor must they be such as to constitute the taking of unfair economic advantage (p. 2 of s.138), or be contrary to good faith and fair dealing (*Treu und Glauben* – s.242 *BGB*; see above, pp. 17 and 52).

IMPOSSIBILITY

German law in the same way as French law has followed the Roman law rule that an objective impossibility at the time of entering into the contract, i.e. one not related to the debtor personally but impossible for anyone, renders the contract void – *impossibilium nulla obligatio* (Art. 306 *BGB*). The distinction is expressed in German as between *Unmöglichkeit*, which is impossible for anyone, and *Unvermögen* which is impossible only for the debtor. In respect of contracts of sale this rule only applies to specific goods and has no relevance to generic goods which the debtor is always obliged to supply even if it causes him greater costs than he had anticipated, provided that such goods are in fact available (Art. 279 *BGB*).[33]

If it is a case of *Unmöglichkeit* and the debtor knew or ought to have known that the performance of the contract was impossible at the time when he entered into it, then he is required to indemnify the creditor for *Vertrauensinteresse* (reliance interest), that is to say to put the creditor in the position in which he would have been had he not entered into the contract, but not exceeding *Erfüllungsinteresse* (expectation of performance interest – Art. 307 *BGB*). This limit is in contrast to what appears to be the French rule on the damages recoverable in quasi-delict which it will be remembered would apparently include loss of the opportunity expected (see above, pp. 62 and 88). The impossibility in question may relate to the non-existence of specific goods or it may be because of some legal impediment.

If however it is a case of *Unvermögen* then in the event of his failure, the debtor must pay damages to the creditor for non-fulfilment of his bargain. Such damages are based on putting the purchaser in the same position as he would have been had the contract been fulfilled.

Because of the view that it should be restrictively interpreted, the strict rule in Art. 306 of the *BGB* will not in practice be applied by the German courts in situations in which they can interpret the contract as containing 'an undertaking of guarantee' by the debtor that performance of his contract is possible, i.e. he accepts the risk of impossibility. So a supplier in such a case will be regarded as having undertaken that the specific goods which are the subject matter of his contract do exist.

It would appear that an 'undertaking of guarantee' is more likely to be discovered by a German court than by an English court faced with a case concerning the application of s.6 of the Sale of Goods Act, where it is considered that only the most express wording would displace the rule in the Act that the contract is void if without the knowledge of the seller the goods are not in existence at the time of contract.[34]

If a German court does indeed interpret the contract as containing such an 'undertaking of guarantee' then in that event the debtor would be liable to pay damages on the same basis as in the case of *Unvermögen*.

IMMORALITY

According to Art. 138 s.1 of the *BGB* a contract is void 'if it is contrary to good morals' and in particular under s.2 a contract is void if there has been exploitation of the need, carelessness or inexperience of another in order to obtain an unfair economic advantage. In business transactions this provision has been most often applied to cases in which there has been an exploitation of a monopoly position to 'throttle' the debtor by limiting his freedom of commercial action, contracts known as *Knebelungsverträge*, or advantage has been taken of a debtor to impose extremely high rates of interest together with the taking of other forms of security.[35]

Since the effect of applying s.138 is that the whole contract is void the courts generally will tend to use the more flexible weapons of Arts 157 and 242 of the *BGB* requiring that contracts be construed and performed in accordance with the concept of good faith of s.9 of the AGBG. This allows the court to strike out terms which are inconsistent with 'reasonable standards of fair dealing in the trade in question'. As a recent example a clause contained in the general conditions of a manufacturer of prefabricated houses which gave the manufacturer the right to delay delivery for up to six weeks after the agreed delivery date was held to be contrary to good faith and therefore invalid.[36] (For further examples see below, pp. 304–305 dealing with standard conditions of contract.)

THE VIENNA CONVENTION

As stated earlier (see above, p. 45) the Convention does not apply to the validity of a contract. Therefore if the contract is under French law the requirements under Art. 1108 of the *Code Civil* for there to be *un objet certain* in order for a valid contract to exist, would still apply. So if the subject matter of the contract had, unknown to the parties, perished at the time of the contract then the contract would be null (Art. 1601 and see above, p. 85 and note 10). Presumably the rule that a contract subject to a condition suspensive that the goods will come into existence will be void for lack of *objet* if they never do so, otherwise than due to the fault of the seller, will also still apply (see above, p. 86).

Equally for an English law contract the rule of English law under s.6 of the Sale of Goods Act as to a contract being void if specific goods have perished at the time when the contract was made will also still apply. So also in a German law contract the similar provision in German law as to *Unmöglichkeit* under Art. 306 of the *BGB* (see above, p. 90). In addition the rules in the national systems relating to contracts being void for immorality would remain applicable.

This is but one of several areas in which the question of which national law applies is of substantial importance and the interrelationship between that law and the Convention can be complex.

NOTES

1. See above, p. 54. That the concept does not exist as such does not mean that the ideas which French law subsumes under the heading are not to be found in English law but simply that they are not collected under one general heading. However the difference does lead to the position that under certain circumstances what French law considers as a rule of law will under English law be treated only as a matter of construction.
2. This traditional division is derived from Roman law which saw all possible obligations as being covered by *dare* (transfer of ownership), *facere* (do or not do some act) and *praestare* (perform or execute), Dig. xliv 7.3.
3. So Weill and Terré s.223 and Ghestin s.510: 'Properly speaking the contract does not have "un objet".'
4. Starck s.471: 'Le contrat n'a que des effets qui consistent dans la création d'une ou plusieurs obligations. Ce sont ces obligations nées du contrat qui ont un objet: livrer une chose . . .'
5. Ghestin s.411.
6. Weill and Terré s.224: 'il s'applique aussi à une chose incoporelle – telle la propriété dit "intellectuelle".' For the 'extensive' meaning of 'choses in action' in English law see Keeton and Sheridan, Kluwer, 1987, p. 225.
7. Mazeaud s.844.
8. Ghestin s.519.
9. Ghestin s.519, p. 576.
10. Req. 15 February 1906, S 1906.1.280 quoted Mazeaud p. 122 and Starck s.476.
11. 'Nec emptio nec venditio sine re quae veneat potest intellegi' (Dig. XVIII.1.8) which Zulueta translates as 'Without a thing sold no sale can be admitted'. Also Dig. XVIII.18.1.15: 'Etsi consensam fuerit in corpus, id tamen in rerum natura ante venditionem esse desierit, nulla emptio est'. 'Even if there is consent as to the specific thing, if it has ceased to exist before the sale, the contract is void'.

    As to the partial destruction, Dig. XVIII.1.57 refers to the case of a house being partially destroyed by fire unknown to both buyer and seller and draws a distinction between whether more than half has been burnt or not. If more than half then the sale is null although the buyer can recover any partial payment already made, but if less than half, then the sale is valid but the price is to be reduced according to the loss in value caused by the fire, Zulueta p. 100).
12. Starck s.477; Mazeaud p. 122.
13. Example given by Weill and Terré s.236.
14. Carbonnier *Les Obligations* s.156 quoted Starck s.499.
15. Starck ss.93 and 94 and Ghestin s.558 quoting Cass. civ. 27 December 1938 DP 1939 1.81.
16. Mazeaud s.842 and Starck s.479. The same principle is applied to contracts of marine insurance. The contract is valid even if the loss or the safe arrival occurred before the conclusion of the contract, unless the assured had personal knowledge of the loss or the insurance company of the arrival of the goods insured. Arts 8 and 9 of Law no. 522 of 3 July 1967.
17. Dig. XVIII.1.8 s.1: 'emptio enim contrahitur, etiamsi nihil inciderit, quia spei emptio est'. 'A valid contract is completed, even though nothing is caught, because it is the purchase of an expectation'. So the contrast is drawn between *emptio spei* (purchase of a hope) and *emptio rei speratae* (purchase of a thing which is hoped for).
18. Mazeaud s.843.
19. Starck s.483.
20. Mazeaud s.843 p. 124 appears to suggest that *all* contracts for the sale of crops after they have been sown and before harvesting are aleatory in that their growth and ripening is beyond the vendor's control and that what the purchaser has bought is the chance of their being fit to be harvested. This is surely going much too far and indeed is inconsistent with his later s.909 on p. 187 dealing with the passing of property and risk in future goods where he refers to the seller's obligation 'to take the necessary care for the harvest'. It must be a matter of interpretation of the contract in the individual case as to where the parties intended that the risk should lie.
21. Weill and Terré s.244.
22. See David and Pugsley s.283.
23. Op. cit. s.285.
24. Op. cit. s.290.

25. The French rule refers to the goods not being 'in existence' whilst the English one to goods 'having perished' which, interpreted strictly, would mean that it would only apply where goods had once existed but no longer do so, i.e. it does not apply if the goods have never existed at all as in the McRae case. Cheshire (pp. 222 and 232) does not favour this interpretation although Atiyah (p. 76) does. If as is generally supposed the rule in the Sale of Goods Act is intended to give effect to the decision in *Couturier* v. *Hastie* 1856 5 HL 673 in which the goods had existed but then perished, and taking into account there is no general rule in English law that for a contract to be valid it must be possible of performance, then Atiyah's view seems preferable.

26. (1951) 84 CLR 377. See further Treitel p. 725. However the limitation to reliance damages was a result of the plaintiff's inability to quantify his loss of expectation to the court's satisfaction rather than on any rule of principle.

27. Delictual is when the damage has been caused intentionally and quasi-delictual when the damage has not been caused intentionally, although in practice the term 'delictual' is used to cover both (Starck vol. 1 p. 5).

28. So in a case decided on 7 March 1972 the *Cour de cassation* approved a decision by the Cour de Paris in which a distributor of films in France was awarded damages against a Japanese company who claimed that the distribution contract was void because it had not received the approval of the Bank of Japan which was required by the International Monetary Fund. The *Cour de cassation* ruled that 'far from giving effect to a contract which it had expressly declared ineffective' the Cour de Paris had established a quasi-delictual fault on the part of the Japanese company by reason of the company not having done what it possibly could to obtain the approval, not having advised the French party of the difficulties involved, and in effect having used these as an excuse unilaterally to break the contract, which justified the award of damages.

    Unfortunately as Ghestin comments, p. 1095, the decision of the Cour de Paris was to refer the estimation of the damages to an expert so it is not possible to know the basis upon which they were assessed.

29. See Atiyah pp. 78–81.

30. Strictly the question of risk cannot arise in relation to purely generic goods (*genera non pereunt*), but only when the goods are coming from a bulk which has been specified (Mazeaud s.904).

31. See *Howell* v. *Coupland* 1876 1 QBD 258.

32. See further s.18 Rule 5(1) of the *SGA* (Atiyah pp. 300 and 301) and s.20(1) (Atiyah p. 321).

33. Generally a mere rise in price even of 100 per cent did not constitute non-availability provided that the goods could be obtained in the market in the quantities required by the contract (RGZ 88, 172), provided that the increase would not ruin the supplier's business (RGZ 98, 21). But the supplier's obligation is not unlimited as regards searching for other sources of supply. As was said in an old case in which a mill, which was the only producer of the brand of cottonseed product in question burnt down: 'The supplier (who was a merchant and not the mill) could not be required to attempt to buy the brand on all German and foreign markets' (Reichsgericht 23 February 1904 57 ERGZ 116). That conclusion, with modern methods of marketing and communication, could be open to reconsideration.

    However, even though the obligation to supply may remain, it is open to the courts to amend the terms of the contract under the doctrine of *Geschäftsgrundlage* where an exceptional change in circumstances has caused the basis of the contract to be altered so that there exists a gross disproportion between the respective obligations of the parties and it would be contrary to the requirement of good faith under Art. 242 *BGB* to require that performance by the debtor should be effected on the original terms. See further Von Mehren pp. 1078–1099; Michael D. Aubry, 'Frustration Reconsidered some Comparative Aspects', 12 *ICLQ* pp. 1177–81.

34. Zweigert and Kotz (pp. 179 and 180) are particularly critical of the rule of s.306 of the *BGB* which they regard as inequitable. They refer to a case before the Oberlandsgericht in Hamburg in which a cargo of 1000 boxes of tomatoes were sold aboard a named ship and described as 'aboard and afloat'. In fact only 106 boxes were loaded. The court held that although this was a sale of specific goods, and delivery was initially impossible, the use of the term 'afloat' is taken by merchants to be an undertaking of the guarantee of performance and so the vendor must pay damages for non-performance. However there have been cases decided the other way – see *Objet, Cause et Lésion* p. 119.

    The Hamburg Court decision may be contrasted with that in *Barrow, Lane and Ballard* v. *Phillip Phillips & Co.* [1929] 1 KB 574 where a sale of 700 bags of nuts lying in a warehouse was held void under s.6 of the *SGA* when it was found that there were only 591 bags to be delivered.

35. So in a case decided by the Bundesgerichtshof in November 1961 a loan at an interest rate of 45 per cent plus security, which consisted of a total guarantee by the debtor's wife and conveyance of a small store and six oil paintings, was held void.
36. BGH (VII ZR 276/83) 28 June 1984. [1984] DB 2341.

7 Cause and consideration

The historical origins of the two doctrines were briefly discussed earlier. Here it is proposed to consider their importance in contract law today and to draw some comparative conclusions.

CAUSE – FRENCH LAW

Article 1131 of the *Code Civil* provides that 'an agreement without "cause", or having a false "cause" or a "cause illicite" is without any legal effect'. *Cause illicite* is defined under Art. 1132 as covering that which is either illegal or contrary to good morals or *l'ordre public*.[1]

The classic explanation of the meaning of *cause* is that it answers the question 'why is the obligation owed?' But in answering that question French law makes a fundamental distinction in contracts, *à titre onéreux*, between the absence of *cause* and a *cause illicite*.[2] The reasoning behind this distinction is as follows. Absence of *cause* in such contracts is a matter of the *objective* determination as to whether or not there exists a genuine counterpart obligation and the motives of the parties are of no account, at least when it is not a matter of an *erreur sur la cause* (see below, pp. 98–99).

The issue of *cause illicite*, however, can only be decided upon in exactly the opposite way, that is by the *subjective* examination of the particular reasons which decided the parties to enter into the contract.

Put another way, in 'absence of cause' one is concerned with the 'cause' of the 'obligation'; in 'illicit cause' one is concerned with the 'cause' of the contract (see further below, p. 99). The bringing together of these two different concepts, both under the heading of 'cause', creates some conceptual difficulties as the French textbook writers freely admit. But the practice is firmly established in the jurisprudence despite the considerable criticisms.[3]

To try to simplify the issue we shall examine first absence of cause and then illicit cause.

ABSENCE OF CAUSE – *LES CONTRATS À TITRE ONÉREUX* AND *SYNALLAGMATIQUES COMMUTATIFS*

Here one looks for the cause in *le but immédiat* – 'the immediate objective' – so that *cause* is found in the undertaking by the other party to execute the obligations which he is required by the contract to perform and which are related to the class of contract involved, sale, lease etc. So it is said 'the cause varies according to the class of contract and not according to the parties to the contract'.[4]

In any contract for sale therefore the *cause* for the buyer is the undertaking by the seller to deliver the goods and transfer the property in them in exchange for the payment of the price. The particular reason why the purchaser requires the goods is irrelevant.

According to French jurisprudence, when the issue of the absence of *cause* arises with this type of contract the question is whether or not there exists any genuine and serious counterpart obligation, looked at objectively and not from the personal viewpoint of the party involved. The court is not concerned with what were the motives of the parties and whether these have been satisfied or not, nor whether or not the respective obligations are the equivalent of each other, or even with the economic sufficiency of the counter-obligation, unless that obligation is so insufficient as objectively to be derisory or effectively non-existent.[5]

The following are some examples where the *Cour de cassation* has held that there was an absence of *cause* and the contract was therefore void:

1. Where the subject matter of the contract was objectively of no use, e.g. transfer of a patent which was no longer valid.[6]
2. Where, under a *contrat de remplacement*, a peculiar type of contract in the last century under which a man liable for military service could validly contract with another to do the service for him, the parties were mistaken and the man was not in fact liable for military service but the replacement still sought to claim the contract price.[7]
3. The sale of a particular model of car which was not marketed in France.[8]
4. The lease of premises intended for use as a greengrocers in a commercial centre with a right of exclusivity for the lessee for which he paid extra. Under the then current legislation it was impossible for the lessor to comply with the obligation to grant exclusivity.[9]
5. Transfer of an authorization to operate a driving school when the authorization was in fact freely available to anyone who complied with the necessary legal requirements and there was no limitation on the number of such schools.[10]
6. Leases when only a token amount of rent was charged, e.g. in one case 10 francs a year and in another 100 francs a month for a golf course.[11]
7. In three cases concerning agreements entered into by a syndicate of banks in relation to the issuing of shares in the Panama Canal Company where the *Cour de cassation* held that the benefits claimed by the banks had no counterpart in any obligations or risks whatsoever.[12]

In contrast was a case where an exclusive option was granted for the sale of a business exercisable within a certain period with a heavy penalty payable if the option was not exercised. After eight days the beneficiary of the option declined to exercise it but refused to pay the penalty and claimed that the obligation was void for lack of *cause*. He succeeded in the cour d'appel but the *Cour de cassation* annulled the decision, stating that the exclusive nature of the option, which prevented the sale during the period stated to another person, was an advantage to the beneficiary, which provided the *cause* for the obligation to pay the penalty.[13]

These decisions illustrate one of the three factors which, despite criticism, still make *cause* important in French law in synallagmatic contracts – the interdependence of the party's obligations each of which possesses some objective reality. If the obligation of one party has no *objet*, e.g. because it is objectively impossible for him to do what he has promised or the *objet* has in reality no objective substance, then the non-existence or lack of substance of the *objet* will mean that the other party's obligations will be null for lack of *cause*. As Weill and Terré have pointed out, if one were to abandon the doctrine of *cause* it would have to be replaced by one of 'interconnection'.[14]

The other two factors which make *cause* important are considered later (see below, p. 99).

ABSENCE OF *CAUSE* POST CONTRACT

On the basis of Art. 1131 of the *Code Civil* the issue as to whether there is a *cause* or not ought only to be assessed at the time when the contract is made, since *cause* is a necessary element in the formation of the contract. As stated in a recent decision, 'la cause, élément nécessaire à la constitution du contrat, doit exister au jour de la formation de celui-ci'.[15] Therefore it should follow that, if there is a valid *cause* at the time of contract, a subsequent failure by one of the parties to perform his obligations cannot be used as a means of seeking a declaration that the contract is void for lack of *cause*. This was confirmed by the *Cour de cassation* (30 June 1987) in censuring a judgement which had annulled a contract for lack of *cause*, when the court held that 'the court of appeal, in not stating that the counter-obligation offered was imaginary or illusory, but in deducing the absence of "cause" from the circumstances of the execution of the agreement, had wrongly applied Art. 1131 of the *Code Civil*.[16]

However, it has been argued, and older cases support this view, that the concept of *cause* does extend to the post-contract period so that the failure by one party to perform his obligations may constitute an absence of *cause* which allows the other party to avoid his. But while the jurisprudence is not wholly consistent, and doctrine is divided, the better opinion seems to be today that any such failure does not entail the contract being void for lack of *cause* and so allow an *action en nullité*, but will allow some other remedy based on the interdependence of the parties' obligations.[17]

Such remedies, for which *cause* can be said to have provided the foundations, are: resolution under Art. 1184 of the *Code Civil* for non-execution of his obligations by the other party (see below, pp. 320–322), the application of the *l'exceptio non adimpleti contractus* (see below, pp. 324–326) or 'the theory of risk' (see below, p. 335).[18]

CONTRATS UNILATÉRAUX

Two forms of unilateral contract only will be considered: those of a loan and those for payment in respect of an existing obligation.

The main interest in relation to contracts for a loan is where the loan contract is linked to that of a contract for sale. The problem, which has also arisen in English law, is as to whether or not the practical 'interdependence' between the two contracts has any legal effect in circumstances in which the sale contract is for some reason defective.[19]

Typically in French practice there is one contract between the credit house and the purchaser, under which the credit house pays the funds to the seller, and a separate contract between the buyer and the seller for the purchase of the goods for which the credit has been arranged. The issue usually arises because the seller either fails to fulfil his contract because he has gone into liquidation, or the contract of sale is subject to rescission either for non-conformity of the goods with their description or for latent defects (see below, pp. 172–174).

It has been argued on a number of occasions before the *Cour de cassation* that the *cause* of the loan was the contract of sale and if that was properly terminated, then so should be the contract of credit since it would be deprived of *cause*. However, the *Cour de cassation* has consistently held that the *cause* of the obligation of the borrower was 'in the provision of the funds necessary for the purchase' and that therefore the validity of the loan was unaffected by the rescission of the contract for sale. The only exception was when the seller and lender were found to be acting 'in concert'.[20] Eventually the problem had to be solved, as far as consumers were concerned, by legislation which tied the two contracts together and established their interdependence.

CONTRACTS FOR PAYMENT IN RESPECT OF AN EXISTING OBLIGATION

The interest here lies in the application of the doctrine of *erreur sur la cause* and in the distinction between that and *erreur sur la substance* – Art. 1110 of the *Code Civil* (see below, pp. 121–123).

A promise which has been made solely in the belief that one was under a particular obligation, e.g. to make a payment, when in fact no such obligation existed, is void for *fausse cause*. *Fausse* here does not mean 'false' in the normal sense of the term but that the cause is non-existent and that the obligation was only entered into in the mistaken belief that it did exist; hence the use of the expression *erreur sur la cause*.

So a promise by a television company to pay compensation to another for each time they transmitted a particular programme created by the other, was held to be void on the grounds that the promise had only been made in the belief that the programme was entitled to the protection of the law of 11 March 1957 on copyright, a belief that was in fact mistaken. As a result there was no *cause* for the promise and the fact that the promise had been made did not prevent the television company from maintaining that it was void under Art. 1131.[21]

Similarly a promise by a theatre proprietor to pay damages to an artist whose equipment was destroyed in a fire in the mistaken belief that he was legally obliged to do so, was held to be void 'pour erreur sur l'effacité juridique de la cause de l'engagement'.[22]

It is obvious that here the *cause* to which reference is being made, while objective, in the sense that there was a pre-existing obligation, which has now disappeared, is at the same time subjective in that the reason for acting because of the obligation was particular to the person.

It is this latter point, the subjective nature of the reason for entering into the contract, which has caused the confusion with the doctrine of mistake. But the two are distinct. It is not a matter of an error as to a substantial quality in that which is the *objet* of the contract (see below, pp. 121–122) but as to the existence at all of any counterpart reason for undertaking the obligation.

This issue will be discussed further when dealing with mistake (see below, pp. 121–122) and the practical consequences noted of the distinction between the two doctrines. It is sufficient here to point out that the existence of *erreur sur la cause* is one of the other reasons why *cause* is important in French law; it supplements the scope of mistake under Art. 1110 of the *Code Civil*.[23]

ILLICIT CAUSE

As referred to earlier (see above, p. 95), when it is a matter of illegality or immorality then in all cases *cause* is the illegal or immoral motive which determined the entry into the contract – *cause impulsive et déterminante*. The distinction was made clear by the *Cour de cassation* in a case decided on 12 July 1989 which concerned the sale by one parapsychologist to another of certain occult material, crystal balls and séance tables, to be used for the purpose of telling the future. A part of the price of 53 000 francs not having been paid, the seller sued for the balance. In giving judgement the court stated that while the *cause* of the purchaser's *obligation* is in the transfer of property and delivery of the item sold, the *cause* of the *contract* is in the determining motive, in the absence of which the purchaser would not have entered into the agreement. As in this case the *cause impulsive et déterminante* was the opportunity to exercise the occupation of telling the future, which is contrary to Art. R.34 of the penal code: the contract was illicit and therefore not capable of being enforced.[24]

It is not necessary that the illicit or immoral *cause* should be the sole reason for entering into the contract, only that it should be one which exercised a significant influence. So not only a contract which relates to the establishment or operation of a brothel will be void but also one which relates to the employment there of a domestic servant.

More controversially it was decided by the *Cour de cassation* on 4 January 1956 in an *arrêt de principe* that a contract *à titre onéreux* was only void if the illicit or immoral purpose was *agreed* by both parties.[25] An action by the lessor of premises for a declaration that a lease was void for *cause illicite* was rejected on the grounds that 'it had not been established that before the granting of the lease the parties had agreed on the operation of a brothel in the premises'.

While it can be argued that the decision has some justification if the claim for nullity is brought against the party who knew nothing of the illicit or immoral purpose of the other, it seems unjust in the opposite case where the innocent party wishes to claim the nullity. The better solution is surely that if the contract was entered into for an illicit or immoral purpose by either party, whether known to the other or not, then in the general interests of society the contract should be void absolutely and, if one party was innocent, then that his interests should be protected by other means.[26]

CAUSE – GERMAN LAW – AND UNJUST ENRICHMENT

As was noted earlier, under French law there are two applications of the doctrine of *cause*. The first concerns the objective concept of *cause* which is a necessary requirement for the formation of the contract. This has no counterpart in German law. Neither does German law contain any doctrine of consideration. As regards the second application, an illicit cause, para. 138 of the *BGB* which was referred to previously (see above, p. 52) and renders void contracts which are 'immoral' applies not just to the content of the contract but also to the motives of the parties. In this sense it closely parallels Art. 1133 of the *Code Civil*.[27]

While not applying the doctrine of the objective concept of *cause* to the formation of contracts, German law has taken over from Roman law the idea that the failure of cause, or the discovery post contract of the non-existence of cause, can be used as the basis for an action for unjust enrichment. The principle is set out in para. 812 of the *BGB*: 'A person who through an act performed by another person or in any other manner acquires something at the expense of the other, without legal justification, is bound to return it'.[28]

ABSTRACTION

One reason why this action has acquired significance in German law is because of the principle of abstraction according to which the legal act which operates to create the obligation to transfer the ownership of property, the contract of sale (*Verpflichtungs-geschäft*), is separate from the legal act which effects the actual transfer (*Verfügungs-geschäft*). The effect of this separation is that the validity of the actual transfer of property (*dinglicher Vertrag*) is only exceptionally affected by the invalidity of the contract for sale or obligational contract.

It follows from the principle of abstraction that a person who has obtained ownership of goods under a valid transfer does not normally lose that right, if subsequently the contract of sale, which resulted in the transfer, is held to be void. The only exceptions to this are when the invalidity is due to a grossly immoral act which may also render void the transfer (s.138 *BGB*)[29] or when the transfer itself is voidable for mistake.

Since the transfer was effective to pass the ownership, the claim of the transferor then becomes one for unjust enrichment under Art. 812 of the *BGB* and the more detailed rules which follow in the succeeding paras 813–822 and are all directly derived from the *condictio* of Roman law.[30]

The basic rule is that as against the transferee who still retains possession, the original owner may demand the return of the goods themselves. However if before such restitution the transferee has become bankrupt, or has resold the goods to a purchaser who buys in good faith, then the rights of the original owner will only be for the enrichment e.g. in bankruptcy a claim which has only just a preference over that of any ordinary creditor, and if the goods have been resold, for the proceeds of sale.[31]

Apart from providing an answer to this particular problem arising from the principle of abstraction, the subject of unjust enrichment (*ungerechtfertigte Bereicherung*) as a whole is extensively developed and of great importance in German law.[32] There is space here only to comment briefly on two distinctive points of German law and compare them with the position in England and France.

UNJUST ENRICHMENT

First there is the provision in para. 818(3) of the *BGB* that 'the obligation to return or to make good the benefit is excluded where the recipient is no longer enriched'. This sub-paragraph has been extensively applied by the courts to protect the recipient in situations in which he has incurred an economic loss as a result of the transaction, at least up to the time when he knows that there is no legal ground for his acquisition or retention of any benefit – see para. 819. So if he has resold at a loss, invested in shares which are now valueless, or spent the money by increasing his standard of living then it is the original owner who is left to suffer the financial consequences of the recipient's behaviour and he can recover only what, if anything, is left of the original benefit.[33]

There is no such general principle in English law.[34] However it now appears that English law will recognize what is known as a defence of change of position where the defendant has acted in good faith, and it would be inequitable in all the circumstances to require him to make restitution or alternatively to make restitution in full. The reception of the defence into English law is very recent and the scope of its application remains to be worked out case by case.[35] Up until now it has been only if on the facts of a particular case it is decided that the *solvens* is estopped from demanding repayment because of representations made by him to the *accipiens*, that the decision of an English court would be likely to be the same as that of a German court.[36] It seems improbable in any event that the English courts will allow the defence of change of position to cover cases in which the *accipiens* has acted imprudently.

Under French law the general rule is that the *accipiens* is obliged to repay the money or return the property to which he is not entitled because the payment to him is not due, i.e. when it is not supported by any valid *cause*.[37] The obligation to repay is objective and not related to the use to which he intended to put the money, e.g. obligation to return the over-payment of child benefit.[38]

There may however be an action in tort by the *solvens* if he can establish that the over-payment was the result of a gross error. This would then result in an award of damages which would reduce the amount to be repaid but would not allow the *accipiens* to retain the whole amount of the over-payment.[39]

As regards the return of property to which the 'accipiens' is not entitled and benefits accessory to either money or property, the rules differ according to whether or not the *accipiens* was in good faith, i.e. whether he was ignorant of the fact that he was not due the payment or not. In summary the rules are as follows (as per Arts 1378–1380 of the *Code Civil*):

- Good faith – only obliged to return the sum of money or property received; can retain interest or profits earned. If property is sold, only obliged to repay sale price. If property is destroyed or damaged due to the fault of the *accipiens*, value to be repaid, but no liability if damage or destruction due to *cas fortuit*.
- Bad faith – profits or interest earned must be repaid. If property is sold, then if the value exceeds the sale price, the repayment is of the value. If property is destroyed or damaged, even if due to cas fortuit, then value must be repaid.

Second, under German law today the general rule is that the right to claim for the unjustified enrichment can only be made against the person with whom the transaction was effected. This is the principle of directness (*Unmittelbarkeit*). So if repairs are carried out to a property by a contractor on the instructions of the tenant who then goes bankrupt, then normally there can be no claim by the contractor against the owner of the property on the grounds of unjustified enrichment.[40]

Such an action *de in rem verso* would in principle be permitted under French law in such a case.[41] But today it would only be allowed if there was no obligation of repair owed by the tenant towards the landlord, i.e. there was no clause within the lease which required the tenant to undertake the work in question, and similarly for other obligations.

ACTION *DE IN REM VERSO*

Generally the formulation of the rule in France today is that

> the action de in rem verso (unjust enrichment) based on principles of equity, which prevent someone enriching himself at the expense of another, lies in every case where the patrimony of one person is enriched to the detriment of the other without a legitimate 'cause', that latter not having the benefit, in order to obtain what is due to him, of any action arising out of contract, quasi-contract or tort.[42]

Where the claim for unjust enrichment is indirect that formulation of the rule for the action establishes two conditions both of which have to be satisfied for it to be valid:

1. The benefit must not have arisen out of a contractual obligation owed by the third party (in the above case the tenant), to the person enriched, as that would create a legitimate *cause*.
2. The party providing the benefit must have no other practically enforceable means of recovery. That he has a contract with the third party will not in itself be a bar to the

action *de in rem verso* if he is unable to enforce a claim because the third party is bankrupt or in liquidation. However what he cannot do is to try to use the action when his remedy against the party is barred because of another provision of the law, to get around that barrier (see the first case quoted in note 42).

English law knows nothing of the action *de in rem verso*. If one follows the traditional path that an action for unjust enrichment is based on an implied contract then clearly any indirect action against a person enriched would fall foul of the rule of privity of contract. Further there appears to be no room for the application of the doctrine of a constructive trust in equity since the requirements for such an action include the intention to create a trust, an irrevocable intention to benefit the enriched party, the existence of a fiduciary relationship between the parties and that the promise is one which is capable of being the subject of a trust, generally the payment of money or the transfer of property. It would be very unusual to find that these requirements were satisfied.[43]

CONSIDERATION

The historical roots of consideration were traced earlier (see above, pp. 21–22) but what is its function in English law today and what is its relationship with *cause*? The most common explanation of its function is that it is the hallmark of a bargain and that English law has decided that it will only accept agreements as being legally enforceable if they do constitute a bargain, unless they are entered into as a deed. Put in another way, English law requires that in order for there to be a binding contract there must be something which the law recognizes as being of value given or promised by one party to the other in exchange for that other's own promise or performance, the exchange constituting a single transaction.[44]

How then does this compare with the doctrine of *cause* as regards 'absence of *cause*', i.e. leaving aside entirely *cause illicite ou immorale* which is the subject in English law of the doctrines of illegality and public policy?

The comparison can only sensibly be made in respect of synallagmatic *contrats à titre onéreux*. Here the promise itself which constitutes the consideration may also in French law constitute the *cause*. So in an ordinary contract for the sale of goods the buyer's obligation to pay the price will be both the consideration supporting the contract and the *cause* of the seller's obligation to transfer the property in the goods. Both are needed for the validity of the contract and both establish the interdependence of the respective obligations of the parties.[45] Further, as regards their substance – what English law would regard as consideration – French law would be very likely to regard as *cause*. Neither system is concerned with comparing the respective values of the obligations, and therefore, as English law puts it, with the adequacy of the consideration, provided that it has some value no matter how small.[46] However from the examples given earlier (p. 96) the approach of French law is more objective than English which does allow the contracting party to 'stipulate for what consideration he chooses'.[47]

But despite the coincidence in their effects it would be misleading to assume that consideration and *cause* in such contracts represent equivalent concepts. *Cause* is related to purpose, even if the purpose is, as was referred to earlier (see above, p. 96) an objective purpose which varies only with the particular type of contract concerned. It is the existence of this purpose which justifies the law in enforcing the agreement. Consideration, however, has nothing to do with purpose but is based on the concept that a promise is only legally enforceable if given in exchange for what the law recognizes as being valuable consideration.[48]

Outside the field of synallagmatic *contrats à titre onéreux* no comparison is possible since in English law neither past consideration nor a promise made gratuitously or out of a sense of moral obligation can support a contract.[49]

Under French law, however, such unilateral promises whether *à titre onéreux* or *à titre gratuit* would be valid contracts provided that they had *une cause légitime*.[50]

The importance of the difference between *cause* and consideration lies outside the mainstream of bilateral commercial contracts where, as we have seen, their practical effect is largely coincident but in the fringe, though nonetheless commercially significant fields, such as the validity of offers and options discussed earlier (see above, pp. 58–59), agreements for additional payments, the settlement of debts, discharge of contracts and actions by a third party to enforce a benefit in his favour.

In all the above instances it can be argued that the technical common law rules, unless strained to or beyond their limits by judicial inventiveness, will operate not to give effect to the intentions of the parties but to frustrate them.[51] Yet none of these problems exists for our civil law colleagues and it cannot seriously be maintained that their legal systems in these respects suffer in relation to our own.[52]

OFFERS AND OPTIONS

Under English law an offer or an option, unless supported by consideration, or executed as a deed, is not enforceable despite its being expressed as valid for a definitive period of time, although one would assume that its being valid for that period represented commercially the intention of the parties.

German law, as stated earlier, is the opposite (see above, pp. 63–64); an offer may not be revoked during its validity period.

French law, although it distinguishes between the *offre, un acte purement unilatéral*, which if revoked while it is valid could expose the offeror to an action in delict by the person to whom it is addressed, and *une promesse de contrat* which once accepted is a valid unilateral contract, equivalent in English terminology to an option, effectively allows today that both offers and options are binding upon the party issuing them.[53]

Both systems give effect therefore to the intentions of the parties without the need for an artificially introduced 'consideration'.

ADDITIONAL PAYMENTS UNDER AN EXISTING CONTRACT

The English rule, established finally in 1809,[54] is that if what is promised to be performed under the contract is no more than that which was originally promised, then any undertaking to pay an additional amount for such performance is void for lack of consideration. So it was thought that what could be a sensible commercial bargain, to pay a contractor who was in difficulties a bonus for extra effort to achieve completion by the original contract date, would be unenforceable at law and such a promise could be defaulted upon by an unscrupulous purchaser with impunity. In a recent decision the Court of Appeal has modified the original doctrine and held that if there was a genuine doubt as to whether or not the party responsible (a sub-contractor) would be able to complete performance of his work and was promised extra to do so, and as a result the promisor (the main contractor) obtained in practice a benefit, then in the absence of economic duress or fraud, such benefit was consideration for the promise.[55]

The decision seems sensible and in accord with commercial realities. The difficulty remains, however, that the factual benefits which the court held that the main contractor obtained by paying extra, such as improved working, were arguably all benefits to which he was already entitled at law under the terms of the original contract. Whether he would have received them in practice, however, given the sub-contractor's financial position, is doubtful. How far therefore the decision establishes a general principle which will be supported remains to be seen.

For a helpful discussion of factual and legal consideration in cases of existing duty see Treitel p. 72 et seq., written before the above-mentioned decision, in which the learned author concludes, 'it may be doubted whether the doctrine of consideration continues in this type of case to serve any useful purpose'. One can only respectfully agree.

The issue does not seem to have arisen directly in French law but following the principle applied in the related situation of *double emploi* it is considered that if there was any genuine counterpart obligation for the promise then it would be held valid.[56]

In the absence of any doctrine of either consideration or cause the issue does not arise in German law.

THE SETTLEMENT OF DEBTS

Under English law an undisputed debt for a sum which is liquidated can only be discharged by the payment of some lesser amount if consideration is given which is other than the part payment itself and outwith what the debtor is obliged to do under the contract.[57] Perhaps the most common example of such consideration is payment plus an undertaking not to enforce a cross-claim which the debtor has against his creditor. Another would be payment at an earlier date than that at which the debt is actually due.[58]

Despite these possibilities, and allowing for the possible equitable remedy under the by now famous High Trees House doctrine,[59] the rule is still inconvenient and a trap for the unwary. So in a case in 1986 in which a commission of 10 per cent had been agreed between the parties, but after a subsequent disagreement an invoice for the 10 per cent was then amended to 5 per cent, initialled and endorsed by the negotiator for the plaintiff 'accepted in full and final settlement', it was decided by the Court of Appeal that as no consideration had been given, the plaintiff was entitled to payment of the full amount of 10 per cent.[60]

DISCHARGE OF THE CONTRACT BY AGREEMENT

Closely related to the settlement of debts is the rule that a contract can only be discharged unilaterally, i.e. the debtor released from his obligations which are to a degree unperformed, if consideration is given for the release which is other than the partial performance of the obligation itself.

FRENCH AND GERMAN LAW

In both the above cases, untrammelled by any constraints imposed by the doctrine of consideration, both French and German law only require an agreement between the debtor and the creditor either to reduce or release the debtor's liability which includes the discharge of the contract.

In neither law does the agreement have to be in any particular form. For German law see ss.397, 518 and 782 of the *BGB* which make it clear that the notarial form for a donation is not needed. Not even writing is needed for the validity of the agreement, although valuable as evidence.[61]

The position is similar under French law. All that is required is agreement between the parties, no notarial form, not even writing, although again the latter is useful as regards proof.[62]

CONSIDERATION AND THIRD PARTIES

The general issue of privity of contract and the rights, if any, of a third party to a contract to enforce it in his favour will be discussed later (see below, pp. 269–271). What needs to be noted here is the English rule that 'only a person who has given consideration may enforce a contract not a deed' or as it was stated some years earlier, 'no stranger to the consideration can take advantage of a contract although made for his benefit'.[63]

The inconvenience, if not actual injustice of the rule is obvious. It is however often argued that it does not exist separately from the doctrine of privity of contract and certainly it seems clear that its abolition or amendment would require a change also to that doctrine. Accordingly an examination of the comparative and very different provisions of French and German law will be made later under that heading (see below, p. 286).

NOTES

1. As referred to earlier (above, p. 87 note 21) the expression *bonnes moeurs* is treated as subsumed under *l'ordre public*.
2. Ghestin s.650 reviews the various terms used by modern French authors to differentiate between one concept of *cause* and another and concludes that they virtually all distinguish between the absence of cause and *cause illicite*.
3. Ghestin on p. 760, having analysed the various concepts proposed by different authors, comments: 'It results in consequence that the unity of the notion [of cause] in its several functions becomes in itself artificial since the immoral cause requires an analysis of the will in order to determine its aim whereas the absence of cause is defined in an objective manner as the absence of a counterpart obligation'.

   F. P. Walton (1925) writing in the *LQR* commented that 'cause cannot mean one thing when there is a question of its lawfulness and mean something quite different when there is no such question' (p. 321). But as Ghestin has observed this is exactly the position which has been reached in contemporary French law.
4. Starck s.668.
5. Ghestin s.667.
6. Bordeaux 23 Nov. 1896 S.98, 2, 297.
7. Req. 30 July 1873 S.1873 1.448.
8. Cass. civ. 1re 12 February 1975, *JCP* 1979 II 18643.
9. Cass. com. 5 October 1981; Bull. civ. IV no. 340 p. 270.
10. Civ. 3e 4 May 1983; Bull. civ. III no. 103.
11. Quoted in Ghestin s.662.
12. Quoted Ghestin s.663.
13. Quoted Starck s.687.
14. Weill and Terré s.270.
15. Cass. civ. 1re 16 December 1986 Bull. civ. I no. 301 p. 287.
16. Bull. civ. IV. no. 263 p. 122.
17. The older leading case is Cass. civ. 14 April 1891 – see *Source Book* p. 479. Ghestin ss.688 and 689 appears to support the view given in the text but does refer to certain decisions which are inconsistent. Weill and Terré take a stronger view in favour of the application of cause post contract following Henri Capitant but admit that 'one does not have to deduce that the disappearance of the "cause" during the execution of the contract puts in question its validity which ought to be assessed at the time when the contract is made. But if, once the contract is entered into and one of its obligations is not performed, the other no longer has to be executed' (S.279 p. 289). To the same effect, in commenting on the case referred to in note 42, Starck says 'It appears therefore that the disappearance of the "cause" during the course of the contract does not affect its validity . . . but does concern its performance . . . it serves to justify the correlation of the reciprocal obligations and provide the basis for "resolution" or if necessary suspension of the obligation deprived of "cause" after the event' (ss.695 and 696).

    Markesinis (1978) writing in the *Cambridge Law Review* for April on cause and consideration makes a similar comment in relation to the English decision in *Taylor* v. *Caldwell* (1863) 3 B & S 826: 'Why should the *contract* be discharged [because of failure of consideration] and not merely the innocent party from *his obligation to perform his part of the bargain?'*

    Both Starck s.1664 and Weill and Terré pp. 498 and 499 also point out later the inconsistency between maintaining that failure of the other part post contract involves a lack of *cause*, which should result in nullity, and the actions of the courts in insisting on the remedy of 'resolution' which is a matter of judicial discretion.
18. See Weill and Terré s.279.
19. In English law as regards consumer transactions the matter is now dealt with under the Consumer Credit Act 1974. Broadly, when there is a connection as defined under the Act between the dealer and the creditor then the consumer has a 'like claim against the creditor' as he has against the dealer. This is a complete reversal of the common law position which was that the creditor was never liable for the breaches of contract by the dealer. Within the context of the Act a 'consumer' is an individual and therefore a partner or sole trader would qualify as such even if the goods were being bought for use in his business but a company would not do so. See for details Croner's *Buying and Selling Law*, Section 5B, Croner Publications Ltd., October 1992.

20. Ghestin s.680.
21. Cass. civ. 1re 6 October 1981; Bull. civ. I. no. 273 p. 272.
22. Chambre des Requêtes 1 July 1924.
23. Ghestin p. 792.
24. Bull. civ. I no.293 p. 294; *Revue Trimestrielle de Droit Commerciale et Droit Economique* no.2 1990 p. 245.
25. Ghestin s.704.
26. Ghestin p. 820.
27. *Objet, Cause et Lésion du Contrat*, Allemagne La Cause p. 123.
28. For a brief survey of the historical background see Brice Dickson (1987) 'The Law of Restitution in the Federal Republic of Germany. A comparison with English law', ICLQ vol. 36 October at pp. 767–70 and other sources cited there. See also Lawson, *A Common Lawyer Looks at the Civil Law* pp. 156–8.
29. Where a contract is held void because of a breach of s.138(2) of the *BGB* then it has been held that 'the invalidity of the primary transaction for an offence to bonos mores immediately includes that of the secondary transaction concluded for the implementation of the primary transaction'.
    For the rules as to the validity of a transfer and the concept of 'good faith' see below, pp. 263–264.
30. For details see Cohn *Manual of German Law*, vol. 1 s.309.
31. Only if the transferee has given away the property to a third party can the original owner reclaim the property itself from the third party ss816(1) and 822. These sections are an exception to the general rule that claims for unjust enrichment only lie directly against the person who received the benefit. If however the property has been sold in good faith then the only remedy is in a claim against the transferee for unjust enrichment; there would be no claim against the third party.
32. For a comprehensive review see the article by Brice Dickson (1987) referred to in note 28 above.
33. This is a major limitation on the ability of the original owner to recover in unjustified enrichment claims in which there is already the weakness that, unlike English law, there is no possibility of a right in rem to trace the goods. While that right only exists if there is an actual trust, or a constructive trust under a fiduciary relationship, and the identity of the property can be established, it is nevertheless a far more satisfactory remedy for the original owner especially where, as is so often the case, the transferee has gone bankrupt, than a mere claim as a creditor. See further on trusts and tracing Keeton and Sheridan's *Equity* Ch. XIX, Kluwer, 1987.
34. The problem in English law is that 'unjust enrichment' is not at the moment generally recognized as a category of law separate from contract or tort and needing a fusion of the rules of equity and the common law, despite the valiant efforts of Goff and Jones (1987) *Law of Unjust Enrichment*, 3rd ed. Interestingly, a general doctrine of 'unjust enrichment' has now been accepted in Canadian law – *Air Canada* v. *Attorney General of British Columbia* (1989) 59 DLR 161.
    At present therefore it seems that the remedies in quasi-contract must be classified as contractual, even though the obligation to repay the benefit received generally rests only on the uncertain grounds of an implied contact. If the obligation is contractual then what the recipient has done with the money or goods becomes irrelevant.
35. In *Lipkin Gorman* v. *Karpuale Ltd* (TLR 7 June 1991) the House of Lords, Lord Goff, stated that a bona fide change of position should of itself be a good defence to a claim in restitution where the change was such that it would be inequitable in all the circumstances to require restitution in whole or part. So while a firm of solicitors was entitled to recover from the casino money stolen from their firm by a partner and used by him for the purposes of gambling, the amount they could recover was limited to that which the casino had won after taking into account the winnings they had paid to the partner. It is not clear if this case is now authority for the defence of change of position where the claim is based on a mistake of fact which has previously been disallowed (see J. Beatson in the *Law Quarterly Review* April 1989 p. 179 and cases cited there).
36. Recovery has therefore been denied in cases where repayment would cause severe hardship to an individual who has been overpaid and the court has been able to find grounds in the form of a representation or a mistake of law in order to do justice in accordance with equitable principles (see *Holt* v. *Markham* [1923] 1 KB 504 and the old cases of *Skyring* v. *Greenwood* [1824] 4 B & C 281 and *Brisbane* v. *Dacres* (1813) 129 Eng. Rep. 641). German courts would have been likely to have reached the same answer in each case applying s.818 (3) of the *BGB*.
37. Article 1376 of the *Code Civil* states that 'Someone who receives by mistake or knowingly that which is not due to him is obliged to make restitution to the person from whom he received that to which he is not

due'. It is not due because it is not supported by any valid cause (Starck s.2064 and the notes to Art. 1376 in the Dalloz edition of the *Code Civil* and cases cited there).

38. See Starck para. 2079 commenting on Civ. 1re 7 February 1984 Bull. civ. I no. 50 where the *Cour de cassation* held that the sums paid by the social security organization in excess of those which it was legally obliged to pay constituted a payment which was not due and its character was irrelevant.

39. 8 June 1983 Bull. civ. V, no. 310 and see Starck s.2067 and note 19 to Art. 1376 of the *Code Civil* in Dalloz p. 870.

40. The principle is not found in the *BGB* but has been applied consistently by the courts (see Dickson op. cit., note 28 p. 778). German law has therefore rejected the *actio de in rem verso*. Originally in Roman law this was an action for which the head of the family, the *paterfamilias*, was held liable in respect of a debt contracted by a person in power, e.g. a slave, which was applied to his benefit. Later in the development of the civil law this action was applied generally to cases in which the benefit which constituted the unjust enrichment was received indirectly through the act of another. It was at one time part of the *Gemeines Recht*, the German common law, and of Prussian law but was rejected by the authors of the *BGB* (see Dickson op. cit., note 28, p. 778, Zimmermann p. 378 et seq. and Zweigert and Kotz p. 234 et seq.).

41. The existence of the action *de in rem verso* was first confirmed in the famous Boudier case in 1892. There a merchant had sold fertilizer to a tenant farmer but had not been paid. The owner of the land terminated the tenancy and the tenant was bankrupt. On learning of the termination and the settlement of accounts between the tenant and the owner, including the value of the unharvested crop, the merchant brought an action against the owner for the value of the fertilizer which had been applied by the tenant to the crop. The action succeeded although there was no article in the *Code Civil* upon which it could be based. The court expressly based its decision on the 'personal and direct profit' which the owner derived from the improvement in the crop due to the use of the fertilizer and that 'the action deriving from the principle of equity which protects against the enrichment of one person by another not being regulated by any legal text, its exercise is not subject to any pre-determined conditions, and that it suffices to establish the action that the plaintiff alleges and offers to prove the advantage which the defendant had obtained from the plaintiff's own privation or action' (Req. 15 June 1892 DP 92.1.596.s.93 included in Capitant les grands arrêts de la jurisprudence civile 916, ed. Dalloz, 1991, at p. 613 et seq.).

42. The formulation given in note 41 was clearly too wide and that in the text was stated in a decision of the *Cour de cassation* in 1915 which also established the principle of subsidiarity. A concession was granted by the town of Bagnères to one Bréchoire for the operation of its thermal baths and casino and Bréchoire was authorized at his own risk to undertake certain improvement works for the fixed sum of 160 000 francs. He engaged contractors for this purpose which included one Brianhaut. The costs exceeding the amount allocated, Bréchoire abandoned the concession and Brianhaut sought to recover his costs for extra work against the town. His action *de in rem verso* was refused on the grounds that Brianhaut could not by that means circumvent the rule that the recovery of additional costs under a firm price contract (*marché forfait*) was contrary to Art. 1793 of the *Code Civil* (Brianhaut was entitled to exercise Bréchoire's rights against the town under Art. 1166 of the *Code Civil*) Civ. 2 March 1915 DP 1920.1.102 Capitant op. cit. p. 621.

A second decision in 1939 confirmed that if the enrichment was a result of a valid contract between the enriched and the third party then again the action did not lie. The proprietor of a business entered into a contract with a couple under which they were entitled for a period to operate the business at their own risk and profit (*contrat de gérance libre*) but at the end of the period the stock in trade of the business was to revert into the ownership of the proprietor. A supplier delivered certain materials for the purposes of the business but at the end of the period had not been paid, and therefore sought in the action *de in rem verso* to recover from the proprietor.

The *Cour de cassation* rejected the claim on the grounds that there is no enrichment without cause when the enrichment has its origins in a valid legal act. That was the case here since the proprietor had become the owner of the materials as a result of the *contrat de gérance* (Civ. 28 February 1939 DP 1940.1.5. Capitant p. 623).

43. See Treitel *Contract* p. 485 et seq.

44. Although this is how it is usually stated in the textbooks, in particular see Fifoot, *History and Sources of the Common Law* p. 398, it is recognized that the founding of the doctrine of consideration within bargain is not without its critics (see Cheshire p. 68 n.5).

45. Markesinis (1978) *Cambridge Law Journal* p. 58, draws the same conclusion. See also Nicholas p. 113 2a. This is not however to say that their function is the same.
46. Per Lord Somervell in *Chappell & Co. Ltd* v. *Nestlé Co. Ltd* 1960 AC at p. 114.
47. Indeed as long ago as 1587 it was said in *Sturlyn* v. *Albany Croke Eliz* 67 that 'when a thing is to be done by the plaintiff be it never so small this is sufficient consideration to ground an action'. So long at least as the promise is the payment of money its amount appears irrelevant.
48. As David has pointed out in his careful comparison between the two, consideration was required in English law precisely because the law did *not* follow the doctrine of *pacta sunt servanda* and therefore had to define those agreements which the law would enforce. French law, because it did follow the doctrine of *pacta sunt servanda* had to temper its application by defining, through the idea of cause, the conditions under which a person would be held in law as well as morally to be bound by his promise (*Les Contrats en droit Anglais* para. 189). Levy sums it up by 'La cause tempère le consensualisme, qui ne sera pas acceptable sans elle' p. 188.

There is here a reflection of the fundamental moral base of French contract law as opposed to the economic base of English law.
49. Consideration is said to be 'past' and therefore in reality no consideration at all when the act relied upon as constituting consideration was performed in advance of the promise to confer a benefit unless such act was done at the promisor's request and the two can be regarded as forming a single transaction. So work completed voluntarily cannot normally constitute consideration for a subsequent promise to pay for the benefit received (*Re Mcardle* (1951) Ch. 669).
50. As regards contracts based on what we would refer to as 'past consideration', since the existence of the act giving rise to the past consideration is the only reason for the promise, then such promise would only be invalid if that act was illusory, i.e. for *erreur sur la cause* (see Ghestin ss.681 and 682 – assuming the *cause* was not *illicite ou immorale*).

With *contrats à titre gratuit*, it is again a question of motive, which will normally be found in the act of generosity itself, and any issue of *cause* will therefore be in respect of a *cause illicite ou immorale*. However the act has apparently to have a 'minimum objective basis'. So if there is a specific reason for the generosity, and this is subsequently found to be non-existent, then exceptionally the contract may be annulled for lack of cause. For example, when a donation was made dividing up property between the donor's children, based on the advantages to be gained from the then existing tax law and subsequently removed by a change in the law with retrospective effect, the *Cour de cassation* on 11 February 1986 approved the decision of the cour d'appel that the donation was null for lack of cause. Bull. civ. I no. 25 p. 22.
51. It is agreed with Chloros (p. 147) and contrary to the views expressed by Zweigert and Kotz (p. 73) that seriousness of intention is not determined by the presence of consideration and that the two doctrines within English law are distinct. However the antithesis surely ought not to be the case, that if there is evidence of a seriousness of intention to be bound at the time when the agreement was made, one party may then escape from the consequences of his actions because of the technicality of the lack of what the law recognizes as consideration. In this regard the views expressed by the above two learned authors at p. 79 et seq. are supported.
52. On the contrary, while there have been Law Commission papers on, and proposals for, substantially modifying the law relating to consideration, France and Germany seem to be satisfied with the provisions of their respective codes in this respect. The doctrine of *cause* was recommended to be retained by the Commission du Réforme du *Code Civil* with only a clarification of the distinction between cause and motive. It is further to be noted that when the Uniform Law for International Sales was prepared the common law doctrine under which an offer may be revoked at any time prior to its acceptance in the absence of consideration was not followed (see Art. 16 of the 1980 Vienna Convention).
53. The French *promesse de vente* contains its *cause* in the terms of the option which must specify, as for the sale itself, the subject matter of the option and the price; otherwise, as for an agreement for sale, it would be void for lack of *objet* and *cause*.
54. In the case of *Stilk* v. *Meyrick* (1809) 2 Camp 317.
55. *Williams* v. *Roffey Bros & Nichols (Contractors) Ltd* TLR 8 December 1989.
56. Ghestin s.666.
57. The rule is an ancient one originating in the action of debt and was established certainly in 1495 and restated in Pinnel's case in 1602. Finally it was confirmed by the House of Lords in *Foakes* v. *Beer*

(1884) 9 App. cas. 605. See further Fifoot pp. 412–5. It was applied in *D & C Builders* v. *Rees* [1966] 2 QB 617 when a small firm of builders under financial pressure was induced by a threat of non-payment and after a delay lasting many months to accept £300 in settlement of a bill for £480. Later they sued for the balance and won. In this case there was no room for the application of the equitable principle referred to in note 42.

58. Decided so in Pinnel's case.

59. This holds that where a promise was made which was intended to create a legal relationship and which to the knowledge of the person making it was going to be acted upon by the person to whom it was made, and which was in fact so acted upon, then the court will uphold the promise in order to prevent the party who made it from exercising his strict legal rights, where it would be inequitable to do otherwise having regard to the dealings between the parties.

60. *Tiney Engineering Ltd* v. *Amods Knitting Machine Co.* 1986 Court of Appeal, unreported, *The Buyer*, Monitor Press, Vol. 8, Issue 10 at p. 7.

61. Cohn vol. 1 s.286.

62. Weill and Terré s. 1084.

63. Per Wightman, J. in *Tweddle* v. *Atkinson* (1861) 1 B & S 393.

8 Mistake and misrepresentation – English law

MISTAKE

The three legal systems with which we are concerned face the same problem although they differ quite markedly in their answers. On the one hand there is the need to maintain the security of contracts once entered into so that business can be carried out with confidence and the interests of *bona fide* third parties protected. It surely should not be permitted that those who freely enter into contracts can avoid them subsequently simply because they realize they made a bad bargain. On the other hand it would appear equally wrong that the law should 'fail to give effect to the reasonable expectations of honest men,'[1] yet that would be so if contracts were enforced when their subject matter or terms were shown to differ in fundamental respects from those which they were reasonably believed to be at the time when the bargain was made.

CATEGORIES OF MISTAKE

It has been proposed[2] to divide mistakes into three categories:

1. Common mistake – where the same mistake is shared by both parties.
2. Mutual mistake – where the parties are at cross-purposes one with another. Strictly, as Cheshire points out, this is not really a matter of 'mistake' but of 'misunderstanding'.
3. Unilateral mistake – where one party is mistaken and the other knows or ought to have known of the mistake.

There is the further difference between common mistake and the other two forms in that with common mistake there is an admitted agreement between the parties. What is denied is that it is of any effect. With mutual and unilateral mistake it is maintained there never was an agreement. Either the parties were at cross-purposes or the purported acceptance lacked validity.

112

Common mistake

We have already dealt with one classic case of common mistake – that of a belief by both parties in the existence of the subject matter of the contract which has, however, already perished at the time of sale. This is the *res extincta* of Roman law for which, and the exceptions to it, see above, p. 88.

Obviously such cases will be rare. Of much more interest are those in which it is claimed that the subject matter, although it exists, is so fundamentally different from that which was envisaged at the time the bargain was made, that the contract is void for mistake.

There was a concept in the Roman law of sale known as error *in substantia* which was limited to mistakes in the material of which the article sold was made (and the sex of a slave). The examples used by the Romans were the sale of an article of bronze instead of one of gold, or one of lead for silver.[3] The doctrine was strict. The sale was only void for mistake if the article was wholly of the incorrect material; if the bronze bracelet contained some gold then the sale was valid. Issues of quality were also irrelevant; if the gold was of an inferior quality to that which the buyer thought he was purchasing then the sale was valid.[4] It did not matter whether the error was common to both parties or was the buyer's alone but the mistake of the latter must not have been due to his negligence.[5]

The Roman texts were quoted extensively by Blackburn J. in *Kennedy v. Panama etc. Co.* and he deduced from them that

> if there be misapprehension as to the substance of the thing there is no contract; but if it be only a difference in some quality or accident even though the misapprehension may have been the actuating motive to the purchaser, yet the contract remains binding.[6]

We shall see later how the Roman doctrine has been extended by French law well beyond its original limits but the use which Blackburn J. and later the House of Lords in *Bell v. Lever Bros*[7] made of it was to restrict its application even more severely. In the Kennedy case the subject matter of the contract was additional shares which the company had issued in order to allow it to finance a mail contract it claimed to have received from the New Zealand Government. It later transpired that the company (although innocent of fraud) had not secured the contract in question and an applicant for the shares who had received them refused to pay any further calls and claimed the return of his money.

Both parties had clearly been mistaken regarding the mail contract but it was held that the applicant had in fact received the shares for which he had applied and that the mistake was one of motive, and did not go to the substance of the contract. This latter was the securing by the applicant of the shares themselves which was indeed what he achieved. The shares were still shares and possessed some value even if they were less valuable than they would have been if the company had secured the mail contract in question.[8]

Blackburn J., in summing up the law, derived as he saw it from the Roman texts, stated:

the principle of our law is the same as that of the civil law; and the difficulty in every case is to determine whether the mistake is as to substance of the whole consideration, going as it were to the root of the matter, or only to some point even though a material point, an error as to which does not affect the substance of the whole consideration.[9]

On this reasoning there would only have been a mistake if there had been a total failure of consideration, i.e. either no shares awarded at all or shares which were completely valueless. Existence and substance come therefore to mean much the same thing.[10]

The well-known case of *Bell* v. *Lever Bros* need only be referred to briefly. There the subject matter was the service contracts of two of their employees, the surrender of which had been negotiated by Lever Bros in exchange for significant compensation payments. In fact at the time of the surrender they could have been terminated by Lever Bros for acts of breach of contract by the two employees concerned. By a majority the House of Lords held that Lever Bros were not entitled to a refund of the payments made.

The reasoning, at least of Lord Atkin, was essentially the same as that of Blackburn J. in Kennedy's case. Lever Bros got what they bargained for: the surrender of the same two service agreements which were the subject of the contract into which they entered. That those service contracts were voidable by them was a matter which related to the quality of the subject matter of their contract and was not fundamental. Three of the Law Lords' statements are worth recording as illustrations of the limited scope of mistake within the English common law:

> a mistake will not affect assent unless it is the mistake of both parties and is as to the existence of some quality which makes the thing without the quality essentially different from the thing as it was believed to be. (Lord Atkin.[11])

Again:

> Does the state of the new facts destroy the identity of the subject matter as it was in the original state of facts?

> [Common mistake] can only properly relate to something which both must necessarily have accepted in their minds as an essential and integral element of the subject matter. (Lord Thankerton.[12])

It is to be noted that in all these quotations, and there are many others to like effect[13] the emphasis is placed on the necessity, if the contract is to be voided, for the mistake to be both fundamental and directly affecting the elementary definition of that about which the parties contracted.[14] A mistake is not sufficient if it relates to some characteristic outwith that definition or is in an assumption on the basis of which the parties entered into the contract which they would not have done had they known that assumption to be false.

The difficulty of establishing common mistake has led to one eminent textbook writer to doubt whether outside res extincta there exists any such doctrine at all in the common law.[15] However in the most recent case to come before the courts, Mr Justice Steyn, in a careful and penetrating analysis of the problem, rejects that view, while at the same time following Lord Atkin in stating that the 'mistake must render the subject matter of the contract essentially and radically different from the subject matter which the parties believed to exist'. He went on:

> while the civilian distinction between the substance and attributes of the subject matter of a contract has played a role in the development of our law, the principle enunciated in Bell v. Lever Bros Ltd is markedly narrower than the civilian doctrine. It is therefore no longer useful to invoke the civilian distinction.[16]

The case itself concerned the sale and leaseback of four identified and numbered machines with a guarantee being provided by Crédit du Nord in respect of the lease. The seller and lessee of the machines was fraudulent; the machines never existed and he defaulted after making the first rental payment. The lessor (AJB) had parted with over a million pounds for the non-existent machines and with the lessee bankrupt called in the guarantee. Crédit du Nord maintained, however, that either there was an express or implied condition precedent to the guarantee that the lease related to four existing machines or alternatively that the guarantee was void for mistake.

Mr Justice Steyn, on the construction of the guarantee, agreed with their first point but also dealt extensively with the issue of mistake. Having made the comments referred to above he went on:

> the real question is whether the subject matter of the guarantee (as opposed to the sale and lease) was essentially different from what it was reasonably believed to be . . . For both parties the guarantee of obligations under a lease with non-existing machines was essentially different from a guarantee of a lease with four machines which both parties at the time of the contract believed to exist.

Accordingly in his judgement the common law test was satisfied and the guarantee was void for mistake.[17]

Common mistake in equity   Even though it may be decided in law that a contract is not void for a common mistake it may still be set aside in equity on terms which do justice as between the parties. In *Grist* v. *Bailey*[18] a property was sold with both parties believing that the existing tenancy was subject to the Rent Acts and the price was fixed accordingly at about a third of that with vacant possession. In fact the tenancy was not so subject and the tenant left. The court decided that the mistake was not sufficient to hold the contract void at law but ordered, in equity, that the parties enter into a fresh agreement to sell at a price based on the giving of vacant possession.

In the case of *AJB* v. *Crédit du Nord* set out above Steyn J. also said that if he had not held the contract to be void at law he would have held that it was so in equity and indicated that this would have been upon terms.

Mutual mistake

Here the problem is that there has been a misunderstanding between the parties of which at the time of the contract neither was aware.

What each party subjectively intended will be treated by the court as irrelevant. It is a matter of how, looked at objectively, they behaved and if one party by his conduct acted so that the other believed they had an agreement on a particular basis then the court will uphold the contract.

So if X agreed to sell to Y certain specific goods by sample and the price is agreed on that basis, the fact that the specific goods are of a higher quality than the sample and would therefore normally command a higher price, is irrelevant. The seller, despite his mistake, is bound by his contract.[19]

It is generally only if the court decides that it cannot deduce from the facts with a sufficient degree of precision the existence of an agreement between the parties that the purported contract will be held void.[20]

Unilateral mistake

The essence of unilateral mistake is that the mistake is that of only one party; the other party either knows of the mistake or certainly would have done if, as a reasonable man, he had thought about it. In commercial situations it is usually a matter of one party seeking to take advantage of a mistake which he knows has been made by the other.

English law under the influence in the last century of the political doctrine of individualism and its legal counterpart, caveat emptor, abandoned any pretence to supporting the concept in contractual relationships of 'good faith'. As a result, it was established that if the one party (usually the vendor) knew of the other's mistake as to an attribute or quality of the subject matter of the contract but took no positive step to encourage it, and had not induced the mistake through fraud, then the contract was valid.[21]

The only exceptions are if the mistake relates either to a term of the contract, e.g. a warranty that the goods possess a particular quality, or where the mistake causes the party to express a fundamental provision of the offer incorrectly and this is known to the other party before he purports to accept it.

In a Canadian case a contractor omitted by mistake the first page of his tender which contained a price fluctuations clause and the purchaser, knowing full well of the error, sought to accept the tender. It was held that a mistake as to price was fundamental and not a matter of motive or underlying assumption and accordingly there was no true agreement between the parties and the contractor was not bound by his tender.[22]

MISREPRESENTATION

A representation is a statement of fact which is made by one party to another pre-contract and which is not a term of the contract, but is intended to induce the person to whom it is made to enter into the contract, and in reliance upon which he does so. A misrepresentation is simply a representation which is not true.

THE POSITION AT COMMON LAW

There was no remedy at common law for a misrepresentation unless it was made fraudulently. The concept of fraud was restricted to cases in which when the false statement was made the representor did not honestly believe it was true. Subjective honesty of belief was the criterion; foolishness or even negligence was irrelevant.[23]

The common law position was altered by the landmark decision of the House of Lords in *Hedley Byrne & Co.* v. *Heller & Partners Ltd.*[24] As a result of that decision it is now possible that where advice or information is given by party A to party B in a pre-contractual situation with the intention of inducing B's decision in A's favour and in the knowledge that, because of A's special expertise, such advice or information will be relied upon by B, then A may owe B a duty of care and so be liable to B in damages for economic loss if the advice or information is given negligently and did in fact induce B's decision.[25]

Further change was made by the Misrepresentation Act 1967. Section 2(1) of that Act provides that if in the pre-contractual negotiations party A makes a misrepresentation which, had it been fraudulent would have given party B a claim in damages, then A is liable to B in damages unless he can prove that 'he had reasonable grounds to believe and did believe up to the time that the contract was made that the facts represented were true'.

It follows that under the Act it is not sufficient for A to prove that he was not negligent; he must show positively that he had reasonable grounds for his belief, which may not be easy.[26]

MISREPRESENTATION IN EQUITY

Where before the Misrepresentation Act a misrepresentation was made 'innocently', i.e. it was not fraudulent, then the only remedy for the injured party was rescission together with a restricted right of indemnity in respect of obligations necessarily assumed under the contract. The right to rescind was in many instances of limited value, in that it gave no proper compensation[27] and, since the contract was only voidable, the right was lost if the goods in the mean time had been sold to a bona fide purchaser for value.

As a result of the Act s.2(2), the court now has the discretion, instead of rescinding the contract, to award damages. For a detailed review of the remedy of rescission and the effects of the Act see Cheshire pp. 279–88.

THE EFFECT OF SILENCE

Generally mere silence cannot constitute a misrepresentation.[28] Further there is no requirement that party A is under any obligation to party B to disclose in the course of their commercial dealings a material fact, even when he knows that party B is proceeding on a false assumption which A could correct, provided that A does nothing to induce or confirm the error.[29]

There is also no general duty of disclosure of known latent defects, although the active concealment of a defect making it impossible for the buyer to discover the fault would be considered as a misrepresentation.[30] So where pigs were sold at market 'with all faults' it was held by the House of Lords that there was no duty on the part of the seller to disclose his knowledge that they were infected with typhoid and he was under no liability to the buyer so long as he did nothing to prevent the latter's discovery of their condition. The use of the expression 'with all faults' negatived any possible representation as to their propensity for not causing damage.[31]

Nor will a court hold that there is a duty of disclosure in negligence which 'will cut across the principles of our law of contract relating to the effect of silence in the course of pre-contractual negotiations'.[32]

Of course if a material fact is disclosed, then the whole truth must be told, since the partial truth may well amount to a misrepresentation because of what is omitted.

The only exception of commercial importance to the rule that there is no duty to disclose is in contracts which are of *uberrimae fidei*, of utmost good faith, of which the contract of insurance is the primary example. In such contracts there is an obligation on the insured to make disclosure of all material circumstances, that is all facts which a reasonably prudent insurer would take into account in deciding whether or at what premium to take the risk. Equally the insurer is under an obligation to disclose to the insured all facts known to him which were material either to the nature of the risk or the recoverability of a claim under the policy which a prudent insured would take into account in deciding whether to place the risk with that insurer.

NOTES

1. So stated by Steyn J. at the opening of his judgement in *Associated Japanese Bank* v. *Crédit du Nord SA* (1989) 1 WLR 255. The same principle, although not in the context of the law of mistake, was enunciated by the Court of Appeal in *Fuel Energy (UK) Ltd* v. *Hungarian International Bank Ltd*, *The Times*, 4 March 1993.
2. Cheshire, Furmstone and Fifoot (cited Cheshire) at pp. 217 and 218.
3. D. XVIII 1.9.
4. D. XVIII 1.10 and 14.
5. D. XVIII 1.14 and XLI 10.5; see also XVIII 1.15.
6. (1867) LR 2 QB 580 at p. 588.
7. 1932 AC 161.
8. Lawson 52 LQR at p. 90.
9. Ibid. note 6.
10. Lawson op.cit. p. 91.
11. At p. 218.
12. At p. 235.
13. See further the article by Lawson, 'Error In Substantia' referred to in note 8, 52 LQR and the judgement of Steyn J. in *Associated Japanese Bank* v. *Crédit du Nord*, above, note 1.
14. By elementary definition is meant the definition of the thing which is just sufficient for it to be identified by type or class, e.g. 'shares' or 'a service contract', not shares or a service contract having certain specific characteristics. So in most instances of the purchase say of a picture or a set of dining chairs it would be sufficient to define them as just that. It would however be different if the purchase was of a Picasso or a set of Chippendale chairs. Then the name of the artist is an essential part of the elementary definition. See further the argument on similar lines in Treitel pp. 218 and 219.
15. Cheshire p. 228.
16. At p. 267.

17. The essential difference as Steyn J. saw it was in the security which was provided by the existence of the machines which were of assistance in the servicing of the debt and, in the event of default, could provide a means of at least partial recovery. But they were certainly not the whole consideration. There was the creditworthiness of the lessee, and although this turned out to be valueless, it seems highly doubtful if the guarantee would ever have been given if Crédit du Nord had not believed that he was in a substantial way of business. Indeed on the facts it was established that they had investigated his financial standing and been impressed with this, by his 'proven ability to obtain government contracts' and reports they had obtained on him from the Midland Bank.

On this basis there is an obvious difficulty in bringing the case within the test which Lord Atkin had established in *Bell* v. *Lever Bros*. For a more detailed analysis see the note by Treitel in the *LQR* vol.104 pp. 501–7.

18. [1967] Ch.532.

19. See for example *Scott* v. *Littledale* (1858) 8 E & B 815.

20. As in *Scriven Bros* v. *Hindley & Co.* [1913] 3 KB 564.

21. See Atiyah *The Rise and Fall of the Freedom of Contract*, p. 466 et seq. The high-watermark of this doctrine was *Smith* v. *Hughes* (1871) LR 6 QB 597 where although the seller knew that the buyer wanted old oats, whereas the sample offered by the seller was new oats, it was held that in the absence of any express warranty or representation by the seller, there was no obligation on the seller to state whether they were old or new. Since the buyer had relied on his own judgement he had no cause for complaint. See further p. 140.

It would have been different if the buyer had thought that the supplier had *warranted* that the oats were old. In that event the mistake would have been as to a term of the contract and the contract would have been void. The distinction appears well established although difficult to justify (see Treitel pp. 229, 233 and 234).

22. *McMaster University* v. *Wilchar Construction Ltd* (1971) 22 DLR (3d) 9.

23. *Derry* v. *Peek* (1889) 14 App. Cas. 337.

24. [1964] AC 465.

25. Such a situation arose in *Esso Petroleum Co.* v. *Mardon* [1976] 2 All ER 850 in which an inexperienced tenant of a newly developed filling station was induced to take the lease by a statement from Esso's sales representative that from his expert knowledge and experience he had estimated the annual throughput in the third year would be 200 000 gallons. In fact it was only about 86000 gallons. Mardon was compelled to give up the tenancy since at that level it was uneconomic and succeeded in his claim for damages.

26. *Howard Marine and Dredging Co. Ltd* v. *A. Ogden & Sons (Excavations) Ltd* 1977 9 BLR 34. Ogdens wished to hire barges in connection with their excavation work. Howard's manager stated from his recollection of Lloyds Register that the barges' payload was 1600 tonnes whereas it was only 1055, which he could have ascertained from the barges' shipping documents. The contract made no mention of the payload. It was held that since this was a misrepresentation which, if fraudulent, would have given rise to a claim in damages, then under the Act Howards had to prove that their manager had reasonable grounds for his belief that the facts stated were true and this they failed to do, since reference should have been made to the shipping documents.

27. *Whittington* v. *Seale-Hayne* (1900) 82 LT 49. In negotiations for a lease an innocent misrepresentation was made that certain premises were sanitary when they were not. As a result the lessees who were prize poultry breeders suffered severe losses primarily arising out of the death of their stock. It was decided that the indemnity to which they were entitled only covered their payment of rates and repairs ordered by the council since these were the only obligations that arose necessarily out of the lease. Their loss of stock and profits was not recoverable.

28. This is supported by the old case of *Keates* v. *Cadogan* (1851) 10 CB 591 in which a landlord, prior to the letting of a house, failed to inform the tenant it was in a ruinous condition. It is interesting that this was one of the examples given by Cicero in discussing advantage and right in business, and sharp practice and the law (On Duties III, pp. 179–84 in Cicero *Selected Works*). Cicero comes down clearly on the side that both morally and legally such a failure to disclose was wrong. For the Roman law position see further p. 124.

Grotius followed the same view where as in this case the failure to disclose was intimately connected with the subject of the transaction (*De Juri Belli ac Pacis Libri Tres* in vol. II of the translation by Kelsey, Oxford University Press 1925 at p. 348).

29. See *Smith* v. *Hughes* discussed earlier in relation to unilateral mistake.
30. Of course in many instances of the sale of goods the buyer's position will now be protected by the Sale of Goods Act 1979 in particular s.14 discussed below, p. 141). However by no means all cases will fall within the scope of the Act. It would have made no difference to *Smith* v. *Hughes*: it only applies to sale of goods and it provides no protection for the seller where the act complained of is that of the buyer (see further below, pp. 124–127 for French law).

    As regards the exception relating to active concealment, this was established in the old case of *Schneider* v. *Heath* (1813) 3 Camp. 505 where on the sale of a ship 'with all faults' the seller prevented the buyer from discovering that, as the seller knew, the ship's bottom was rotten.
31. In such a case today it is possible that such a statement would fall under s.13(1) of the Unfair Contract Terms Act and therefore be subject to the requirement of 'reasonableness' (see the discussion in Yates and Hawkins, (1986) *Standard Business Contracts*, Sweet and Maxwell in ss 6G(3) and 9b(1).
32. *Banque Keyser Ullman* v. *Westgate Insurance Co.* in the Court of Appeal [1988] 2 Lloyds Rep. 513 quoted at p. 566 and see the note by F.A. Trinidade in LQR vol. 105 p. 191.

    Even more strongly the Court of Appeal in *Bank of Nova Scotia* v. *Hellenic Mutual War Risks Association (Bermuda) Ltd* (The Good Luck) said 'where it was held, where a duty of care was claimed to arise by virtue of an implied term under a tripartite agreement and also in tort, if the plaintiff failed in contract he must necessarily fail in tort'.

    The court had also this to say as regards the duty of disclosure in a tripartite arrangement: 'it was regrettably immoral if a party to such a commercial arrangement were willing because of his own commercial advantage to keep silent about such [fraudulent] conduct but immorality of conduct did not by itself provide a basis for implying a term in the contract. It was desirable that in a tripartite commercial arrangement one party should not be free to prefer its own commercial advantage if it knew that another party was actively defrauding the third, and it would be salutary if there were a duty on each party to tell the defrauded party what was going on . . . however such a term could not be implied'. TLR 20 April 1989.

9 Mistake, fraud and the obligation to inform – French law

MISTAKE

As indicated earlier the French law of mistake originated with the Roman doctrine of error *in substantia* but then moved far beyond the limited Roman concept which was, as we have seen, restricted to cases in which the material of which the item was made was wholly different from that which the purchaser had intended to buy. The test here is objective; the result would be the same for any purchaser.

Under the twin influences of consensualism and the moral teachings of the canon law the law had developed by the time that Pothier wrote in 1761: 'the mistake annuls the contract not only when it is as to the thing itself but when it relates to the quality of the thing which the contracting parties had principally in mind and which makes the substance of that thing'.[1]

MISTAKE UNDER THE *CODE CIVIL*

The *Code Civil* Art. 1110 states: 'Error is only a cause of the nullity of an agreement when it relates to the very substance of the thing which is the "objet" of the agreement'.[2] The contract may also be null under Art. 1116 for *dol* (see below, pp. 124–127). Whether the authors of the code intended that this should restrict the application of nullity for mistake to cases which fell within Pothier's formulation, or perhaps even to a stricter objective definition, is not clear. It seems probable that they had in mind Pothier's famous example of the contract which was void for mistake because the purchaser intended to purchase silver candelabra but instead was sold ones which were silver-plated. Here the mistake was one which related to the 'substantial qualities of the thing which determined consent'. But this would not have been so if it was not the nature of the metal but the artistic quality or antiquity which was the determining factor in the decision to purchase the candelabra.[3]

DEVELOPMENTS IN THE JURISPRUDENCE

It is clear that the term 'substance' in Art. 1110 has come to be interpreted by the courts as meaning 'the essential qualities of the thing without which the party would not have contracted'.[4] One can note here the change from Pothier from whom the *erreur* must have been of both parties, to the more subjective notion of the *erreur* being only of one party (see further, p. 124).

But the courts in the latter part of the last century and more particularly during this century have moved even beyond this point so that the interpretation of the 'essential qualities' may be either 'objective' taken in a broad sense or, with certain qualifications, 'subjective'.

Essential qualities – broadly objective

In the first instance the 'essential qualities of the thing determinative of the will to enter into a contract and in the absence of which the purchaser would not have done so,'[5] for example 'to buy a Corot', lie in the characteristics of the subject matter of the sale itself. No one intends to purchase a picture by a famous artist and pays a substantial sum for it, only to be sold a copy.

The seller must have known, or from the circumstances of the sale, e.g. in an antique shop, must be taken to have known the essential qualities of the object which not only that purchaser had in mind but any other purchaser would as well. The qualities are not specific to that purchaser and it is in that sense that they may be considered as objective.[6]

Contracts can be annulled on account of their objective qualities. Examples include: items sold as authentic antiques which are mere copies, pearls which are only cultured and not natural, land which is sold as building land when it is not, a farm which was leased as easily restorable when the work would be very costly and of long duration, a car which was sold second-hand with an incorrect manufacturing date, a lease of premises at a high rental which were stated to be 'desirable' but were in fact in a deplorable state and with construction work going on next door, a demolition contract for some concrete works where the exceptional hardness of the concrete was known to the employer, but not to the contractor.[7]

Essential qualities – subjective

In this case the 'essential qualities' can be determined only by an examination of the particular purchaser's objective in view of which he entered into the contract.[8] In order, however, for a mistake in the existence of such qualities to justify annulling the contract, the seller must in this instance have been made specifically aware of the fact that it was the presence of those particular qualities which constituted for the purchaser the determining objective.

This is illustrated in a well-known case of the sale of a property which had been advertised as having an area of 7800 m². The purchaser's intention, *known to the vendor*, was to divide the land into lots for resale. In fact the area was not more than 5119 m² and therefore unsuitable for the purchaser's objective. The *Cour de cassation* confirmed the cour d'appel's decision that, *given the knowledge of the vendor as to the purchaser's intentions*, the area of the property was an 'essential quality' which justified the finding that the *erreur* was of the 'substance itself', of that which was the *objet du contrat*.[9]

A somewhat similar case concerned the sale of a Louis XV chest of drawers which was also annulled for *erreur*. From the negotiations the vendor knew that the antiquity of the chest of drawers was the quality which the purchaser had principally in mind and without which he would not have made the purchase. This was said by the court to be further evidenced by the vendor carefully avoiding any 'exclusion of guarantee of antiquity knowing that such a clause would avoid the conclusion of the contract of sale'.[10]

If however the vendor is unaware and cannot be expected to be aware of the particular objective of the purchaser in respect of the qualities of the *chose objet du contrat*, then the purchaser's subjective intentions will not give rise to the nullity of the contract. An example of this was the purchase of a Delacroix because of the buyer's belief, unknown to the seller, that it had hung in the painter's bedroom. In fact it had not, and the court refused to annul the sale for *erreur*.[11]

Motives unrelated to the essential qualities

Motives which are unrelated to the 'essential qualities' of the object, e.g. the purchase of a wedding dress in anticipation of a daughter's wedding, which is then cancelled, would never justify the nullity of the purchase unless the parties had made it an express term of the contract.

Mistakes and terms of the contract

In some of the examples given above it could be argued that the *erreur* was actually in a term of the contract and as such would have enabled the purchaser to proceed for breach of contract. Indeed under French law the same set of facts, say the sale of a second-hand car, could give rise to four possible actions: an action *en nullité* for *erreur* or *dol*; an action *en résolution* for failure by the vendor to perform his contractual obligations under Art. 1184 of the *Code Civil* (see further below, pp. 319–321); an action for *vice caché* under Art. 1641 (see further, pp. 170–172); or a delictual action for damages for failure by the vendor to comply with his pre-contractual obligation to provide information under Art. 1383 (see further, pp. 127–128).

ENGLISH LAW COMPARISONS

Two points immediately arise in comparing the above cases with English law. First, what difference does it make under French law whether or not the vendor also knew of the mistake assuming, if he did know, that he said or did nothing to mislead the purchaser? Second, what about the doctrine of *caveat emptor* or at least for the purchaser to have exercised reasonable prudence?

To the first question the answer from a practical viewpoint is: very little. If the vendor knew of the mistake and said nothing then he will be liable for *dol* under Art.

1116 and the contract will be null (see below, pp. 125–126). There is no ability here to behave immorally as in the case of the vendor in *Smith* v. *Hughes* or in the examples given by Lord Atkin in *Bell* v. *Lever Bros* (see above, pp. 113–114).[12]

If the vendor did not know and believed that for example the article was a genuine antique, then the contract is still null under Art. 1110: 'It would be then a double erreur and a contract formed by two "erreurs" is a misunderstanding which cannot bind the parties'.[13] There is no test here, which is almost impossible, as we have seen, to satisfy, that 'the mistake must make the contract something different in kind from which it was believed to be, or destroy the identity of the subject matter' (see above, pp. 114–115).

As to the second question, there is no doctrine of *caveat emptor* in French law, which took over from Roman law the concepts that contracts for sale were to be made in good faith and hidden defects must be disclosed, and more recently has developed a doctrine of *l'obligation precontractuelle de renseignements* (see below, pp. 127–128).

However the party mistaken will not be allowed to take advantage of his mistake if it was due to an act of negligence on his own part.

ERREUR INEXCUSABLE

If the party mistaken has acted negligently, then he will be unable to obtain the nullity of the agreement. What amounts to negligence is to be decided on the facts of the individual case taking into account the age, experience and above all the person's professional qualifications related to the subject matter of the contract.

So where an architect purchased land and was warned by the seller of the existence of a town development plan, the architect had to discover for himself that the land was in fact unsuitable for the purposes of construction of the building which he had intended, and the *Cour de cassation* approved the judgement below that his claim to annul the contract for *erreur* should be dismissed.[14]

Generally the *erreur* of the party mistaken is *inexcusable* when he could and ought, taking account of his particular circumstances, to have informed himself of the facts in question, or made known to the other party the qualities in the subject matter of the contract to which he attached particular importance.[15]

DOL ET L'OBLIGATION DE RENSEIGNEMENTS

DOL – ORIGINS

The origins of the French law of *dol* are to be found in Roman law. Under the Roman law of sale the seller was bound to warrant the absence of fraud and that included 'artful concealment'.[16] It was concealment to withhold the existence of a neighbour so that the estate being sold appeared larger than it was which, if the purchaser had known, would have caused him not to conclude the contract.[17] *Dolus* was also defined as 'any craft or deceit employed for the circumvention or entrapping of another person',[18] a definition which has recently surfaced again in French law (see below, p. 126).

It was further considered as *dolus* not to disclose a material defect in the thing sold of which the seller was aware and generally *dolus* became the opposite of *bona fides* on which was based the contract of sale.[19] There is a clear interrelationship derived from Roman law between the French law of nullity for *erreur* and *dol* and the obligations relating to the provision of information and for *vices cachés* (see below, pp. 127–128). All can be regarded as manifestations of the more general principles of *bona fides*.

DOL UNDER THE CODE

Article 1116 of the *Code Civil* provides that *dol* is a cause of nullity when *les manoeuvres* practised by one of the parties are such that it is evident that without such *manoeuvres* the other party would not have contracted. The French *les manoeuvres* is virtually untranslatable. Usually it is rendered by 'artifices' although the author has a preference for 'machinations' as bringing out more clearly their dishonest nature.[20]

In any event the term is wide enough to cover a variety of actions such as the issue of false documents or the giving of false information, provided that the action is carried out with the intention to deceive. It is the intention to deceive which is significant rather than the specific character of the act itself. Even deliberately causing the other party to lose his wits by drinking too much may count!

There is no need for the *manoeuvres* to be a series of actions designed to deceive; a simple falsehood will be sufficient provided that the requisite intent is present. However such statements must be distinguished from what the Romans referred to as *dolus bonus*, *le bon dol*, that is the mere exaggeration of the qualities, value or cheapness of the article, which is tolerated by custom and is to be expected within the trade in question. But even then regard has to be had in deciding upon any particular case as to the professional qualifications, age and experience of the purchaser in relation to the seller.[21]

DOL COMPARED TO *ERREUR*

While, as we have noted, *erreur* must relate to the 'essential qualities of the thing determinative of the will of the party to enter into the contract' (above, pp. 121–122) this is not the case with *dol*. The deception may affect simply the motives of the party for entering into the contract or the qualities of the subject matter of the contract, which in either case may be purely personal to the party deceived. So if a person is deceived into buying a house in a particular town in the false belief induced by his vendor that he is about to be appointed to a position in the local authority there, then that would be a case of *dol*.

DOL MUST PROCEED FROM THE OTHER PARTY

A limitation on the scope of *dol* is that in accordance with Art. 1116 it must proceed from the other party to the contract. In practice this has been extended to include his agent or someone with whom he was acting in concert, but the rule can still create difficulties in the type of situation we examined earlier in relation to *cause* in *contrats unilatéraux* (see above, p. 98).

A married couple entered into a loan agreement with a credit company in order to purchase a second-hand car. The car never arrived and the borrowers, having been deceived by the garage proprietor, had not repaid the loan. The credit company sued for its return. The *Cour de cassation*, overruling the cour d'appel held that the contract of loan was not nullified by the fraud of the garage proprietor since he was not a party to that contract. Nor was the contract null for *vice du consentement* since the *erreur* related only to motive.[22] The same position applies to contracts for suretyship.

MUST *DOL* ACTUALLY CREATE *UN ERREUR?*

Traditionally it has been thought that the *manoeuvres*, in order to give rise to *dol*, must create an *erreur* in the mind of the victim. There must have been not only an intent to deceive but an actual deception.[23] However this view has been challenged in a decision by the Cour de Colmar which has argued that Art. 1116 of the *Code Civil* does not refer to *erreur* but only to the fact that 'without the "manoeuvres" the other party would not have contracted'. If therefore the one party has practised *manoeuvres* with the intention of inducing the other to act in a manner which they would not otherwise have done, then that can constitute *dol*. The act in this case consisted of a daughter and son-in-law keeping her 75-year-old mother confined under circumstances in which out of sheer exhaustion she signed a formal donation in their favour to the exclusion of her son, which the court annulled for *dol*.[24]

DOL INCIDENT AND *DOL* PRINCIPAL

The medieval lawyers derived from Roman law a distinction between the *dol* which had induced the contract to be entered into at all, and which therefore led to the contract itself being declared invalid, and the *dol* which affected only the terms of the contract. In the latter case the party deceived would still have entered into the contract had he known the truth but only on different terms. This distinction led to a difference in the remedies available. If the *dol* was *principal* then the deceived party could claim both rescission of the contract and damages. If it was only *incidens* then his remedy was limited to an adjustment of the contract terms, generally the price which he would have paid, if there had been no deception.

The general view of 'doctrine' today, supported by a recent decision of the *Cour de cassation*, is that the distinction is unnecessary and should be avoided.[25] Once the existence of *dol* as a factor determinative of the will of the creditor to enter into the particular contract has been established, then it is for the creditor to decide whether he wishes to claim nullity plus damages or to leave the contract in existence and limit his claim to one for an adjustment of the price.

The fact that *dol* is *une faute* also allows the creditor to proceed in an action for damages in 'delict' under Art. 1382 of the *Code Civil* and the *Cour de cassation* has held that he can do so even though the action for nullity under Art. 1116 was barred by prescription.[26] This ability to proceed under Art. 1382 means additionally that it is not necessary for the creditor to establish a deliberate *faute* but simply that the debtor behaved negligently. So a claim for damages may be made on the grounds of a failure of the debtor to comply with his obligation pre-contract to provide information (see below, p. 128).

CAN SILENCE/RETICENCE CREATE *DOL*?

As from the time of an *arrêt de principe* of the *Cour de cassation* in 1971 the answer has been that 'dol may be constituted by the silence of a party hiding from his co-contractor a fact which, if it had been known to him, would have stopped him from entering into the contract'.[27] This concept of *réticence dolosive* has been applied in a large number of cases both as between professionals and laymen and also even when the vendor was not a professional.

Some examples are: the sellers of a property, knowing the intention of the purchasers to turn it into a hotel, failed to warn them that the supply of water was insufficient for such usage;[28] the sale of a business without revealing a planning scheme for the elimination of a level crossing which was likely to cause a significant diminution in the number of customers;[29] and failure to disclose the widening of a road.[30] These examples contrast sharply with the judgement given by Lord Atkin in *Bell* v. *Lever Bros* where he maintained that the seller of the roadside garage who knew of the plan to build a bypass which would divert all the traffic away from the business, was entitled to keep quiet about it, and shows the wide divergence in this area between the two legal systems (see above, p. 117).

OBLIGATION DE RENSEIGNEMENTS (DISCLOSURE OF INFORMATION)

Apart from the obligations of disclosure which arise from the concept of *dol*, there now appears to be within French law a much wider obligation on a party in pre-contractual negotiations to advise the other party as to facts within his own knowledge which he could not expect, in the circumstances of the case, the other party to be aware of, and which he knew or ought to have known would either cause the other party not to enter into the contract at all, or at least only on different terms. While the obligation is assimilated to that of *réticence dolosive* discussed above and to that of *vices cachés* (below, pp. 170–174), it seems to exist as a separate doctrine in its own right based on the principle of *bonne foi*.[31]

So in a decision of the *Cour de cassation* in 1981 it was held that the vendor company and its manager, professionals in property development, had an obligation to inform the purchasers, who lacked experience in such matters, of the position regarding the roads and services of the land which they were purchasing for development. Their failure to do so rendered the contract null.[32]

After some hesitation the *Cour de cassation* seems now to have concluded that there is an obligation on the part of a bank which lends money against the security of a guarantee to advise the guarantors as to the already hopelessly indebted state of the borrower towards the bank. Failure of the bank to do so was held to be a 'breach of its obligation to contract in good faith and to constitute therefore "dol par reticence" '.[33]

The basis of the obligation to disclose has been described variously as one of acting 'honestly' or 'in good faith' or 'in conformity with the legitimate confidence that the one party may have in the other'. The obligation is therefore particularly applicable where the one party is a professional and the other is a layman as regards the subject matter of the contract in question; or because of his position, as in the case of the bank, the one party has access to data denied to the other. But it can apply also to the layman: 'even a person dealing with a professional is not dispensed from supplying him with information in his possession the absence of which would affect consent'.[34]

Each case, however, will be looked at on its own facts and account taken of all the circumstances involved. These will include the nature of the contract, the significance of the failure to inform on the consent of the other party, the relations between the parties, their respective professional skills or otherwise, and the possibility and costs for the party allegedly deceived of discovering the facts. So for example it would not be expected that a tenant of a short let during the season would visit the premises in advance to determine their condition, whereas someone taking a lease of shooting rights could be expected to visit them in advance in order to determine the position regarding the game to be found there.[35]

As regards consumers the obligation to provide information pre-contract has now been reinforced by law no. 92–60 of 18 January 1992 which provides that:

> All professional sellers or providers of services must before the conclusion of the contract put the consumer in a position to know the essential characteristics of the goods or services. The professional seller of goods must also advise the consumer the period during which it is foreseeable that the parts necessary for the use of the goods will be available on the market. That period must be brought to the knowledge of the seller by the manufacturer or importer.

ENGLISH LAW COMPARISON

MISREPRESENTATION

While they may be said to be aimed largely at the same mischief, and while there are some similarities between fraudulent misrepresentation and *dol*, there are also wide differences. The definition of fraud is narrower than *dol* and that of misrepresentation narrower than *manoeuvres*. But the major distinction is the acceptance in French law of the *dol par réticence* and the virtual denial in English law of misrepresentation by silence.

At one time it could be said that the English doctrine of non-fraudulent misrepresentation was wider than any remedy available under French law, which required that not only should the statement have been false but it should have been made with an intent to deceive. However the position now is that once the obligation to inform the creditor is established, then it is no longer necessary to show that the failure to inform was intentional.[36]

DUTY TO INFORM

As we would expect from the fact of English law not accepting silence as constituting a misrepresentation, other than in exceptional circumstances, it also does not accept a general obligation to inform during pre-contractual negotiations. It follows that the French doctrine of *obligation précontractuelle de renseignements* cannot really be compared with that of 'innocent misrepresentation'. The attempt to establish in English law such an obligation to inform was made by Lord Mansfield in *Carter* v. *Boehme* in 1786: 'good faith forbids either party by concealing what he privately knows to draw the other into a bargain from his ignorance of that fact and his believing the contrary'. But, as Atiyah has demonstrated, the attempt failed with the rise of economic liberalism.[37]

A further effort was made by Lord Denning in 1975 to establish a broadly based doctrine of 'inequality of bargaining power' which would allow the court to grant relief if 'the bargaining power of one party is grievously impaired by . . . his own ignorance coupled with undue influence brought upon him . . . by one who may be moved solely by his own self-interest'.[38] However, the suggestion fell on deaf ears despite the view of the authors of Cheshire that 'it could be a fruitful source for future development of the law.[39] Indeed 'inequality of bargaining power' and the French 'inequality of information' have an obvious connection. As has been observed in French doctrine, 'The good faith of a professional includes the obligation to put the layman on the same level of knowledge as himself so that they can deal on equal terms.'[40]

But it is difficult to see how the duty to inform in French law could be established easily in English law since it is a part of a series of concepts, error *in substantia*, obligation of contracting in good faith, a general duty to disclose latent defects and *dol par réticence*, none of which are part of English law.[41] Essentially there is a conflict between a law which increasingly seems to base contractual obligations on the grounds of morality to the detriment perhaps of commercial security, and one which places the security of commercial transactions before the requirements of morality.

If there ever is to be a convergence of the two then it is surely English law which must make the move of replacing its more rigid concepts with the greater flexibility and disposition to correct the imbalance of the knowledge of the parties, which is characteristic today of the approach of French law to the pre-contractual stage.

It is interesting to note that in New Zealand there has recently been an attempt made to develop the concept that there exists within the common law a general duty in contract to act in good faith – see the article by Michael Whincup in the *Law Society's*

Gazette for 29 September 1993 commenting on the New Zealand High Court decision in *Livingstone* v. *Roskill* [1992] 3 NZLR 230. However the reasoning of the learned Judge who decided that case, and the authorities upon which he relied do not appear convincing, and it is agreed with Michael Whincup that English law is far from accepting any such general principle. Equally the reason normally given for this refusal, that it would promote uncertainty, which means giving precedence to certainty over fairness, seems increasingly out of line with modern judicial thinking in other legal systems.

NOTES

1. *Traité des obligations* (1761) B.29 no. 18 (edn of 1827).
2. The second paragraph refers to *erreur sur la personne* with which it is not proposed to deal. For those interested see Nicholas pp. 92–4 for a brief account in English.
3. Weill and Terré s. 167 on p. 174.
4. Civ. 28 January 1913 S.1913 1.147 quoted Weill and Terré p. 175.
5. Starck s.388 and *Source Book* (2nd edition) p. 357: 'la qualité que l'acheteur avait principalement en vue et sans laquelle il n'aurait pas acheté'.
6. Starck s.390: 'On notera encore – et surtout – que les qualités dites "substantielles" ont, en général, un caractère *objectif* en ce sens, qu'à les supposer établies, elles eussent été determinantes pour tout individu'.
7. See the cases listed in Starck s.389 and the notes on p. 133. The judgement in the demolition case 14 October 1931 (Cour d'Appel de Paris 4th Ch.D.1934 II.128) is given in Von Mehren and Gordley p. 1033. The concrete was both of an exceptional hardness and contained an unusually high proportion of steel reinforcement, facts unknown to the contractor Marchand et fils but known to the employer Ciment Verre. This case may be contrasted with a number of English decisions such as *Bottoms* v. *York Corporation* (1892) in which it has been held that, in the absence of any express warranty or representation by the employer, unexpected difficulties in the performance of the contract, even if anticipated by the employer from his own knowledge, did not entitle the contractor to any remedy. See Hudson *Building Contracts* 10th edn, pp. 269 and 270 and *Davis Contractors* v. *Fareham UDC* [1956] AC 696.
8. Starck s.391.
9. D.P. 1932 I.129 Note Josserand (the Villa Jacqueline case) *Source Book* p. 349.
10. Orleans 21 January 1931 D.H. 1931.172 *Source Book* p. 324.
11. Tr.civ. Seine 8 December 1950. 1951.50 quoted Weill and Terré p. 177.
12. The examples given by Lord Atkin are set out in Cheshire p. 235. They all involve A having no remedy in circumstances in which his loss could have been avoided had B been commercially honest and disclosed the truth although, as Lord Atkin makes clear in the absence of any warranty or representation, it is irrelevant whether B knew of A's mistake or not since the mistakes all relate to motive. Only, as we have seen below (p. 174) if the mistake is both as to the fundamental nature of the subject matter of the contract and is shared by both parties is there the possibility of the contract being void.

    Even then, as Lawson has pointed out, this latter requirement is illogical. English law, having no general obligation of disclosure and unilateral mistake being normally of no effect, if A's right to maintain that the contract is void were to be dependent upon B's sharing in A's mistake, then B, while strenuously denying that his conduct was fraudulent, would be bound to maintain that he knew all along of the mistake which A was making. This puts a 'premium on a particularly shameless form of lying' (Lawson, *A Common Lawyer looks at the Civil Law*, reprinted Greenwood Press, Connecticut 1977, at p. 97).

    Under French law, however, B is in a dilemma. Either he acted in good faith and shared A's mistake and the contract is void for *erreur ex pacto*; or he knew of A's mistake and kept quiet which would mean the contract was null for *dol*. Note by Josserand *Source Book*, 3rd edition, p. 325.

13. Starck s.390 p.134.
14. Civ. 1re sect. civ 2 March 1964. Quoted Weill and Terré note 327, p. 185.
15. See Starck s.418.
16. Dig. XVIII.1.43.2.
17. Dig. XVIII.1.35.8 and see 'Three Notes on the Text' by David Daube *LQR* vol.73 p. 379.
18. Dig.IV.3.1.2.
19. Dig.XIX.1.13: 'If the seller knew [the timber was unsound] but was silent and so deceived the buyer he will have to make good all losses which have fallen on him in consequence of the purchase'.
20. This is brought out clearly when comparing the two terms in Roget's *Thesaurus*. Compare also the definition by Labeo D.IV.3.1.2 where he refers to *dol* as being *machinationem*.
21. Weill and Terré p. 192 and note 365.
22. Chambre commerciale Gaz.Pal. 1978, somm.103. Starck s.448.
23. Starck s.430.
24. Colmar 30 January 1970 JCP 70 II 16609. See for commentary Starck ss.432–4 who approves of the decision, but it remains a matter of controversy. See Weill and Terré pp. 189–90 note 351. They suggest that while the decision to nullify the act was clearly correct, it could have been based on the narrower ground of the theories of *captation* and *suggestion* which have been used specifically to nullify donations obtained through fraudulent or deceitful *manoeuvres*, without bringing into question the traditional definition of the requirements for *dol*.
25. See Weill and Terré s.184; Starck s.446 and Ghestin s.440; Cass. com. 2 May 1984, Bull.civ. IV no. 145, p. 123.
26. Cass. civ. 4 February 1975 JCP 1975 II 18100.
27. Cass. civ. 3e 15 January 1971.
28. Cass. civ. 7 May 1974 Bull. civ. III no. 186.
29. Cass. com. 21 May 1977 JCP 1977 IV. 35.
30. Cass. civ. 13 February 1967 Bull. civ. I no. 58.
31. See Ghestin ss.475–566 and his summary in *Contract Law Today*, pp. 155–65 and Starck ss.272–9. Also a recent decision of the *Cour de cassation* in which the judgement of the cour d'appel was quashed because they should have investigated whether or not the conduct of the purchaser, a local authority who were negotiating the resale of the land, in not disclosing to the seller the initiation of a revision to the zoning regulations, which would increase the value of the land, did not constitute a failure to act in good faith which would nullify the sale. Cass. civ. 27 March 1991 Bull. civ. III no. 108.
32. 3e Chambre civil 3 February 1984 D.1981 p. 457. As Ghestin comments, the assimilation of *dol* with *l'obligation précontractuelle de renseignements* of the professional seller is enlarging the scope of the remedy for *dol* in that it is no longer being required that the vendor had an intention to deceive – an essential requisite for a finding of *dol*. However it appears that where the vendor is not a professional, then a finding of 'intention to deceive the other party in his decision to enter into the contract' will be required in order to provide legal justification for a finding of *dol*. Cass. civ. 12 November 1987; Bull. civ. I no. 293 p. 211. Ghestin p. 476.
33. Epoux Pougnand of 10 May 1989 (inédit), the subject of a report in *Revue Trimestrielle de droit civil*, 'Formation du Contrat' by Jacques Mestre, 1989 p. 738, who points out the importance of the decision as confirming that Art. 1134 para. 3 of the *Code Civil* applies not merely to the performance of contracts *de bonne foi* but also to their formation.
34. 1re Chambre civil 24 November 1976 Bull. 1. no. 370 p. 291. A private individual who sold his second-hand car to a garage proprietor failed to disclose that the person who had sold the car to him had rewound the kilometer to zero.
35. See Ghestin s.500 on p. 554 and cases cited in note 133.
36. The *Cour de cassation* quashed a decision which had rejected a plea for nullity by the purchasers of a mobile home which was being bought with the objective of establishing it permanently on a particular site, without the judges having examined if the seller was not under an obligation to draw the purchaser's attention to the regulation that a special official permit was required for such a purpose (D.1982 IR p. 526).

    As Weill and Terré have observed, the dominant principle is no longer that 'the buyer ought to enquire' (or as we would say 'let the buyer beware') but that the 'seller should be fair and honest' (s.183 on p. 194).
37. Atiyah p.168.

38. In *Lloyds Bank Ltd* v. *Bundy* [1975] QB at p. 339.
39. Cheshire p. 300 after quoting Denning's views *in extenso*.
40. Th.Ivainer (1972) 'De l'ordre technique à l'ordre public technologique' JCP 1972 I 2495 nos 37 et seq, quoted in Harris & Tallon at p. 164.
41. Nicholas in *Contract Law Today* p. 178 and the concluding section to Part 4, p. 188 et seq.

10 Mistake – German law

GENERAL BASIS

The general basis for the German law of mistake is to be found in s.119 of the *BGB*. A party is entitled to rescind his 'expression of will' (*Willenserklärung*), for mistake when he would not have made the declaration had he known and appreciated intelligently the true facts of the situation, and the mistake relates to either: s.119 (1) the expression or content of the *Willenserklärung* itself, or s.119 (2) the characteristics of a thing or person which are regarded in business dealings as essential.

MISTAKE AS TO EXPRESSION

A mistake as to expression occurs when the intentions which a person has formed quite correctly are not expressed properly in the declaration which he makes. So if a person visiting the Stock Exchange makes a movement of his hand which corresponds to a signal used in the Exchange for effecting an order, and it is treated as such by a broker, the visitor will be entitled to rescind.[1]

Again a person may make an error in the expression of his figures so that they do not correspond to the intentions which he had correctly formed. This will be treated as an error as to content and therefore grounds for rescission if there is, say, a confusion between the prices of two different items or it was the common intention of the parties that the price should be fixed at the 'market price' and the mistake is simply one of calculation.[2] However this type of mistake is to be distinguished from one in which a person, because of an error in his own calculations, decides to make a particular purchase because he believes it to be advantageous. This does not allow him to rescind since it is then only a mistake as to motive.

MISTAKE AS TO ESSENTIAL QUALITY

The distinction made in the previous paragraph between an error as to expression of the *Willenserklärung, Geschäftsirrtum* and motive (*Motivirrtum*), is not always easy to draw. However of perhaps more practical importance is the second paragraph of s.119 which refers to the 'qualities of the person or thing considered in business dealings as essential'.[3]

The value of an article is not considered as an 'essential quality' so the purchaser cannot rescind because he believed the article to be worth more than its true value.[4] However the age or authenticity of an antique, the year of manufacture of a vehicle, the creditworthiness of the other party to a credit transaction, but not to one for cash, are all examples of 'essential qualities'.[5] Although generally the mistake will be that of the purchaser it can sometimes be that of the seller. So where a painting attributed to a particular painter was sold and later turned out to have been painted by a different, much better known painter, it was held that the seller was entitled to rescind the sale agreement on the ground of mistake.[6]

For mistake to apply, it is not necessary that the other party knew of the mistake but it is necessary that he knew, either by implication or expressly, that the party mistaken regarded the quality as essential. This will be determined by examining the circumstances of the transaction. Knowledge will be implied if the transaction is of such a nature that the quality in question would be treated by anyone as being essential. The authenticity of an antique is obviously an essential quality of the purchase where this is made from a specialist dealer. However this would probably not be the case where an article was bought cheaply in a bazaar.[7]

Express knowledge depends on the party mistaken having made known to the other, prior to the purchase, that he regards as essential that particular quality.

It is to be noted that the mistake is subjective in that no account is taken as to whether or not the person mistaken was himself at fault. The French doctrine of the mistake being excluded as a cause for rescission if it was *inexcusable* (see above, p. 124) does not apply in German law.

COMPENSATION FOR NEGATIVE INTEREST

Because German law allows for the contract to be annulled, even if the mistake is that of one party only and even if the party mistaken was himself careless, this much wider right to rescind than that which exists under either English or French law creates the need for a means to protect the interests of the other party and the security of commercial transactions.[8]

For this reason German law requires that the party mistaken, if he exercises his right to rescind, must compensate the other for the costs which he has incurred, the so-called 'negative interest' or *Vertrauensinteresse*, by relying on the mistaken party's declaration of intention to enter into the contract. This is intended to put the other party in the same position as he would have been had he not relied upon such a declaration.

The compensation would include therefore costs and expenses incurred in the negotiation of, and preparations for, the contract and also the loss of profit that could have been earned on another opportunity which has been forgone because of the seller's expectation that the contract would materialize.[9]

Since the effect of mistake is to render the contract voidable rather than void it would be open to the party mistaken to affirm the contract rather than to claim rescission and pay compensation.

The obligation to compensate does not, of course, apply if the other party either was aware, or ought to have been aware (i.e. his failure to be aware was due to his own negligence), of the grounds upon which the mistaken party was entitled to claim the nullity of the contract (s.122 (2) of the *BGB*).

RESCISSION AND CONTRACTS OF SALE

There is an important practical limitation on the application of the rules relating to mistake in regard to contracts of sale. As soon as the risk in the goods has passed to the purchaser, he is no longer entitled to exercise his rights to rescind under s.119(2) but is limited to the particular rights relating to defects which are contained in ss.462 and 463 of the *BGB* (see further below, pp. 209–210). This would not however apply if the mistake was one as to content of expression since this situation is not covered by the particular rules relating to defects.

Dannemann on p. 26 refers to a case in which the deputy head of a school made a mistake in transaction when he ordered 25 'gros' rolls of toilet paper mistakenly believing that 'gros' meant large when in fact it is an old-fashioned expression for twelve dozen. The school was allowed the right to rescind the contract for 3,600 rolls of toilet paper. LG Hanau 30.6.1978 NJW 1979, 21. This is the kind of case in which rescission for mistake would still be allowed after the risks in the goods had passed to the purchaser since it is a mistake as the quantity and not quality for which there is no remedy under Art. 459 *BGB*.

Also the doctrine of abstraction which was considered earlier (see above, pp. 100–101) will usually apply. Although therefore the contract may be rescinded, the transfer of the goods will not be, and the rights of the parties will be decided according to the principles discussed previously of unjust enrichment (see above, pp. 100–102). But today in cases of fraud even if the doctrine of abstraction is applied by the courts they may well in that event hold the transfer as well as the contract affected by the fraud so that both will be rescinded.

MISTAKE AND THE FORMATION OF THE CONTRACT

The mistakes which have been referred to above relate, as Cohn has pointed out,[10] to the declaration of the one party itself and not to the agreement (*Vertrag*). It would be possible for both declarations to be made without either containing a mistake in the declaration itself and yet for no contract to be formed because they did not correspond with each other. Cohn comments that *Raffles* v. *Wickelhaus* would have been treated by a German court as one of dissent, in which no contract was ever formed because the declarations were ambiguous, and not as one of mistake.[11]

MISTAKE AS TO THE BASIS OF THE CONTRACT

As we have seen, motives are not taken into account under s.119(1) of the *BGB* but are taken into account under s.119(2) when they concern the characteristics of the thing which is the subject of the contract or of the person with whom the contract is made. However a mistake, in principle by both parties, or at least by one party with the other being aware of the erroneous supposition and raising no objection to it, and which, if the parties had been aware of the truth, would have affected or been incorporated in good faith into their respective declarations of intention, may give rise to the right, if not to have the contract rescinded, then to have the terms adjusted. This is referred to as the doctrine of *Wegfall des Geschäftsgrundlage*.[12]

Only something which is independent of the wills of the parties, and fundamental to the underlying basis upon which their contract is founded, so that it would be contrary to good faith under s.242 of the *BGB* to maintain the contract in its original form, may fall within the scope of the doctrine. Generally if the contract can be maintained, then the courts will seek to make an appropriate adjustment to its terms so as to maintain an equilibrium between the obligations of the parties. Only exceptionally, if it proves impossible to do so, will the contract be declared void.[13]

The doctrine, which was enunciated by Oertmann, will be considered further in what Horn et al. refer to as its 'objective form'[14] when discussing frustration of the contract and the related doctrines in the civil law (see below, pp. 345–346).

It appears that the doctrine could apply, even on a contract for the sale of goods after the risk has passed to the purchaser, although the dividing line between the rules relating to the doctrine in its subjective form, which is closely related to a mistake common to both parties, and those relating to latent defects is a matter of contention in modern German law.[15]

FRAUD

Under s.123 of the *BGB*, if a person has been induced to make a declaration of intention by fraud, then he is entitled to rescind. German law does not accept the distinction between *dolus causam dans* and *dolus incidens* which was certainly at one time part of French law though, as referred to earlier, would appear now to have been abandoned (above, pp. 126–127). Indeed German law goes further and will treat as fraud *dolus eventualis*, that is, a statement made in the knowledge that it was possibly false and accepting the consequences were it to be so, if the party making the statement also knew that it might decide the other to enter into the contract.[16]

The deception need not be as to an essential quality. Unlike the case of mistake, the contract will be voidable for fraud even if the fraud affected only the motives of the deceived party. Nor need the deception constitute the sole determining reason why the victim entered into the contract provided that it was one reason.[17]

It is also not necessary for the party committing the fraud to have had any intention of injuring the other. It is sufficient for him to have behaved 'disloyally'.[18]

The contracting party will be responsible for any fraudulent acts which may be committed by those engaged by him to assist in the negotiations for the contract whether he knew of their fraudulent acts or not.[19]

The fraud need not, however, be that of the other party to the contract or his representative. It can be that of a third party if the person to whom the declaration was made knew or by reason of any negligence did not know of the fraud (s.123(2) of the *BGB*).[20]

In this respect German law is wider than French law, which restricts the right of the party deceived to the case in which there was actual knowledge by the other party to the contract of the fraud of the third party and does not extend the right to the case in which, however easily, the other party could have known of it.[21]

Additionally, if a party to the principal contract who is fraudulent can be said to have been acting for the benefit of the other party in arranging a related contract, say for suretyship, then that related contract itself may be voidable on the grounds of his fraud.[22] Again, this is going further than would French law which has consistently held that the fact of the principal contract being void for fraud does not affect the contract of suretyship in the absence of proof of complicity.[23]

DOES MERE SILENCE CONSTITUTE FRAUD?

Silence only constitutes fraud if there is a duty to provide information. There is no general obligation under German law for one party to give information to the other during the pre-contractual negotiations. Whether or not the duty exists is determined in the individual case taking into account all relevant facts such as business usage and the relationships of the parties and following the principle of good faith.

If the seller knows of some fact relating to the goods being sold which could affect the purchaser's decision to purchase and knows that the purchaser is both unaware of its existence, and not capable in the circumstances of discovering it then the court may find that he is under a duty to disclose. Indeed fraudulent failure by the seller to disclose a fault in the goods will give the purchaser a right to claim under s.463(2) of the *BGB* without the need for the purchaser to prove that the deception caused him to make a mistake.[24]

The courts will more readily find that a duty to disclose exists where the seller is a professional and the purchaser a layman, and especially if the failure to inform could be dangerous to the purchaser. The seller is then obliged to give all the information necessary to allow the purchaser to enter the contract in full knowledge of the obligations which he is assuming. In the particular case of second-hand cars it now appears to be the rule that the professional seller must give information which is not readily available to the purchaser, such as the fact that the car has been involved in a serious accident.[25]

However, as between professionals the obligations of the seller are reduced. So in a case where a manufacturer of certain machinery sold his goods exclusively to specialist dealers he was not obliged to mention in his mounting instructions that failure to follow these could create a safety hazard. However, if previous instructions were incorrect then he must make the position clear in any new instructions which he issued.[26]

If information is given, then it would be fraudulent if there were only a partial disclosure and only that which was favourable was disclosed and that which was unfavourable was withheld.[27] In much the same way it would be contrary to good faith if information was given which was honestly believed by the person providing it to be true at the time, but he subsequently discovered it to be false and failed to disclose this fact.[28]

NOTES

1. Example given by Ranke and Boulin para.70 on p. 300.
2. See the cases quoted in Rodière (ed.) *Les Vices du Consentement*, note 25 on p. 125.
3. This is the suggestion made by Zweigert and Kotz on p. 96 vol. 2 and by Rodière (ed.) op.cit. p. 124.
4. RG HRR 1932, 224.
5. Age and authenticity of an antique RGZ 124,116; year of manufacture of a vehicle quoted Ranke and Boulin para. 73 p. 300; creditworthiness of the other party RGZ 66,385.
6. Bundesgerichtshof (VIII ZR 135/87) 8 June 1988 [1988] DB 2399.
7. Rodière (ed.) op.cit. note 20 on p. 124.
8. See further Sabbath *ICLQ* vol. 13 p. 814 et seq.
9. Jauernig, note 3 under s.123 of the *BGB*: 'Zu ersten sind zum Beispiel Vertragsabschlusskosten, infolge Ablehnung oder Unterlassung anderweiten Geschäfts entgangener Gewinn'.
10. S.148 on p. 81.
11. S.160 on p. 85. The author agrees with Cohn that this is a more logical way of approaching the issue.
12. An example quoted by Rodière (ed.) is that of a contract of sale which was concluded in the belief that the sale was state-aided (note 22 p. 123). Horn et al. refer to BGH NJW 1976, 565, a case in which the contract was held void because the football player who was being transferred was barred (note 25 p. 142).
13. Ranke and Boulin s.78 on p. 302.
14. Horn et al. p. 142 refer to the distinction made by Larenz between the 'subjective' foundations of the contract which are akin to a common mistake and the 'objective' foundations which are related to the question of the effect on the contract of subsequent events, completely changing the basis upon which the contract was expected to be performed, and rendering its performance for the debtor intolerable.
15. See BGH NJW 1976, 565 (transfer of a football player who was in fact barred; contract held void). As referred to earlier (see above, pp. 123–124) the same issue arises in French law but does not cause the same difficulty since the remedies for *vices cachés* are not regarded as being the exclusive actions open to the purchaser after delivery of the goods.
16. Rodière (ed.) op.cit. p. 131 para. B II and note 62.
17. RG 3 April 1933, Warn. 1933 no. 92.
18. RG 30 April 1925, RGZ III 5,7.
19. BGH 17 Nov. 1960 BGHZ 33, 302.
20. BGH 47, 227 ff.
21. Weill and Terré p. 197 note 389.
22. BGH NJW 1962, 2195.
23. 'Le dol du débiteur principal est sans effet sur la validité du cautionnement, puisqu'il n'émane pas du créancier' Cass. com. 27 July 1986 JCP 1986 IV p. 294. For the case of complicity see Cass. com. 25 March 1974 Bull. civ. no. 104 p. 83.
24. BGH (V ZR 21/88) 7 July 1989 [1989] DB 2426.
25. BGH NJW 1967, 1222.
26. BGH (VI ZR 179/84) 4 February 1986 [1986] DB 1113.

27. So on a contract for a guarantee, while there is no obligation to give information relating to the debtor's financial position, it would constitute a fraud if only favourable information was provided and that which was unfavourable was not disclosed (RGZ 91,81).

28. The claim in this instance for damages would be in delict under Art. 826 of the *BGB* – see Markesinis p. 659 and the cases cited there.

11 Performance obligations

GENERAL

It is often stated that a distinction between the English common law and the civil law is that under common law contractual obligations are strict whereas under civil law they are fault-based. According to this view if, under an English contract, a party fails to comply with an obligation then he is in breach of his contract whether he is at fault or not. That when he entered into the contract he undertook to do the impossible is no defence.[1] His only possibility of obtaining relief is then under the doctrine of frustration (see below, pp. 316–319).

Traditionally under the civil law, however, a party is only to be held in breach of contract if he was at fault in his failure to comply with his obligations. A clear expression of the 'fault' principle is to be found in ss. 275, 276, 280 and 285 of the *BGB*.[2]

The distinction is partially correct. French and German law do generally require that there should be an element of fault present in the behaviour of the party concerned in order to support an action for damages for breach of contract – a requirement which is derived from Roman law.[3] Equally, however, the courts by the way in which they have interpreted and supplemented the code provisions have reduced to some degree that practical importance of the 'fault' principle and brought their respective laws, in terms of the results achieved, closer to the common law. The ways in which this has been done will be shown in the following sections.

Further, the requirement of 'fault' in the sense of proving negligence is not present under either French or German law in the specific actions for hidden defects which apply after the delivery of goods or the *réception* (*Abnahme*) of works (see further below, pp. 150–151).[4]

Equally, while the common law does apply what has been referred to as 'a guarantee for results' for contracts for the sale of goods and construction works, this principle is by no means universal.[5] In a wide range of contracts for services, whether of professional people such as doctors, lawyers, consulting engineers or accountants, or of others, like technicians engaged in repair and maintenance work, the common law does not imply into their contracts any such guarantee. Under those contracts the 'debtor', to use the civil law term, is responsible only for using 'reasonable skill and care', which means that he can only be liable for breach of contract if he can be shown to have been negligent, i.e. at 'fault', unless the terms of the contract provide otherwise.[6]

Within the limitations of this book it is possible to examine and compare only briefly the most common of the obligations for performance in commercial contracts which, within the common law are implied terms, and within the civil law are usually *règles supplétives* or exceptionally *règles impératives* (see above, p. 8). Attention will therefore be concentrated on:

1. Conformity of the goods/work/services with the implied contract terms relating to description/quality and fitness for purpose.
2. Latent defects/*vices cachés*.
3. Time of delivery/performance.

CONFORMITY OF THE GOODS/WORK/SERVICES WITH THE CONTRACT – ENGLISH LAW

The obligations of the seller or contractor are based either on express terms or on terms which are implied by law. While the express terms may extend the seller/contractor's implied obligations, terms which exclude or limit these may be either invalid or subject to the test of 'reasonableness' under the Unfair Contract Terms Act (see below, pp. 295–296).

IMPLIED TERMS CONTRACTS OF SALE

Sale by description

The rule is contained in s.13 of the *SGA* 1979. Where there is a sale by description there is an implied condition[7] that the goods will correspond to that description. The implied condition will apply whenever the buyer is relying on the description, e.g. to unascertained goods which he has not seen. It will also apply even to sales of specific goods unless it is clear either that the buyer is purchasing the item because of its unique qualities or that he is in no way relying on the description. Reliance by the buyer has been said to be 'the natural index of a sale by description'.[8]

Quality

Where the seller is selling in the course of a business, there is an implied condition under s.14(2) of the *SGA* that the goods are of 'merchantable quality' except if, before the contract is made, the defects are drawn to the buyer's attention or the buyer examines the goods and the defect ought to have been revealed by such examination.

The main difficulties which have arisen in connection with this section of the Act have been in the interpretation of the phrase 'merchantable quality'. The following conclusions are drawn from the wording of s.14(6) of the Act[9] and recent decisions of the courts:

1. Where goods are suitable for more than one purpose then they must be suitable for those purposes for which goods of that sort are commonly bought, but not for every possible purpose.[10]

2. Goods are not of merchantable quality if, although they are still usable, they do not correspond to the purposes for which such goods are commonly bought in that they are unreliable, unsafe, uncomfortable or, in respect of an expensive passenger vehicle, the buyer's ability to drive it 'with pride in the vehicle's outward and interior appearance'.[11]

3. The requirement of merchantable quality applies also to second-hand goods. With such goods, commonly motor vehicles, it is a question of whether, having regard to the price, age and defect complained of, the goods were as fit for their purpose as could reasonably be expected.[12]

4. Goods which are only suitable for use, if applied or operated under certain specific conditions, will only be regarded as being of merchantable quality if appropriate warnings or instructions are provided.[13]

5. Goods are not of merchantable quality if they do not continue to be fit for the purpose for a reasonable time, which is to be determined from the nature of the goods and their quality.[14]

6. The price at which the goods are bought may be a relevant factor in determining whether the goods are of merchantable quality or not. If goods could have more than one use, then the price paid may be an indicator as to the use intended, e.g. a second-hand car bought at a low price for spare parts only and not as a road vehicle. However if a high price is paid because of the buyer's mistaken belief in a quality of the goods, which is not a term of the contract, it will be irrelevant.[15]

7. Strangely, merchantable quality does not imply that the goods are of any specific quality. If goods are sold in various grades then it is sufficient that they would satisfy even the lowest grade at which goods of that description would commonly be sold unless the price paid by the buyer is clearly appropriate to a higher grade and the difference in price is such that the buyer can resell only at a substantially lower price.[16]

Fitness for purpose

Section 14(3) of the *SGA* deals with the position where the buyer has either expressly or impliedly made known to the seller the particular purpose for which he requires the goods and the seller is selling in the course of a business. There is then an implied condition that the goods are reasonably fit for that purpose unless the circumstances show that the buyer did not rely, or that it was unreasonable for him to rely, on the seller's skill or judgement. The following points arise:

1. The purpose need not be specific; it may indeed be quite general, as for example the sale of a product to be compounded into animal feedstuffs where its fitness for any animal should have been within the seller's reasonable contemplation.[17]

2. Provided that the buyer has made known the purpose to the seller, then the onus is on the seller to establish that the buyer did not rely on his skill and judgement or that it was unreasonable for him to do so. This may be easier for the seller to do, the more generally the purpose has been expressed, and when that general purpose

covers a wide range of possibilities, only one of which is the buyer's particular purpose, and that is one which the seller could not reasonably have been expected to contemplate.

So a requirement that goods shall be fit for export hardly differs from their being of merchantable quality.[18] If the buyer wants the goods for export to some particular territory which has unusual characteristics, and wishes to rely on the seller to provide goods to meet these, then he must specify the territory in question in a way which shows that he relies on the seller's skill and judgement.[19] The implied condition, as Atiyah points out, is only that the goods shall be 'reasonably fit for the buyer's purpose' and if that purpose is highly unique within a broad category of purposes then it is necessary for the buyer to specify that unique purpose.[20]

3. What has been said above under merchantable quality regarding durability of the goods and instructions or warnings as to their use applies equally to cases of fitness for a particular purpose.

LATENT DEFECTS – ENGLISH LAW

Unlike the civil law, the common law does not have particular provisions which relate to hidden defects. It has, however, clearly been established judicially that the seller's liability under s.14(3) is strict so that although he could not have discovered the hidden defect he will still be liable for it.[21] The same position would appear to apply as regards merchantable quality for which again liability is strict unless the buyer examines the goods before the contract is made and the examination ought to have revealed such defect.

But while the implied condition under s.13 that, on a sale by description the goods will comply with that description, applies to private sales, neither paras (2) nor (3) of s.14 apply to sales made otherwise than by the seller in the course of his business. Here the old rule of *caveat emptor* still holds good. This is in sharp contrast with French and German law where the rules relating to latent defects apply to all sales, whether made in the course of business or privately. The status of the seller does, however, in French law affect the remedies to which the purchaser is entitled, and in both laws the extent to which the seller can exclude or limit his responsibilities (see below, pp. 172, 173 and 209).

TIME OF DELIVERY/PERFORMANCE

Time of delivery of the goods in ordinary commercial contracts is generally held to be of the essence of the contract. It follows that failure to deliver by the contractual date will be a breach of a condition of the contract and the buyer will be entitled to reject the goods.[22] If no time has been stated then the seller must deliver within a reasonable time.

CONTRACTS FOR SERVICES

As was indicated earlier (see above, p. 140), contracts for services differ significantly from those relating to the sale of goods. According to the Supply of Goods and Services Act 1972 s.13: 'in a contract for the supply of services where the supplier is acting in the course of a business there is an implied term that the supplier will carry out the services with reasonable skill and care'. There is therefore no guarantee of a result and the supplier's liability depends on proof of his negligence. This means that the supplier of the service will only be liable if he has failed to exercise the reasonable skill and care to be expected of an ordinarily competent member of his profession or trade.

The test is therefore an objective one and not one related to the degree of particular skill which that person happens himself to possess.[23]

TIME FOR PERFORMANCE

Time for performance will only be regarded as of the essence if the contract specifically states this or the nature of the contract or other circumstances show that it ought to be so considered. However, failure to complete on time or any extended period of time allowed under the contract will be a breach of contract for which the supplier is liable in damages.

If the time is not stated in the contract then there is an implied term that the supplier will carry out the services within a reasonable time, which is a question of fact in any given circumstances.[24]

CONTRACTS FOR WORKS

Although the contractor's obligations for building or engineering works will normally be set out specifically in the contract documents, there will still be times when it is necessary to rely on the terms which are implied by law. These are that the contractor:

- will carry out his work in a good and workmanlike manner, and
- will supply materials of good quality and reasonably fit for purpose, although this latter obligation will be excluded if, in the selection of the materials, the employer placed no reliance on the skill and judgement of the contractor;[25]
- where the employer is relying on the contractor's skill and judgement, that he will provide a house which is fit for human habitation or a structure fit for its intended purpose.[26] This warranty will not apply to the extent that the contract shows that the employer is relying upon his own architect or consulting engineer and that it is the contractor's obligation to carry out the work in accordance with the documents provided to him and the instructions he receives from the architect or engineer.

The above obligations are strict so that it is no defence for the contractor to say that he had exercised reasonable care and no need for the purchaser to prove negligence.

144

Altogether different are the obligations of the architect or consulting engineer whose reponsibility for design in the absence of special facts or circumstances is limited to the exercise of all reasonable skill and care in conformity with the usual standards of his profession. On the law as it now stands the only situation in which an architect or engineer could be held to warrant the fitness for purpose his design would be if either:

- there was an express term in his contract to this effect, or
- on the particular facts of the case the court were to imply *as a matter of fact* that he had so warrantied his design.

In the case of *Greaves & Co. Contractors* v. *Baynham Meikle and Partners* the Court of Appeal did find such a warranty implied as a matter of fact but declined to answer the question as to whether or not such an obligation could be implied *as a matter of law* if say an engineer were employed to design a bridge.[27] Subsequently, however, the Court of Appeal in *George Hawkins* v. *Chrysler (UK) and Burne Associates* confirmed that 'it is not open to this court except where there are special facts and circumstances to extend the responsibilities of a professional man beyond the duty to exercise all reasonable skill and care in conformity with the usual standards of his profession . . . as the law stands at present a warranty of fitness for purpose *will not be implied as a matter of law* where the consulting engineer is retained to advise or design.[28]

Returning to the implied liabilities of the contractor the main problems which have arisen in English law have been connected with the specific UK system of nominated sub-contracting and nominated supply contracts. Under that system, which applies especially to building contracts, the architect on behalf of the employer invites tenders for the carrying out of specialist work or the supply of particular materials and then nominates to the building contractor the firm whom the architect selects to carry out the work. However, the sub-contract or purchase order is then placed by the building contractor with the nominated firm so that the only direct contractual relationship which exists is between that firm and the main contractor.

The problems with the system are covered in detail in specialist works on the subject e.g. Keating on *Building Contracts*, Sweet and Maxwell, 5th edition, 1991. However, the following brief summary of the obligations of the main contractor is provided as a basis upon which to compare the position as it applies under French and German law.

1. The main contractor is liable for the good quality of the materials or work provided by the nominated firm.
2. The main contractor will not be liable for the fitness for purpose of the materials provided or work performed by the nominated firm where it is clearly established that the choice of the material or the method of working was made by the employer or his professional advisers and no reliance was placed upon the judgement of the main contractor.

3. If the main contractor is himself expressly responsible under the terms of his contract for the design of the works, or at least for that part to be performed by the nominated sub-contractor, then whether the main contractor carries out the design himself or it is undertaken by the nominated firm, the main contractor will be strictly liable.

4. If, however, design is not expressly included within the main contractor's contract, but is undertaken by the nominated firm, then it appears unlikely that the main contractor has any liability for such design, and the employer can only be protected by the nominated firm entering into a collateral warranty with the employer.[29]

As an eminent German construction lawyer has pointed out, there is an inherent conflict in the English nomination system between economic reality and legal principles.[30] From a legal and, it is considered, commercial viewpoint, a main contractor should have total responsibility for *all* his sub-contractors, but with responsibility must go control. To the extent that the employer, through the nomination system, deprives the main contractor of the choice of firm to carry out the work and the terms upon which he is to be employed, and creates an economic relationship as between himself and the nominated firm, then it is only to be expected that the main contractor will seek to protect himself from the acts or defaults of the nominated firm and to put these on to the employer. The author has argued elsewhere for changes to the nominated system which in its present form seems only to be of benefit to lawyers.[31]

COMPARATIVE NOTE ON LATENT DEFECTS

In view of the importance which is attached to this subject in the civil law, especially in France, it is interesting that it receives only a minor mention in the leading English textbooks. So in the latest edition of Keating *Building Contracts* the subject is not even included in the index although the expression 'latent' defects does appear at places in the text, e.g. p. 53.

The primary reason for this is that the effect of the handing over of the works to the employer and the issue of the certificate of the completion or practical completion is determined, not as a matter of law, as it is in France and Germany, but by the terms of the contract between the parties which, subject to the provisions of the Unfair Contract Terms Act (see below, pp. 295–298), they are free to settle as between themselves. So with that proviso, what rights the employer possesses after the issue of the certificate of completion/practical completion as regards defects not revealed at that time, is to be decided according to the contract. Under the standard English forms those rights are to require the contractor to make good those defects as notified to him by the engineer/architect during the contractual period of defects liability. There may also be, depending on the provisions of the contract, a right at law to claim damages.

As regards defects which are apparent at the time when the contractor applies for the certificate of completion/practical completion, but which are not significant enough to affect the issue of the certificate, these are required to be identified by the engineer/architect and listed at the time when the certificate is issued.[32] However, the effect of failure by the architect/engineer to include a patent defect on the list is again a matter to be decided according to the construction of the particular contract.

In principle the entitlement of the contractor to be paid the retention money, constituting the balance of the contract price, depends on the fulfilment by the contractor of his obligation to complete the works in accordance with the contract. It is suggested therefore that the contractor, having been paid the first half of the retention money due on practical completion, could not deny the obligation to make good a patent defect, although due to the architect/engineer's error, it had not been included on the defects list. This would be so even if the wording of the defects liability clause were such as to suggest, if read literally, that it applied only to defects which 'arose during the Defects Liability Period', and therefore by implication excluded those obvious at the time of practical completion.[33]

It will be seen subsequently that under both French and German law the effects of the issue of the completion certificate are in general that the employer has no remedy in respect of defects which were apparent at the time of completion but which were not made the subject of an express reservation at that time (see below, pp. 186 and 228).

NOTES

1. See above, p. 88. Also *Jones* v. *St John's College Oxford* decided in 1870 LR 6 QB 115 and the comment in Hudson: 'there is nothing legally offensive in undertaking a task not in fact capable of being performed' p. 351. For a modern illustration of the principle see *Eurico* v. *Phillip Bros* [1987] 2 FTLR 213 where the buyer, under an FOB contract having the right to nominate a main Italian port, nominated Ravenna which was a port into which the vessel was unable to enter because of her draught. It was held by Lord Donaldson in the Court of Appeal that 'the parties to a contract are free to agree upon any terms which they consider appropriate including a term for one of the parties to do the impossible . . . if they do so agree and the other party fails to perform he will be liable in damages'.
2. Section 275(1): 'The debtor is relieved from his obligation to perform if the performance becomes impossible because of a circumstance for which he is not responsible occurring after the creation of the obligation'.
    Section 276(1): 'A debtor is responsible, unless it is otherwise provided, for wilful conduct and negligence'.
    Section 280(1): 'Where the performance becomes impossible because of a circumstance for which the debtor is responsible the debtor shall compensate the creditor for any damage arising from the non-performance'.
3. Fault or negligence was clearly an important issue in contractual liabilities under Roman law – see Buckland and McNair pp. 258 et seq. In discussing *la faute contractuelle* Weill and Terré state that 'fault is clearly at the base of the dispositions governing contractual liability which appears most clearly if one examines Art. 1137 of the Code civil relating to the obligation of someone charged with preserving something in their possession, who must exercise all the care of a reasonable man' s.395 on p. 399.
    An example would be goods left in the seller's possession after the completion of the sale and therefore now the property of the purchaser. If they are lost or damaged it would be for the purchaser to prove this was due to the fault of the seller. This is the same as the Roman rule in those circumstances that: 'the seller does not suffer for anything which happens without any wrongful intention or fault on his part', Inst. III. 23.3 (According to Dig. XVIII.6.3. the vendor was also liable for *custodia* but whether

147

this added any further liability is unclear – see Buckland pp. 560 and 561.)

4. See Treitel, *Remedies*, s.20.

5. Zweigert and Kotz (p. 194) do not make this distinction and equate liability under contracts for sale, services and work equally, which is clearly not the case.

6. *Bolam* v. *Friern Hospital Management Committee* [1957] 1 WLR 582 approved by the House of Lords in *Whitehouse* v. *Jordan* [1981] 1 All ER 267. For the distinction between the supply of an article, e.g. a set of false teeth (strict liability), and the performance of a service, extraction of a tooth (liability only for negligence) see *Samuels* v. *Davies* [1943] KB 256 approved by Lord Scarman in *IBA* v. *EMI Electronics* (1980) 14 Build LR1. For a useful discussion on the distinction between the supply of goods and supply of services see Atiyah pp. 24–7.

7. For the meaning of 'condition' and the distinction between conditions, warranties and other terms see above, p. 25.

8. *Harlington & Leinster Ltd* v. *Christopher Hull Fine Art*, *The Times* 22 December 1989, per Nourse LJ in the Court of Appeal.

9. The section reads 'Goods are of merchantable quality . . . if they are as fit for the purpose or purposes for which goods of that kind are commonly bought as it is reasonable to expect having regard to any description applied to them, the price (if relevant) and all other relevant circumstances'.

10. *Aswan Engineering Establishment Co. Ltd* v. *Lupdine Ltd and Thurgar Bolle* [1987] 1 WLR 1. Pails were bought for holding waterproofing compound. Exported to Kuwait and stacked six pails high they were exposed to very high temperatures for several days and eventually collapsed under their own weight. It was held that the pails were of merchantable quality as they were fit for use when exported to most parts of the world even when stacked six high.

11. *Rogers* v. *Parish (Scarborough) Ltd* [1987] QB 933.

12. *Business Appliances Specialists Ltd* v. *Nationwide Credit Corporation* [1988] RTR 332.

13. *Wormwell* v. *R.H.M. Agriculture (East) Ltd* [1987] 1 WLR 1091.

14. *Lambert* v. *Lewis* [1982] AC 225.

15. This was the position in *Harlington & Leinster Ltd* v. *Christopher Hull Fine Art* cited in note 8 above. The case concerned the sale of two paintings by one dealer to another which were, unknown to the seller, forgeries. The court held that the attribution of the pictures to the artist was not a term of the contract. Since, as Lord Justice Slade held, the only defect in quality of the painting related to the identity of the artist, which was no part of the description of the goods, there was accordingly no room for the application of s.14 of the Act.

The majority of the court took no account of the paintings having been sold for £6000 although they were virtually worthless.

16. *B.S. Brown & Son Ltd* v. *Craiks Ltd* [1970] 1 All ER 823.

17. *Ashington Piggeries* v. *Christopher Hill Ltd* [1972] AC 441.

18. See the *Aswan Engineering* case referred to in note 10 above.

19. See the *Aswan Engineering* case.

20. Atiyah p.188.

21. 'By getting the seller to undertake to use his skill and judgement the buyer gets an assurance that the goods will be reasonably fit for his purpose and that covers not only defects which the seller ought to have detected but also defects which are latent in the sense that even the utmost skill and judgement on the part of the seller would not have detected them', per Lord Reid in *Kendall* v. *Lillico* [1969] 2 AC 31, at p. 84.

22. However this will only apply if the terms of the contract are sufficiently explicit as to the date by which delivery is to be performed. The use of such expressions as 'as soon as reasonably practical' or 'without delay' are unlikely to be regarded as sufficient. *British and Commonwealth Holdings* v. *Quadrex Holdings Inc.* (1989) QB 842, and see the discussion in Treitel p. 701.

23. *Wimpey Construction UK Ltd* v. *Poole*, *The Times* 3 May 1984. However if a person has been employed because of some special expert skill which he claims to possess and is paid accordingly, then it is arguable that he should be judged by that standard. *Duchess of Argyll* v. *Beuselinck* [1972] 2 Lloyds Rep. 172.

24. Section 14 of the Supply of Goods and Services Act 1982 and see *Charnock* v. *Liverpool Corporation* [1968] 3 All ER 420 based on the common law rules which were codified by the Act.

25. *Young and Marten* v. *McManus Childs* [1969] 1 AC 154, 1.

26. *Hancock* v. *B.W. Brazier (Anerly) Ltd* [1966] 2 All ER 901 and as to the design liability for fitness of the

structure for purpose see the judgement of Lord Scarman in *IBA* v. *EMI Electronics* (1980) 14 Build LR 1.

27. (1975) 3 All ER 99.
28. (1986) 38 BLR 36.
29. As regards materials to be provided by a nominated supplier the House of Lords in *Young and Marten* v. *McManus Childs Ltd* (1969) 9 BLR 77 laid down clearly that if the employer selected the material then there is no liability for fitness of purpose but the contractor is still responsible for the quality of the materials since if they turn out to be defective the employer would be left without a remedy, and the contractor can pass on the responsibility to the supplier.

    If, however, a firm is nominated which will not accept such responsibilities, then usually the contract provides that the main contractor can refuse to accept the nomination. Alternatively his own obligations in respect of the nominated works are restricted to those which are contained within the terms and conditions which are acceptable to the nominated firm – see, e.g. clauses 36.4 and 36.5 of the JCT 80 *Form of Contract* and clause 59A of the *ICE Conditions*. These follow the decision in *Gloucester County Council* v. *Richardson* [1969] 1 AC 480 where it was held that a main contractor was not liable for defective work of a nominated supplier where his rights against that supplier were severely restricted by the terms of the supplier's quotation which he had been instructed to accept and to which he had no right to object.
30. Dr Christian Wiegand Dr.jur Rechstanwalt in *The Liability of Contractors*, Centre for Commercial Law Studies Queen Mary College 1986 at p. 132.
31. *Contracting for Engineering and Construction Contracts*, Gower Press 1988, pp. 213 and 214.
32. It is arguable that under the JCT 80 *Form of Contract* the architect has no power to give a certificate of practical completion if there are patent defects unless these are of a very minor character. See *Jarvis and Sons* v. *Westminster Corporation* [1970] 1 WLR 637. However under the *ICE Conditions*, 6th edition, it is specifically allowed that there may be work outstanding at the time of the issue of the certificate of substantial completion, which could include defective work, provided that the contractor gives an undertaking to complete this during the defects liability period. The author agrees with Keating that the extent of the outstanding work is limited by the requirement that the works must be fit for use by the employer – Keating p. 882.

    Model Form MF/1 for electrical and mechanical contracts allows for the taking over certificate to be issued when there are minor defects not affecting the use of the works for the purpose intended and provides that a list of these should be scheduled to the certificate.

    In practice, under all three forms of contract, the certificate is issued with a schedule of outstanding and defective work which is to be completed by the contractor. It is the responsibility of the architect/engineer to ensure that the items outstanding/defective do not affect the use of the works for the purpose intended, that they are listed and are to be completed within specific times during the defects liability period.
33. See Keating p. 530 and generally Hudson 10th ed. pp. 250–8.

12 Performance obligations under civil law – general

English law, as was indicated earlier (see above, pp. 143–146), has no separate regime in respect of latent defects. Nor, with one exception – the buyer's loss of his right to reject the goods for breach by the seller of a condition – does English law limit the rights of the purchaser after acceptance or completion as regards defects in the goods supplied or work performed. Unless excluded by the express terms of the contract, and subject to these being valid under the Unfair Contract Terms Act (see below, pp. 295–296), the right to claim damages for defects which were latent at the time of acceptance/completion continues under the normal common law rules for breach of contract until the expiry of the statutory period of limitation. As Treitel has observed, 'in common law countries the remedies ordinarily available for breach of contract apply to the case of defects in the subject matter of a sale'.[1]

The same is also true in common law countries in respect of contracts for works, although in practice the liability of the contractor after completion is often limited by the express terms of the standard form contracts in common use.[2]

The position is however quite different in those civil law countries, including both France and Germany, which have developed particular regimes for the obligations owed by the seller in respect of *vice caché* in the goods, which are discovered within a limited period after acceptance, and the remedies to which the purchaser is entitled. Both countries also attach a special legal significance to the *réception* (German *Abnahme*)[3] for contracts for works and again both apply particular, although rather different sets of rules, to defects in buildings or in other constructional works which only appear after *réception*.

Reference has also been made to the right within the civil law to claim damages for breach of contract, being based originally on the debtor being at fault (see above, p. 140). Today, however, in certain instances, particularly in French law, no proof of fault is necessary – only the existence of the damage and the causal link between the damage and the act of the debtor.

Three issues are therefore involved:

1. The existence of particular regimes covering the liability of the seller/contractor, and the rights of the purchaser, for latent defects after acceptance/*réception*.
2. The acceptance of the goods or the granting of *réception*/*Abnahme* produces specific legal results.

3. The liability of the debtor to pay damages without proof of fault exists only in particular instances and not as a general rule.

These are issues which are peculiar to the civil law and apply, although in differing ways, to both French and German law. It is convenient to consider each of them generally before proceeding to a more detailed examination of the rights and liabilities of the parties under contracts for the sale of goods, the carrying out of work or the provision of services.

THE PARTICULAR REGIMES FOR *VICE CACHÉ*

The reason why civil law systems do not share the simplicity of English law in having only one type of action for latent defects in goods sold or work executed is that they took over from Roman law two particular actions which the Romans had developed to deal specifically with hidden defects. These actions, while having the advantage from the purchaser's viewpoint of there being no need to prove fault, have corresponding disadvantages in terms of the remedies which they provide and the very short periods within which they must be exercised.

As a result the various civil law systems have sought in differing ways to overcome these disadvantages by allowing other actions alongside those derived from Rome, but in so doing have created a multiplicity of actions the dividing lines between which are often difficult to define.

Because the Roman actions have been so largely absorbed into French, and even more so into German law, a brief description will provide an introduction to the modern actions for *vice caché* under the respective codes.

THE ROMAN ACTIONS

Early Roman law was based on the concept of *caveat emptor*. But progressively the rights of the purchaser were improved. With the development of the consensual contracts of good faith the vendor became liable under the action *ex empto* for fraud which included the fraudulent concealment of a defect known to him but not to the purchaser and which was not patently obvious.[4] Then the purchaser could also proceed *ex empto* if the vendor had stated during negotiations that the item sold possessed a particular quality which it later transpired that it did not, or was free from a defect, which in fact it did possess. Further, such a statement did not have to be in the form of an express warranty provided that it was not a mere 'puff'.[5]

There was also the possibility for the purchaser to obtain from the vendor an express stipulation regarding the quality of the goods or the absence of defects.

In all these instances the vendor was liable *quod actoris interest* so that he could recover not merely the price of the goods but also other losses which he had suffered. A famous example is given in the Digest of the ability of the purchaser to recover the value of the house which had collapsed because of the unsound timber which he had purchased, provided that the seller had been aware that the timber was defective.[6]

However, in the absence of an express stipulation, when the action could be made *ex stipulatu*, the weakness of these actions from the viewpoint of the purchaser is that they were based on the bad faith of the vendor and necessitated proof by the purchaser of the vendor's knowledge of the defect.[7]

THE AEDILITIAN REMEDIES

As a result, and because of the notorious frauds which were practised in the slave markets, the *curules aediles* introduced the edicts which established what have become known as the Aedilitian Remedies. Under these the vendor was responsible for disclosing at the time of sale all non-apparent physical defects and defects of character which affected the use of the slave. Failure to disclose, *whether the vendor knew of the defect or not*, gave the purchaser two alternative rights.[8]

First, he could return the slave and obtain restitution of the purchase price. Both parties had indeed to be restored to the position they would have been in if the sale had not been concluded. This was the action *redhibitoria* which had to be brought within six months of the defect having become apparent.[9] The same remedy applied if the vendor had failed in his promise that the slave possessed some particular quality or was free from some particular defect.

The alternative remedy, the action *quanti minoris*, was for the difference in the purchase price between what the slave was worth with the defect and what he would have been worth without it. The limitation period for this action was twelve months.

These remedies, which applied also to the sale of cattle in the market, could be excluded by express agreement between the parties.

ASSIMILATION OF THE CIVIL LAW AND THE AEDILITIAN REMEDIES

Originally the Aedilitian Remedies applied only to slaves and cattle although this was later extended to all sales but not to other contracts.[10] In parallel, however, the action *ex empto* was extended to cover cases in which the vendor did not know of the defect in the goods and had not given an express warranty against defects. So a vendor was liable under the action *ex empto* for the soundness of the timber for a building even though he was unaware of the defect unless he had expressly disclaimed liability, which amounted to an implied warranty against latent defects.[11]

Further, any such disclaimer would not be valid if the vendor knew of the fault since this would be bad faith and an action *ex empto* was always *bonae fidei*.[12]

As to the purchaser's remedy in such cases of implied warranty, this depended on whether the vendor knew of the defect or not. If he did know and had concealed the defect, then the purchaser could claim his full damages. If he did not know, then the purchaser was limited to the Aedilitian Remedies of either *redhibitoria* or *quanti minoris*.[13]

So in Justinian's time the two sets of remedies, those of the *ius civilis* and those of the *aediles* were effectually merged with one major exception: the period during which the remedies might be exercised. Even with the abolition of the office of the *aediles* and their specific jurisdiction the distinction remained and was continued with the reception of Roman law in the Middle Ages.

If the remedy sought was for *redhibitoria* then the limit was six months and if for *quanti minoris*, the limit was twelve months, however the action was brought. For the *actio empti* proper, based on the bad faith of the vendor, to which was assimilated knowledge of the hidden defect, and which alone of the three actions carried the right to damages, the prescription period was the traditional one of 30 years.[14]

THE POTHIER RULE

There was one further development after Justinian which was to be influential in French law, though not in German. In a text dealing with the soundness of a receptacle, Labeo refers to the 'vendor answering for soundness in every case except where soundness did not form part of the bargain and Pomponius agrees'. This text was later used by Pothier to justify holding a professional seller or merchant, whether a fabricator or not, liable for all damages due to the goods not being fit for the usual purpose for which they were intended, even when he did not know of the defect.[15]

This rule has now been adopted by the jurisprudence into French law by holding under Art. 1645 of the *Code Civil* that 'the seller who knows of the defects to which it is appropriate to assimilate the seller who by his profession is not permitted to be unaware of them, is liable in addition to the restitution of the price he has received, to all damages suffered by the purchaser'.[16]

MODERN CODE PROVISIONS

With minor modifications the actions *redhibitoria* and *quanti minoris* have been carried forward into contemporary French and German law. While German law has remained faithful to the principle that these actions are the only ones open to the purchaser after acceptance for defective goods, other than for fraudulent concealment of a defect or the breach of a guaranteed attribute (see below, pp. 207–208), French law in its attempt to do justice between the parties, but with less logical rigour, has allowed actions after delivery for the seller's failure to fulfil his delivery obligations (see below, pp. 174–175).

THE ROMAN ORIGINS OF *RÉCEPTION* (*ABNAHME*)

Under the Roman contract for building works the stage of completion was marked by the *adprobatio operis*. This could be either a demonstration by the contractor to the employer that the work had been executed properly in accordance with the contract, or if the contract so required, a formal declaration by the employer based on his own examination or by someone technically qualified on his behalf, that the works were approved. This declaration of approval had to be made objectively in good faith. In either event, from the time that the *adprobatio operis* was made, the employer could no longer claim in respect of defects unless these had been fraudulently concealed, the risk in the works for accidental loss or damage passed to the employer, and the employer was bound to pay for the work.[17]

Although the modern codes have each established a particular regime in respect of the contractor's liability for latent defects, the general principle that *réception* (*Abnahme*) in all other respects brings to an end the contractor's liabilities, other than for defects reserved at *réception* (*Abnahme*), still applies. As an example the *Cahiers des Clauses Administratives Générales Applicables aux Travaux de Bâtiment Faisant l'Objet de Marches Privés* (General Administrative Clauses for Contracts for Private Building Works) contains the following clause:

> La Réception libère l'entrepreneur de toutes les obligations contractuelles autres que celles prévues à l'article 15.2. La date de Réception est le point de départ des responsabilités et garanties instituées par les articles 1792, 1792–2, 1792–3, 1792–6 et 2270 du Code civil.

La Réception itself is defined by Art. 1792.6 of the *Code Civil* as 'The act by which the Employer declares he has accepted the Works either unconditionally or with reservations'.

There is no parallel here with English law which leaves it entirely to the discretion of the parties to a construction contract to decide upon the meaning that they are to attach to words such as 'completion', 'acceptance' and 'takeover'. None of these has any defined legal meaning and does not constitute a 'juristic act' in the civil law sense.

LIABILITY, WHETHER FAULT-BASED OR NOT

In civil law countries the issue of fault or non-fault-based liability raises three questions. First, in the absence of proof of fault is the debtor under any liability at all? Second, if liability is dependent on fault is the creditor responsible for proving the debtor's fault or is it for the debtor to prove that he was not at fault? Third, without the creditor needing to prove fault, is the debtor under a limited form of guarantee liability, derived from the Roman actions described above, but which does not extend to the payment of damages? There are differing answers to these questions according to whether the contract is classified as one for sale, for works or for services and there are specific provisions which only apply post acceptance/*réception* (*Abnahme*).

The detailed answers to these questions are given in the succeeding chapters on performance obligations under French and German law in respect of contracts for sale, works and services (Chapters 13–16).

However, there is the general question to be considered first, of the distinction between obligations which are intended to achieve a particular result, and obligations which are only for the performance of services, to be carried out certainly according to the standard of skill to be expected of the class of person undertaking the work, but without the undertaking that a specific result will be attained.

The distinction was one which was known to the Romans but within the context only of the difference between the contract for the hiring of labour (*locatio conductio operarum*) and the contract for the production of a piece of work which could be a physical thing or a service, e.g. the transport of a column (*locatio conductio operis*).[18]

In modern French law the distinction has been applied generally to contracts for sale as well as for work and services. In modern German law the distinction again appears in the contrast between the obligations of a contractor and those of a professional person such as a doctor, though not an architect (see below, pp. 234–235). This general distinction is the subject of the next section.

FRENCH LAW AND LIABILITY

It was noted earlier that English law makes a sharp distinction between the implied strict liability of a seller of goods, or of a contractor supplying a product, and a person only supplying services such as a professional man or a technician who is only under an implied obligation in the performance of such services to use reasonable skill and care.

French law, equally, but for quite different reasons, draws a not dissimilar distinction.[19] There is the first the obligation under which the supplier/contractor is responsible for achieving a result, an *obligation de résultat*, and his fault is presumed from the fact that he failed to do so. He is only then excused from liability if he can establish that he was prevented from performing that obligation by *une cause étrangère*. In practice this is hardly to be distinguished from the strict liability of English law and when applicable answers affirmatively the first question posed.

Alternatively the supplier/contractor may be under an *obligation de moyens*, when he is only liable if he can be shown to have committed negligent or incompetent acts which *un bon père de famille*, the French equivalent of a reasonable man, would not have done if placed under the same conditions. Here the answer to the first question is 'no' and to the second question that the creditor must prove the debtor's default.

The difference is fundamental under French law, as indeed is the similar distinction under English law, because of the obvious difficulty for the creditor of carrying the burden of proof if the obligation is classified as being one of *moyens*.

Where the two laws differ is that in English law the application of the distinction is reasonably clear-cut and well established.

Under French law, since the distinction was developed by the jurisprudence and is in only a few instances alluded to in the *Code Civil* and, given the lack of detailed reasoning and establishment of general principles in the judgements of the *Cour de cassation*, it is difficult to set down clearly either the dividing line between the two or to find the principle upon which the distinction is drawn. It is not made easier by the fact that the classification applies to the *obligation* and not to the *contract* and that there are many instances of the same contract containing the two different obligations.[20]

A transport operator, e.g. SNCF, is under an *obligation de résultat* for the safety of a passenger during the period of the contract of transport, i.e. from the moment he started to board the train until he had descended. At one time it was considered that the transport operator was then under an *obligation de moyens* for the passenger's safety while on the station premises. Now it has been decided by the *Cour de cassation* that the transport operator's responsibility, otherwise than during the journey, is delictual and not contractual.[21]

There is no single or simple means of deciding in French law whether an obligation is one of *résultat* or *moyens*. There are only certain criteria which have been proposed by doctrine and to a degree adopted by the jurisprudence. None however is on its own decisive, and while one can discern certain general trends, as in the case of doctors, for effecting a cure (*obligation de moyens*), and transport operators for the safety of their passengers when in transit (*obligation de résultat*), in the ultimate each case is decided pragmatically. One can only refer therefore to the primary criteria as being guidelines.

Criteria used by the French doctrine and courts and comparison with English law

The will of the parties This is the primary criterion provided that the will of the parties as expressed in the contract is not in conflict with a rule of *ordre public*. Clearly if the parties have expressly written into their contract certain specific guarantees of performance then these will be regarded by the courts as *obligations de résultat* although it would still be prudent to define them as such in the contract documents themselves.

In the same way as under English law it is also open to the parties by an express term in the contract to extend what would otherwise be an *obligation de moyens* into one of *résultat*, e.g. that of a doctor to effect a cure. What is less certain is the right of the parties to go the other way and reduce what would normally be an *obligation de résultat* into one of *moyens*. This would only be effective if the obligation concerned was not one of *ordre public*.

In certain instances, e.g. the liability of the architect under Art. 1792 for a defect in the works under the *garantie décennale*, the *Code Civil* specifically makes the obligation one of *ordre public* and prohibits any attempt to exclude or limit liability (Art. 1792–5). In the same way the jurisprudence has established that a professional seller in a contract of sale with a purchaser, not being a professional of the same speciality and possessing the same level of technical skill, cannot exonerate himself for his liability for *vices cachés* under Art. 1643 of the *Code Civil*.[22]

Other examples where the concept of a clause being disallowed as being contrary to *ordre public* have been those where the obligation which it was sought to avoid related to personal safety.

The risk involved in achieving the result If there is a large element of risk in obtaining the result, so that it would be unreasonable to hold the debtor strictly liable for its achievement, then the obligation will be considered to be one of *moyens*. This is given as the reason why a doctor, surgeon or lawyer does not generally have an *obligation de résultat* towards his client. The doctor is not held responsible for curing his patient; nor the lawyer for winning his case but only for a fault in their professional conduct. But a lawyer is under an *obligation de résultat* for his attendance at court at the time required.

However, if the result envisaged by the contract ought to be attained by the use of methods and equipment which the debtor should normally have at his disposal, as for example a railway company carrying passengers safely, or a supplier delivering goods free from defects, then the obligation will be one of *résultat*.

A similar distinction is made in English law but the reasoning is not wholly convincing. Many of a doctor's acts are of a simple routine nature in which the risk level is low. Equally a supplier or contractor may be operating at the limits of technology.[23]

Moreover, while the obligation of the doctor as regards using professional skill to cure the patient is usually considered to be only one of *moyens*, it is different when it comes either to the supply of an article, e.g. an artificial limb, or a defect in the equipment to be used.

In a case virtually identical to *Samuels* v. *Davis*[24] the *Cour de cassation* decided that the obligation of a dentist was to provide a dental plate which was satisfactory for its purpose, i.e. an *obligation de résultat*, since this was a technical act and not a medical one, but only under a duty 'to be conscientious and conform to the practice of his profession', i.e. an *obligation de moyens* in respect of its installation.[25]

But there does appear to be a difference between the two legal systems when it comes to the supply of items incidental to the provision of medical services. As Atiyah observes, it has never been suggested in England that the supply of blood for a blood transfusion would be regarded as falling within the implied warranties of the sale of goods.[26] In France, however, a patient who was given contaminated blood was successful in a claim for damages which was decided in contract even though there was no fault proved on the part of the centre which supplied the blood. As the *Cour de cassation* said, 'the debtor could not establish according to Art. 1147 of the Code Civil that their failure to comply with their contract was due to "une cause étrangère" so clearly the obligation was considered as one of *résultat*'.[27]

Again it seems that where a radiographer or anaesthetist uses equipment then he will be under an *obligation de résultat* that the equipment itself is not defective. The distinction is drawn here again between a 'medical' and a 'mechanical' act. The former, related to the treatment of the patient, is only one of *moyens*. The latter, concerned with the correct functioning of the equipment itself, is one of *résultat*.[28]

The part played actively by the creditor If the role of the creditor is active, so that he has the opportunity of avoiding the risk, then the obligation is likely to be one of *moyens*. If he is passive, then it is likely to be one of *résultat*. This reasoning has been applied mainly in cases of safety. The passenger sitting in the train can do nothing to prevent injury if there is an accident. The obligation of the railway company in respect of his safety is one of *résultat*.

However, the operator of a chairlift is only under an *obligation de moyens* in respect of the operations of the skier in getting on and off the chairlift in which the skier plays an

157

active part.[29] Similarly the proprietor of a riding school hiring out horses is only under an *obligation de moyens*.[30]

Other instances are more difficult to understand. The operator of dodgem cars at a funfair has been held to be under an *obligation de résultat* at least once the victim was inside the vehicle. No reasoning was given, so one can only think that perhaps the court considered that the operation involved an element of risk of human injury attributable essentially to the operator who ought to have been exercising proper control especially over young people.[31]

Provision of services   As discussed above, the provision of services by a member of the 'liberal' professions such as a doctor is only an *obligation de moyens* unless the contract between the parties provides otherwise. The same applies to other professions but not, as in England, to those of an architect, consulting engineer or *bureau d'études* so far as their responsibility arises under Art. 1792 of the *Code Civil* for defects in the works not apparent at *réception* and which are covered by either the *garantie décennale* or the *garantie biennale*. Their liability is then presumed and they can only escape on proof of *cause étrangère* which would be either *force majeure*, the defect being due solely to the fault of another party for whom they were not responsible, or the fault of the employer. They are therefore under an *obligation de résultat* (see further below, pp. 187–188).

It is only when the claim against the architect or other professional is made under the *droit commun*, and not under Art. 1792 that proof of fault is required, and even then it appears that the burden of such proof is not all that difficult to satisfy.[32]

As regards pure engineering services for work which does not fall within the scope of Art. 1792, e.g. demolition, the consultant will generally be under an *obligation de moyens* if his responsibility was limited to the giving of advice, but under an *obligation de résultat* if he was also responsible for supervising the carrying out of the work.[33]

Another distinction between English and French law is in the provision of services such as those of a garage mechanic. In England the mechanic would only be required to exercise 'reasonable skill and care in the carrying out of his work', although if the contract required the provision of spare parts then their supply would be subject to the strict liability rules of the Sale of Goods Act.

In France, however, if the services relate to a tangible rather than to an intangible activity, then, although the jurisprudence is not constant, the obligation will tend generally to be regarded as one of *résultat*. So a garage is under an *obligation de résultat* in respect of work done on a vehicle, while a travel agency is generally only under an *obligation de moyens* although this can change according to the nature of the services provided by it to its clients.[34]

GERMAN LAW AND LIABILITY

Although German law refers to the contractor's obligations to produce results, *BGB* 631, the French *obligation de résultat* has no real equivalent in German law. The basic practical distinction in German law is between the guaranty obligations based on the Aedilitian Remedies, independent of fault, and the obligation to pay damages for breach of contract which is dependent upon fault, unless it is for breach of a promised quality in the goods *'Zugesichter Eigenschaft'* Art. 459(2) *BGB*.[35]

In these latter cases where fault is required, proof by the debtor that he was not at fault would therefore exonerate him from liability for damages, even if the obligation were one which, under French law, would be classified as an *obligation de résultat* and from which therefore the debtor could only escape liability on proof of *cause étrangère*. While the effect of establishing *cause étrangère* will always be that the debtor is not at fault, the reverse is not true.[36]

Further, French law draws, as we have seen, a pragmatic distinction between the *obligation de résultat* and that of *moyens* so that, e.g. it cannot be said that the qualification of the contract as being a *contrat d'entreprise*[37] is sufficient to decide upon the nature of the contractor's obligations. In German law the nature of the debtor's obligations depends primarily upon the characterization of the contract.[38]

Categorization of contracts

In this context the *BGB* distinguishes between three types of contract:

• The contract for sale (*Kaufvertrag*)
• The contract for work (*Werkvertrag*)
• The contract for services (*Dienstvertrag*)

The contract for work (*Werkvertrag*) has an important subdivision known as *Werklieferungsvertrag* which is a contract for the production of a particular piece of work, usually an item of machinery, which is to be manufactured from materials supplied by the manufacturer. Such a contract would under both English and French law generally be classified as a contract for sale although perhaps for English law not a 'pure' contract of sale. This may be of some importance under English law in certain circumstances.[39] The distinction is of very considerable significance under French law.[40]

Although *Werkvertrag* has been translated as contract for work, and indeed includes all forms of building and constructional contracts and those for engineering works, it also covers contracts such as those for the commissioning of a painting by an artist, the production of an entertainment or sporting event, the writing and application of software programs and the carrying out of repairs.

The *Dienstvertrag* covers both a contract of employment (*Arbeitsvertrag*) and generally contracts for the hire of professional services, e.g. a lawyer. The distinction between such a contract and a *Werkvertrag* is that under a *Dienstvertrag* the person whose services are engaged is responsible only for the provision of such services and not for the achievement of a result. Under the *Werkvertrag*, however, the debtor undertakes to produce the completed work and achieve the result which is the subject matter of the contract. One important distinction in contrast with English law is that a contract with an architect is classified as a *Werkvertrag* whilst in English law this would be a contract for services.[41] Contracts with doctors are regularly classified in the same way as in English law as a *Dienstvertrag*.[42]

If the contract involves both the supply of an item and the provision of services, e.g. a contract under which a dentist supplies and fits a set of false teeth, then the contract will be treated as falling into two categories. The fitting falls into the category of a contract for services (*Dienstvertrag*) and the supply will be a contract for work (*Werkvertrag* – *BGH* 9 December 1974, NJW 1975, 305). The importance of the distinction lies primarily in the guarantee obligations which are assumed by the dentist under the *Werkvertrag* and are independent of fault but the difference in periods of prescription is also significant. It is six months for the guarantee obligation under the *Werkvertrag* (five years for buildings), running from the date of the *Abnahme* but the normal 30 years for the liability for negligence under the *Dienstvertrag*.

Table on p. 162 summarizes the principal distinctions between the obligations owed by the debtor for default under each of the three forms of contract. The succeeding Chapters 13–16 provide more detailed explanation. However four major points of contrast with French law will be discussed first.

Burden of proof – negligence Where negligence has to be established as a basis for liability, e.g. in a contract for medical services, French law requires that the creditor is responsible for proving the debtor's fault. Under German law, however, once the creditor has established the treatment concerned and the causal link between this and the injury suffered, the burden of proof shifts to the debtor who must establish that objectively neither he nor those for whom he is responsible were at fault (*BGB* Arts. 282 and 278; Volkommer/Jauernig para. 3 p. 283 and *BGH* NJW 1988 2939).

Remedies and defects – works contracts Unlike French law which imposes extensive *obligations de résultat* for defects in buildings and other constructional works (see below, Chapter 14), German law applies the limited guarantee remedies derived from the Roman Aedilitian Remedies to contracts for works as well as to contracts for the sale of goods. However these remedies are secondary to the primary right of the purchaser under a *Werkvertrag* to require the contractor to produce a work which has the promised qualities and which is free from defects (*BGB* 633, 1) and, if the contractor defaults in removing the defect, the right of the purchaser to do so himself and recover from the contractor the costs involved (*BGB* 633, 3). The right to claim damages only applies if the contractor was at fault.

After *Abnahme* these rights only apply to defects which are discovered subsequently or which were known at the time and in respect of which the purchaser reserved his rights[43] other than for the right to claim damages under Art. 635 of the *BGB* for a defect due to the debtor's fault.

Defects – sale of specific goods Again French law permits the purchaser on a contract for the sale of specific goods, in addition to his guaranty rights for *vices cachés*, an action in damages and/or termination if the seller delivers goods which are not fit either for normal use or that which was required by the contract.[44] Under German law delivery of defective specific goods will count as performance of the contract and the purchaser is restricted to the limited guarantee remedies based on the Aedilitian Remedies. The only exceptions are if the goods lack a specific promised quality or if the supplier has been at fault in the sense of having behaved in bad faith by deceiving the purchaser about the quality of the goods. In these two cases the purchaser would have the *alternative* remedy of claiming damages (see further pp. 207–208).

The position is however different on the sale of generic goods, i.e. commodities which are sold at so much per unit of measure or goods which are sold by type, class or kind. A new car sold by model would fall into the category of generic goods (*Gattung*), Volkommer – Jauernig p. 186 s.2.

Sale of generic goods   Although under German law the purchaser has the right to treat the delivery of defective generic goods as constituting performance of the contract, and to exercise the guaranty remedies of *Wandlung* or *Minderung*, his principal right is to require the seller to replace the defective goods with ones which are in conformity with the contract.

This right is not in the nature of a guaranty (*Gewährleistungsanspruch*), but an extension of the initial obligation of the seller to perform his contract (*Erfüllungs-anspruch – BGH* 10 January 1958, NJW 1958, 418 and *BGH* NJW 1985, 3526).

If therefore the seller fails to replace the defective goods with ones which comply with the contract, the purchaser can claim damages for non-performance either under Art. 326 if replacement is delayed beyond the period of notice, or under Arts. 279 and 280 if the replacement is impossible for the seller, i.e. subjectively impossible, but remains possible objectively. (See Volkommer – Jauernig pp. 278 and 279 and references given there.)[45] For the distinction between subjective impossibility (*Unvermögen*) and objective impossibility (*Unmöglichkeit*) see above, p. 90 and note 33 p. 93.

Despite the difference in the legal basis of the remedies, the short period of prescription of six months from delivery applies also to this right of requiring replacement in the same way as for *Wandlung* or *Minderung*.

French law has no need of any special rules governing generic goods since the purchaser has the right to refuse to accept delivery of defective goods as constituting performance of the contract whether these are specific or generic.[46] He also has the right under a commercial contract of generic goods, after giving notice to the seller to deliver conforming goods, to purchase replacement goods and charge the seller with the cost, without having to obtain a court order.[47]

Secondary factors affecting debtor's liabilities

Taking account of the above, the secondary factors which affect the nature and extent of the debtor's liabilities under the three contract forms, are therefore whether or not:

• the debtor gave the creditor an express undertaking as to quality or performance;

- the debtor was at fault in the performance of his obligations; and
- the defective performance occurred before the passing of the risk in the goods (*Kaufvertrag*) or the *Abnahme* of the work (*Werkvertrag* or *Werklieferungsvertrag*).

The position is summarized in the table set out below. The division in question 3 of the default of the debtor into three categories, impossibility, delay and defective performance, is necessary because German law has no unitary doctrine for breach of contract. The *BGB* only provides for damages for breach of contract in two cases: impossibility of performance and delay in performance. In order to cover other cases, where performance is rendered, but is in some way defective, and for which there do not exist particular rules under the Code, jurisprudence and doctrine developed the so-called 'positive breach of contract' (*positive Vertragsverletzung*). This would cover compensation for damage to other legally protected interests of the purchaser but not damage to the object of the sale or the works themselves (*BGH* 24 November 1976 NJW 1977, 379 and see further below, p. 213).

Question	Kaufvertrag	Werkvertrag	Dienstvertrag
1. Is the debtor liable under the guaranty obligations for cancellation (*Wandlung*) or the reduction in price (*Minderung*) independent of proof of fault?	Yes.	Yes, after he has been given notice to remedy the defect and has either failed or refused to do so.	No.
2. Is the debtor liable for the payment of damages for defects as an alternative to the guaranty obligations?	Yes, if the thing lacks a promised quality, or the seller has fraudulently either concealed the defect or represented the thing has certain qualities which it lacks.	Yes, if the defect is due to the debtor's fault or the works lack a promised quality.	No.
3. Is the debtor liable for the payment of damages if, due to his fault:			
(i) performance becomes impossible?	Yes, before the risk in the goods passes to the creditor.	Yes, before *Abnahme*.	Yes.
(ii) performance is delayed?	Yes, but normally only after notice.	Yes, but normally only after notice.	Yes, but only after notice.
(iii) performance is defective?	Yes, but only for injury or damage other than to the goods themselves.	Yes, but only for injury or damage other than to the works themselves.	Yes.

In the above table the obligations of a debtor under a *Werkvertrag* have been stated according to the provisions of the *BGB*. In practice, as regards contracts for buildings and other constructional works, these will normally be determined under the standard conditions of contract known as the *VOB* (see further below, p. 222).

NOTES

1. Treitel *Remedies for Breach of Contract* s.98.
2. See for example clause 36.9 of MF/1 which limits the contractor's liability to the remedying of the defect and excludes all liability of the contractor for damages consequent upon the defect other than for death or personal injury caused by the contractor's negligence. It is to be noted that this clause purports to exclude the contractor's liability for damages even in the event of 'a wilful disregard of the consequences of an act or omission of a contractor'. Such conduct would certainly constitute a *faute lourde* under French law, the liability for which a professional cannot exclude. Cass. com. 6 July 1961; Bull. civ. III no. 315 p.273.
3. For the definitions of *Réception* and *Abnahme* under French and German law respectively see below, pp. 185 and 227.
4. Dig. XVIII 1.43 s.2: 'A seller must warrant the absence of fraud on his part and it is fraud . . . if one is guilty of artful concealment'. Also Dig. XXI 1.4 s.4: 'An action ex empto will lie if the seller did not declare a mental or moral defect (of a slave) of which he was aware'.
5. Dig. XIX 1.6 s.4: 'If you sell me a vessel stating it to be of a certain capacity or weight I can sue you ex empto if there is a shortage'. Also Dig. XXI 1.19: 'It must however be understood that there are some statements which a seller is not bound to make good, namely those are merely laudatory . . . . For as Pedius says there is a great difference between a statement which is mere puffing and a promise to make good what is stated'.
6. Dig. XIX 1.13.
7. Dig. XIX 1.13 s.1.
8. Dig. XXI 1 s.2: 'It is to be understood that a seller, even though he was unaware of the existence of faults, liability for which is decreed by the aediles, must nevertheless be held liable'.
9. Dig. XXI 1.1 s.1.
10. Dig. XXI 1.63.
11. Dig. XIX 1.13.
12. Dig. XIX 1.6 s.9: 'If a man has sold what he knew to be charged or to belong to someone else with a clause negativing liability on that account, damages must be given for his bad faith under the action ex empto because the action is bonae fidei'. Tr. Zulueta.
13. Dig. XIX. 1.13: 'the unwitting seller of a diseased herd or of unsound timber will have to make good in the action ex empto only the amount by which the price would have been reduced had the buyer known the truth, whereas, if the seller knew, but was silent and so deceived the buyer, he will have to make good to the buyer all losses which have fallen upon him (the buyer) in consequence of the purchase'. Compare this with the *caveat emptor* principle in English law and the case of Smith and Hughes discussed earlier (pp. 119–120).
14. See generally Zimmermann pp. 322–5.
15. Pothier (1768) *Traité du contrat de vente*, Part II, Chapter 1 pp. 223–5: 'There is a circumstance in which the seller even although absolutely ignorant of the defect in the thing sold is nevertheless responsible for the damage which the defect causes to other property of the purchaser; that is when the seller is a workman who sells the works of his trade or a merchant who sells articles of commerce which it is his business to sell; this workman or merchant is held liable for all the damage which the purchaser suffers by reason of the defect in the thing sold being used for the purpose for which it was intended even when the workman or merchant claim to be ignorant of the defect'.

    The reason Pothier gives for this is that the workman must be a master of his trade and no one ought to publicly claim to practise a trade if he does not have the necessary knowledge to carry it out well. Ignorance is to be counted as a fault. It is the same for the merchant whether he is a fabricator or not. If he is not a fabricator then by publicly practising the trade of a merchant he must only sell goods which are fit for the usage intended and cannot claim ignorance of their defects. If he is a fabricator then he must only employ good workmen for whom he is responsible.
16. See Chapter 13 note 19 on p. 181.
17. Dig. XIX 2.24.
18. See Zimmermann at p. 394 and the sources there quoted.
19. The need for the distinction in French law arose out of the requirement to reconcile two apparently contradictory texts of the *Code Civil*, Arts. 1147 and 1137. Under Art. 1147 the debtor can only avoid

liability for damages for the non-execution of the contract or its late execution, if he can show that this was due to a *cause étrangère*. Under Art. 1137 a person responsible for looking after something, e.g. specific goods after their sale and prior to their delivery to the purchaser, is only under the obligation to exercise *tous les soins d'un bon père de famille*, i.e. all the care of a reasonable man.

The concept that there were two possible contractual degrees of responsibility of a debtor, one for achieving a definite result – *obligation de résultat*, from which the debtor was only exonerated by proof of *cause étrangère* and one for only exercising care, an *obligation de moyens* – was originated by Demogues in 1928 in his *Traité des obligations*. As the concept was developed the *obligation de moyens* became equivalent to a delictual fault under Art. 1382 for which the proof of fault belonged to the creditor, while that of an *obligation de résultat* became equivalent to the objective liability *en plein droit* (see further Viney s.530).

20. As a classic example, while a restaurant proprietor is only under an *obligation de moyens* as regards the quality in terms of flavour of the food which he provides, he is under an *obligation de résultat* in respect of its being fit to eat and leaving his client well at the end of the meal (Poitiers 16 December 1970).

21. Cass. civ. 17 March 1989; Bull. civ. I no. 118 and note by Patrice Jourdain in *Rev. trim. dr. civil* 1989 p. 548 et seq.

22. See Chapter 13, p. 172 and note 19.

23. The 'state of the art' defence in contractual claims against a supplier or contractor has not however been accepted in either English or French law – see *IBA* v. *E.M.I. Electronics Ltd* (1980) 14 Build LR for the English law position, and Cass. civ. 30 Nov. 1983, Bull. cass. no. 235 at p. 191 for the French position. In the latter case the *Cour de cassation* held that the use of a biological system, even though in standard use at the time of the plant's construction and considered to be valid and the best available, did not constitute a *cause étrangère* which would relieve the contractor, liable under Art. 1147 of the *Code Civil* to produce a plant free from defects, from his responsibility.

24. [1943] KB 526.

25. Cass. civ. 1re 15 November 1988: 'although a dental surgeon is only under a simple "obligation de moyens" in respect of the treatment which he carries out, like a supplier he is under an "obligation de résultat" of a set of dentures and is obliged to deliver them free from defects'.

26. Atiyah, pp. 24 and 25.

27. The contract in this case was between the National Centre for Blood Transfusions and the health and social security service responsible for the hospital where the patient was being treated. Through no fault of the centre the donor who provided the blood was infected with syphilis. The patient was able to sue in contract under the doctrine of *stipulation pour autrui* since the contract was made for her benefit (see further below, pp. 277–278).

28. See Viney p. 654. The jurisprudence is not consistent.

29. Cass. civ. 11 March 1986 and a decision of the Cour d'Appel Chambéry 11 March 1987. However as regards the proper working of the equipment the operator is under an *obligation de résultat*. Cass. civ. 16 July 1980 and see the discussion in Starck s.1038 on p. 363.

30. Cass. civ. 16 March 1970 *Source Book* p. 405.

31. Cass. civ. 12 February 1975; *Source Book* 3rd ed. pp. 404 and 405. The proprietor is under an *obligation de résultat* for the safety of the driver during the ride. However before and after the person enters the car, the proprietor is only under an *obligation de moyens* in regard to his safety. Cass. civ. 30 October 1968 D.1968.650 and 2 November 1972 D. 1972.

The decision of 12 February 1975 has been criticized on the grounds that the attraction of dodgem cars is the banging of one car into another and that it is unreasonable to hold the proprietor responsible for an injury caused by the very nature of the activity – Starck s.1043 on p.365.

The operator of a merry-go-round was similarly held under an *obligation de résultat* for the safety of the fair-goer during the period of the ride in a case involving a young girl who fell and was fatally injured (Cass.civ. 18 February 1986 Bull. civ. I no.32).

32. Cass. civ. 10 July 1978 (Delcourt). Although this case was decided under the earlier version of Art. 1792 which distinguished between major and minor works of construction, the judgement is still valid today for situations not covered by the present text of Art. 1792. Malinvaud s.113 and n.2 p. 149 and s.177 pp. 213 and 214. For comments on proving fault see Malinvaud s.92 and works cited under n.1 on p. 119.

33. Cass. civ. 1, 8 January 1985. A company which was a specialist in the methods of demolition of a building using explosives was held responsible for the damage caused because 'the contract was not limited

simply to the giving of advice but included the control of the operations'.

34. Cass. civ. 16 February 1988 in which it was held that the court below had justly decided that the repairer responsible for the carrying out of maintenance work on a vehicle was under an *obligation de résultat*. Liability was avoided in this and in other cases because the repairer established the absence of causality between the work done and the subsequent accident.

Contracts with travel agencies may be considered either as contracts of *mandat* or as *contrats d'entreprise*. Although the agency's obligations are often referred to as *obligations de moyens* little is required to establish proof of the agency's fault. Further, agencies will be treated as being under an *obligation de résultat* in respect of their undertaking to book tickets and to provide their clients with the appropriate tickets and reservations and this will extend to the bad selection of the carrier. Cass. civ. 5 January 1961 BI no. 7 and Cass. civ. 31 May 1978; Bull.civ.I, no.163.

35. The two most important exceptions for which fault is not required are: the liability of the seller of generic goods to deliver them in accordance with the contract; and the liability of a seller for breach of a warranty that the goods concerned will possess some quality which he has expressly guaranteed.

As regards a *Werkvertrag* fault is not required if the contractor has expressly guaranteed a certain characteristic.

36. Chabas p. 454 draws the distinction in these terms: 'To know if there has been fault one ought to ask if a wise person would have acted as the debtor did. To know if there has been Force Majeure one ought to ask if it would have been impossible for a wise person to have acted otherwise than the debtor did'. It follows that although a person may not have committed any fault this will not necessarily result in it being a case of *force majeure*.

37. Malaurie p. 394: 'the qualification of a contract as being a "contrat d'entreprise" is not sufficient to decide upon the system of rules governing responsibility: a "contrat d'entreprise" may give rise sometimes to "un obligation de moyens" and sometimes to "un obligation de résultat" according to the "objet" of the obligation which is imposed upon the contractor'.

38. In answering the question, 'As regards the scope of contractual obligations does your law know the distinction between "obligations de résultat" and those of "moyens"?' Andras Kneip answered, 'No, in German law the distinction only serves to distinguish between a contract for works and one for services'. *Définition et domaine de la responsabilité contractuelle* ed. Rodière, Institut de droit comparé, l'Université de Paris.

39. The distinction is important in relation to: obtaining the return of a deposit; the time at which property passes; and maybe the effect of a retention of title clause – see Atiyah pp. 21 and 22.

40. The principal differences are: on a contract of sale of goods to be manufactured the property and risk would pass to the purchaser on completion of the goods ready for delivery while with a *contrat d'entreprise* the property passes when delivery is made; the rules relating to *vices cachés* differ even when the *contrat d'entreprise* includes the supply of equipment and in particular a clause limitative of the contractor's responsibility may be valid if it is a *contrat d'entreprise* which would be invalid if it were a contract of sale (Cass. com. 4 July 1989 B.IV no.210); and the provisions of the Law of 12 May 1980 relating to reservation of title only apply to contracts for sale.

41. BGHZ 31, 227. The same applies for an engineer (BGHZ 58, 225).

42. BGH NJW 73, 1399.

43. However *Abnahme* or completion of the work is not a bar to a claim for damages for defects caused by the fault of the contractor, nor is it necessary for such a claim that the purchaser has reserved his rights at the time of the *Abnahme* BGB 640(2) does not refer to Art. 635 but only to Arts. 633 and 634 and this appears to have been deliberate. BGHZ 61, 369, commentary by Schlechtreim/Jauernig pp. 716 and 717 and Lorenz p. 83.

44. Cass. civ. 8 November 1988; Bull. civ. I no. 314 p. 213: 'The obligations of a seller are not limited to the guarantee for "vices cachés" but equally impose upon him an obligation to deliver an item which is in conformity with the use for which it is intended; in case of a failure by the seller to meet this obligation the purchaser may bring an action for termination of the contract and recovery of damages.'

45. The seller will however be relieved of liability if there is no practical market in which the goods can be purchased (see further below, p. 207).

46. For specific goods see above, note 44. For generic goods it has been stated by the *Cour de cassation*, Cass. civ. 1 December 1987; Bull. civ. no. 325 p. 233 that 'in order to appreciate the extent of the delivery obligations of a seller of generic goods, it is necessary to take into account the characteristics of the goods in consideration of which the sale was concluded'.

47. The purchaser may also reimburse himself for his loss of profit (Cass. com. 1 June 1959 JCP 1959 II 11206). The right of *remplacement* is particular to commercial contracts. For non-commercial contracts the purchaser would have to apply to the court for an order. See further *Droit commercial* Dalloz 9th ed. pp. 778 et seq.

13 Contracts for sale – French law

Because, as indicated earlier (pp. 151–152) French law took over from Roman law the concept of a separate regime of liability in respect of latent defects (*vices cachés*), it is necessary to consider separately the position before and after completion of delivery. However, it will also be seen that in what appears to be an effort to do justice in particular cases, French jurisprudence has extended the responsibilities of the supplier pre-delivery into the post delivery period with what French authors admit to as being confusing results.

OBLIGATIONS OF THE SELLER PRE-DELIVERY

DELIVERY

Article 1604 of the *Code Civil*, relating to delivery, only refers to 'delivery being the transport of the goods sold into the power and possession of the Purchaser'. However, in the absence of any general provision in the *Code Civil* corresponding to s.13(1) of the Sale of Goods Act, the courts have extended this Article to cover the obligations of the supplier to deliver goods the characteristics of which correspond in terms of identity, quality and quantity with the terms of the order.

The supplier is obliged to deliver that which was ordered. If he delivers something different (an *aliud*) then he has failed to perform his contract.[1]

The supplier must also deliver goods whose characteristics correspond to the terms of the order and the purchaser is not bound to accept anything different (Art. 1604 of the *Code Civil*).

So where the hinges and the colour of the wood of a new piece of furniture differed from those ordered, the purchaser was entitled to reject even though the differences did not materially change the item's appearance.[2]

It was also stated by the *Cour de cassation* in another case that 'in deciding on the extent of the seller's obligations in respect of unascertained goods account must be taken of the characteristics of the goods in consideration of which the sale was concluded which may be aesthetic in character'. So if a car of the type ordered is delivered but has defects in the body paintwork, the purchaser can still reject it if he had made it known that he intended to purchase a car whose paintwork was faultless.

This will still apply even if all models of that type of car show the same imperfections. The purchaser is entitled to expect the goods to be without defect.[3]

If the quality of the unascertained goods is not specified in the order then they must be of medium standard (Art. 1246 of the *Code Civil*). This is in contrast with the English rule on merchantable quality (see above, pp. 141–142). As regards compliance with approved technical quality standards such as the French AFNOR, this will not relieve the supplier of liability if the goods are in fact defective for the purpose for which they are required and the seller as a professional should have known that this would be so. However such cases will normally be dealt with under the provisions relating to *vice caché* (see below, pp. 170–171).

The seller is also under an obligation to deliver goods which are fit either for the normal purposes for which such goods are required or for the purposes which have been defined specifically in the contract. These are very much the same obligations as those found in s.14 of the Sale of Goods Act.

The seller is further responsible for providing all necessary information relating to the usage of the goods especially if there is any danger involved.

The obligation of the supplier in that event is not just to describe the precautions which must be taken but also to warn the purchaser of the consequences if he fails to do so. As was said by the *Cour de cassation* when holding the manufacturer of a pesticide liable 'He had not signalled as he had the obligation to do the serious danger which the product presented to the eyes and the simple recommendation to avoid prolonged contact with the skin was not sufficient to warn those using the product against this particular danger and to lead them to take special precautions for their eyes' (Cass. com. 14 December 1982 Bull. civ. IV p. 309).

This obligation to advise is the more severe the greater the degree of professional skill and expertise of the seller in the field in question. He may even as an expert be required to establish from the purchaser the purpose for which the purchaser requires the goods in order that he can then advise him as to their suitability.[4]

A further illustration is that of a case in which a shipyard was held responsible for not having advised the purchaser that the price of a secondhand dredger including the costs of its renovation would be greater than the purchase of a new one (Cass. com. 16 March 1982 Bull. civ. IV no. 92). Strictly in those cases the obligation is one which relates to the seller's pre-contractual obligation to advise rather than his contractual obligation to give information as to the use of the product but it is not always easy to distinguish between the two. So in a case where a spray gun had been supplied with instructions as to its use, but the attention of the purchaser had not been drawn to these, with the result that the gun was defective the first time it was used, the *Cour de cassation* agreed that the seller had failed in his contractual obligation to provide the purchaser with advice (Cass. civ. 7 February 1979 D. 1979 I.R. p. 188).

However, the obligation to provide advice whether this is classified as pre-contractual or contractual is restricted by the terms of the contract itself. Where two computers had been ordered, but the purchaser an information technology contractor was unable to install them at the offices of his client because of their unsuitability for purpose, it was held that the supplier was not liable because he had had no contact with the client and had supplied exactly that which had been ordered (Cass. civ. 5 December 1989 Bull. civ. IV no. 306 and RTD.com 43(3) July to September 1990).

In the same way if the purchaser requires the goods for a particular purpose of his own, then he must in the same way as under English law (see the Sale of Goods Act s.14(3) above, pp. 142–143) advise the supplier accordingly, if he wishes to hold the supplier responsible for their suitability for that purpose.

On facts which are reminiscent of the Aswan Engineering case (see above, p. 148), apples were exported to Venezuela which had to be destroyed because the dye on the paper in which they were wrapped had run and marked them indelibly. The *Cour de cassation* quashed the decision of the cour d'appel, on the grounds that the quality of the paper and dye were sufficient for all normal uses which was established by the fact that there had been no previous complaints. Their suitability for a tropical climate could not be required if the purchaser had not made known to the supplier the particular use intended.[5]

ACCEPTANCE

Although the concept of acceptance of goods by the purchaser is known under French law it is not a defined term under the *Code Civil*, as is *réception* for works contracts, nor does it appear in practice to be applied as strictly especially in regard to non-professional purchasers. As is the case with any creditor the purchaser is only obliged to accept what is offered to him if it conforms with the requirements of the contract (Art. 1243 of the *Code Civil*). If, however, the purchaser fails at the time of delivery to protest to the seller regarding goods which are visibly not in conformity with the contract then in theory he has renounced his right to reject for failure to deliver, such renunciations being known as *agréation*. The same applies if the goods are complex and require testing in order to verify their compliance with the contract. The purchaser should carry out such testing within a reasonable period after delivery or lose his right to reject on the grounds of non-conformity.

In principle, therefore, the acceptance of the goods by the purchaser without reservation brings to an end the obligations of the seller relating to delivery for defects which were obvious or could have been discovered by a reasonable examination and the purchaser is obliged to pay the contract price.[6] His only remedy, then, is for defects which were hidden at the time of delivery as provided for under the special rules of Art. 1641 et seq. of the *Code Civil* – see below.

Unfortunately this neat distinction between defects which should have been discovered by the purchaser on the delivery of the goods or within a reasonable time afterwards, if they required a period of testing, and those which were hidden, has not been followed consistently by the courts. In a number of instances an action for termination has been allowed even when the goods were manifestly not in accordance with the contract and yet have been accepted by the purchaser without protest particularly if the defect was in the design.[7]

In practice, therefore, it is uncertain in any particular case what attitude the court will take. It has been suggested that this may differ according to whether the contract is between a professional seller and a non-professional purchaser or between two professionals, and that this may account for the difference in the judgements rendered by the first *chambre* of the *Cour de cassation* and those of the *chambre commerciale*.[8]

RULES APPLYING ONLY TO COMMERCIAL CONTRACTS

In commercial contracts the purchaser has the right if there are minor differences in the quantity or quality of the goods from those ordered to claim for a reduction in the price, *réfaction*. Also the seller may claim *réfaction* as a defence to an action by the purchaser for termination and the court can order that the purchaser is obliged to retain the goods although at a reduced price determined by the court.[9]

If the undelivered goods are *choses de genre* then, after giving the seller notice with a definite time limit, the purchaser may purchase replacement goods of the same quality. If he has to pay more, the seller is liable to him for the difference; if he is able to buy for less, then he retains the difference as damages.

HIDDEN DEFECTS (*VICES CACHÉS*)

As stated above, in principle, once the goods have been accepted without any reservation, the purchaser's rights are limited to those which are provided under Arts. 1641 – 6 of the *Code Civil* based on the Roman actions discussed earlier (see above pp. 151–153). However, as also stated above, and will be discussed in more detail later (see below p. 175), this principle is not always strictly applied and the purchaser may be allowed a choice of actions.

Conditions for the actions for *vices cachés*

According to Art. 1641 of the *Code Civil* the supplier 'is obliged to guaranty the thing sold against hidden defects which make it unsuitable for the use for which it was intended or which so reduce its suitability for that use that the purchaser would not have bought it, or would only have paid a lesser price, if he had known of them'. The following points arise from that definition.

1. The purchaser must establish that there was a defect inherent in the goods and that such defect existed at the time of contract or at the latest at the time of delivery. It is sufficient if the defect originated before delivery even if it only manifested itself later as, for example, with foodstuffs improperly sterilized. Equally it has been deduced that a TV set which caught fire was defective before delivery because it was established that the defect was in the internal wiring/components of the set and that it had functioned normally without any intervention by the purchaser before the fire.[10]

2. The defect must be shown to be one which rendered the goods unsuitable either for

the normal purpose for which such goods are purchased, or, if it was a special purpose, that such purpose had been known to the seller. So a brewery which bought a sterilizer to a lactic fermenting agent, the presence of which prevented the preservation of the beer, was not entitled to bring an action under the guaranty against the seller, since the sterilizer was not made for this purpose and the seller had no knowledge of the purchaser's intentions.[11]

3. The seller will not be responsible for a defect which arises out of the defective design which is provided by the purchaser or if the individual items supplied, while manufactured in accordance with the purchaser's specifications, fail to meet the purchaser's requirements when they are assembled together with one another.[12]

4. The defect must have been hidden. Obviously if the seller can establish that the purchaser actually knew of the existence of the defect and its adverse consequences then the guaranty cannot apply. Further, the defect is only hidden if the purchaser may legitimately be in ignorance of it. 'There are hidden only those defects which pass unnoticed to the eyes of purchasers of normal diligence'.[13]

The question arises as to whether this issue is to be decided objectively or subjectively. As Ghestin has observed, the courts do not follow strictly either path but take into account 'the technical competence normally to be expected of a person of that profession, the nature of the defect itself, the circumstances in which the purchaser was able to examine the goods before delivery and finally the nature of the goods in question'.[14]

The character of the purchaser as a professional or layman as regards the goods purchased will clearly have a significant influence on his ability to have discovered the defect. What would constitute a *vice caché* in a car sold to an ordinary person would not do so if the purchaser were the owner of a garage, provided at least that the defect was of a nature which ought to have been discoverable by such a professional purchaser.[15]

However, all the factors enumerated by Ghestin will be applied in arriving at an answer. Even a professional purchaser is not required to know of a defect if it could only be discovered by taking the goods concerned, e.g. a boat, to pieces.[16]

5. If it is public knowledge that the goods have a high risk of being defective the purchaser cannot invoke the guarantee; if a risk is foreseeable then the purchaser is required to make an even more careful examination. Secondhand goods are in principle subject to the guarantee but in deciding what is a defect account must be taken of the normal wear and tear to be expected according to their character and age.[17]

REMEDIES OF THE PURCHASER

THOSE BASED ON THE AEDILITIAN ACTIONS

Under Art. 1644 of the *Code Civil* the purchaser has a choice of remedies derived from the Roman actions. He may opt 'either to return the thing and obtain the return of the price, or to keep the thing and to have returned to him part of the price, as may be determined by experts'. The first is known as the *action rédhibitoire* and the second the *action estimatoire*.

Normally the purchaser is free to choose which action to take and the court is bound to respect his choice unless the defects are only minor, and do not affect the use for which the goods are intended, in which event the purchaser will be restricted to a reduction in the price. If, on the other hand, the defects have caused the loss of the goods then the purchaser may demand the restitution of the price even though he cannot restore the goods (Art. 1647 of the *Code Civil*).

If the vendor was ignorant of the defects in the goods then these were the only remedies open to the purchaser except that he could recover his expenses occasioned by the sale (Art. 1646 of the *Code Civil*). Previously the definition of these costs was so extended by the courts that they were virtually the equivalent of damages. Today, because of the extension of liability placed upon a professional seller, so that the issue arises only on sales by an occasional, non-professional seller, they have become much more restricted. So on the sale of a vehicle by a non-professional seller, which is rescinded for *vices cachés* which were unknown to the seller, the purchaser is entitled to the return of the purchase price and the cost of the vehicle licence but not to the cost of repairs which he had incurred and which were attributable to the *vices cachés*.[18]

REMEDY IN DAMAGES

According to Art. 1645 of the *Code Civil*: 'if the seller knew of the defect then in addition to the repayment of the price which he has received he is liable to the Purchaser for all damages'. This again followed from Roman law (see above, pp. 151–153) since the seller who knew of the defect will have acted in bad faith. However, by a series of steps of judicial inventiveness, and following Pothier's rule that the professional seller *spondet peritiam artis*, ('pledges himself to the skill of his profession') and 'ignorance of the defect is to be counted as *culpa*', the courts have now arrived at the position that as a matter of law the professional seller is 'held to know the defects in the items which he is selling' or in an alternative formulation 'has no right to be ignorant of them.'[19]

As a result the present position is that:

1. The professional seller cannot escape liability by showing that he was not at fault, or in no way could have discovered the defect or that he acted in good faith. The simple answer is that the professional seller or manufacturer is held as a matter of law to know the defect. It is not a matter of fact which is capable of being disproved.[20]
2. The rule applies equally to professional sellers as well as to actual manufacturers.[21]
3. It appears that the rule in contracts under Art. 1150 of the *Code Civil* that damages are limited to those which were either foreseen or could have been foreseen at the time of entering into the contract, unless the default is due to *dol*, will not apply if the

seller is a professional. He will be liable for all damages arising out of the *vice caché* provided that the purchaser can establish a causal link between the two.[22]

4. The professional seller or manufacturer cannot exclude or limit his liability by the insertion of appropriate clauses in the contract, except in the situation when both parties are 'professionals of the same speciality'. This phrase has received only a limited application in the courts. In general it would appear that clauses excluding or limiting responsibility for *vices cachés* are only likely to be effective when the contracting parties are both manufacturers working in the same industry and that, say, one is supplying parts to be fitted into a machine being assembled by the other and the purchaser has an equivalent level of technical knowledge to that of the vendor in relation to the goods the subject of the contract. If however one of the parties is a client organization, say an operator of transport, and the other a specialist in the supply of vehicles and spare parts, then a clause limiting or excluding the supplier's liability for *vice caché* would be unlikely to be upheld.[23]

The onus of proving that the parties were 'professionals of the same speciality' would fall upon the seller.

PERIOD FOR THE EXERCISE OF THE RIGHTS

It will be remembered that Roman law only gave a very limited period of time within which the purchaser could exercise either of the two actions specific to hidden defects. French law, in common with other continental systems, has followed this practice and according to Art. 1648 the actions resulting from the *vices cachés* must be brought within *un bref délai* (a short period).

There is little in the way of set rules for determining the period of the *bref délai*. It seems from the jurisprudence that the starting point is when the purchaser actually had effective knowledge of the defect rather than when objectively he should have known of it.[24] However it is left in the sovereign power of the judge of the facts to determine the actual length of time within which, in the particular circumstances of the case, the action should begin, provided that they state clearly the date on which the purchaser had effective knowledge of the defect. Ghestin has commented that generally the action will be considered inadmissible if the delay exceeds nine months and admissible if it does not exceed four months.[25]

Often the appointment of an expert will be necessary to determine the cause of the problem which has arisen and whether or not it arose before delivery. The issue of a writ requesting the appointment of an expert, even *en référé*,[26] is now sufficient to satisfy the requirement to act within *un bref délai*.

When the parties have engaged in negotiations in order to find the causes of the defect and how it should be remedied, then it seems that the action will be commenced within the *bref délai* provided that the purchaser acts quickly after the negotiations have broken down, even if this is a year from when the defect was first discovered.[27]

RELATIONSHIP OF THE ACTION FOR *VICE CACHÉ* WITH OTHER ACTIONS

Nullité pour erreur

The facts which give rise to the possibility of an action for *vice caché*, that in the circumstances and without his being at fault, the defect was unknown to the buyer at the time of acceptance and that the defect has made the thing unsuitable for the purpose agreed between the parties which will be either its normal use or a special purpose made known by the buyer to the seller, are essentially the same as those which will support an action for *erreur sur la substance* under Art. 1110 of the *Code Civil* (see above, pp. 121–123).

If therefore in the case of a sale of goods the purchaser elects to bring an action for nullity on the basis of *erreur*, is this subject to the rule requiring such an action to be brought within a *bref délai*? Different answers to this question have been given at different times by the various chambers of the *Cour de cassation*. However at the moment the answer is clearly that the requirement to bring the action within *un bref délai* does not apply to action *en nullité pour erreur*. The First Chamber of the *Cour de cassation* in the second of two judgements exactly a year apart has stated that the short period for an action for *vice caché* under Art. 1648 of the *Code Civil* does not apply to an action for nullity for mistake and that 'it is of no real importance in this respect that the error invoked was the result of a hidden defect making the thing unsuitable for the purpose for which it was intended'.[28]

In writing on this decision in the *Revue Trimestrielle de Droit Civil* Professor Philippe Remy commented that 'it confirms the confusion [between the action on the guaranty and that for nullity for mistake] in giving to the purchaser in the same factual circumstances, the choice between two actions, the one long and the other short; the action long probably driving out the action short'.[29]

The same applies if the action is for *nullité pour dol*. A short time after he had bought a car the purchaser was involved in an accident, the wheel falling off the vehicle. A year later he brought an action for rescission for *vice caché* which the cour d'appel did not allow since it was outside the *bref délai*. The *Cour de cassation* quashed the decision since it was the obligation of the judge to give the proper legal effect to the facts without being bound by the way in which the case had been pleaded by the parties. The facts showed that the wheel nuts had been soldered to the wheel because the threads were worn. It was no longer a matter of *vice caché* but of possible *dol* which had not been examined by the cour d'appel.[30]

Breach of contractual obligations

There are two situations in which, apart from the action for *vice caché*, the purchaser may have a contractual action against the seller relating to the quality or lack of fitness for purpose of the goods sold. First he may bring an action based on a failure to deliver that which has been promised. Second, the contract will often contain a contractual guarantee against defects which may run for an extended period of time from delivery or acceptance.

Failure to deliver according to contract In the same way as the *Cour de cassation* has allowed actions in nullity for *erreur sur la substance*, even if it would have appeared that the action should have been one for *vice caché*, it has also allowed actions based on a failure to deliver goods which were not fit for the purpose intended and did not restrict the purchaser after delivery to the action for *vice caché* or to the contractual period of guarantee. These judgements have been based generally on a failure by the vendor in design and have clearly been intended to avoid the adverse consequence to the purchaser of the *bref délai* under Art. 1648 which would apply if the action were for a *vice caché*.[31]

A recent example will illustrate the distinction between the action under the *garantie des vices cachés* and the action based on *inexécution de contrat*. An agricultural contractor had entered into an exclusive contract with a co-operative for the spreading of carbonate of lime and for this purpose had purchased a tractor. From the time of delivery he had established the fact that the tractor did not develop the power expected but nevertheless he had used it. Four years later and after various mechanical problems the tractor had finally ceased to function.

As a result the contractor had then brought an action against the seller for the damages he had suffered as a result of the unsuitability of the tractor for the purpose intended. The Caen cour d'appel had rejected his claim since it had not been made within a *bref délai*. The contractor challenged the decision because he asserted that the tractor did not comply with the purpose for which it had been specially ordered. He maintained that the cour d'appel had failed to distinguish between the action for *vice caché* and the action for non-performance of the contract for the failure of the goods to conform to the requirements of the contract.

The *Cour de cassation* accepted the contractor's argument, quashed the judgement of the cour d'appel and in consequence asked the court to which the case would be sent for rehearing to examine if the seller had not failed in his delivery obligations which are not restricted by the *bref délai* of Art. 1648 of the *Code Civil*.[32]

Droit commun et faute lourde There can be one problem for the purchaser, however, if the action is brought under the *droit commun* as opposed to that of the *vice caché*. As noted earlier, under the regime of the *vice caché* the professional seller is assimilated to one who knew of the defect in the goods and therefore cannot avail himself of the protection of any clause in the contract limiting his responsibilities, which includes the payment of damages, unless the purchaser is a professional of the same speciality.

But in principle under the *droit commun* clauses which limit the responsibility, even of a professional seller, are valid, at least in transactions with a commercial or professional purchaser, and the purchaser does not have to be of the same speciality as the seller.[33] The only general exceptions are if the debtor is guilty of *dol* or *faute lourde* which is assimilated to *dol* (Cass. civ. 24 February 1993). Traditionally *faute lourde* has been considered to be an act of gross negligence or extreme foolishness which, although not intended to injure the other party, would nevertheless result in doing so. More recently it has been said to be 'behaviour of extreme seriousness, akin to *dol*, showing the inaptitude of the debtor to fulfil the contractual task which he has undertaken' (Cass. com. 3 April 1990 Bull. IV no. 108). The use in the handling of goods of lifting equipment which was manifestly inadequate for the purpose was held to be *faute lourde* (Cass. com. 13 November 1990 Bull. IV no. 271).

Les juges de fond may also characterize a default as *faute lourde* if it relates to an obligation which is essential to the fulfilment of the contract and the non-performance of which will have serious consequences for the creditor. So a bank which failed in its obligation of security to verify strictly the identity of a person claiming access to a strong-box could not apply a clause limiting its liability contained in the contract under which it let the strong-box (Cass. civ. 15 November 1988). One is reminded of the now abandoned English law doctrine of 'fundamental breach' which still seems to be alive in France.

The lower courts have on occasions found a default in the manufacture of goods to be a *faute lourde* in order to avoid giving effect to a clause limiting the manufacturer's responsibility and where the defect constituted also a *vice caché* these decisions have been upheld by the *Cour de cassation*, e.g. Cass. com. 6 July 1961 Bull. III no. 148. However, although it was decided to be *faute lourde* to supply pesticide not suitable for the purpose for which it was intended, in that it destroyed the vines which it treated (Cass. civ. 22 November 1988 Bull. I no. 595), the jurisprudence is not wholly consistent when the action is one for non-conformity as opposed to one for *vice caché*, e.g. the kiwi fruit case quoted in note 33 above. It seems that with non-conformity, while there is a definite tendency towards finding a production defect to be *faute lourde*, it still remains a matter of judicial discretion.

BREACH OF A CONTRACTUAL GUARANTY

Most contracts will contain a clause, often entitled 'guaranty', under which for a limited period of time, usually no more than two years, and often considerably less, the supplier will be responsible for making good defects in the goods supplied, subject usually to the purchaser having operated and maintained the goods in accordance with the instructions of the supplier.

It is well established that this contractual guaranty is quite separate from the legal guaranty in respect of *vice caché* under Art. 1641. So the rules of the legal guaranty will not apply to the contractual guaranty. There is no question of the contractual guaranty having to be exercised, according to Art. 1648, within a *bref délai*,[34] although in practice periods are usually stated within the contractual guaranty itself. The fact of the seller having failed to carry out his obligations under the contractual guaranty is sufficient to allow the purchaser to bring an action to compel him to do so or to bring an action for rescission together with a claim for damages.

Equally, the fact that the purchaser has not complied with some provision of the contractual guaranty, relating for example to repairs only being carried out by technicians approved by the vendor, does not prevent the purchaser from exercising his rights under the legal guaranty when the goods are subject to a *vice caché* occurring during design/manufacture.

Finally, provisions of the contractual guaranty which seek to limit the purchaser's rights, e.g. to replacement of defective parts, will not affect the purchaser's rights under the legal guaranty if the seller is a professional.

OBLIGATION OF SECURITY

Additionally it now appears that there is also an obligation of security under the *droit commun* which has been expressed by the *Cour de cassation* as 'only to deliver products free from any defect or fault in manufacture of a type which would create a danger for people or their goods'.

The case in which this obligation was clearly expressed concerned the purchase by a couple of a mobile home. Two days after they had taken delivery they were both found dead in the vehicle having been asphyxiated by carbon monoxide leaking from a gas heater which was defectively designed, the vehicle having inadequate ventilation. An action was brought by the heirs of the couple against the Belgian company which had the right to sell the vehicles in France and the French re-seller. Although the *cour d'appel* rejected the claim for *vice caché* because the action was brought outside the period of the *bref délai* they nevertheless allowed an action in damages and this was upheld by the *Cour de cassation* because the sellers were in breach of their obligation of security which was expressed in the terms stated above.

It has been commented that the obligation of security is independent of the action for *vice caché* since that action is essentially for the defect in the thing purchased with the remedies as referred to earlier of *rédhibition* and *estimatoire*. The liability to pay damages is only incidental to the action for *vice caché* in circumstances where the seller actually knew, or is taken as a professional to know, the existence of the defect and is therefore guilty of bad faith. This is to be contrasted with the action for breach of the obligation of security which is essentially one for damages in respect of physical harm to the purchaser or damage to the other goods of the purchaser (Cass. civ. 11 June 1991, Bull. civ. I no. 20 and commentaries in the RTD com. (1) January to March 1992 and RTD civ. 91 (1) January to March 1992).

TIME FOR DELIVERY

French law has the same basic rule as English law that it is for the parties to fix the time for delivery in the contract and if they fail to do so then it is for the court (*les juges de fond*) to decide on what is a reasonable time within which the seller should deliver the goods.[35] There, however, the resemblance ends and indeed French law proceeds in almost an opposite direction to English law. It seems that in this, as in other instances, English law is far more geared towards commercial, and in particular international trading practice, than is French law.

English law, it will be recalled, holds generally that in mercantile contracts a time clause will be regarded as a condition of the contract the breach of which entitles the purchaser immediately to terminate the contract (see above, p. 143 and note 22) and to claim damages.

MISE EN DEMEURE

French law by contrast starts from the position that a delay in itself by the seller is not sufficient to put the seller in default. The purchaser must give the seller a formal notice (*une sommation*), or an informal notice such as a letter accepted by the *juges de fond* as being equivalent, requiring performance (Arts. 1139 and 1146 of the *Code Civil*). It is the issue of this notice, the *mise en demeure*, which places the seller legally in default (*en demeure*), and entitles the purchaser to claim damages for delay from that date.

This requirement is not perhaps surprising if under the terms of the contract the period/time for delivery was only indicative, and it would seem that in cases of doubt French courts will tend to presume that this was so, rather than that the period/time was mandatory.[36] It is more surprising if there was a firm period/term stated for delivery which is now past. However, this may well be the case since the mere fact *on its own* of the contract containing a firm delivery period/time which has expired will not generally be sufficient to put the seller in default.[37] The issue will depend on the decision by *les juges de fond* within their sovereign power as to whether or not the provisions of the contract relating to the time for delivery were sufficiently clear and rigorous that they could be said to constitute the tacit intention of the parties to dispense with the need for the notice. The inclusion of a penalty clause, the requirement *livrable de suite*, a fixed period for completion under threat of cancellation and an express provision in the form of agreement for a firm delivery period overriding the seller's general conditions of contract, are some instances where the courts have decided that the necessity for the *mise en demeure* was implicitly renounced by the parties.[38]

It is however always a risk to trust the court's discretion. This is why purchasers will normally seek to take advantage of one of the exceptions to the rule requiring notice, especially that allowing the requirement to be excluded by the express terms of the contract.

Exceptions

1. When the goods can only be delivered within a certain period to be of any use to the purchaser. Starck gives the example of a merchant who ordered goods to re-sell at a particular fair. If they are not delivered by the time the gates of the fair are closed, then the merchant can immediately claim damages (Art. 1146 of the *Code Civil*).[39]
2. When the seller has stated that he does not intend to deliver.[40]
3. When the parties have expressly provided in the contract that a *mise en demeure* is not required. It is again for *les juges de fond* in exercise of their sovereign power to decide as to whether or not the parties have expressed their intentions with

sufficient clarity. This is the most important exception and one which the purchaser will normally seek to follow. An example taken from a set of standard French conditions of contract reads 'Les pénalités sont applicables *sans mise en demeure préalable*, sur simple confrontation des dates d'expiration des délais contractuels . . . et des dates d'achèvement des travaux correspondants . . .'[41]

APPLICATION TO RIGHTS TO TERMINATE

Where the purchaser wishes to terminate the contract for the default of the seller, the general rule under French law is that termination requires a judgement of the court (see below, pp. 322–323). Since however the application to the court constitutes a *mise en demeure* there is no advantage to be gained by issuing one separately.

Contractual rights to terminate

There is an important exception to the general rule if the parties have expressly provided in their contract for termination in certain specified cases of default. These clauses however are construed strictly by the courts since they are a derogation from the *droit commun*.

The clause must at least provide that the purchaser can terminate *de plein droit*. In this case he must still give a *mise en demeure* before he can exercise his rights, but he can then do so without the need to obtain the judgement of the court. If additionally the contract provides for the right of termination to be exercised *de plein droit et sans sommation ni formalité judiciare*, then even the need for a *mise en demeure* is avoided and the right could be exercised immediately. Careful drafting of the clause is essential.[42]

If a *mise en demeure* is needed then it should state the period within which the seller is required to deliver which, because of the requirements of good faith, must be reasonable in the circumstances of the case. This period is then mandatory on the seller.

Provided that the contract contains a firm period/time for delivery then the obligation of the seller is one of *résultat* so that he can only avoid liability by proving *cause étrangère*.

COMMERCIAL CONTRACTS

In commercial contracts there is an even stronger emphasis placed on the requirement for the strict compliance with the terms of the contract and of its execution in good faith.[43] Also, taking account of the needs of commerce, there is more room for the purchaser to act independently in the case of default by the seller, without his having first to obtain an order from the court. If therefore there is a serious default by the seller in the delivery of generic goods (*choses de genre*) then the purchaser has the right, after issue of a *mise en demeure*, but without the need for a prior order of the court, to determine the contract and purchase replacement goods at the seller's expense.

If the purchase price exceeds the contract price then the purchaser may claim the difference from the seller; if he purchases at a price lower than the contract price then he keeps the benefit.

The right of *remplacement* however only applies to *choses de genre* and not to a sale for a specific item of machinery.[44]

NOTES

1. Delivery of seeds of mangelwurzels instead of those of sugar beet (Cass. civ. 11 October 1966 Bull. civ. I no. 466, p. 353).
2. Cass. civ. 1 December 1987, Bull. civ. I no. 324, p. 233.
3. Cass. civ. 1 December 1987 Bull. civ. I no. 325 p. 233 and Cass. civ. 4 April 1991, Bull. Civ. I no. 130.
4. Cass. com. 14 November 1977 Bull. civ. IV no. 253 p. 216 in which a supplier was held partially responsible for the loss suffered by the purchaser when, knowing that the goods had different properties once put into use, according to the method in which they were cut, he had failed to obtain information from the purchaser at the appropriate time as to the usage to which he intended to put the goods. In a recent decision the *Chambre commerciale* of the *Cour de cassation* has gone even further and held that the seller of an item of equipment has two obligations: to inform himself as to the requirements of the purchaser and to advise the purchaser of any technical constraints in the use of the piece of equipment and of its suitability for achieving the purchaser's objective. The seller of equipment, it appears, must take the initiative in holding discussions with the purchaser so that he can satisfy himself that what he is supplying will meet the purchaser's needs. Cass. com. 1 December 1992, Bull. civ. IV no. 391 and see RTD com. 46(3) July–September 1993.
5. Cass. com. 19 March 1973 Bull. civ. IV no. 125, p. 109.
6. A decision of the *Chambre commerciale* of the *Cour de cassation* 12 February 1980 in quashing a judgement of the *Cour d'Appel* who had pronounced the rescission of the contract on the grounds that the wood delivered was not suitable for making furniture, stated clearly that the court could not pronounce the rescission since 'the judges had found that the agents of the purchaser had checked the goods and accepted them without reserve'. (Bull. civ. IV, no. 80, p. 61). It is to be noted that the purchaser was a professional.

    Ghestin, *La Vente* s.764 sets out a judgement of the *Cour de Bordeaux* which in part states 'if the nature of the defect complained of is such that it is obvious, which normally may not escape the attention of the purchaser, the acceptance without reserve of the goods, implies on the part of the purchaser, above all in commercial matters, his acknowledgement that the goods conform to the contract from which it follows that an action in rescission based on Art. 1184 is no longer open to him' (23 May 1977, Gaz. Pal. 1978, 94). Again there is the reference to transaction being a commercial one.
7. Observation on the decision by the Ass. Plen. 7 February 1986 in *Les grands arrêts de la jurisprudence civile*, at p. 724.
8. *Contrats civils et commerciaux*, Dutilleul and Delebecque, Dalloz, Paris 1991 at. p. 222 and notes 3 and 4. While the *première chambre* since 1983 has been in favour of allowing the action for rescission under the *droit commun*, so protecting the purchaser from having to satisfy the need to act within a *bref délai* as required by Art. 1648 if the action is for *vice caché*, the *chambre commerciale* has not followed this route. See also Ghestin *La Vente*, ss. 775 and 776.
9. The differences must be minor and not affect the use for which the goods are intended (Cass. civ. 1 April 1924 S.19251 371. However in a case involving crayfish tails of second-rate and not first-rate quality the price was reduced by a half (Cass. com. 23 March 1971 B.IV no.89). There is no power for the court to require the purchaser to keep a larger quantity of the goods than ordered although he must pay a supplement if he does so. For the right of the seller to claim *réfaction* and for the court to order the purchaser to retain the goods at a reduced price see Cass. com. 4 June 1980, Bull.civ.IV no.230, p. 194.
10. Cass.civ.28 November 1979 Gaz.Pal.3 April 1980. Also Cass.civ. 1 re 2 December 1992 – machine had only worked 960 hours before a fire; no evidence of ill-use, lack of maintenance or sabotage. *Cour d'Appel* entitled to find that fire was due to *vice caché* which could only be a manufacturing defect.

11. Rouen 31 May 1938 Rec.du Havre 1938.2.237.
12. Cass.com.4 December 1973 inedit. cited Ghestin, *La Vente* p. 803.
13. Cass.com. 15 December 1977 Gaz. Pal. 1978 1.Somm, p. 107.
14. Ghestin, *La Vente* p. 773.
15. Cass.civ. 18 December 1962 D.1063.J.114.
16. Cass. com. 20 April 1970, Bull. civ. IV no. 125, p. 116.
17. The purchaser, even if he is a layman, is still expected to make a careful examination within the limits of technical competence to be expected of someone such as himself. So he would not be expected to discover a defect which would only be revealed if the vehicle were placed on an elevated ramp. Versailles 1re Ch.3 February 1989, D.1989 IR, p. 92.
18. Cass. com. 12 December 1984, Bull. civ. IV no. 349.
19. See Zimmermann p. 335 and the references there to Pothier, *Traité de contrat de vente* n.214 and *Traité des obligations* n.163. The modern rule, which also restricted the amount of the costs occasioned by the sale which could be recovered from the seller ignorant of the defect, started with two decisions of the First Chamber of the *Cour de cassation*, one of 24 November 1954 and one of 19 January 1965 in each of which the court stated: 'but whereas under the terms of Article 1646 of the Code civil a seller who is ignorant of the defects in the thing is only held liable for the restitution of the price and for reimbursing the purchaser the costs occasioned by the sale, it results on the contrary from the provisions of Art. 1645 of the same code that the seller who knew of the defects, *to whom it is proper to assimilate one who by his profession is not allowed to be ignorant of them,* is held, in addition to the restitution of the price which he has received, liable to the purchaser for all damages . . .'. Bull. civ. 1954 I no. 338 p. 285 and D.1965, 389 Gaz. Pal. 1965.1.359. For the judgements and an extensive review of these cases and subsequent jurisprudence see *Les grands arrêts*, p. 710 et seq.
20. This follows from the terse statement of the Commercial Chamber of the *Cour de cassation* on 27 April 1971: 'every manufacturer is held to know the defects affecting the thing manufactured'.
21. So held by the First Civil Chamber of the *Cour de cassation* in a decision of 21 November 1972. The defect was a brake failure and it was sufficient for the court that the defendant was a garage proprietor by profession even though the evidence given by the court expert in the court below had been to the effect that the defect was not discoverable by a careful and well-informed professional (Bull. civ. I p. 244 no. 257). Also, 'the professional seller is in the same way as the manufacturer presumed to know the defects in the goods which he sells' (Cass. civ. 18 October 1977, Bull. civ. III no. 348, p.263).
22. The general rule does not apply if the debtor has been guilty of *dol* or, according to the jurisprudence, of *faute lourde* – gross misconduct. Since, as referred to in note 20, the professional vendor is held to know of the defects in the goods which he sells it would seem to follow logically that he must be guilty of either *dol* or *faute lourde*. It will be remembered that *dol* is present if the vendor fails to disclose a fact which if he had known of it would have stopped the creditor from entering into the contract (see above, p. 127). There would appear to be no decision of the *Cour de cassation* directly on the point but the formulas used by the court in cases involving a professional seller that he is responsible for 'all damage' or 'the totality of the loss' suffered by the purchaser clearly supports this view (Ghestin, *La Vente* p. 903).
23. Cass. com. 3 December 1985 Bull. civ. IV no. 287 p. 244 where the contract in question was between a shipyard constructing a tanker and a manufacturer of the defective tanks.
24. Cass. com. 24 November 1982 Bull. civ. IV no. 381 p. 312 where the court quashed a decision of the *Cour d'Appel* on the grounds that they had based their decision not on when the purchaser had effective knowledge of the defects but on when they thought he ought to have know of them due to his technical expertise.
25. *La Vente* p.790.
26. Art. 2244 of the *Code Civil* introduced by Law no. 85–677 of 5 July 1985. The reference to *en référe* is to the accelerated procedure under Art. 484 et seq., 808 et seq. and 872 et seq. of the New Code of Procedure under which an application can be made as appropriate either to the President of the *Tribunal de Commerce* or the President of the *Tribunal de Grande Instance* in urgent cases for interim measures.
27. See Malaurie and Aynes p. 242 and decisions cited in n.55.
28. Cass. civ. 28 June 1989. Bull. civ. I no. 268, p. 178.
29. January-March 1990 p. 100.
30. Cass. civ. 16 April 1991 Bull. civ. I no. 144 and see *Revue trimestrielle de droit commercial et de droit économique* no.1 1992 at p. 218.
31. An action by the purchaser of a burglar alarm system which it appeared was unsuitable for the site which

was close to the sea and subject to bad weather and never worked properly was disallowed by the *Cour de Poitiers* because the proceedings were begun outside the contractual guarantee period and the *bref délai de l'article 1648 du Code Civil*. The decision was quashed by the *Cour de cassation* because the court below should have considered if the fault in design did not constitute a failure to deliver goods which were suitable for the normal purpose intended. Cass. civ. 14 February 1989 Bull. civ. I no. 83 p. 53, commented on in the *Revue trimestrielle de droit commercial et de droit économique*, no. 4, October–December 1989 p. 712.

32. Cass. civ. 29 January 1991, Bull.civ.I no.41 and *Revue trimestrielle de droit commercial et de droit économique*, vol.4, 1991, p. 637.

33. Cass. civ. 20 December 1988, Bull. civ. I no. 373 p. 252. In this case a large quantity of kiwi plants had been ordered by a nursery but a part of those supplied were not of the variety ordered. Relying on a clause of his general conditions of sale printed on the back of his invoices, the seller denied liability for loss of profits but replaced the plants. The wording of the clause was ambiguous in that it was not clear whether it applied to an error in the variety of the good supplied or not. The court referred therefore to trade practice which established that 'the guarantee of authenticity of the variety was limited at the choice of the seller to the replacement of the plants or the refunding of the costs to the exclusion of the payment of damages'. The court therefore accepted the seller's argument.

  The *Cour de cassation* held that the court below had not been at fault in referring to trade practice to resolve the ambiguity in the clause in the conditions of sale. Further, as it was not a matter of an action for *vice caché*, but of conformity of the goods supplied with those ordered, the validity of the clause was not restricted to cases in which the purchaser was of the same speciality as the vendor. They therefore confirmed the judgement. See the *Revue trimestrielle de droit commercial et de droit économique*, no. 3, July–September 1989, p. 522.

34. Cass. com. 2 May 1990 Bull. civ. IV no. 132 commented on in the *Revue trimestrielle de droit commercial et de droit économique*, no. 1, January–March 1991, p. 90.

35. Cass. civ. 10 April 1973, Bull. civ. III. no. 274.

36. Ghestin, *La Vente* p. 721 and note 27.

37. Weill and Terré para. 418. They refer to the present law as being opposed to the pre-revolutionary French law which did put the debtor into *demeure* by reason only of his not having delivered by the firm date and followed in this respect the Latin maxim *dies interpellat pro homine*. Nicholas translates this as 'the arrival of the due date takes the place of the creditor in demanding performance' (Nicholas p.234). As will be seen later (p. 216) this maxim does form part of German law. For a historical account of the development of the maxim, see Zimmermann, p. 798.

38. Penalty clause Cass. civ. 7 March 1969 JCP 70.II 16461; *livrable de suite* Req.7 March 1933: DH 1933, 218; fixed period for completion under threat of cancellation Cass. civ. 29 October 1986, judgement set out in Joanna Schmidt-Szalewski p. 544; agreement overriding vendor's general conditions of sale Cass. civ. 9 February 1977, Bull. civ. 1977 I p. 60.

39. Example given in Starck p. 469 quoting Com. 2 April 1974, D.1974 IR 152.

40. Req. 4 January 1927, DH 1927, 65.

41. *Cahier des clauses administratives générales applicables aux marchés de travaux de grand équipement* Électricité de France, December 1981, clause 20.2.

42. Joanna Schmidt-Szalewski para. 529, pp. 543 and 544.

43. Malaurie refers to 'the rigid strength of business morality' – 'La morale des affaires est une morale de fer'.

44. Cass.com. 20 January 1976, B.IV no.26.

14 Contracts for works – French law

OBLIGATIONS OF THE CONTRACTOR

In respect of the quality of the works to be performed, the contractor is obliged to:

1. Execute the work in accordance with the terms of the contract and the plans, specifications and instructions which are given to him by the architect.[1]
2. Perform his work in accordance with the professional standards of skill which ought to be exercised by a contractor having his particular specialist skills and experience.[2]
3. Provide materials which are suitable for the purpose for which they are required unless he can exonerate himself by proof that the defect in the materials was due to a *cause étrangère*.
4. Draw the attention of the architect to the disadvantages, faults or defects which may result from errors or omissions which he is led to notice in the documents which are provided to him and in the orders which he receives.[3]

Three important comments may be made on the above in comparison with the obligations of a contractor under English law. First, French law sees the duly qualified contractor as being a professional who is 'master of the rules of his art' and the more of a specialist he is, the higher the degree of competence he is expected to show in the performance of his obligations.

Under English law the obligation is to carry out the work in a good and workmanlike manner in accordance with the plans and specifications prepared by the architect. English law as regards workmanship does not appear to draw any real distinction as between the skills of one contractor and another. The level of skill to be shown is that of a reasonably competent contractor in the field of work in question.

Second, in respect of materials the contractor can only avoid liability for defective materials if he can establish *cause étrangère* which effectively means either an event of *force majeure* or a default by the client. It is no excuse that the defect in the materials was not discoverable by any means known at the time or that the materials corresponded to a technical standard then in force.[4] In practice this creates a result virtually identical to that under English law although the reasoning is different.

French law reaches its conclusion on the contractor's liability because of a presumption of his responsibility to execute the works free from defects.

The contractor held to execute works free from defects, is responsible for the defects due to imperfections in the material used except only if he can show that the improper execution was due to a 'cause étrangère' which could not be imputed to him. The sole fact that the contractor was unable to know at the time of construction of the defect inherent in the material did not constitute a 'cause étrangère' which relieved him of his responsibility.[5]

English law is more concerned with the 'chain of liability' argument that in the absence of the contractor being strictly liable the employer would have no remedy at all because of the doctrine of privity of contract (see below, pp. 270–271). This problem is most acute when the supplier is nominated by the employer.[6]

There is no need for French law to be concerned with the problem of establishing a 'chain of liability' since the employer has *une action contractuelle directe* against the vendor of the defective material.[7] Moreover the problems associated with nomination hardly exist since in France the nominated system is virtually unknown. In the French standard form of building contract it is provided that the contractor is responsible for the supply of all materials and the employer does not have the right to nominate a supplier, unless the special conditions provide otherwise. Other standard forms contain no right for the purchaser to nominate but only a right to supply materials himself.[8]

As regards the responsibility of the employer who does instruct the contractor as to the materials to be purchased, or supplies them himself, French law draws a sharp distinction between the employer who possesses an acknowledged technical competence (*notoirement compétent en la matière*) and one who does not.[9] If the employer is acknowledged to be technically competent, and issues the contractor with precise instructions, then this may relieve the contractor from liability if these result in the supply of defective materials.[10] Even so, it has been decided in administrative law that if the contractor does not make any reservation based on his own knowledge and experience, then he is not discharged from his responsibility to provide the employer with advice. He may not follow blindly the employer's orders.[11]

If alternatively the client is technically not competent then the contractor is not freed from his obligations by accepting the employer's choice.[12] He should examine the materials and, if he has doubts as to their suitability, then he must warn the employer with reasons for his reservations and obtain a definitive decision from him. If the employer were to confirm his instruction then the employer would assume the total responsibility. However the contractor should still not follow the employer's instructions if to do so would mean constructing a building the solidity of which in his professional opinion would be seriously in doubt. To do so would put the contractor at fault.[13]

As will be apparent, the French concept of the contractor as a 'master of his art' has wide consequences since the obligation of the contractor to advise the employer, especially if he is not acknowledged to be technically competent, is not limited to choice of materials but extends to the methods of construction and, in the absence of an architect, to the planned scope of the works. He must know if these are unsuitable, e.g. construction on sloping ground without the necessary levelling.

That brings in the third issue: that of the requirement for the contractor to warn of possible difficulties or errors arising out of the drawings or instructions which he has received even if these come from the architect. Although the contractor is not expected to do a detailed check of the architect's drawings and calculations he is expected to use his skill and experience as a 'master of his art' to draw the architect's attention to any matter which he considers may create a problem. As it has been said, 'he must not carry out with his eyes shut that which has been ordered' nor without making reservations must he undertake work in accordance with drawings which he considers contain a mistake.

This is clearly a wider responsibility than that which is provided for under English law. There are two earlier cases before the official referee which are sometimes used to support the contention that there does exist a duty to warn.[14] However, having regard to later authority these have been held as supportable only on the basis of some special relationship between the parties which could support a finding of reliance by the building owner on the contractor but not otherwise.[15] There is no room under the standard forms of building and civil engineering for any implied term since none is necessary to give business efficacy to a contract under which in design matters the employer has chosen an architect/engineer upon whose judgement he is content to rely.[16] As regards liability in tort, given the express and detailed wording of the contract forms, this can be no wider than the liability in contract, and could only exceptionally arise in a particular case on a finding of 'special relationship and reliance' sufficient to bring the case within the *Hedley Byrne* principle for the recovery of what is economic loss unless there is alleged to be injury to persons or damage to property other than the defective works.[17]

RÉCEPTION

As stated earlier (see above, p. 154) there are specific guarantees under French law which apply after the issue of the *procès verbal de réception*. However *réception* both acts as the trigger for those guarantees but also substantially brings to an end the contractor's other obligations in respect of the quality of the works and transfers the risk in the works to the employer. The act of *réception* is therefore of primary importance in the French law of contract for works.

DEFINITION

Réception under the *Code Civil* Art. 1792–6 is the act by which the employer signifies his acceptance of the works with or without reservations. It is a single and unique judicial act.[18] The architect is not strictly a party to the *procès verbal de réception* although it would be normal for him to sign it. His signature is only there to record that he has satisfied his obligations of having properly advised the employer and either of his approval that *réception* should be granted with the reservations if any as stated, or that he disapproves, so that he is protected against any action by the employer for having failed in his duty to provide proper advice.

Despite the wording of Art. 1792–6 the issue of a *procès verbal* (certificate) is not a condition for *réception* to be granted. *Réception* can be tacit but it must then be established that the employer had intended to effect *réception*. The mere taking possession without proof of such intention or the issue of a document for administrative purposes which declares that the works have been completed will not be sufficient. It is essentially a matter of showing an intention by the employer to accept the works as being a fulfilment of the contract, except for any express reservations made at the time, with his rights in the future being to require the performance of the guaranty obligations contained in Art. 1792, *Code Civil*.[19]

The responsibility to apply for the *procès verbal de réception* is that of the contractor and if he has not done so then under a contract for public works the *Conseil d'Etat has held that the taking of possession did not constitute réception*.[20]

CONSEQUENCES OF *RÉCEPTION*

For all practical purposes *réception* brings to an end the contractual obligations of the contractor under the *droit commun*, i.e. for purposes of the ordinary contractual responsibilities. These only remain in respect of damage not covered by the specific guaranties under Art. 1792 of the *Code Civil* (see below, pp. 189–195). This could be either faults not affecting the solidity of the works or their suitability for the purpose for which they were intended, referred to as *dommages intermédiares*, or for work not classified as the construction of an *ouvrage*, e.g. renovation. In either case the employer must prove the contractor was at fault (Cass. civ. 9.2.1988 D.1988 IR 83).

For contracts subject to the administrative law the *Conseil d'Etat* has ruled that the contractual responsibility of the contractor ends at the conclusion of the guaranty period which runs from *réception*, usually for one year under Art. 44 of the CCAG (*Cahier des clauses administratives générales*) except in the case of fraud or dishonesty or a fault which by its nature is assimilated to a fraud or *dol*.[21] The omission by a contractor of an important element of the works, the very serious foreseeable consequences of which he could not have been ignorant because of his particular expertise, has been held by the *Conseil d'Etat* to constitute a fault assimilated to *dol* even though there was no proof of an intent to deceive. The period of the contractor's liability to the employer was therefore 30 years and an action was accordingly allowed after the expiry of the *garantie décennale*. C.E. 3 April 1991.

It also brings to an end the contractual responsibility of the architect except again for an action outside the scope of the specific guaranties, or an action based on the default of the architect in falling to advise the client as to reservations which ought to be made.

The issue of the *procès verbal de réception* is the starting point for the specific guaranties under Art. 1792. It is also therefore the beginning of the period of prescription, either ten or two years, applicable to those guaranties. Further, the jurisprudence has consistently held that the ten-year period of the *garantie décennale* applies equally to contractual faults to which the guaranties do not apply (Art. 2270, *Code Civil*).[22] This applies however serious the default except in the case of fraud or *faute dolosive* which requires proof, if not of the intent of the debtor to cause the damage, at least of a deliberate breach of contract with the certain knowledge of the damage which would result (Cass. civ. 4 February 1969 Bull. I no. 60 and Cass. civ. 26 May 1988 J.C.P. 88 IV 267). It seems therefore the civil law is in this instance more demanding than the administrative law.

It follows that if the *réception* is not given that the contractor and architect will continue to be under their respective contractual obligations and that the particular periods of prescription relative to the guaranties will not start to run (see above, note 20). Although this was a decision under administrative law the same would apply under civil law.

After the *réception* the contractor and architect are only responsible to the client for defects which are 'hidden' at the time of the *réception* and defects which were apparent but which were made the subject of reservations. If the defect was apparent, but no reservation was made, then the client has no claim against the contractor.[23] He may, as stated earlier, have a claim against the architect for failing to advise him of the necessity of making the reservations.

However the courts have sought to improve the position of the employer. A defect will only be regarded as 'apparent' if it was discoverable by an employer 'normally diligent' and account will be taken of the technical competence of the employer and the nature of the defect. Also a defect will be treated as 'hidden' if, although its existence was known at the time of the *réception*, its serious effects only became apparent afterwards and were not discoverable beforehand. The principles which are applied are similar to those used in connection with *vices cachés* in contracts for the sale of goods (see above, pp. 170–171). The decision in each case is left by the *Cour de cassation* to the *appréciation souveraine du juge du fait*.[24]

DEFECTS AFTER *RÉCEPTION* OR THE SUBJECT OF *RÉSERVES* AT *RÉCEPTION*

These defects are covered by three separate guaranties under Art. 1792 of the *Code Civil*. They form the most comprehensive set of such guaranties in any civil law system.

The legal status of the guaranties under Art. 1792 of the *Code Civil* in the administrative law is that although they are not, according to consistent rulings of the *Conseil d'Etat*, *ordre public*, and they can therefore be modified by the parties or by the *juge administratif*, in practice, with a few exceptions noted below, the rules relating to the guaranties are followed in the administrative law. The administrative courts are said to apply the 'principles from which articles 1792 and 2270 draw their inspiration and not their literal text'.

Garantie de parfait achèvement

This guaranty which applies under Art. 1792–6 has the following characteristics:

1. It runs for a year from *réception*.
2. It applies to all defects and faults in, or non-conformity of, the works which were the subject of reservations made at the time of *réception* or which occur during the year and are advised by the employer to the contractor in writing.
3. It applies only to the contractor in respect of his work and not to the architect or others.
4. The contractor is obliged to remedy such defects, faults or non-conformity and if he fails to do so then the employer may engage others to do it at the risk and cost of the contractor. The guaranty does not depend on proof of fault but the contractor would have recourse against others if the defect were their responsibility or might even exonerate himself.[25]
5. The guaranty does not apply to defects due to wear and tear or normal usage.
6. The guaranty is not exclusive. The *garantie décennale* applies also during the year after *réception*.[26]
7. It is now specifically stated in the code – Loi no. 90–1129 of 19 December 1990 in force from 1 December 1991 – that for civil contracts the guaranty, like the others under Art. 1792, is of *ordre public*, i.e. the contractor cannot under the terms of the contract exclude or limit his liability. However, this is not the case with public works contracts. The *garantie de parfait achèvement* is regarded in public works contracts as being a matter of the contractual obligations of the contractor. It is therefore possible for the public authority to agree to a lesser period than twelve months.[27]

Garantie décennale

Persons giving the *garantie* These guaranties are given by all those who are termed *constructeurs* under Art. 1792, which covers architects, contractors, technical experts or other persons bound to the employer under a contract for works but not sub-contractors. It includes therefore what in England would be termed 'consulting engineers', *bureaux d'études techniques (BET)*, which are offices of mixed professions offering design, engineering and consultancy services and also under the 1978 law the *bureaux de contrôle* which are technical quality control organizations required to be employed for insurance purposes (see below, pp. 198–199). Such an organization is, however, only responsible within the scope of the work for which it is engaged by the employer, Loi 78–12 4 January 1978 Art. 9, and is only subject to the *garantie décennale*.

Also certain suppliers known as *EPERS* (*éléments pouvant entraîner la responsabilité solidaire*) are made jointly and severally responsible with the *constructeur* to the employer under the conditions established in Art. 1792–4. Their position is considered after we have examined the responsibilities of the *constructeurs* themselves.

Persons for whose benefit the *garantie* is given Obviously the primary person to whom the *garantie* is owed is the employer but it also extends to any subsequent owner of the works. However, the fact that the *garantie* can be exercised by a subsequent owner does not prevent it from being exercised by the original employer if he still has a direct interest in the matter, e.g. a seller who is obliged to repair the deficiencies in a building.[28] This is in total contrast with English law which has consistently rejected the idea of a transmissible warranty.[29]

Scope of the *garantie décennale* Under Art. 1792 the *constructeur* is responsible for all damage, even that resulting from a defect in the soil (foundations) which affects the solidity of *un ouvrage* (works) or which, affecting one of its constitutive elements or one of its items of *équipement*, renders the works unsuitable for the purpose for which they were intended. Note that the word *équipement* is wider in meaning than the English 'equipment'. It was said by M. Richomme that 'the equipment function was fulfilled by the parts for the fitting out of the area within the covered enclosure of the Works'.[30] Recently supports for the basins in hotel bathrooms were held to be within the meaning of *équipements*.[31] The English term will be used from now on in this wider sense.

The *constructeur* is not liable if he can prove that the damage arose from *une cause étrangère*.

Definition of the works (*ouvrage*) Within the definition of *un ouvrage* are included buildings, factories and all types of civil engineering works including those for infrastructure purposes such as bridges, and also those for recreation such as swimming pools and tennis courts and underground works. Works of a minor or temporary nature are excluded.

Constitutive elements of *un ouvrage* would include the foundations, the structural framework, the roof, and the walls.

Application of the *garantie* under Art. 1792 The *garantie* covers two different situations:

1. A defect affecting the solidity or stability of the structure itself.
2. A defect in either one of the constitutive elements of the structure, or in an item of equipment, which renders the works unfit for the purpose for which they were intended.

There is an additional *garantie décennale* under para. 2 of Art. 1792 relating to equipment in a building which is *indissociable* and a *garantie biennale* under para. 3 for equipment which is *dissociable*. These will be considered later after the meaning of 'building' as opposed to 'works' has been examined. In practice it is the *garantie* under Art. 1792 itself which is of the widest application and greatest importance.

There have been few difficulties with the *garantie* in 1. It should be noted that it does not require that there should be an immediate risk of collapse but does include defects affecting durability. So serious cracking which would lead the works to deteriorate during bad weather would be covered.

There have been far more problems with 2 in deciding whether or not the defect is sufficiently serious to affect the use for which the works were intended. Many of the cases have concerned the leaking of walls and roofs and have given rise to some fine distinctions. Leakage into a living room would be covered by the *garantie* but not just into a balcony.[32] In administrative law the leaking of water into a classroom has been held to render the building unfit for its intended purpose but a similar leakage into the covered playground area at the same school was held not to do so.[33]

Defects in the wooden floor of a gymnasium due to the failure of the glue to adhere the parquet blocks to the base was decided to make it unsuitable for use but not a similar defect in the floor of a house.[34]

However, if the defects are such as to make the premises dangerous for those using them, this will be considered as making them unsuitable for the purpose intended.[35]

Other systems within the works such as drainage, pipework and so on will equally be subject to the *garantie* if the works are rendered unfit for use as a result of their being defective.

As regards items of equipment within a building such as lifts, this would depend on the seriousness of the defect and the number of storeys in the building as to whether or not the defect was such as to make the structure unsuitable for use. The same reasoning would apply to a central heating system. Is the defect such as to make the works unfit for use?

The more difficult question is that relating to items of machinery in a factory. Are these to be submitted to the *garantie décennale* if a major failure were to prevent the factory from being used for the purpose intended; say a total breakdown in the boilers which provided the steam for a laundry? The answer would appear to be 'yes' although each case is to be assessed on its merits by the *juge de fait*. It does however raise an even more difficult issue as to the damages which are payable in that event. Are these restricted to the repair of the equipment and of any other part of the works damaged because of the failure of the equipment, or do they extend to the loss of profits suffered by the enterprise? Another example would be the failure of a heating system which prevented operation of the air conditioning, essential to the maintenance of the correct temperature in the computer room (see further below, p. 192).

In administrative law it has been decided by the *Conseil d'Etat* that the damages recoverable are not limited to the remedying of the defects but extend to all damages suffered by the purchaser subject to the condition that they are connected directly with the defects affecting the works. As a result the reduction in rent suffered by the lessor of premises during the time that they were under repair by the contractor were held to be recoverable. Decision of the *Conseil d'Etat* of 9 December 1968 and of 23 April 1986.

The position under the civil law does not appear so clear. Malinvaud and Jestaz – s 88 and 141 have suggested that while it was clear under the previous version of Arts. 1792 and 2270 that damages consequential on the defects were recoverable, and they cite numerous decisions to this effect, they doubt if this is so under the present text, certainly as regards items of industrial equipment which were previously excluded, because of the width of the liabilities to which this would expose those liable under the guaranties.

Fault The *garantie* is not dependent upon proof of fault. There is a presumption of responsibility such that the contractor or architect, or other person to whom the *garantie* applies, can only escape liability if he can prove *cause étrangère*, or that the defects arose solely in work which was outside his scope of responsibility. So the architect originally employed on a project was not held responsible for defects arising out of the repair of defective work after *réception* for which he was not employed in the capacity of architect nor over which he had any management responsibility.[36] An architect has also been relieved of responsibility when he was able to establish that the defects were due solely to faulty execution of the work by the contractor and that he had satisfied his obligations of supervision.[37] Equally, in an administrative case where it was held that the defects were due solely to errors in design which were the responsibility of the architect and the client, the contractors were relieved of responsibility and the liability was shared 70 per cent by the architect and 30 per cent by the client.[38]

Cause étrangère does not, however, cover cases in which the work has been performed in accordance with the then currently approved techniques which only later were discovered to be defective. The so-called 'development risk' rests with the architect and contractor.[39]

The same principle applies in administrative law. In a case before the *Conseil d'Etat* concerning the watertightness of the roof of a school in which it was not established that there was any fault of the architect in design or of the contractor in the choice of materials and both corresponded to the technical standards in use at the time, the contractor and the architect were nevertheless held jointly and severally liable. The court stated that they could only escape responsibility on proof of *force majeure* or fault of the employer.[40]

Defects covered As indicated above it is only defects which were hidden at the time of *réception* which are covered by either the *garantie décennale* or *biennale*. If the defect was apparent and made the subject of a reservation at the time of the *réception* then it is covered by the *garantie de parfait achèvement* (see above, p. 188).

Buildings and associated equipment Under Art. 1792–2 there is an addition to the *garantie décennale* in regard to items of equipment which form part of *bâtiments* (buildings) as opposed to *ouvrages* (works). The presumption of responsibility is extended to damage which affects the solidity of elements of equipment of a building but only when they are indissociable from the foundations, walls, roof, framework and services of the building. They are regarded as being indissociable when their dismounting, removal or replacement cannot be affected without damage to those parts of the building.

The first issue which arises is the definition of a *bâtiment* which is more restricted than an *ouvrage*.

The essential requirement is that it should provide shelter against the elements. A secondary requirement is that people should move about within the structure otherwise than purely by chance or only very occasionally.[41] For the purpose of compulsory insurance, it appears that there may be a third requirement for a structure to be classified as a building. That is that it should be constructed above ground – see below, p. 198. So a factory is a building but a separate store-room in which people only go exceptionally, is probably not. On the other hand a warehouse in which people do normally work using fork-lift trucks to move and stack stores would fall within the requirements. There are obviously difficult dividing lines. Is a separate boiler-house in which someone only goes on an occasional basis for maintenance purposes to be considered a 'building'? The answer is probably 'no'.

The second issue is as to the meaning of *solidité*. It would appear to relate to the soundness or durability of the item rather than to its qualities of performance in terms of output.

Equipements   It is thought that the intention of the legislator in introducing the new law in 1978 (*loi Spinetta*) had been to draw a distinction between elements of equipment which were related to the construction of the building and those which were installed in the building for industrial use. So items of equipment which were necessary for the building to be used as such, e.g. the waste disposal or central heating system would be included under the *garantie décennale* but not the machine tools in the factory.

However, this intention has not been expressed in the drafting of Art. 1792–2 which would seem to apply to both items of equipment, at least if they are *indissociable* in the sense referred to above of not being able to be removed, dismounted or replaced without damaging or removing the fabric of the building, e.g. the flooring or wall tiles. It has been commented by French writers that this concept of being *indissociable* is a far from happy one. It makes the applicability of the *garantie* under Art. 1792–2 depend on whether or not the item can be removed without disturbance to the building itself, which is related to the method of installation and not, which would be more logical, to the useful life of the item concerned.[42]

As has recently been established, however, the question of 'indissociability' is irrelevant if the defect in the item of equipment is such as to make the works or building unsuitable for the purpose for which they were intended (e.g. the supports for the basins in the hotel bathrooms referred to above, p. 189 and note 31).

The same ruling has been applied to the defects in a boiler of a central heating system causing the breakdown of the air conditioning which was necessary for the correct functioning of the computers.[43]

Garantie biennale

The other items of equipment in a building which are not indissociable are the subject of a *garantie* of good operation for at least two years from *réception* (Art. 1792–3).

This text raises several problems of interpretation. First it refers to *bon fonctionnement* (good operation or working order) as opposed to *solidité*. If, as indicated above, the term *solidité* refers only to the soundness or robustness of the item, because it is indissociable from the structure, then it would make sense that the *garantie biennale*, which is concerned with items not affecting the structure such as wall-mounted radiators, should be subject just to a *garantie* of their good operation.

However, does it follow that if the item is indissociable and suffers only from a defect affecting its *bon fonctionnement* but not its *solidité* that it escapes from either the *garantie décennale* or *biennale*? This could be the case of a large machine fixed to the floor of a factory in such a way that to dismount it would necessitate disturbing the factory floor. Malinvaud and Jestaz discuss the question but without arriving at a clear answer.[44] The *maître de l'ouvrage* may in these circumstances have the remedy of *une action directe* against the supplier or manufacturer of the machine for *vice caché* or *non-conformité* (see below, pp. 195–196).

Indeed the question has been raised as to the circumstances in which the guaranty does apply. As referred to earlier, if the defect in the item renders the works unsuitable for the purpose for which they were intended, which seems to be interpreted widely by the *juges de fait*, the question of whether it is dissociable or not is irrelevant. Account also does not appear to be taken of the anticipated life of the item. As has been commented, 'the legislator has distanced himself from technical reality'.[45]

Second, there is the question of who gives the *garantie*. While it is clear that it is not the *bureau de contrôle*, what is the responsibility of those enumerated in Art. 1792–1 as being *constructeurs*, even though they may have had nothing to do with the item of equipment in question? This has been called in question for contracts subject to administrative law[46] and also by Malinvaud and Jestaz for private works contracts.[47]

Third, there is the relationship between the period of the *garantie* and the obligations of the professional seller relating to *vices cachés*. It will be remembered that although the purchaser must exercise his action for *vice caché* within *un bref délai*, this period runs from when the defect is discovered, and that the courts will refuse to give effect in the case of a professional seller to a clause limiting his responsibilities to a period commencing from delivery (see above, pp. 176–177). Further, the normal periods of prescription of 30 years or ten years for commercial contracts would apply.

Yet it would appear from the wording of Art. 1792–3 and from Art. 2270 relating to the periods of prescription that it is permissible for the *garantie* to be limited to a period of only two years from *réception* and that this would apply to any action in respect of *vice caché*.

At the time of writing this conflict does not appear to have been resolved although the most probable answer seems to be that if the defect was of any importance at all the court would find that it was one which affected the purpose for which the works had been intended and therefore subject to the *garantie décennale*.

Finally, it is to be noted that the *garantie* applies only to buildings as defined earlier (see above, pp. 191–192) and not to civil engineering works.

SUPPLIERS

As regards the rights of the employer against a supplier, a distinction is drawn between those defined as *EPERS* (see above, p. 188) and those non-*EPERS*.

EPERS

Under Art. 1792–4 these suppliers are stated to be liable jointly with the main contractor in respect of his obligations under Arts. 1792, 1792–2 and 1793–3. They are defined as manufacturers of a piece of work, a part of a piece of work, or an item of equipment which is: designed and produced in order to comply, on being put into service, with specific requirements defined in advance; and put into place by the main contractor without modification and in conformity with the instructions of the manufacturer.

For the purpose of Art. 1792–4 those who import a piece of work, a part of a piece of work or an item of equipment from abroad are also considered as manufacturers.

In effect the manufacturer *EPERS* has taken over from the architect or main contractor the tasks of designing and fabricating a part of the works or an item of equipment and providing all necessary information as to how it is to be installed, leaving to the main contractor only the task of putting it into place.[48]

So in one leading case the *Cour de cassation* quashed a decision of the Cour de Nimes which had held that the manufacturer of ready mixed concrete which was intended exclusively for the construction of particular works or parts of work such as pavements or foundations was responsible under Art. 1792–4. The *Cour de cassation* held that in the state in which it was delivered, the product was neither in itself a piece of work, a part of a piece of work or an item of equipment but a construction material.[49] A similar decision was reached as regard tiles.[50]

On the other hand the manufacturer of a heat pump which formed part of a heating system which included a wood-fired boiler was held liable under Art. 1792–4 on the basis that despite its incorporation into the heating system

> the pump was designed to be put into operation without modification for the purpose of a defined function of generating heat according to the characteristics and performance specified by its manufacturer, and did not require any modification in order to be installed in the system, the contractor who installed it only having to follow the instructions given by the manufacturer for this purpose.[51]

If the manufacturer is liable under Art. 1792–4 then the employer has the right to proceed against him jointly with the contractor responsible for the installation of the item manufactured and to recover from him all the damage which results from the defect.

Two points are to be noted from the particular wording of Art. 1792–4. First, the joint liability is only between the manufacturer and the contractor who has installed the work or item of equipment concerned. Second, there is no reference in the text to the case in which the work or item of equipment is installed by a sub-contractor. It has been suggested that this was an omission when the law was enacted and that the courts should not follow the literal wording of the text but treat the act of the sub-contractor as that of the main contractor.

Administrative law

Traditionally, according to the *droit administratif*, the only parties who can be bound by the *garantie décennale* are those who have a direct contract with the *maître de l'ouvrage* (the employer). Therefore since the *fabricant* who is made responsible *solidairement* with the main contractor under Art. 1792–4 is not directly in contract with the *maître de l'ouvrage*, it would not appear open to the *juge administratif* to utilize the principles of Art. 1792–4. Accordingly under the *droit administratif* the supplier who is classified as *EPERS* is in no different position from any other supplier to the main contractor.

It remains to be seen whether the *Conseil d'Etat* may not at some time in the future change its position in this matter and align the *droit administratif* with the *droit civil*.[52]

Suppliers non-*EPERS*

At the time of writing the responsibility of a supplier non-*EPERS* is that which was established by the *Assemblée plénière* in their decision of 7 February 1986:

> le maître de l'ouvrage, comme le sous-acquéreur jouait tous les droits et actions attachés à la chose qui appartenait à son auteur: qu'il dispose donc à cet effet contre le fabricant d'une action contractuelle directe fondée sur la non-conformité de la chose livrée. . . (the employer in the same way as the sub-purchaser has the benefit of all the rights and actions attaching to the thing which belong to its original purchaser; he possesses therefore to this effect a direct contractual right of action against the manufacturer based upon the non-conformity of the thing delivered).

The main consequences which follow from this were described in the note of the case by Benabent to be:

> a) the failure to comply with the contractual obligations is to be determined exclusively by reference to the terms and conditions of the initial contract [in this instance between the manufacturer of a product and a sub-contractor].
> b) the clauses relating to responsibility, and those limiting the manufacturer's responsibilities, contained in the initial contract, if valid under that contract, apply as against or for the benefit of the subsequent purchaser.
> c) the extent of the damages recoverable will be those foreseeable at the time of the initial contract.
> d) when the period of prescription is transmitted with the thing then the period is that of the initial contract and begins to run from the time of the initial contract, so in the example given in the note if the original period was 10 years under the commercial contract of sale, followed afterwards by a works contract of 3 years, the Maître d'ouvrage would only have 7 years in which to act against the manufacturer.[53]

The question of the validity of the above reasoning and of the foundation of *une action contractuelle directe* on the transmission of a right accessory to the thing transferred, has been questioned by Ghestin in his note to the decision by the *Assemblée plénière* of 12 July 1991 (see below, pp. 273–274). At the moment however this remains the dominant theory and it was applied in a case decided by the third civil chambre of the *Cour de cassation* on 15 February 1989 and referred to by Ghestin apparently with approval.[54] The case concerned steam boilers installed in a hospital and although the court held that the *maître de l'ouvrage* did indeed have a direct contractual right of action against the manufacturer, this right was time-barred under a clause in the original contract between the manufacturer and the installer which limited the liability of the manufacturer to one year, and this period had expired at the time when the defects first appeared. As Ghestin comments: 'the maître d'ouvrage may not possess greater rights than the contractor in contract with the manufacturer himself possesses'.

SUB-CONTRACTORS

In regard to the main contractor the obligations of the sub-contractor have been expressed by the *Cour de cassation* in the following terms: 'the sub-contractor is under an *obligation de résultat* which includes the execution of his works free from hidden defects at the time of *réception* (29 May 1984 B.III no. 106).

However sub-contractors have been specifically and intentionally excluded from the definition of *constructeurs* under Art. 1792–1 nor are they included within Art. 1792–4.[55] They are therefore outside the scope of the *garanties légales* of Art. 1792 (Cass. civ. 20 June 1989 Bull. civ. no. 146).

As regards the rights of the employer against the sub-contractor it has been decided recently by the *Assemblée plénière de la Cour de cassation* that any action by the *maître de l'ouvrage* (the employer) against the sub-contractor can only be delictual and not contractual and therefore depends upon proof of fault. However this also means that the sub-contractor cannot avail himself of the period of prescription of ten years under the *garantie décennale*.[56] It is to be noted that unlike English law after *Murphy* v. *Brentwood District Council* (see above, p. 189, note 29) there is no rule under French law which restricts the right of the employer in recovering damages from the sub-contractor in delict for economic loss. Liability depends on the normal rules relating to proof of fault and the establishment of a causal link between the fault and the damage.[57]

Nor, since the liability of the sub-contractor would be for a proven fault under Art. 1382 of the *Code Civil*, would the sub-contractor be able to set up as against the employer any clause limiting his responsibilities contained in the contract between himself and the main contractor. It is strongly arguable that such would necessarily follow from the fact of the employer not being a party to the sub-contract but additionally the delictual responsibility for fault is *ordre public* and cannot be excluded.[58]

RESPONSABILITÉ SOLIDAIREMENT ET 'IN SOLIDUM'

French law distinguishes between two situations in which two or more debtors may be responsible jointly to the creditor.

The first case – referred to as *solidarité* – is when the debtors are liable under the same contract having the same *objet*. There is a common obligation which is shared between them. Each is responsible for the whole of the debt and the creditor may bring an action against either one or more of the debtors. In general also there are what are termed 'secondary effects' of the *solidarité* which are based on the concept that there is mutual representation as between the debtors; a legal notice given to one binds all the debtors.

The provisions governing the situation of *solidarité* are almost exactly parallel to those which apply in English law to contracts in which there are joint obligations of the contractors.

However the second situation, termed *in solidum*, has no true parallel in English contract law although in tort it has some similarity with the rules applying to joint tortfeasors.[59]

The responsibility *in solidum* arises in contract when either two or more of the parties bound by different contracts to the *maître de l'ouvrage*, or one or more of such parties and a party liable to the *maître de l'ouvrage* in delict, are responsible for a 'shared fault' which causes the totality of the damage. The essential requirement is that the faults of the two or more parties involved have concurred together to produce the defect. It is not necessary that the faults themselves should be of the same nature or derived from the same source.

So an architect and a consulting engineer contractually responsible for the design and supervision of the works were held liable *in solidum* with a sub-contractor responsible in delict for the supply and installation of the work when a system for heating and the supply of hot water to a building was defective, their respective faults having combined together to produce the whole damage.[60]

As regards the primary effect for the parties held responsible *in solidum*, there is no distinction between this and the responsibility *solidaire*. Each may be sued by the debtor for the whole loss which he has suffered. The difference only arises in the secondary effects which cannot apply to the obligation *in solidum* since the concept of mutual representation upon which the secondary effects are based is not present.[61]

ADMINISTRATIVE LAW

Essentially the administrative law follows the same principles both as regards the obligations of *solidarité* and *in solidum*. However if an administrative court finds an architect or engineer liable *in solidum* with a contractor for defective work then while the contractor can be ordered to carry out the necessary remedial works the architect/engineer can only be made to pay for the costs involved.

One further difference is that where the default of the architect/engineer is in

197

respect of their duty of supervision then a distinction is made by the administrative law according to the degree of seriousness of the default. If it is only a light degree of fault then the obligation of the architect is not *in solidum* but *subsidiare* and in that event the architect is only responsible to indemnify the client if the contractor is in liquidation.

ENGLISH LAW COMPARISON

As referred to above the concept of *in solidum* is quite unknown to English law but the same effect may be achieved in certain instances from the English rules on causation and concurrent causes. If there are two breaches of contract both contributing to the loss and both of approximately equal effect, then the plaintiff can recover the whole of the loss from either party. Keating refers specifically as an example of this to the case of the employer claiming for defects caused both by the architect's defective design and the contractor's defective work.[62] He suggests that provided the cause in either event contributed materially to the loss the employer could recover in full from either the architect or the contractor, but obviously not twice over, and with the party who is held liable being able to recover from the other under the Civil Liability (Contribution) Act 1978.

ASSURANCE

French law imposes a system of compulsory insurance of which the main features are:

1. The system applies to buildings but not to works of civil engineering. The same definition of a building which was referred to earlier (see above, pp. 191–192) would appear to be restricted to those which are above ground.[63]
2. There are two different policies. The one known as a policy *de dommages* is subscribed to by the *maître de l'ouvrage* and the other, known as a policy *de responsabilité* is subscribed to by all those who are responsible under Art. 1792 of the *Code Civil*.

   Where the buildings are constructed by the state for its own purposes, or by a local authority which has been authorized by the appropriate administrative authority, the requirement for the policy *de dommages* does not apply.
3. The policy *de dommages* must come into effect at the time of the commencement of site work and must cover all the costs of the work of making good any damage to the works, the nature of which *constructeurs* (as defined in Art. 1792-1, e.g. contractors, architects, engineers), manufacturers or importers or the *contrôleur technique* are responsible under Art. 1792 of the *Code Civil, without any examination of responsibility*. The policy applies for the benefit of the *maître de l'ouvrage* and subsequent purchasers and takes effect from the end of the period of the *garantie de parfait achèvement* and runs until ten years from the date of *réception*.

   The effect of this is that funds are immediately available with which to carry out the repair works without any need to establish liability.

4. The policy *de responsabilité* must be taken out by everyone who is liable under Art. 1792. It runs from the time of the opening of the site until the expiry of the period of the party's obligations under Art. 1792. The policy must provide that it remains in force during this period without the payment of any further premiums. This removes the risk of the policy lapsing due to the contractor going into liquidation.[64]

In practice the policy taken out by a contractor (*la police individuel de base*) will cover his liabilities in the period before *réception* and during the period of the *garantie décennale*, both for the costs of making good any damage to the works but also any damage to adjacent buildings and any indirect damages.

In consequence of the existence of the two policies it might be thought that any disputes as to liability would become disputes between the two insurance companies concerned. There are obviously such disputes but the main problem remains that of knowing whether or not the damage which has occurred is covered by the *garantie décennale* at all.

TIME FOR PERFORMANCE

The contractor is under an obligation to hand over the works at the time stated in the contract and unless otherwise specifically provided for in the contract he is only relieved from this obligation if he is delayed due to *une cause étrangère*, that is to say an act or default of the employer, or *force majeure*. Under the standard conditions of contract for the construction of buildings in the private sector (NF P 03–001) the acts of the employer would include variations ordered by him to the works or suspension of the works subject to the contractor providing the necessary justification and not being himself at fault. Default of the employer would include delays by him in the performance of his obligations including the obligation to pay according to the contractual terms of payment provided that as regards delays in payment the contractor had given at least fifteen days' written notice by recorded delivery.

Force majeure is defined extremely restrictively as an event which is 'unforeseeable, irresistible and external to the debtor'. Also it must not have been due to his fault. The unforeseeability is determined at the time of entering into the contract and is strictly applied. A natural event such as rain, snow and so on must be of a wholly exceptional nature, 'a true calamity never experienced since records have been kept', as was stated in one case. The use of a method approved at the time of construction by the Scientific and Technical Centre for the building industry but later amended has also been held not to be *force majeure*.[65] The event must be insurmountable regardless of the extra expense to which the contractor may be put in overcoming the obstacle to the performance of the contract.

Strikes will only exceptionally constitute *force majeure*. In a leading case in which two companies brought an action against EDF for cutting off the electric power supply and causing them a loss of production it was held that EDF were protected by *force majeure*. The strike had been unforeseeable at the time of the contract. It was irresistible because EDF were unable to replace their work force and had to meet first the demands of their priority users. Finally it was an event exterior to EDF because it had been provoked by a political decision of the government.[66]

The term *force majeure* is regrettably used at times in English contracts without being defined (see clause 25.4.1 of the JCT 80 Form of Contract) which can only lead to uncertainty given that the term has no defined meaning within English law (see the author's article on the subject in the *Contracts Management Journal* of the Chartered Institute of Purchasing and Supply, December 1990).

REMEDY OF THE EMPLOYER

The remedy of the employer is damages for delay. Unless the delay is due to *dol* the level of damages is that which was foreseen or should have been foreseen at the time of entering into the contract (Art. 1150, *Code Civil*). French law does not distinguish between liquidated damages and penalties. A clause fixing the amount of damages payable in respect of delay entitles the employer to the recovery of that sum, neither more nor less (Art. 1152, *Code Civil*), although under that article the court may now amend the amount stipulated in the contract if it is either derisory or excessive. In making that decision the court may take into account the objectives of the clause which can include pressurizing the contractor to complete on time.[67]

In the same way as with contracts for the sale of goods the employer can only claim to put into effect a penalty clause if either he has given the contractor a notice to complete (*mise en demeure*), or the contract contains provisions that make it clear that the parties intended the contractor to be in default without such notice (Art. 1230, *Code Civil*).

Although it has been held[68] that, on a lump sum contract with a fixed completion period, the court may not refuse to allow the employer to put into effect a penalty clause without examining whether or not the parties had the common intention to dispense with a *mise en demeure*, it is far preferable from the employer's viewpoint to include an express clause to this effect – see for example the clause set out above p. 179.

NOTES

1. This principle was set out in Art. 1.112 and 1.113 of the Standard (Norme) of l'Association Française de Normalisation (AFNOR) of 1948, P 03–001, and although the Norme has subsequently been revised the statement is still valid: 'Each contractor is obliged to conform with the provisions of his contract and with the written documentation and diagrams which accompany it and also with the details which are supplied to him by the Architect and the orders which he receives from him'.
2. This principle is again expressed in Norme P 03–001 of the edition of 1948, clause 1.111, and although not included in the latest edition still remains valid. See also Cass.civ.1re 7 April 1965. D.65 som.p. 108.
3. According to Norme P 03–001 of 1989, Art.05.4, the contractor is under the obligation stated in the text

both before starting work and during the course of executing the works.

4. Cass.civ.3e 22 Oct.1980, JCP 1981.IV.14.
5. Cass.civ.3e 22 Oct.1980, Bull. civ. III no. 162; 17 May 1983, Bull. civ. III no.115 and 30 Nov. 1983, Bull. civ. no.253.
6. See *Young and Marten* v. *McManus Childs* (ch. 11, n.29 on p. 146).
7. Cass.civ. 1 29 May 1984, D.85.213,2e. 'The employer has a direct right of action against the supplier of material installed by the contractor in respect of the guaranty for a hidden defect in the material arising during its manufacture, which action is necessarily contractual'. This was confirmed by the Assemblée plénière in a decision on 7 February 1986: 'The Building Owner, in the same way as the subsequent purchaser, has the benefit of all the rights attaching to the item which belong to the person from whom it was purchased'. Bull.civ.Ass.plen.no.2 D.1986.293.

   The later decision by the assembly on 12 July 1991, in which it was held that the employer did not have a contractual action against a sub-contractor but a right in delict, is not considered to have changed the position so far as a supplier of material or equipment is concerned. Dalloz *Recueil* 1991 36a cahier – Sommaires commentes p. 321 and note by Professor Ghestin *Recueil* Dalloz 1991 38 cahier Jurisprudence p. 549.

   It would seem that the distinction being drawn is between an obligation which, in English terms, 'runs with the item the transfer of whose ownership is the subject of successive contracts', and an obligation of a third party to the contract, which is created immediately by the contract itself. The former gives rise properly to an action in contract. The latter can only give rise to an action in delict since 'agreements only have effect as between the contracting parties' (Art. 1165 of the *Code Civil*. This is the principle of *effet relatif du contrat* (see further below, pp. 272–273).

8. NF P 03–001 1984 ed. Art. 04.3: 'The Contractor is responsible for the supply of all materials and for their construction into the Works. As a result, subject to the particular conditions of contract, the Employer may not instruct the Contractor to obtain the materials or supplies from suppliers whom he designates nor require him to use materials or supplies belonging to the Employer. At the same time the particular conditions of the contract may foresee the supply of special materials, items or machinery. In this case the Contractor has the right to require that he is provided in due time with the instructions necessary for ordering them. In any event the Contractor has the right to refuse to use materials supplied by the Employer which do not satisfy the quality requirements appropriate for the purpose for which they are intended.'

9. 'In case of defects in the construction the responsibility of the contractor will only be wholly or partially discharged even although he only followed the instructions of the Building Owner in the method of construction or the use of materials, if he can establish that the Building Owner was generally recognised as technically competent in the matter.' Cass.civ. 4 February 1980 Bull.Cass.no.11 p. 8. The choice of materials made by a building owner who was technically incompetent would not discharge the contractor from liability (Cass.civ. 7 December 1976, Bull. Cass.no. 443, p. 336).

10. Cass.civ. 3e 10 July 1972.
11. CE 23 May 1962 and other cases cited under note 123 Caston Vol. 1 p. 251. For the obligation to provide advice CE 24 July 1987, Entreprise Jean Lefèbvre Dr. Adm., 1987 no. 493: 'When the Building Owner has insisted upon the use of materials which have proved to be defective the contractor who accepted this decision without making any reservation is not as a result discharged from his obligation to give advice. However this obligation does not extend beyond that of the usual knowledge which a normal person of his qualifications ought to possess'. In this case as the materials were experimental and their deficiency was only known after the date of the decision by the building owner to use them, neither the architect nor the contractor were held responsible.

12. Cass. civ. 7 December 1976, Bull.Cass. no. 443, p. 336.
13. Cass.civ.1re, 4 October 1961.
14. *Equitable Debenture Assets Corp.* v. *William Morris* 2 Con. LR 1 and *Victoria University of Manchester* v. *Hugh Wilson & Lewis Wormsley* 2 Con. LR 43.
15. Per Judge Peter Bowsher QC in *University of Glasgow* v. *Whitfield* 19 Con. LR 111 at p. 140.
16. Per Judge Peter Bowsher QC at p. 139. The powerful dissenting judgement of Dixon J. in the Canadian case of *Brunswick Construction* v. *Nowlan* 1974 21 BLR 27 at p. 40 is to the like effect that the obligations of the contractor are to be found within the 'four corners' of the contract and nowhere else. See also the views of Duncan Wallance QC in Construction Contracts p. 43. A duty to warn may arise under the general obligation of the contractor for workmanship but it is suggested only in respect of

those matters of detail left to this discretion or where to comply with the architect's or engineer's design would put him in breach of statutory obligations with which he is bound to comply. Cf Humphrey Lloyd QC in *The Liability of Contractors*, p. 144.

17. *Tai Hing Ltd* v. *Lin Chong Hing Bank* [1986] AC 80 (PC): 'Their Lordships do not however accept that the parties' mutual obligations in tort can be any greater than those to be found expressly or by necessary implication in the contract'. See also Hilary Nichols 'Contractor's Duty to warn' 5 Con.LJ p. 176.

18. Since the law of 4 January 1978 came into force there is only one *réception*. Previously there had been a provisional and then a final *réception*. The act of *réception* must be pronounced *contradictoirement*, that is to say the contractor must either be present when the *réception* is given or have been duly notified of the intention to pronounce the *réception*. In the former case the contractor will sign the certificate (*procès verbal*) as evidence of his agreement, especially to any reservations stated in the certificate. If he is not present then he must be notified, usually by providing him with a copy.

The Norme P 003–001 provides that the contractor is either provided with a copy forthwith at the meeting or is sent a copy within five days. This is important especially if there are any imperfections to be remedied since it is provided in Art. 15 of the 1989 version that unless otherwise agreed the contractor has 90 days from the day of the *réception* in which to carry out the necessary remedial work.

19. Exceptionally the employer has the right under the *droit commun* (the general law) to require the contractor to remedy defects not covered by the guaranty obligations of Art. 1792, i.e. minor defects not affecting the solidity of the works or making them unfit for the purpose intended (see further below, p. 186). In addition the employer would have an action in delict against a sub-contractor to whom the guaranty obligations under Art. 1792 do not apply (see further below, pp. 273–274).

20. The Conseil d'Etat stated: 'in the absence of any initiative to apply for the *réception* taken by the Contractor, no *réception* even tacit could be held to have taken place, even although the Building Owner had taken possession of the Works without reservation; from which it follows that the contractual relationships between the Building Owner and the Architect and Contractors were not at an end and therefore the lower administrative tribunal were wrong in deciding that the latter could no longer be sued for breach of contract.' 31 May 1989, pp. 64–253.

21. CE 28 February 1986 and Art. 44–1 of the CCAG which states that 'at the end of the guarantee period the Contractor is no longer bound by his contractual obligations'. The matter is not however free from doubt. It can be argued that the *réception* itself brings the contractor's contractual obligations to an end (see Caston vol. 1 p. 163). In any event as from the date of *réception* such obligations are limited to those which arise under the guaranty period, normally one year from *réception*, and which require the contractor to remedy defects for which reservations were made at *réception* or which arise during the year (otherwise from fair wear and tear or normal use) so that the works are in the same state as they were at the time of *réception* or after the correction of the defects noted at that time.

The difference between the civil and the administrative law is due to the fact that under the civil law the guaranty (*garantie de parfait achèvement*) is imposed by Art. 1792–6 of the *Code Civil*, whereas under the administrative law it is a contractual obligation.

22. Such contractual liability for minor defects under the *droit commun* has also been held by the *Cour de cassation* to be subject to a period of prescription of ten years from *réception* (Civ.3e 11 June 1981 and see Malinvaud, pp. 149 and 150).

23. Although this is not stated expressly in the law of 1978 the jurisprudence is constant on the point (Caston vol. 1 p. 155 et seq. and Malinvaud p. 97). 'The *réception* of the Works eliminates responsibility for any apparent defect or default in conformity which has not been made the subject of a reservation', unpublished decision of the *Cour de cassation* quoted in Malaurie and Aynes note 110, p. 412.

24. Cass.civ. 3e 23 November 1976 Bull.cass.415 p. 316 and Cass.civ. 3e 27 April 1977, Bull.cass.no.178, p. 137. See also Malinvaud pp. 115 and 116 who shows how the jurisprudence has placed the responsibility on the contractor to establish that the defects were apparent both in their existence and their effects or were known to the building owner. Also Cass.civ.3e 10 January 1990 Bull.civ.III no.6 in which the *Cour de Cassation* agreed that a cour d'appel were within their *pouvoir souveraine* in deciding that defects were hidden, and therefore fell under the terms of the *garantie décennale*, when although they were noted at the time of the *réception*, the full extent of the defects only became apparent later.

The knowledge of the defect covers both the cause of the defect and the injurious consequences which follow from it. Where a defect consisted of the infiltration of rain water, but it had not rained on the day when the building owner took possession and he was not therefore aware of the damage which would result, and the defect itself was only apparent to a professional and not to a layman such as the building owner, the defect was not considered to be apparent and the contractor remained responsible. *Cour d'appel de Limoges*, 14 December 1992, *La Semaine Juridique* [JCP] Ed. G, no.16, 1993.

25. It is suggested by Caston that the contractor could exonerate himself if he were to establish that the defect was due to the fault of the architect, p. 174 para.259.

26. Cass.civ.3e 4 February 1987 Bull.cass.no.16 p.11. The same principle applies to contracts under the administrative law (CE June 1989, no.73–946).

27. CE 28 February 1986, Entreprise Blondet: 'it is permissible for a public authority to provide for a period less than a year'.

28. Cass.civ. 3e 20 April 1982, Bull.civ.III no.95.

29. There could be no such transmissible warranty in contract due to the doctrine of privity. The possibility of any in tort was firmly rejected by Lord Keith in *Murphy* v. *Brentwood District Council* when he said in relation to the liability of a builder in negligence for economic loss that once such a duty was recognized, 'it would open on an exceedingly wide field of claims, involving the introduction of something in the nature of a transmissible warranty of quality' which none of their Lordships was prepared to accept.

30. Rapport de M. Richomme, *député* when the law of 4 July 1978 was going through parliament. He was contrasting *équipement* with the construction function which he said comprised 'the works of services, foundations and of covering and enclosing'.

31. Cass. civ. 3e 23 January 1991 *Recueil* Dalloz 41e cahier Jurisprudence; note by Raymond Martin.

32. Cass. civ. 3e 30 March 1989 reported *Le Moniteur* 16 June 1989.

33. CE 5 July 1967.

34. CE 10 May 1967 and CE 23 October 1970.

35. CE 21 February 1986.

36. Cass.civ. 3e 3 May 1989 D. 1990.

37. Cass. civ. 3e 19 June 1984 arrêt. no. 847.

38. CE 24 January 1990 no. 59.052 reported *Le Moniteur* 2 March 1990.

39. 'The sole fact that a technique current and considered as valid in accordance with the (unified technical documents – codes of practice mandatory for public works and frequently applied to private works) in force at the time when the technique had been employed, did not constitute a cause for exonerating the contractor from his contractual responsibilities' Cass.civ. 3e 22 October 1980, Bull. civ. no. 161, p. 120.

40. CE 2 February 1973 (Trannoy).

41. The distinction between *un ouvrage* and *un bâtiment* was considered in an article by Malinvaud and Jestaz in the *Revue de Droit Immobilier* July to September 1985. The essential requirement in their view is that for a structure to be a building it must have as its primary purpose the intention of providing shelter for people. It is this which distinguishes a school, a hospital or a factory from a storehouse. The former are used regularly for the shelter of those working while the latter are visited only occasionally by a workman for the purpose of maintenance. See to the same effect the ministerial response (JO Deb. Ass. Nat. 25 April 1979, p. 6827).

42. See for example Malinvaud and Jestaz, s.146 pp. 183 and 184.

43. Cass. civ. 3e, 12 May 1982, JCP 1982.IV.257.

44. S.147 pp. 184 and 185.

45. Caston, p. 304, s.546.

46. Dufau, p. 254 and n.638 refers to the discretion which may be exercised by the *juge administratif* in deciding upon those liable under the *garantie biennale* and that it is not certain that all the *constructeurs* in the wide meaning of Art. 1792–3 would be included.

47. They suggest that based on the wording of the Article the only persons liable under the *garantie biennale* would be those responsible for the design, choice, manufacture, installation or the inspection and testing of the item of equipment.

48. See Circulaire no. 81–04 of 21 January 1981 of the Ministère de l'Environnement at Cadre de Vie reproduced Caston vol.2 p.629 et seq. One of the conditions for a manufacturer to be included within the definition of an *EPERS* is that the manufacturer is responsible for the design of his product and replaces what would otherwise be the design responsibility of the architect or contractor – condition 1 given on p. 630.

49. Cass.civ. 3e, 24 November 1987, Bull.civ.III no.188.

50. Cass.civ.3e, 4 December 1984, no.202.

51. Chambery, 12 September 1990, Soc. Clyma Carrier. C.Perrot et autres, Dalloz Informations Rapides, confirmed Cass. com. 20 January 1993, D 1993 IR52.
52. Dufau, pp. 240–41.
53. Cass. Ass. Plen. D.86.293 and Source Book 3rd ed. pp. 445 et seq.
54. Bull. civ. III no.35.p. 20 quoted Ghestin *La Vente* p. 1046.
55. Malinvaud and Jestaz, p.204, para. 168.
56. 12 July 1991 and note by Ghestin *Recueil* Dalloz 1991, 38e cahier, p. 549 et seq.
57. Viney, vol. IV, p. 308.
58. Starck, vol. 1 *Obligations Responsabilité delictuelle* p. 564.
59. While there is some similarity the English doctrine is narrower in scope. Tortfeasors are joint only where each concurs in the act causing the damage, not simply two separate acts which each contribute to the damage. As has been said the *injuria* and the *damnum* must be the same. The Koursk [1924] p. 140. In the French concept of *in solidum*, provided the *damnum* is the same the *injuria* can be different.
60. Cass. civ. 3e, 25 March 1980, Bull. Cass. no. 69, p. 48.
61. Cass. civ. 1re, 29 November 1966. See Caston, p. 357, n.40.
62. Keating, pp. 193–6.
63. See Malinvaud and Jestaz pp. 260 and 261. The standard clause in Art. 234–2, *Code des assurances*, defining *un bâtiment* was annulled by the Conseil d'État on 30 November 1979 but the principles of the definition still apply as regards insurance. See Caston vol.2 p.577 and the extract from a decision of the Cour de Paris of 11 May 1988 reproduced there in which the court held that in principle buildings were structures above ground.
64. Discussed Malinvaud and Jestaz, pp. 270–72.
65. Cass.civ.3e 17 May 1983, Bull.civ.III no.115.
66. Chambre mixte, 4 February 1983, Gaz.Pal.1083 p. 163.
67. Cass.com., 27 March 1990, D. 1990, 390.
68. Cass. civ., 17 November 1971, Bull.civ. III, no. 564.

15 Contracts for sale – German law

SOURCES

The German law relating to the sale of goods is to be found in a number of different sources:

- Book 1 of the *BGB* – the general part.
- Book 2 of the *BGB* – the law of obligations: ss. I–VI dealing with general obligations, and s. VII the particular obligations of sale, title 1 and other titles, e.g. 24 relating to unjust enrichment.
- Book 3 of the *BGB* – the law of property, in particular ss. I–III.
- Book 3 of the *HGB*, in particular ss. I and II.
- The *AGBG* (*Allgemeinen Geschäftsbedingungen Gesetz*) the German Standard Contracts Act.
- The *EGBGB* (*Einführungsgesetz zum Bürgerlichen Gesetzbuche*), which was revised in 1986, in particular as regards the choice of the applicable law to the contract to bring in the Rome Convention on the Law Applicable to Contractual Obligations.
- The practices of merchants and the decisions of the courts.

In considering any issue it is necessary therefore to take into account not just the specific provisions relating to sale but also all the other general obligations which have been 'factored out' (see above, pp. 14–15).

It must also be remembered that in general the rules of both the *BGB* and *HGB* as to the rights and obligations of the parties have the status of the *ius dispositivum* (*supplétive*) and in accordance with the principle of freedom of contract the parties may vary these rules by the express terms of the contract within the limits of good faith (*nach Treu und Glauben*).[1]

Comment was made earlier on the almost universal usage within Germany of standard conditions of contract which invariably modify the rules as expressed in the code, except for the few cases where these are of the *ius cogens* (mandatory). Such standard conditions are now subject to the *AGBG* but are still of great importance in determining the obligations of the parties. A prime example of this is the *VOB* (*Verdingsordnung für Bauleistungen*), the regulations for the award of public works construction contracts which contains in Part B the general conditions of contract which are also often applied in the private sector by agreement between the parties. Where these conditions do apply to a contract they are more important in deciding on the rights and obligations of the parties than the few Articles in the *BGB* dealing with *Werkvertrag* (works contract).

OBLIGATIONS OF THE SELLER

DEFECTS – SPECIFIC GOODS

If, before the passing of the risk in the goods, which will generally coincide with delivery (but for exceptions see below, p. 247), performance of the contract becomes impossible for a reason for which the supplier is responsible, then the purchaser has the normal rights in respect of non-performance by a debtor of an obligation due to his fault. He may rescind the contract or claim damages (Arts. 280 and 325, *BGB*).

This would apply if, say, a piece of antique china was broken due to the seller's negligence, including that of his assistants, while being packed ready for despatch. If the seller is not responsible for the damage, say the goods are accidently damaged by fire before they can be despatched, then both parties would be released. It would, however, be open to the purchaser, if the damage were insured by the seller, to maintain the contract and require the seller to assign to him his claim against the insurance company for compensation (Art. 281, *BGB*). Of course in this instance the purchaser would have to make payment of the purchase price. If payment had already been made, and the purchaser did not wish to demand assignment of the insurance claim, then he would be entitled to require the refund of the purchase price (Art. 323(2), *BGB*).

If responsibility for the damage were disputed then it would be for the seller to prove that he was not responsible (Art. 282, *BGB*). This reversal of the proof of negligence is a significant attenuation of the fault principle in German law.[2]

GENERIC GOODS – DEFAULT IN DELIVERY

As an exception to the fault principle a seller of generic goods (as defined earlier, see above, p. 161) is responsible for a failure to deliver the goods, whether it is due to his fault or not, provided only that delivery of goods of that type or class remains possible (Art. 279, *BGB*). A sale will not be one of generic goods if the source from which they are to be derived is either defined in, or implicit in, the terms of the contract (RGZ 91,312).

Additionally the application of the principle that contracts should be executed in good faith (Art. 242, *BGB*) may serve to relieve the supplier in circumstances in which it 'has become so difficult to obtain objects of the class in question that it cannot fairly be expected of anyone' (RGZ 57,116). This concept of *Unzumutbarkeit* has also been applied to cases in which the goods have been considered as generic only within a particular market, e.g. where the purchase was for goods to be obtained within the home market the supplier's obligation did not extend to the procurement of goods from overseas (see Jauernig [Vollkommer] s.280 at p. 278 bb).

However, in practice German firms are not inclined to accept the risk that they may be held under an absolute liability and therefore will normally qualify their quotations with such phrases as *richtige und rechtzeitige Selbstbelieferung vorbehalten* which protected the seller when his own supplier failed to deliver (BGHZ 92,399), or *Lieferungsmöglichkeit vorbehalten* ('subject to delivery being possible' – BGH NJW 58,1628).

Distinction between delivery of an *aliud* and a defect in quality

A distinction is drawn between a defect which results in a non-conformity (*Identitätsfehler*), i.e. the delivery of an *aliud*, and a lack of quality in the goods (*Qualitätsfehler*). In the first instance the purchaser is entitled to demand either specific performance or to claim damages in accordance with the rules on delay and impossibility. In the second he is limited to the remedies under the guaranty for *Wandlung* or *Minderung* (see further below, pp. 209–210) which must be exercised within the very short period of six months from delivery and do not, except in the case of fraud or the absence of a promised quality, entitle him to damages. Additionally he may have a claim for positive breach of contract and a right to damages for *Mangelfolgeschaden* (see below, pp. 212–213).

The distinction is not easy to draw. In the case of a contract for the sale of a consignment of Auslese wine, the wine only tasted like Auslese because it contained certain prohibited additives. It was held that this was the delivery of an *aliud* and not of defective goods.[3] Equally, when imported scrap metal was to be delivered and the contract expressly provided that goods of domestic origin were to be excluded, and the seller in fact delivered goods of domestic origin, then this was again held to be a misdelivery and not a matter of a qualitative defect.[4]

But while the delivery of Yugoslavian beechwood in place of Roumanian was only a defect, that of winter wheat in place of spring wheat was held to be an *aliud*.[5]

DEFECTS AFTER THE PASSING OF THE RISK–SPECIFIC GOODS

To a greater extent even than in French law a distinction is drawn in German law between the obligations and remedies which apply before and after delivery. German law has incorporated the old Roman rules limiting the rights of the purchaser after taking delivery of specific goods to the choice of the two remedies of *Wandlung* (redhibition)[6] and *Minderung* (reduction in the price) except in the following cases:

- if the seller has given an express guaranty as to some quality which the goods should possess, and they do not, the purchaser may as an alternative claim damages (Art. 463, *BGB*); and
- if the seller has fraudulently either concealed the defect or misrepresented their quality or condition the purchaser may again as an alternative claim damages (Art. 463, *BGB*).

The purchaser's rights are further restricted because of the six-month prescription period for the exercise of these remedies (see below, pp. 213–214). German law has not adopted the French doctrine that the supplier's obligation to deliver includes the requirement that the goods must be in conformity with the purposes of the contract, in order to defeat the short period of prescription, as French law has done with the *bref délai* of Art. 1648 of the *Code Civil* (see above, pp. 174–175). On the contrary, German law will treat delivery of specific goods, even if defective, as performance of the contract and leave the purchaser to his special remedies under the *BGB* as referred to above.

DEFECTS – GENERIC GOODS

For generic goods the purchaser has a right to decline to accept defective goods as performance of the contract and may require their replacement with goods which do conform.

Alternatively he may accept the delivery of the defective goods as performance of the contract and exercise the right of *Wandlung* or *Minderung* as if they were specific goods. Or again, as an alternative to any of the above he has the right to claim damages for the lack at the time of the passing of the risk of an express promised quality or for the fraudulent concealment of a defect (Art. 480(2), *BGB*).

DELIVERY, TRANSFER OF RISK AND ACCEPTANCE

Under Art. 459, *BGB*, the point in time at which the seller warrants that the goods are free from defects, and have the qualities which have been promised, is when the risk passes to the purchaser. For sales contracts there is no express requirement for the purchaser to accept the goods. However, if at the time of accepting them he knows of a defect and fails to make a complaint or reservation about it, then he will lose all remedies in respect of such defect (Art. 464 *BGB* and BGH 50,366). However Art. 464 does not apply to knowledge which is acquired after acceptance (BGH NJW 58,1724).

As to commercial sales, and the purchaser's duty to examine the goods, see Art.377 of the *HGB* referred to below, p. 214.

The passing of risk is defined under Art. 446 of the *BGB* as being the delivery of the goods which, unless the contract provides otherwise, is at the seller's place of business (Art. 269, *BGB*). However when, as is quite normal in commercial transactions, the seller is instructed by the purchaser to deliver the goods, then the risk passes to the purchaser at the time when the goods are delivered to the firm responsible for transporting them (Art. 447, *BGB*). This would not apply if the seller as part of the contract had undertaken the delivery or such an undertaking can be inferred from the contract because for example of the nature of the goods. Risk would then pass on actual delivery to the purchaser.[7]

Difficult questions can also arise when the contract concerns machinery which is to be installed under the supervision of the vendor and then tested. If this is regarded as a contract of sale then most probably the risk would pass to the purchaser on delivery to the site where the machine is to be installed. But if the contract is categorized as a *Werklieferungsvertrag* then the risk would pass on *Abnahme*, which would be after the machine has passed its tests. Obviously it is important that this issue is dealt with expressly in the terms of the contract rather than left to the uncertainties of the law.

As in French law the defect will be regarded as being in existence before the passing of the risk, when it exists in embryo', *in keim*, and its existence only manifests itself after delivery.

REMEDIES FOR HIDDEN DEFECTS

If after delivery specific goods are found to be defective then the purchaser has the right as stated earlier either to rescind the contract (*Wandlung*) or to retain the goods and claim a reduction in the price (*Minderung* – Art. 462, *BGB*).[8]

If the goods are generic then as an alternative the purchaser can require the delivery of goods which are free from defects and in default of compliance by the seller can claim damages (see above, p. 161).

Under the *BGB* there is no right on a contract for the sale of goods as opposed to one for work (see below, pp. 227–228) to require that the seller should make good the defect by repairing the goods, although this right is often contained in the seller's standard conditions and an attempt made to substitute it for the purchaser's rights under the code. In fact a revision to the code, Art. 476a, refers to the seller being obliged to bear all the costs necessary to effect the repair if this right is agreed upon by the parties in their contract, in lieu of the claim for *Wandlung* or *Minderung*.[9]

However, under the *ABGB* Art. 11 no. 10(a), the seller cannot in his standard conditions deprive the purchaser altogether of the rights of rescission or reduction in price in respect of new goods, although he may require that they are suspended while at his option he seeks either to rectify or replace the goods or assigns to the purchaser his rights against one of his sub-suppliers allegedly responsible for the defect. But the purchaser's right at his option to rescind or claim a reduction in price would revive if the seller failed within a reasonable time to effect the rectification or replacement or the purchaser failed to obtain satisfaction from the sub-supplier.

The particular provisions in Arts. 10 and 11 of the *ABGB* rendering certain contract terms void only apply directly to contracts with consumers. However, with some relaxation to take account of business practice, and the greater experience and commercial judgement to be expected of businessmen than consumers, the same rules will be applied by the courts indirectly to business contracts through s.9 of the *ABGB*. This makes standard terms void whether in business or consumer contracts if 'they place the other party at an undue advantage to such an extent as to be incompatible with the requirements of good faith'.[10] (See further below, pp. 304–306.)

THE REMEDY OF *WANDLUNG*

The aim of this remedy is that the parties should restore each other to the position which existed before the contract. However, consistent with the principle of abstraction the exercise of the remedy only creates a contractual obligation to transfer the ownership; it does not operate directly itself to transfer the property back to the seller (Arts. 467 and 346 of the *BGB*).

Difficulties with *Wandlung* may arise if the goods are no longer in the same condition as they were when delivered. The position is complex and only an outline will be given here.[11] Under Art. 467 of the *BGB* the general rules relating to the rescission of contracts in Arts. 346 et seq. are to be applied.

Somewhat anomalously the right to rescind is not lost if the goods are accidentally destroyed while in the purchaser's possession (*BGB* 350).[12] Nor more reasonably will it be lost if the goods are destroyed because of the defect itself.

If however the goods are destroyed or they deteriorate significantly due to the fault of the purchaser, then the right to rescind is lost (Arts. 467 and 351 *BGB*). Further, in this case if the destruction or deterioration occurs *after* the action for rescission has been filed then the purchaser will be liable to the seller in damages (Arts. 347 and 989). The purchaser must also return any benefit which he has received from the use of the goods.

Equally, the seller must return the price which he has been paid for the goods together with interest and any object which he has taken in part payment. Also he must compensate the purchaser for any administrative expenses (*Vertragskosten*) which the latter has incurred relating to the contract and its termination as well as paying compensation for expenditure on the subject matter of the contract (*Ersatz von Vorwendungen*) e.g. customs duties and costs of transport, adaptation and installation (Arts. 467 and 347, *BGB*). These costs are therefore more extensive than those *occasionés par la vente* – (see above, p. 172), as to the costs recoverable under Art. 1646 of the *Code Civil*.

REDUCTION IN THE PURCHASE PRICE

The purchaser may prefer to retain the goods and claim a reduction in the price. In that event the reduction to which he is entitled is determined objectively in accordance with Art. 472, *BGB*. This is important if the goods were sold at a discounted price as in the following example:

Value without defect	=	12,000 DM
Value defective	=	8,000 DM
Contract Price	=	9,000 DM
Y	=	Reduced contract price

Formula for reduction: $\dfrac{12,000}{8,000} \times \dfrac{9,000}{Y} = Y = 6,000 \text{ DM}$

CHOICE OF REMEDY

So long as the purchaser has not exercised his right one way or the other then he is free to choose either remedy and there is no requirement that a defect, to justify *Wandlung*, must be more serious than that for *Minderung*, provided that the purchaser acts in good faith.

ANCILLARY OBLIGATIONS OF THE SELLER

Even though they may not be expressly stated in the contract, the seller is under certain obligations additional to those relating to the delivery of goods free of defects. These will cover the provision of information necessary for the purchaser to supply and operate the goods, especially complex equipment, and to inform the purchaser as to any dangers involved. The goods must be properly packaged in order to avoid the risks of damage in transit. They must also not constitute a danger to the health of the purchaser or members of his family.

REMEDIES IN DAMAGES

The general matter of remedies for breach of contract in German law are discussed in more detail later (pp. 337–343). However there is one issue which must be dealt with now. It is a particular characteristic of German law that it has no single concept of breach of contract as such. When the *BGB* was drafted the authors considered that there were only two circumstances which could amount to a breach of contract: an impossibility of performance (*Unmöglichkeit der Leistung*) for which a party was responsible, or a delay (*Verzug*). If therefore an action was brought for breach of contract it had to be put into one of these two categories and then the rules appropriate to the proper category applied.

It was quickly realized that not all breaches of contract could be put into one of these two categories, especially those which related to ancillary obligations such as the supply of correct information.[13] The German courts therefore introduced the doctrine of positive breach of contract (*positive Vertragsverletzung*) in order to fill the gap left by the code. The remedy is accordingly subsidiary to those stated in the code.

CIRCUMSTANCES IN WHICH A PURCHASER CAN BRING AN ACTION IN DAMAGES FOR FAILURE IN PERFORMANCE

The purchaser can only bring an action for damages in two cases. The first is where the supplier has guaranteed that specific goods possess some particular quality at the time of the passing of the risk in the goods (Art. 459(2), *BGB*). The guaranty must form part of the supplier's contractual obligations such as for example a guaranty that a machine will produce a particular output, that its energy consumption will not exceed a stated figure, that a vehicle is of a particular power or that goods are suitable for a certain specified use. Mere statements in sales literature or in the course of pre-contractual negotiations as to the benefits to be obtained from the purchase of the machine would not be sufficient. Liability under the guaranty is not dependent on the proof of fault on the part of the seller.

The action for damages is stated in Art. 463, *BGB* to be an alternative to the claim for either *Wandlung* or *Minderung*. This is in line with the general principle of German law that the action for rescission (*Rücktritt*) excludes the right to claim damages for non-performance (see below, p. 348).

A similar right exists in respect of generic goods which lack some promised quality at the time when the risk in the goods passed to the purchaser. Again the remedy is made alternative to either *Minderung, Wandlung* or in this instance the right to demand delivery of goods free of defects.

However, it is accepted that the purchaser who is entitled to damages (*Mangelschaden*) because of the failure of a guaranteed quality has two alternatives. He may retain the goods and claim damages (*kleiner Schadenersatz*), being the reduction in value of the goods because of the lack of the guaranteed quality, together with the costs of remedying such deficiency. Otherwise the purchaser may return the goods and demand full damages for breach of contract (*grosser Schadenersatz*).

In either event the purchaser will be entitled to claim for any detriment which he has suffered directly due to the lack of the guaranteed quality, including any loss of profit which he has suffered.

The purchaser may also be entitled to recover for other consequential losses in which he has been involved because of the damage caused to his legal interests, other than the goods themselves, and which arise indirectly out of the defect (*Mangelfolgeschaden*), provided that the guaranteed quality can be said to have been intended to protect him against the loss in question (BGHZ 50,200). In that case adhesive which had been guaranteed for the fixing of ceiling tiles failed and the tiles fell off shortly after having been installed. The purchaser was held to be entitled to recover damages in respect of the costs which he incurred in carrying out the repair work as he had followed carefully the instructions for using the adhesive which were intended to protect him against risks of that kind. See also cases quoted Jauernig (Vollkommer) s.463, 4aa, p. 501.

The second case in which a purchaser can bring an action for damages is where the seller has fraudulently concealed a defect in the goods or their lack of a particular quality. This will include the failure of the seller to provide information relating to the goods when he must be taken to have known of its importance to the purchaser and the purchaser had no means of knowing it for himself. Classic examples are the reading of a milometer on the sale of a secondhand car or a failure to disclose that the vehicle had been in an accident.

The same rules on damages apply as in the case of a failure of the goods to possess the guaranteed quality.

In contrast to French law there is no concept of the professional seller being equated to one who knew of the defect before delivery and is therefore liable in damages because of a latent defect in the goods without there being any need to prove fault (see above, pp. 172–173). The restrictions in the German law of sale of the purchaser's right to claim damages in respect of defective goods has often caused German law to be referred to as a 'seller's law'.[14]

Relationship with positive breach of contract

The defect in the goods may be responsible for injury to other interests of the purchaser. Although as regards the goods themselves the remedies of the purchaser, in the absence of either a guaranteed quality or fraud, will be limited to those of *Wandlung* or *Minderung* and will exclude any right to damages, the question arises as to whether or not the purchaser can claim damages for the injury caused by the defective goods to his other interests.

Interests of the purchaser will not only cover other property of his but may, through the concept referred to above of ancillary obligations of the seller, extend to the protection of his family[15] or his economic interests, as on the sale of business that the seller should not immediately exercise a competitive activity in the same district.

A claim may be allowed under the doctrine of *positive Vertragsverletzung* referred to above if the purchaser can establish that such injury was caused by the fault of the supplier in the performance of his obligations. So if due to the negligence of the supplier a machine, on being put into service, catches fire and causes damage to other property of the purchaser, then in addition to his rights in respect of the defective machine, the purchaser can claim damages for the effects of the explosion on his other property. What he cannot claim for, in the absence of a guaranteed quality in the machine or fraud, are damages to cover his expectation interest in respect of the machine itself, unless he bring his claim within the scope of products liability (see below, pp. 284–285).

The damages recoverable for a breach by the supplier of his ancillary obligations will be those which compensate the purchaser for the damage suffered. On the measure of damages see below, pp. 341–343.

Period of prescription

Except where the defect is fraudulently concealed by the seller, the period within which a claim must be brought either for a defect or for damages because of a lack in the goods of a guaranteed quality is limited to six months from the date of delivery.[16] When goods are delivered by handing them over to a transport firm for delivery to the purchaser, then the period will run from the time when the purchaser or his representative ought to have examined them. If the seller has to instal, commission or test the goods then the period runs from the time when such work or testing has been completed.

It is important to note in particular that this extremely short period of guaranty runs not from the time at which the purchaser discovered, or even could have discovered, the hidden defect but from the date of delivery, whether it was discoverable within the six months or not.

The harshness of this rule has been criticized in Germany but is generally explained on the basis of an assumption that the purchaser, having been put in control of the goods by the delivery, will then examine them so that he can at once take them into his charge.

Indeed in commercial sales under Art. 377 of the *HGB* the purchaser is required to examine the goods immediately after delivery and to advise the seller of any defects.[17] If the purchaser either fails to do so, or fails to give notice to the seller of a defect which such examination ought to have revealed, then the goods will be considered to be approved and the purchaser loses all rights to complain other than for defects which such examination would not have revealed. However, once any such non-discoverable defect does appear then again it must be notified immediately to the seller. The same provision applies if the seller's attempts to repair the goods fail and the purchaser demands a reduction in the purchase price (Oberlandesgericht München, 23 U 3798/85 6 December 1985 [1986] DB 961).

These rules apply also if the goods delivered are of a different kind or quality unless the difference is so great that the seller could not have expected them to be approved by the purchaser (Art. 378, *HGB*).

Although the trader must make any claim in respect of defective goods 'without delay', where there was a hidden fault in material which was being used to manufacture a whole series of goods, the trader was held to be in time even though he had only reported the defect after he had realized that it was not an isolated fault (BGH (VIII ZR 195/85) [18 June 1986] DB 2123).

It has also recently been decided that a loss by the trader of his contractual rights because of a failure to give notice immediately of faulty goods, does not affect his right to claim damages in tort if those goods cause further damage (BGH (VIII ZR 334/86) 16 September 1987 [1987] DB 2351).

The Federal Supreme Court has also held that a claim may be made in tort after the expiry of the contractual period of limitation of liability (six months from delivery) for damages directly connected with the remedying of the defect itself, where the defect was in a small part of the entirety of the goods purchased, but resulted in use to damage to the whole and there was not substantial identity between the defect and the resultant damage. In one case a tyre on a secondhand car, when it was sold by the dealer, did not conform to the regulations for the type of tyre to be fitted to that kind of vehicle. There was a blow-out which caused an accident. The claim in contract was barred by prescription but a claim in tort was allowed for violation of the integrity of the creditor's property (BGH 5 July 1978 NJW 1978, 2241).[18]

This line of argument strongly resembles, but goes further than, that of 'the complex structures theory' developed by the House of Lords in premises cases in which they have suggested that there could be a claim in tort where damage has been caused to the remainder of the structure by a defective component supplied by a separate contractor or a sub-contractor.[19]

That the policy nature of the argument of the German Federal Supreme Court is intended to redress to some extent the unfairness created by the limited nature of the contractual remedies available to the claimant, and the short prescription period for contractual claims for defects, is clearly shown in the judgements of the court, in particular that of 24 November 1976. Having pointed out that the purchaser could not claim compensation for the cost of repairs to the equipment purchased due to the failure of a particular small component switch (because under the law relating to warranties damages are only claimable for the breach of an express warranty of quality), and any claim for positive breach of contract could not relate to the object of the sale but only other legally protected interests of the purchaser, the court went on, 'thus the buyer would be largely without a remedy if he could not fall back on claims in tort'.[20]

The doctrine may be contrasted with the far superior and more logical reasoning of the German courts as regards defective premises where they clearly anticipated the House of Lords decision in *Murphy* v. *Brentwood District Council* (1990) 3 WLR 414[21] that the real subject matter of the claim was for economic loss and that the defective premises had existed in a defective state from the time at which they were built. As the Federal Supreme Court said, there could be no damage to the owner's property where what became the owner's property as it was completed was already defective. The loss suffered by the owner was that the premises which he had had constructed were less valuable than he contracted for, and that was economic loss for which under Art. 823(1), *BGB* there is no recourse in tort (BGHZ 39,366).

One could wish that this reasoning had been brought to the attention of the English courts before they reached the disastrous decision in *Anns* v. *Merton London Borough Council* [1978] AC 728, now of course overruled by *Murphy*, that such damage constituted in tort 'material physical damage'.

In practice the general rule of Art. 477 is clearly unsatisfactory for many modern manufactured goods where defects may well not be detectable or manifest themselves within six months. The Federal Court has however kept strictly to the wording of the Article and has not followed suggestions that the period should run from when the defect was either discovered or discoverable.[22] Nor is it satisfactory that as regards professional sellers there is no general remedy in damages for hidden defects as now exists in French law (see above, pp. 172–173) and under the common law and the Sale of Goods Act.

At the same time the court has, as referred to above, by allowing parallel remedies in contract and tort and expanding the remedy in tort, in certain instances arguably beyond the tort boundary and into the area which is proper to contract, sought to remedy the perceived injustice. In other instances the Federal Supreme Court has either interpreted the contract having regard to pre-contractual negotiations and the obligation of good faith under Art. 157, *BGB*, so as to find a contractual guaranty running from the date of discovery of the hidden defect, or has interpreted the wording of a contractual guaranty included within the contract to like effect.[23]

Finally, under the Standard Contract Terms Act, s.11, para. 10f, a reduction in the period of the statutory guaranty below six months is not permitted in standard conditions of contract for consumer transactions in respect of new goods and through the application of s.9 of the Act this may apply also in the case of a business contract if the reduction is unreasonable (BGH 90,278). For the impact of s.9 generally see below, p. 304. A reduction of the two-year statutory prescription period for claims against the transport company to three months in the standard conditions of contract of a local haulage firm was held invalid (BGH 19 May 1988 [1989] DB 106).

Despite all the efforts of the courts to assist purchasers and the impact of the Standard Contract Terms Act, there is no doubt that in the area of the liability of the supplier for hidden defects German law fully deserves its reputation as a 'seller's law'. There is also the inevitable problem of uncertainty caused by the need for judicial intervention, if not invention, to mitigate indirectly the injustices caused by the statutory provisions, e.g. the short prescription periods and the limited right to claim damages for defective goods. It seems likely, however, at the time of writing that eventually there will be some statutory reforms in this area, possibly along the lines of the Vienna Convention, which is now part of German law for international sales of goods, and which will bring German law more into line with English law.

Period of prescription – positive breach of contract This is a problem which has been considered many times by the courts both for contracts for sale and those for works. For sales contracts the general outcome is that where the damage arises out of a defect in the debtor's primary obligation to supply the goods then the short period of six months applies. When however the damage arises out of the defective performance by the debtor of one of his secondary obligations, and unconnected to the defect, e.g. the provision of advice or an ancillary service, then the 30-year period will apply.[24] The distinction appears highly artificial especially given the disparity between the two periods.

TIME FOR DELIVERY

The German rules governing the contractual significance of provisions relating to the time for delivery and the remedies available to the purchaser are considerably more complex than those of English law.

The first point to note is that only exceptionally is the purchaser entitled to rescind the contract or claim damages because of the simple failure by the supplier to deliver on time. The general rule is that the purchaser must as a first step give the supplier a notice (*Mahnung*) demanding performance of the contract which can only be given after the supplier has failed to satisfy his obligation to deliver. It is this notice which strictly puts the supplier into default (Art. 284(1), *BGB*).

There are exceptions to this general rule, the most important of which are when:

- the contract clearly specified the definitive date by which the contract must be performed and the date has passed;[25]
- the terms of the contract were such that the supplier was bound to proceed urgently

with the work in question, e.g. *schnellstmöglicher Reparatur* (to effect repairs as quickly as possible – BGH NJW 63,1823 Jauernig Vollkommer p. 289. 5 ex.bb;
- the contract is a *Fixgeschäft* – see further below;
- the nature of the contract was such that performance was only possible if it were completed on or before a certain date;
- the contract itself stated that no notice was necessary.

The rule and the exceptions to it may be contrasted with the requirements in French law for the *mise en demeure* (see above, pp. 178–179).

Of the exceptions listed above the first is the most important in practice and also the one which causes some difficulty in deciding whether or not the contract has specified the date for performance with sufficient certainty. For example 'latest 10th April' or 'end of February' have been held sufficiently definitive not to require the issue of a *Mahnung*, but '30 days after invoice' and '160 working days after commencement of work' have been held insufficient so that in those instances a *Mahnung* was necessary (see Jauernig Vollkommer note 5, p. 289). It will be recalled that this exception does not exist under French law which requires a *mise en demeure* even if the contract has a fixed date which has passed (above, p. 178).

If either a *Mahnung* is given, or exceptionally is not required, and the supplier is late, then the effect is that the supplier is obliged to compensate the purchaser in damages for his *Verzug*, delay in performance, provided that this is due to his default (Art. 286(1), *BGB*). These are 'delay' damages and not damages for failure in performance. For the distinction see below, p. 341. If fault is disputed then, as referred to earlier (see above, p. 206) the onus of proof that he was not at fault is on the supplier. Further if the contract is for the supply of generic goods then under Art. 279, *BGB*, the supplier is liable even in the absence of fault.

If at this stage the performance of the supplier is no longer of any interest to the purchaser by reason of the delay, then the purchaser can refuse performance and demand compensation for non-performance (Art. 286(2), *BGB*). In this instance there is no need for the purchaser to issue the supplier with a *Nachfrist* (see below, p. 218).

The reason for the goods no longer being of interest to the purchaser must result from the delay, as for example a delay in the supply of seasonal goods, say for Christmas. But a fall in the price of the goods or the fact that there is a sales problem not connected with the delay would not constitute circumstances which would justify the purchaser in claiming the goods were no longer of interest to him.[26]

TERMINATION FOR DELAY

Although, if he has given a *Mahnung* or one is not required, and the supplier is in default, the purchaser can claim damages for delay, he must still accept the delayed performance as performance of the contract, i.e. he has no right to terminate or claim damages for non-performance unless he has given the supplier notice or legally notice is not required (Art. 326, *BGB*). This second notice is referred to as a *Nachfrist*. In practice, following judicial authority, the two notices are often combined (RG 50.262), but the notice must contain two essential features.

First, it must state that the seller is required to perform his contract and give a reasonable period within which this must be done. However, since the seller is already in default of his contractual obligations, a provision in standard conditions of contract which is too generous in the further time allowed to the seller will be void, even in business transactions, for breach of para. 9 of the Standard Contract Terms Act[27] (see below, p. 304). The purpose of the *Nachfrist* is not to make it now possible for the defaulting seller to complete his obligations, but so that he has a last chance to fulfil his contract in the manner intended. The additional period as allowed by the *Nachfrist* is not a substitute contract period (BGH NJW 85,857).

Second, it must declare clearly that if performance is not effected within the period of the notice, the purchaser will refuse performance.

Exceptions to the need to issue a *Nachfrist*

The primary exceptions are:

- if as a result of the delay in delivery, the performance of the contract is no longer of interest to the purchaser (Art. 326(1), *BGB*) e.g. seasonal goods delivered after the end of the season;
- if the contract can be interpreted as meaning that either expressly or by implication the seller has waived his right to the protection of the *Nachfrist*.
- if the contract falls within the definition of a *Fixgeschäft*, that is to say a contract under which there is a definite fixed period/time for completion of delivery and it can be inferred that the purchaser was entitled to rescind if performance was not rendered accordingly (*BGB* 361). That would be the case if 'the time of performance was so important that the business transaction "stands or falls" with its achievement' (BGH BB83, 1813). See further the commentary in Jauernig (Vollkommer) s.361 pp. 383 and 384.

In commercial contracts under Art. 376 of the *HGB* a purchaser has the absolute right (as opposed to one drawn by inference), if a definite time/period for completion of delivery is fixed, either to terminate or claim damages for non-performance if the seller is in default or, provided he acts immediately, to insist that the seller performs his contract.

Comparison of the *Fixgeschäft* with 'time of the essence'

It is tempting but misleading to compare the *Fixgeschäft* with the English doctrine of 'time of the essence'. It will be recalled that under English law in commercial contracts there is a presumption that the time of delivery is of the essence (see above, p. 143). Further, it is commonplace in the purchaser's standard conditions of contract to provide that this is the case, thus giving the purchaser the right to terminate if he so chooses the next day after the failure to deliver. Nor is it relevant what loss, if any, the purchaser has suffered as a result of the failure to deliver on time. The purchaser can in truth take advantage of the delay, if he so wishes, to avoid a bargain which has now become inconvenient to him.[28]

However, under German law there is a reluctance to apply Art. 376 of the *HGB* unless the facts of the particular case show that the parties did indeed consider that the time of delivery was such that the contract 'stood or fell' according to whether it was achieved or not. A mere provision in the general conditions of contract would certainly not be sufficient to achieve this. Not only would the stipulation as to the time or period for delivery have to be specific, even to the day, but there would have to be in addition further evidence that the parties had agreed in this particular case on the vital importance of the achievement by the seller of his delivery obligations.

POSITIVE BREACH OF CONTRACT

Reference was made earlier (see above, pp. 162, 213) to the doctrine of positive breach of contract. If the seller is responsible for the breach of some ancillary obligation, which is nevertheless fundamental to the performance of the contract as a whole, then the purchaser may have the right not to proceed with the performance of his own obligations and claim damages for non-performance against the defaulting seller. Further, this right is not dependent upon the purchaser having previously given the supplier notice.

The right of the purchaser in this instance not to proceed further with his own performance of the contract does not amount to termination (*Rücktritt*).

The principle has been applied to contracts for successive deliveries where in making the initial deliveries the supplier was in breach of an obligation which gave rise to a claim for *positive Vertragsverletzung*, e.g. damage caused by the goods to other property of the purchaser. Assuming the damage was significant, the purchaser could refuse to accept other deliveries and claim damages.

ANTICIPATORY BREACH

It is comparatively rare in commercial practice that one party to a contract will advise the other that he does not intend to carry out his contract. More commonly one party may state that he will only proceed with performance if the other will agree to changes in the price or other conditions. Again a party may not openly inform the other as to his intentions but may act so that the other has every justification for believing that he has no intention of performing.

In any of the above events, provided that the intentions of the debtor are sufficiently clearly established, the purchaser can act immediately without the need for the issue of a *Mahnung* or *Nachfrist*. It appears that the purchaser can either exercise the remedies, as provided for under Art. 326, of either termination or claiming damages, or can refuse further performance of his own obligations and claim damages.[29]

NOTES

1. Important exceptions to the principle are Art. 276, *BGB* para.2 under which a party cannot be released in the terms of the contract from responsibility for his intentional conduct; and Art. 476 under which the vendor cannot escape from his liability for defects in the goods sold which he has fraudulently concealed.

2. 'The placing of the burden of proof for the non-responsibility of the impossibility on the debtor alters the Fault Principle in favour of an objective guaranty of responsibility' Jauernig Vollkommer p. 281 commenting in para. 1a on Art. 282.

3. BGH (VIII) ZR 247/87.23 November 1988 [1989] DB 1513. The delivery of a robot without an arm essential for its proper performance was also an *aliud*, not a defect (BGH (VIII ZR 72/89) 27 June 1990 DB 2016). So no obligation to notify the vendor immediately.

4. Case decided on 4 December 1968 and quoted Langen pp. 147 and 15.

5. Quoted Ghestin *La Vente* p. 821. The winter as opposed to summer wheat case is a decision of the BGH, NJW 68,640; see Jauernig Vollkommer, p. 522, para. 4a.

6. *Wandlung* is literally 'an undoing of the sale' (Jauernig Vollkommer, p. 497 note 1 to Art. 462, *BGB*. It is governed in practice by substantially the same rules as apply to termination (Art. 467, *BGB*).

7. For example goods whose delivery required the use of a specialized vehicle which the purchaser could not be expected to possess.

8. There is no direct statement in the *BGB* that the defects must be hidden as is contained within Art. 1641 of the *Code Civil*. See comments by Ghestin *La Vente* para. 734, p. 780 pointing out that it is implied because the seller is not liable if the purchaser knew of the defect or was ignorant of it because of his gross negligence unless the seller had fraudulently concealed it. In commercial sales it is to be implied from Art. 377 of the *HGB* which requires the purchaser to make an immediate examination of the goods but also allows him a claim for a defect which appears later if the defect was not discoverable on examination.

9. Should the seller default, then in his undertaking to effect a repair it seems probable that the purchaser would have an action for damages (Treitel *Damages*, p. 95).

   However a clause which requires the purchaser just to accept an obligation to repair in place of his rights under the code will always be held void even in a commercial contract (Abderrahmane s.380). So will a clause in a seller's general conditions limiting the purchaser's rights to claim for faults at the time of delivery, thus excluding the right to claim for a fault not immediately apparent since this contravenes the *AGBG* (BGH (VIII ZR 152/84), 3 July 1985 [DB 2556]).

10. A significant deviation from a legal norm or a restriction of a fundamental right inherent in the nature of the contract will be contrary to s.9 of the *AGBG*. So in a set of general purchase conditions a period of three years within which claims in respect of defects in the goods could be made was held void as it was too great a departure from the legal norm of six months (BGH VIII ZR 292/88) 17 January 1990 [1990] DB 578). A clause contained in the general conditions of a manufacturer of prefabricated houses which gave him the right to delay delivery for up to six weeks after the agreed delivery date was similarly held void as being contrary to good faith (BGH (VII ZR 276/83) 28 June 1984 [1984] DB 2341).

11. For a more detailed treatment see Treitel *Damages* pp. 385 et seq.

12. The anomaly arises because at this point the risk of accidental loss will have been transferred to the purchaser.

13. On this point and positive breach of contract generally see Horn, Kotz and Lesser, p. 105 et seq.

14. E.g. Cohn, p. 134.

15. Professor Zweigert, in commenting on how a German court would have decided *Frost* v. *Aylesbury Dairy*, in which the milk which was purchased from the dairy was contaminated with typhoid germs, as a result of which the purchaser's wife died, stated that the German court would probably have allowed a claim in damages on the basis of a positive breach of a contractual obligation to protect the health of the purchaser and his family. The seller would only escape liability if he could prove absolutely no fault by either himself or his employees in the preparation and handling of the milk (Art. 282, *BGB*). 'Some Comparative Aspects of the Law Relating to the Sale of Goods' *ICLQ* Supplementary Publication no. 9 1964 at p. 3.

    There could of course be no claim for damages for breach of the warranty against defects in the absence of fraud.

16. Note that this is delivery and not passing of the risk.

17. The German text uses the word *unverzüglich* which is legally defined in Art. 121 of the *BGB* as 'without delay attributable to the fault of'. As Abderrahmane points out since the term is legally defined it is subject to the control of the Federal Supreme Court, unlike the equivalent provisions in French law.

18. The tort period of limitation would be the three years from the damage being known to the victim.

19. The theory was first developed in *D&F Estates* v. *Church Commissioners* [1989] AC 177 and was further developed in *Murphy* v. *Brentwood District Council* [1990] 3 WLR 414. However its scope of application is unclear. It is considered that it probably only extends to work in a building which is specialist non-building work such as electrical and heating installations. See Keating, pp. 164 et seq.

20. BGHZ 67,359; judgement set out in English in Markesinis p. 368 et seq. The quotation in the text is on page 372.

21. RGJW 1905,67 and BGHZ 39,366 referred to in BGHZ 67,359, the judgement of which is set out in English in Markesinis p.368 et seq.

22. See the judgement of the BGH of 5 July 1978 NJW 1978,2241 referred to in note 15 above and reported in English in Markesinis p. 374 et seq. The court stated, 'the Court of Appeal believes that the period of limitation amounting to six months according to para 477(1) BGB had only begun to run when the plaintiff was able to perceive the cause of the accident with the necessary degree of certainty . . . . However this view of the law is erroneous.'

    After pointing out that there had been cases in which the court had considered the short period of limitation in order to avoid gross injustice, the decision went on to state that these had all been instances of *Mangelfolgeschaden*, i.e. damage not to the goods themselves but to other legally protected interests of the purchaser.

    As a final recognition that perhaps they wished to leave the door just open for the future the court did finally say before deciding that the contractual claim was caught by the six-month period of limitation that 'it need not be decided here whether . . . despite the clear wording of Art 477(1) BGB a case might exist in certain circumstances for postponing to a later date the moment when the period of limitation begins'.

    However there appears to be no decision of the BGH allowing this possibility for defects in the goods themselves.

23. See the decisions cited Abderrahmane p. 214, notes 129 and 130.

24. In a recent case the debtor, on delivering petrol to the pumps of the creditor, negligently filled the tanks which should have contained 4 star with 2 star and vice versa. This caused damage to the engines which it was the creditor's business to tune. The error was discovered only after the elapse of the six-month prescription period. The BGH held that the debtor had violated a secondary contractual duty, which was to fill the petrol into the correct tanks, and allowed a claim for damages (BGH 26.4.1989 NJW 1989, 2118).

25. German law did therefore retain the maxim *dies interpellat pro homine*, unlike French law (see above, p. 178).

26. See the cases quoted in the examples given by Jauernig p.352.

27. Silberberg p.45 commenting on para. 10.2 of the Standard Contract Terms Act.

28. See the comments by Atiyah on p.109.

29. There is some dispute as to the basis on which a creditor may act under German law in the case of what English law would refer to as 'anticipatory breach'. Some writers see it as analogous to the rights provided under Art. 326 for irregular performance; others as an application of the doctrine of positive breach of contract and yet others as an independent doctrine developed by the courts. See Horn et al. p. 105; Zweigert and Kotz, p. 185 and Treitel *Damages*, pp. 380 and 381. Whatever the basis, if the actions of the debtor amount clearly to an unequivocal refusal to perform (at least on the terms of the original contract – see BGHZ 65,357) then the creditor can take immediate action.

16 Contracts for works – German law

Reference was made earlier (see above, p. 51) to the German Standard Conditions for Construction Works, the *VOB*, and their importance in comparison with the provisions of the *BGB*. The difficulty as regards the application of the *BGB* is that the rules they establish are really only applicable to simple, short-term contracts and do not take into account the complexities and time-periods of modern construction contracts. For that reason the terms of the *VOB* are of more practical importance in determining the rights and obligations of the parties specific to construction works in contracts to which the *VOB* applies. Its use is mandatory for public construction works and it is frequently applied by agreement to works within the private sector.

It is to be noted that the *VOB* actually exists in three parts. Part A sets out the rules which must be followed in establishing a *VOB* contract. Part B is the general conditions of contract themselves and Part C contains the general technical conditions. It is essential in order to establish a *VOB* contract that the regulations are followed, in particular those in s.10 of Part A.

These provide that the contract documents must prescribe that the general conditions of contract relating to the execution of construction works (DIN 1961 edition 1992) and the general technical specifications in contracts for construction works (DIN 18299–18451) are to form part of the contract. Additions to, or the amendment of these general conditions and general specifications is strictly controlled.

The general conditions must not be altered, with the proviso, however, that clients who regularly award contracts for construction works may add supplementary conditions to take account of their special requirements, but these may not conflict with the general conditions. Special conditions which depart from the general conditions may only be introduced to the extent required by the nature of the work and its execution.

Similarly the general technical specifications may not be altered but may be added to or amended, but only to the extent necessary to meet the requirements of a particular case. These must be clearly set out in the description of the works (*Leistungs-beschreibung* or *Leistungsverzeichnis*) which contains a description of each item of the works prepared by the architect.

A particular point to be noted from Art. 1(2) of Part B of the *VOB* is that the order of precedence of the contract documentation puts the specification (*Leistungsbe-schreibung*) first even above the special conditions of contract. This is in marked contrast with English contractual practice, e.g. clause 2.2(1) of the JCT 1980 form, under which the form of agreement or special conditions of contract would normally be given priority. The *Leistungsbeschreibung* has been described as the 'heart of a *VOB* contract'.

Failure to comply with the rules set out in Part B may lead the court to conclude that the parties did not intend to enter into a *VOB* contract. This can have two unfortunate results. First, the court may decide that the rules of the *BGB* should be applied and the intention behind the *VOB* of providing a reasonable and balanced contract appropriate for works of long duration will not be achieved. An example of this occurred when a contractor in contract with a private client amended the *VOB* conditions as he thought to his advantage by providing that the 2-year defects liability period would only be interrupted if he accepted that there was a defect or when the client had taken legal action against him. According to the *VOB* the period is interrupted by notice in writing from the client of a defect. The Dusseldorf court of appeal decided that this was such a major change that the 5-year defects liability period of Art.638(1) of the *BGB* would be substituted for the 2-year period of the *BGB* and that the whole contract was subject to the provisions of the *AGBG* as it was not a *VOB* contract in its entirety (OLG Dusseldorf 13.12.1991). Second, the exemption of certain provisions of the *VOB* from the application of the Standard Contract Terms Act, *AGBG*, may no longer apply since the courts have held that such exemption is only applicable if the *VOB* is used in full and not if only individual clauses from the *VOB* are used.[1] Even minor amendments to the payment terms may be sufficient for the court to decide that a *VOB* contract has not been used in its entirety and therefore to invalidate terms of the contract, contrary to the *AGBG*, which would otherwise be protected.[2]

OBLIGATIONS OF THE CONTRACTOR (*AUFTRAGNEHMER*)

Obligations of the contractor (para.633 *BGB* s.1) are that:

1. The works must be constructed so that they possess the quality which he guarantees.
2. The works must be free from defects which either prevent or limit the use for which they are required, which is either the use to be normally expected or as may be stipulated in the contract.

These obligations are also contained in the *VOB* and in addition, according to ss.4.2 and 13 of the *VOB* the contractor must execute the works 'in accordance with the contract on his own responsibility and in compliance with the recognised rules of sound engineering practice'.[3] As in French law the contractor is regarded as being a 'master of his art'.

Accordingly he is required to be aware of the latest developments in technology within the industry and of the applicable standards to which the works in question ought to be constructed.

The term 'defects' in s.13.1 of the *VOB* is to be construed objectively and not in relation to the subjective knowledge which the contractor either had or ought to have had at the time of performing the work. Even, it has been said, if the defect was completely unforeseeable by the contractor, having regard to the scientific and technical knowledge available at that time, and the work was carried out in accordance with the then accepted standards of technology, the contractor will still be responsible.[4] This follows the same principles as those which apply in French law (see above, p. 183 and the cases referred to in notes 4 and 5 to Chapter 14 on p.201).

The contractor is strictly responsible under para. 278 of the *BGB* for the default of those whom he employs to carry out work which is specific to the construction of the works forming the subject matter of the contract – those who are referred to as *Erfüllungsgehilfen*. This clearly includes sub-contractors. However it would appear that it does not cover those who simply supply materials which are not specific and are available for general use. If therefore under the *BGB* the main contractor is to be responsible for defects in such supplies then it is through his own failure to select competent suppliers or properly to test the materials delivered.

However, under s.4 of the *VOB* the contractor must execute the work strictly in accordance with the specification (*Leistungsbeschreibung*). Since the specification will normally be objective and allow the contractor freedom of choice of materials, this includes work to be performed by his sub-contractors and suppliers. He cannot avoid this liability by proving that he was not personally at fault or that the defect in the work done or the materials supplied could not have been detected at the time.

MATERIALS SUPPLIED BY THE CLIENT (*AUFTRAGGEBER*)

German construction law and practice contain no provisions equivalent to those under the English system of nomination of sub-contractors and suppliers and the use of the nomination system is virtually unknown.

However the *VOB* conditions do foresee the possibility that the client[5] may himself supply certain of the materials. In that event the client, under s.4.3, sub-para.2 of the *VOB*, is responsible for the quality of the building materials or components which he supplies and for the performance of any other contractor employed by him who is associated with the works, the subject matter of the contract. The contractor should give notice to the client of any doubts which he has concerning such materials, components or performance of such other contractors, and preferably before starting work. While the client remains responsible for such materials, components or work of others, the contractor will be responsible for his own failure to give notice, if the matter was one which he should have been able from his professional ability to identify.

Similarly for defects in the works after completion, the contractor under s.13.3, *VOB* is not responsible for defects in the materials and components supplied by the client or arising from the work of a previous contractor, provided that he has given notice in writing as required by s.4.3 of the *VOB*. It follows that he would not be liable for a defect arising after completion in materials or components supplied by the client or arising from the work of another contractor, even if he had not given notice, provided that the defect was hidden and he could not reasonably have been expected to discover it.

REQUIREMENT OF THE CONTRACTOR TO WARN

As noted above, the contractor in order to protect himself is required to give notice to the client if he has doubts about the quality of materials or components being supplied by the client or the work of another contractor. However there is also a more general duty on the contractor to warn the client if he considers that the instructions he has received regarding the execution of the works are incorrect or would lead to a danger of accident (para. 4.3 of the *VOB*).

The contractor also has an important duty to warn the client as regards defects in the work of another contractor who has carried out work with which his own work is interrelated, e.g. where he is constructing a building on ground which has been prepared by another contractor. It would appear that in such a situation the contractor is obliged to check positively that the work of the first contractor is suitable for his purposes and if not, to advise the client accordingly. He is not entitled to rely solely on the client or his architect/engineer but must use his own specialist knowledge. If his warnings are ignored then there may in the ultimate be an obligation on the contractor not to proceed with a construction which he considers to be defective and dangerous (BGH 4 July 1980 NJW 1981, 50).

The extent of the duty to warn is illustrated by a recent case decided in Nurnberg. A contractor was required to lay paving stones on ground which had been compressed by another contractor. The work of compression had not been done correctly and the question arose as to the liability of the paving contractor for having gone ahead without warning the *Auftraggeber*. The court decided that the paving contractor had a duty to check the work of the other contractor by looking, feeling and measuring and 'normal checking of load bearing capacity' but without actually exploring the ground. However, as he could have checked by the use of a simple iron bar which would have revealed the incorrect compression, and failed to do so, he was responsible for the resultant defects in his work during the defects liability period.

The contractor's duty to warn is therefore significantly more extensive than that under English law and, in terms of a positive duty to satisfy himself as to the proper state of the work performed by others with which his own work relates, it goes further than French law.

DEFECTS PRIOR TO COMPLETION (*ABNAHME*)

The basic right of the client is to have the works performed in accordance with the contract. If therefore work is found to be defective during the course of the contract's execution then the contractor is obliged to correct this. Further, if such defects are due to his fault then he is bound to compensate the client for the damage resulting (para.4.7, *VOB*).

Should the contractor fail to make good the defects then the client may give the contractor a reasonable period of notice to do so, with a statement that he will withdraw from the contract should the contractor not comply (para. 4.7, *VOB*).

If the contractor fails to correct the work within the period stipulated, the client may withdraw from the contract and have the work carried out by others at the contractor's risk and expense, without prejudice to any claim he may have for further damages (para. 8.3(1) and (2), *VOB*).

However if the defect is such that it 'endangers the object of the contract and the Client's confidence in the workmanlike execution is shaken in such a way that he cannot under any circumstances be expected to abide by the contract', then the client has no need to give the contractor the opportunity to remedy the defect and can withdraw from the contract immediately (BGH 6 May 1968, BGHZ 50,160 quoted Lorenz pp. 73 and 74).

If, because of the defective work and the time it will take to remedy it, the contract is no longer of interest to him, the client may, as an alternative to having the work corrected, give up further implementation of the work and claim full damages from the contractor for non-performance (para. 8.3(1) and (2), *VOB*).

This right of the client to withdraw and claim damages for non-performance, because as a result of the defects the contract is no longer of interest to him, is not provided for in any of the English standard forms. It is a peculiarity of German law which is contained within Arts. 280 and 326 of the *BGB*.

It has been suggested by Treitel that this remedy has its counterpart in English law in the provision that a breach will justify termination if it constitutes 'a substantial failure', or in another phrase, 'substantially deprives the purchaser of what he bargained for'.[6]

There is no doubt that, apart from any express rights under the contract, a client under English law can rescind a contract for anticipatory breach on the grounds of its having been repudiated by the contractor if the conduct of the contractor is such that he has demonstrated that he has 'neither the ability, competence or will to complete the work in the manner required by the contract'.[7] This is similar language to that which was used by the BGH in the case referred to above, but that case was concerned with the client's right to withdraw without giving notice, not with the right to withdraw because of lack of further interest due to the effect of the failure to correct defective workmanship. Nor does the right in English law to rescind and claim damages for non-fulfilment of the contract depend essentially on the non-continued interest of the client in the contract, but rather upon the seriousness of the breach and the likelihood of the contract ever being completed. This was the real issue in the Sutcliffe case referred to in note 7 above. Of course the two will often coincide but they may not, and while it would appear that German law in the circumstances of the breach looks primarily to the non-continued interest of the client, English law looks more to the nature of the breach and the chances of the contract ever being fulfilled.[8]

COMPLETION (*ABNAHME*)

Abnahme may take two forms. *Formliche Abnahme*, which is the act of physical reception of the contractor's work by the client accompanied by the express acknowledgement by the client that he accepts the work as complying with the contract. *Fikitive Abnahme*, which is when there has been no formal acceptance but either the contractor has given written notice to the client that the work has been completed or the client has started to utilize the works.[9] Under *VOB* clause 12.5(1) acceptance is deemed to have occurred twelve days after the notice and in the alternative under clause 12.5(2) the works are deemed to have been accepted six days after the usage began unless otherwise agreed.[10]

If it is not a *VOB* contract and the client has started to use the works then he must have a reasonable time of several weeks within which to examine them after commencement of use, the actual length of time being dependent on the nature of the project (BGH 28 April 1992).

If there are serious defects in the works then the client is entitled to refuse the *Abnahme* until they have been rectified, para. 12.3 *VOB*. Other defects which are known at the time must be made the subject of a reservation. If the *Abnahme* is *formliche* then this must be done in the record (*Niederschrift*) of the meeting, para. 12.4 *VOB*. If the *Abnahme* is *fikitive* then the defects must be notified within the periods of twelve or six days respectively, *VOB* 12.5(3).

The concept of removal of defects, which could even involve the production of a new work, is very much a part of a legal system such as the German one which sees the contract in terms of the production of a specified result. There seems no reason in principle why if work is seriously defective, and the only means of remedying the defect is to dismantle or take down what has been built and re-construct it, that the client should not be entitled to exercise this remedy subject perhaps to the rule on disproportionate expenditure.[11]

Even this rule may apparently be qualified if the defect is regarded as 'important', as is illustrated by a recent case in the Higher Regional Court, Hamm on the application of *VOB* s.13 paras 6 and 7. Where on a contract for a house it was specifically stated in the contract that bricks of a particular kind and colour would be used so as to satisfy the aesthetic requirements of the client, and the contractor used bricks of a different colour, then this constituted an 'important defect' which entitled the client to require a completely new work, even if the costs were disproportionate. The client was not limited to a remedy for a reduction in the price. While this case was decided under the guaranty clause of the *VOB* no.13 it is considered that the principle should also be applied to clause 12.3 – *Abnahme* – which uses the same expression, *wesentlicher Mangel* (important defect).

REMEDIES OF THE CLIENT AFTER *ABNAHME*

1. The client can only exercise the rights given him under ss.633 and 634 of the *BGB* in

respect of defects in the works of which he was aware at the time of the *Abnahme*, provided that he reserved his rights at that time. This is also stated expressly in the *VOB*, clause 12.5(3) which requires the client to make any reservations in respect of known defects within the time limits specified in the clause.

2. If the client did reserve his rights, or the defect was hidden at the time of the *Abnahme*, then the primary right of the client is to have the defect made good. Both the *BGB* and the *VOB* require that the contractor be given notice by issue of a *Nachfrist* of the reasonable period within which he must remedy the defect. If on the expiry of the notice the defect has not been removed the client will be entitled to exercise his other rights, but can no longer claim to have the defect remedied nor can the contractor any longer claim to remedy the defect.

   The giving of the notice is not required if the immediate enforcement of his other rights are of special interest to the client. This is most likely to be the case if the client has by now lost confidence in the contractor's abilities and has decided that he must either finish the work himself or have it finished by others.

3. The other rights under the *BGB* Art. 634 which the client can exercise after failure by the contractor to comply with the notice to remedy the defects, assuming that the contractor has not been shown to be at fault, are similar to those which applied in respect of the sale of goods: rescission or reduction in the price and generally the same rules apply.

   However, rescission is not an appropriate remedy for construction works since it would involve both parties in returning the benefit which they had received. This is obviously impractical. The remedy which is applied therefore is termination (*Kündigung*), as under Art. 8.3 of the *VOB*, which means that the effects are not retrospective.

   Rescission (*Rücktritt*) could possibly be applicable to a contract for purpose-built machinery which, it will be remembered, is classified as a *Werklieferungsvertrag* and subject to the rules applicable to contracts for works as opposed to those for the sale of goods.

4. Under para. 13 of the *VOB* there is no mention of the remedy of rescission but only that of a reduction in the price. This could however be to nil value if the works were useless (BGH 29 October 1964 BGHZ 42,232).

   The Standard Contract Terms Act, *AGBG*, allows for the right of rescission to be excluded in contracts for buildings or other construction work (Art. 11, s.10 (b)).

   The question which then arises is whether or not the client can, in addition to a reduction even to nil in the contract price, claim from the contractor the extra costs of the construction of a replacement. In practice such a case would almost certainly involve a serious defect attributable to the default of the contractor and in that event such additional costs ought to be recoverable.

THE RIGHT TO CLAIM DAMAGES

It may not be sufficient for the client to have the right to claim a reduction in the contract price. He may additionally have suffered a financial loss as a result of the defects in the works, either because they have caused damage to other parts of the works or to other property, or because his profits have been reduced while the defects were being repaired.

The basic principles under German law are that damages can only be claimed if the contractor was at fault and that damages are an alternative remedy to either rescission or reduction (*BGB* p. 635). Under the *BGB* therefore the client has in practice the alternative, if he can prove fault, of either restricting himself to claiming a reduction of the price (his restitution loss) or of claiming damages which would include his loss of expectation interest.

Proof of fault would most commonly be based upon a failure to comply with the technical rules of art applying to the contractor or with specific instructions from the client or his architect/engineer.

In addition to his own faults, the contractor would also be responsible in damages for the faults committed by those whom he had engaged specifically to help him execute part of the works (*Erfüllungsgehilfen*), e.g. sub-contractors.

Under the *VOB* s.13.7 the contractor is only liable to pay damages for defective work if there is both an essential defect, i.e. one seriously affecting the use for which the works were intended, and which is due to his own fault or faults of those for whom he is responsible, *Erfullüngsgehilfen*. Further, the damages are generally limited to compensating the client 'for the damage to the structure, for the construction, maintenance or alteration of which the work found defective was intended to serve.'

The contractor will only be liable to the client for loss or damage beyond this (which would include damage to other property, injury to employees of the client or loss of profits arising out of the defect) in certain limited cases, where the defect:

- was due to deliberate intention or gross negligence, or
- constituted an offence against the appropriate technical regulations, or
- consisted in the lack of a characteristic guaranteed in the contract
- and could have been covered by insurance on reasonable terms.[12]

However, it is not certain that damage to other property of the client or injuries to personnel can validly be excluded under standard conditions of contract, if due to the fault of the contractor.

CLAIMS BASED ON POSITIVE BREACH OF CONTRACT

In addition to claims which relate to the works themselves, there can be claims for a breach by the contractor of his ancillary obligations under the contract or for damages consequential upon defects in the works under the doctrine of positive breach of contract.

It must be remembered that this doctrine only applies if there is no other remedy available. There is a remedy under Art. 635 for damages for defective work which is due to the default of the contractor. However this remedy applies only to consequences which have been described as 'the mirror image' of the defect. It is dangerous to use the English word 'direct' since much that under the English law of damages would be classified as direct is under German law considered as *Mangel-folgeschaden* and recoverable, if at all, under the remedy of positive breach of contract for the contractor's negligence. Gerhard Dannemann, p. 31, gives as an example of what would be considered as covered by a positive breach of contract, damage caused to goods under a roof by the negligent work of the workman engaged on the roof's repair.

Other examples quoted by Kelley and Attree, on p. 133, are where fire damage was caused to a building by a ruptured oil pipe or insufficient insulation (BGHZ 58,305 and BGH NJW 1982,2244).

Perhaps the most important area for the application of the doctrine of positive breach of contract is in the provision of instructions for the use of the works, the issuing of warnings to the client or the giving to the client of specialist advice. While the primary area of this responsibility for instructions and advice is in relation to safety, it extends also to advice regarding economic efficiency at least where the contractor is an expert and the client cannot in the circumstances have been expected to know the limitations of the works being constructed – BGH in WM 1987, 1303 – construction of a new type of generating plant; output affected if an auxiliary item of plant failed. Held contractor under a duty to warn.

These claims for positive breach of contract have a special importance, because unlike claims for defects in the works themselves, they are not subject to the short periods of prescription referred to in the next section but to the general prescription period of the *BGB* of 30 years.

There is an important difference here with contracts for sale where the short period of prescription of six months does apply to claims for positive breach of contract for damage to other legally protected interests of the purchaser, when they arise out of defects in the goods themselves.

But there is a difficult dividing line to draw between damage which is a 'mirror image' of the defect and covered therefore under Art. 635, so subject to the short prescription period, and damage due to a positive breach of contract. An example would be a central heating system installed in a block of flats which was defective and resulted in damage to other parts of the works which the contractor had an obligation to safeguard. Ranke and Boulin consider that this would be a breach of a positive obligation on the grounds that the obligation to safeguard was ancillary to the contract.[13] See also Jauernig/Schlechtreim s.635 no. 4, on pages 707 and 708.

PRESCRIPTION PERIODS UNDER THE *BGB*

The prescription period for claims for removal of a defect, cancellation, reduction or compensation is one year for 'work on land' and five years for 'buildings', the periods running from the issue of the *Abnahme*.

For *Werklieferungsverträge* the period is the same six-month period as for contracts for the sale of goods, but runs from the *Abnahme*.

The dividing line between a 'building' and 'work on land' is not easy to draw. In practice it would appear that the courts tend to favour an extensive definition of 'building' in order to avoid the shorter prescription period which can cause hardship. The definition in paragraph 1 of the *VOB* Part A is 'all types of building and civil engineering work by means of which a structure is created, maintained, modified or removed'.

The factors which will favour the classification of the work as building works are that they are permanent works and that they are related to the structure itself. The works do not have to be strictly 'buildings' but as stated in the above definition will include all forms of constructional works such as bridges. Also classified as building works have been reconstructions and improvements at least when there was a requirement for planning based on the original construction and the part reconstructed or modified constituted an integral and permanent part of the whole structure. So also the supply and fixing of parts of the building prefabricated off-site has been held to be building works. The definition has been applied even in the case of the installation of a night storage heating system, a central heating system, lifts and in one instance a burglar alarm system in a departmental store, although this last example was not followed in another case.

On the contrary, work has not been classified as building work when it was an improvement or modification which was not an essential part of the structure itself or of its maintenance or utilization, and was not an integral with the structure.

PRESCRIPTION PERIODS UNDER THE *VOB*

The periods under the *BGB* are not mandatory and they are reduced by Art. 13(4) of the *VOB* so that the five-year period generally becomes two years although there are special rules for particular types of construction. So for example for works undertaken by the highways department it is five years for bridges, four years for complete main roads and two years for other works. Although generally reduction of the statutory prescription periods is not permitted for standard conditions of contract under s.11(10)(f) of the *AGBG* this is specifically allowed for an entire *VOB* contract under Art. 23(5) of the *AGBG*.

However, the effect of the short period of prescription is somewhat mitigated by the fact that the *VOB* also states in Art.13(5) that the defects liability period starts again in respect of the defective part repaired once the defects have been completed and accepted unless the contract provides otherwise.

TIME FOR PERFORMANCE

GENERALLY, UNDER THE *BGB*

Under Art. 636 of the *BGB* the client has similar rights if the works are not completed on time to those which apply under Arts. 634 and 635 in the case of defects. Having given notice to the contractor to complete, unless a notice is not required, he is then entitled to rescind or claim a reduction in the contract price or in the alternative, if the delay is due to the default of the contractor, he can claim damages. Such damages could include liabilities of the client to third parties, the rental which the client is obliged to pay for alternative premises and compensation for loss of use including loss of profits (see further pp. 340–343 for the principles upon which damages are assessed under German in contrast to English and French law).

Penalties and liquidated damages

German law distinguishes sharply between penalties and liquidated damages and with effects which are fundamentally different from those under English law.

As in English law a penalty is a sum included in the contract in order to exert pressure on the contractor to fulfil his obligations. Unlike English law, however, a penalty clause is valid and enforceable against the debtor if the non-performance is due to his fault (Arts. 339 et seq., *BGB*).

Further, the penalty constitutes the *minimum* level of the damages which the client can claim if there is non-performance or delayed performance and is not dependent upon the client being able to prove loss (BGH 27 November 1974, BGHZ 63,256). If the client can establish a claim for damages in excess of the penalty, therefore, he is entitled to recover these *in addition to* the penalty (Arts. 340(2) and 341(2), *BGB*).

If the penalty is for delayed performance then the creditor is entitled to claim both the penalty and fulfilment of the contract (Art. 341(1), *BGB*).

On acceptance (*Abnahme*) the client if he wishes to claim a penalty must reserve his right to do so (Art. 341(3), *BGB* and clause 12.5(3) of the *VOB*).

Although there is provision under Art. 343, *BGB* for the reduction by the court of penalties which are excessive, this does not apply if the penalty is promised by a merchant in the course of carrying on his business (Art. 348, *HGB*). For definition of a merchant see above, p. 32. Effectively it includes any significant company or commercial partnership but not necessarily a construction company since these do not come within the definition under s.1(1) of the *HGB*.

Again as in English law liquidated damages are a genuine pre-estimate of the damage which the client would be likely to suffer from the breach. They are not referred to in German statutory provisions except for s.18(d) 5 of Art. 11 of the *AGBG*. This makes it void in standard conditions of contract in consumer transactions to include a liquidated damages clause if the damages either:

- exceed the amount normally to be expected in cases to which the agreement applies, or

- prevent the other party from proving that the party stipulating the damages either did not suffer any damages or that they were substantially less than the liquidated amount.

The courts place similar restrictions on the level of liquidated damages in commercial contracts by the use of the general good faith clause although not so strictly. However it has been held that where the damages included within the standard conditions attached to a large-scale construction contract were expressed as a percentage of the contract price then they were only valid under the *AGBG* if a figure was also stated as the maximum amount due under any circumstances (BGH (VII ZR 167/86) 22 October 1987 [1988] DB 108).

It follows from the principles set out in the *AGBG* that when the contract is on the client's standard conditions, if the contractor can show that the actual loss suffered by the client was less than the liquidated damages, then he will only be liable for such lesser sum (if any) which represents the client's actual loss. Also if the client can prove that his actual loss was in excess of the liquidated damages then he can claim for the actual loss which he can substantiate (BGH 16 June 1982 NJW 1982, 2316).

This is again the opposite of the English rule (see further below, pp. 316–317). However, there is no direct judicial control on liquidated damages outside of the *AGBG*, i.e. on individually negotiated contracts; only indirectly through the general principles of 'good faith, good morals and fair dealing' (see Arts. 138 and 242 of the *BGB*, above, pp. 50, 52).

COMPLETION UNDER THE *VOB*

Very sensibly the *VOB*, in the obligations which it imposes on the contractor as to timely performance, does not limit itself to the completion of the works. Clause 5 sets out three obligations which the contractor must fulfil in due time and clauses 6.6 and 8.3 provide the remedies for non-compliance. The three obligations are:

- to commence the work according to the contract terms;
- to provide on site the men, materials and equipment necessary for the execution of the works according to the contract terms;
- to complete the works on time.

Interestingly the separate provisions as to progress contained in the work programme are only considered part of the contract terms if this is expressly agreed in the contract.

If the contractor fails to comply with any of the above contract terms the client may either maintain the contract and, if the failure of the contractors is due to his fault, claim damages, or give the contractor reasonable notice to perform the contract, stating his intention to withdraw from the contract if the performance is not fulfilled.

The claim for damages under Art. 6.6 is limited to those which can be demonstrated and it can only include loss of profit, e.g. losses due to the inability to use or let the premises, if the non-performance was deliberate or due to gross negligence.

The client's rights if he withdraws are those under clause 8.3 which were discussed earlier under the heading 'Defects prior to completion' (see pp. 225–226).

Penalties

The *VOB* simply applies the rules of the *BGB* Arts. 339–45. It clearly states that the penalty is only recoverable if on the *Abnahme* the client has reserved this right (clauses 11.4 and 12.5(3)).

If the client terminates under clause 8 then under sub-para. 7 of that clause a penalty on a time basis may only be calculated up to the time when the contract was terminated. In the absence of any special clause to the contrary this seems to be the position in general for liquidated damages under English law (see Keating p. 235 paragraph (h)). However, both the ICE Conditions and the JCT 80 do provide that in the calculation of the sums due from the contractor to the employer on determination for default there are to be included damages for delay and it is arguable that these are the liquidated damages which would be due under the contract up to the actual date of completion.[14]

Extensions of time

There are no express provisions within the *BGB* covering the rights of the contractor to an extension of time. The *VOB*, however, under clause 6.2(1) defines that the terms established for the execution of the work shall be extended when the work is obstructed by:

- something for which the client is responsible;
- industrial action imposed by a trade union either on the contractor or a firm working directly for him;
- *force majeure* or other circumstances beyond the control of the contractor (see p. 344).

Weather is not considered as a reason for an extension of time if it was normal for the season in which the works were to be constructed.

RESPONSIBILITY OF THE ARCHITECT

As referred to earlier (see above, p. 159) the contract between an architect and the client is classified as a *Werkvertrag* so that the architect has the same responsibility as the contractor that the work he performs is suitable for the purpose intended and without defects. In this respect his responsibility is more onerous than that of an architect under English law. The architect's duties will normally cover design, tendering for the works, preparation of the contract documents, preparation of the drawings necessary for the execution of the work by the contractors and the overall management and supervision of the work on site. Where a number of contractors are employed, as is often the case, then the architect has the task of the coordination of their work.

The architect and each of the contractors will have separate contracts with the client and the normal rule is that where there are separate contracts each contractor is responsible only for his own defaults. However since the purpose of the obligations of the architect and the contractor are the same, i.e. to produce works which are free from defects, then the architect and the contractor are jointly liable (*Gesamtschuldner*) to the client if the works are defective (see Jauernig (Schlechtreim) s.631 at p. 694 n.8).

The architect also has a problem in that at the moment the prescription period for his liability to the client may be longer than that of the contractors. If the architect is responsible on a project for the supervision of the remedial work of the contractors necessary in order to correct defects, then his responsibility runs for up to five years from the *Abnahme*. Although the contractor's defects liability period is two years under the *VOB*, the period starts to run again in respect of the defective work which has now been repaired. Only then, after he has completed his own work, does the architect's own prescription period of five years start to run.

The architect can reduce this extended liability by not including in his contract the *Leistungsphase* 9 of paragraph 15 of the *HOAI* (*Honorarordnung für Architekten und Ingenieurs*, fee order for architects and engineers). This represents 3 per cent of the fees, but by giving this up the architect can fix his own defects liability as five years from *Abnahme* for the project and state that his own work finishes when he has approved the contractors' final invoices. If, however, *Leistungsphase* 9 is included, then the architect's liability would be as stated above and could well in practice extend for ten years after completion of the project (*OLG* Koln 19.11.1991).

Nevertheless, the risk for the architect because of the joint responsibility situation and of the fact that he is compulsorily insured, is considerable, and the more so when a number of smaller contractors are engaged on the project. It is then the architect against whom the client is likely to proceed and while the architect would have rights against the defaulting contractor, the value of these would necessarily depend on the ability of the contractor to pay.

NOTES

1. BGH 107,82 and BGH NJW 87,2734.
2. In a case of 14 February 1992, the Federal Court decided that even reducing the period for interim payments from eighteen days to seven days and the final payment period from two months to two weeks, meant that the contract was not entirely a *VOB* contract. This could affect the client's rights, for example to the benefit of Art. 16.3(2) which provides that acceptance by the contractor of the final payment without reservation shall exclude subsequent claims. This could be argued to be contrary to Art. 10(5) of the *AGBG* the application of which to *VOB* contracts is specifically excluded by Art. 23(5) of the *AGBG* when it is an entire *VOB* contract.

3. This is the official German translation of the *VOB* text, July 1990, although it states in cases of doubt that the German language version should be consulted as being the authoritative text. This reads: 'Der Auftragnehmer hat die Leistung unter eigener Verantwortung nach dem Vertrag auszuführen. Dabei hat er die *anerkannten Regeln der Technik . . . zu beachten*'. Dr Christian Wiegand has translated this as 'observance of the professional standards of the construction industry' (*The Liability of Contractors* p.133) but the official version is to be preferred.

4. See contractors' liability for design under German construction law in Dr Christian Wiegand, *The Liability of Contractors*. He refers to the Blasbach Valley case decided by the Higher Regional Court of Frankfurt, 27 May 1981 NJW 1983, p. 456, an appeal which was rejected by the BGH 21 October 1982 (unreported).

5. The German term *Auftraggeber*, literally 'order giver' will be translated throughout as 'client'. But it is to be noted that as regards a sub-contractor a main contractor is also an *Auftraggeber*.

6. Treitel *Remedies* s.264 and the same author *Contract* pp. 671 et seq.

7. *Sutcliffe* v. *Chippendale and Edmondson* [1971] 18 BLR 157.

8. It may well be the case that there is no doubt that the contract will ultimately be completed, because although the defects are serious the contractor's reputation is such that one can be confident he will rectify them. However the consequences of the resultant delay may mean that the client cannot gain the benefit from the contract which he had anticipated because the building will not be ready in time to meet a seasonal demand. In German law it appears that the client under those circumstances would be able to withdraw from the contract. In English law it seems unlikely that the client could do so unless initially time had been made of the essence of the contract. See Keating pp. 154 and 221.

9. See RG 24 April 1925, RGZ 110, 404, 406–407 quoted in Lorenz, note 472 p. 83.

10. Although the parties may agree on a longer period a provision in the standard conditions of contract applying to a sub-contractor that the *Abnahme* would only be given for the sub-contractor's work when it was given by the client for the whole building, has been held to be void under *AGBG* 9 and 10(1) – see further below, pp.304–305). The application of the clause would have extended the twelve days to three months (BGH 11 April 1991).

11. It is provided under Art. 633(2) *BGB* that the contractor is entitled to decline to remove a defect if this would involve him in a disproportionate outlay. This is stated also in Art. 13.6 of the *VOB* with the addition that if the contractor does so decline, then the client may demand a reduction in the contract price.

12. A recent decision of the federal court has, however shown that even in the case of ordinary rather than gross negligence, the contractor may be liable for damages which extend beyond the mere compensation for loss or damage to the construction *baulichen Anlage* which the works were intended to serve. A contractor built a tennis hall which had large windows in the roof. These became defective and had to be replaced. The federal court found that there had only been ordinary negligence but that the contractor was still liable in addition to replacing the windows at his own cost, to pay for higher costs of electricity and the loss of income which the client had incurred, because of their close connection with the actual damage. He was not, however, liable for damage which had occurred to the floor due to the entry of water, since this was not closely enough connected with the *baulichen Anlage* and was regarded as *darüber hinausgehenden schaden*, additional damages, only recoverable for gross negligence. *BGH* 12 March 1992.

13. At para. 224 on p. 95.

14. Clause 63(1) of the 6th edition of the ICE Conditions stating the employer's right to determine the contractor's employment for default states that this 'does not release the Contractor from any of his obligations or liabilities under the Contract'. Then in sub-clause (iv) it refers specifically to the engineer certifying 'the costs of completion, damages for delay in completion (if any) and all other expenses incurred by the Employer'. Although the reference is to damages for completion it is thought that this in fact refers to liquidated damages under clause 47 and means that these are recoverable up to actual completion subject to any limitation contained in the contract. The words '(if any)' could refer to sub-clause (4)(b) of that clause which covers the possibility of 'nil' being inserted in the Appendix for the amount of damages and provides that in such event no damages shall be payable.

Abrahamson in commenting at pp. 281 and 282 on the 5th edition, which contained similar wording to that in sub-clause (iv) above, also makes the suggestion that the employer would be entitled to recover liquidated damages for the delay between the contract completion date and actual completion by another contractor.

Keating has submitted at p. 594 that on termination under JCT 80 the architect in certifying the amount of 'any direct loss or damage caused to the Employer by determination' could include damages for delay. It is again thought that these damages would be the liquidated damages included within the contract, although Keating does not cover the issue, and that since these are the damages due because of the determination, they would be payable from the original contract date up to the actual completion date but still subject to any maximum stated in the contract. Hudson however has suggested under the wording of the earlier RIBA clause 25(3)(d) that the contractor would be liable for ordinary damages (Hudson p. 633 and note 70).

17 Transfer of property and risk

The two issues of when the property in goods passes from the seller to the purchaser and when the purchaser takes over the risk in the goods are interrelated in that one would normally expect that risk would follow property, or as it is expressed in the Latin maxim, *res perit domino*.

However this maxim is not Roman law. There the transfer of ownership was effected only by a conveyance (*traditio*) together with the payment of the price or the granting by the seller of credit.[1] The risk in the goods however passed as from the date when the contract of sale was 'perfect'. That was when the identity, price and quality of the goods had been established and the sale was unconditional.[2]

The two could well coincide as when in a market sale the goods were handed over against payment of the price.[3] However delivery could be delayed and if in the meantime the goods perished or were stolen, then, provided that the seller had exercised all possible diligence in looking after them,[4] the loss was borne by the purchaser who still had to pay the contract price – *periculum emptoris*

The Roman rules are an appropriate place from which to begin a comparative examination of those prevailing in the three systems under review because directly or indirectly they have to a degree entered into each of them although each has rejected some Roman rules in favour of their own native solutions.

The Roman rule as to the transfer of property, but without the qualification as to payment or credit, entered easily into German law which already in its old law required that there should be a transfer of physical seisin of the goods together with a will to transfer ownership.[5] This concept has been retained in the *BGB* under which there must be both an agreement between the parties to transfer the property plus delivery of possession in order for the property to pass to the purchaser (Art. 929, *BGB* and see above, p. 15).

But the *BGB* rejected the Roman rule as to transfer of risk and followed the old German law that the risk in the goods is transferred only on delivery of possession either directly to the purchaser or to the carrier where the contract is one for the sale of goods by despatch which are either specific or if generic have been concretized – *periculum est vendoris*[6] (see above, p. 208).

Under both English and French law the contract acts to transfer property without the need for a separate conveyance and the normal rule is that risk follows property – *res perit domino*. French law had in this instance abandoned the Roman rules before the enacting of the *Code Civil*. English law, which at one time had much the same rule as the old German law, that the transfer of property depended on the transfer of possession, had changed by the fifteenth century to the modern rule that on the sale of a specific item the bargain itself was sufficient to transfer the property.[7]

In all three legal systems, therefore, the rule of *res perit domino* generally applies, although the point at which ownership changes differs. In German law it is on delivery, assuming there is agreement to this effect between the parties; in French and English law when the contract for specific goods is, largely in the same sense as Roman law, 'perfected', or for generic goods when these have been ascertained or *individualisées*.

However these rules only apply unless the parties express otherwise in their contract and this was indeed the position in Roman law. If the parties are well advised, or utilize standard conditions of contract, then almost certainly they will change the rules otherwise implied by law since commercially the linking of property and risk suits neither party. The seller wants the transfer of property as late as possible and if possible not until he has been paid in full. The reverse applies to the risk, which he would like the purchaser to assume as early as possible. Obviously the interests of the purchaser are the opposite of these. He wants the property as soon as he can obtain it, especially if he wishes to resell to a third party, while he does not want the risk preferably until after he has accepted the goods or works concerned.

The contract may well therefore contain terms negating the implied terms of the SGA or the 'suppletive' provisions of the codes and which will reflect the respective bargaining strengths of the parties. The importance of the implied or suppletive provisions is that first they provide the base from which the express terms must be drafted. Second, they will apply to the not inconsiderable number of contracts in which either the parties do not include express terms or it is decided that those terms do not form part of the contract.[8] Those provisions will now be considered in some detail. For this purpose each system will be examined and compared under four headings:

- Sale of specific goods
- Sale of unascertained goods
- Sale of future goods
- Contracts for works.

Then the general issue of the passing of risk will be considered for each system. The validity and application of retention of title clauses which are extensively used in all three systems, and the effects of the transfer where the possessor is not the true owner, will be dealt with in the following chapter.

SPECIFIC GOODS

ENGLISH LAW

Goods are specific if they are identified and agreed upon at the time when the contract is made.[9]

The property in specific goods passes at the time when the parties intended it to pass. In determining their intentions account must be taken of: the terms in the contract, the conduct of the parties and the circumstances of the case. Unless a different intention appears five rules are established for determining the intention of the parties (ss.17 and 18 Sale of Goods Act 1979) for specific goods. In summary these rules are:

1. Where there is an unconditional contract and the goods are in a deliverable state then the property passes when the contract is made and it is immaterial whether the time of delivery or payment or both are to be postponed.
2. If the seller has to do something to put the goods in a deliverable state, then property passes when this has been done and the buyer notified accordingly.
3. If the goods have to be weighed, measured, or tested etc. in order to ascertain the price, when this has been done and the buyer notified accordingly.
4. If the goods are delivered on approval or on sale or return, when the purchaser gives his approval or acceptance or otherwise adopts the transaction.

The presumption under rule 1 only applies if the contract is 'unconditional', i.e. is not subject to a condition precedent which suspends the operation of the contract or the passing of the property in the goods until the occurrence of some event. In modern practice it seems that the courts will find quite easily either that the contract was conditional or that there was a contrary intention of the parties. This is probably because, as stated earlier, property and risk generally go together, and for the goods to be at the purchaser's risk before delivery, when he has no possibility of control or supervision over them, may appear wholly unreasonable.[10]

FRENCH LAW

The provision in Art. 1583 of the *Code Civil* is framed in almost identical terms to that of rule 1 for determining the intentions of the parties under s.18 of the SGA.

> The sale is perfect between the Parties and the property is acquired in law by the Purchaser in respect to the Seller from the moment when there is agreement on the thing and the price, although the thing has not yet been delivered nor the price paid.

The transfer of the property in the goods is then strictly not an obligation of the seller but follows as a matter of law as an immediate and direct result of the agreement between the parties. However the article is not of *ordre public* and the parties may provide in their agreement that the transfer is to be delayed until the happening of some specified event.[11]

French law draws a distinction between sales which are *en bloc* and those which are not. A sale is *en bloc* when the goods have to be weighed, counted or measured solely for the purpose of ascertaining the price and not for the purpose of identifying the subject matter of the sale (Art. 1586 *Code Civil* and Cass. civ. 1 February 1983, JCP

1984 II 2041 referred to in note 1 to Art. 1586 Dalloz *Code Civil*). So the sale of the harvest of a standing crop of maize was a sale *en bloc* (Cass. civ. 8 October 1980 D. 1981 IR 445 referred to in note 2 to Art. 1586 Dalloz *Code Civil*). Such a sale is treated in the same way as a sale of a specific object so that the contract itself is sufficient to transfer both the property and the risk to the purchaser from the moment of the contract. In the case of the sale of the crop of maize therefore the risk of loss through inclement weather was borne by the purchaser.

French law is here the direct opposite of rule 3 of s.18 of the SGA. However, as Atiyah points out, rule 3 is a weaker presumption than either rules 1 or 2 and could quite easily be displaced on the facts of a particular case (see Atiyah p. 296).

Where the sale is not *en bloc* but by weight, number or measure then the sale is not perfect in the sense that the goods being sold remain at the risk of the seller until they have been weighed, counted or measured; but the purchaser may demand delivery or damages, if he has cause, in the case of non-performance of the contract (Art. 1585, *Code Civil*). Here the acts of weighing, counting or measuring are necessary in order to determine the *objet* of the sale for example the sale of so many hectolitres of wine to be taken from a vat which contains a larger quantity.

It is to be noted that although the text of Art. 1585 refers to 'the sale not being perfect', it is only in the sense that the transfer of the property and risk in the goods is delayed until the operations have been performed. (Although only risk is referred to in the text, by implication this includes property.) So it was stated by the *Cour de cassation* (4 December 1957):

> by virtue of Art. 1585 the sale by weight, counting or measure, is only perfect from the viewpoint of the transfer of risk and property when the goods have been weighed, counted or measured, but binds the parties to the obligations which they have contracted for from the moment that they have agreed upon the thing and the price.

The purchaser was accordingly entitled to termination of the contract and to an award in damages on the winding up of the vendor but not to the recovery of the goods the property in which had not been transferred because they had not been measured.[12]

GERMAN LAW

The contract of sale does not operate to transfer the property. Under the principle of abstraction (see above, p. 100) the property may be validly transferred even though the underlying contract of sale is invalid. The property is transferred under Art. 929(1) *BGB* by a valid agreement that it should be transferred (*Einigung*) together with actual delivery of the thing unless the purchaser is already in possession when the *Einigung* alone is sufficient.

However, in two cases the requirement for actual delivery is not needed. First if there is an agreement between the parties that the owner should continue to hold the goods as 'direct possessor' while the other party becomes the 'indirect possessor' (Art. 930, *BGB*) Besitzkonstitut. This enables the 'direct possessor' to obtain a loan from the 'indirect possessor' and continue trading as if in all respects he were the

241

owner of the goods, say his office equipment, while giving the 'indirect possessor' security for the loan. This is known as *Sicherungsübereignung* and gives the 'indirect possessor' a preferential position in the case of the 'direct possessor's' bankruptcy, in that he can claim a separate sale of the assets concerned in order to satisfy his outstanding loan. However the *Sicherungsübereignung* must have been entered into in good faith otherwise in bankruptcy proceedings the court may declare it void.[13]

Second if a third party is in possession and the owner assigns his claim to possession in favour of the purchaser (Art. 931, *BGB*).

UNASCERTAINED GOODS

ENGLISH LAW

Unascertained goods in English law may be either future goods, i.e. those to be manufactured or grown, generic goods or part of a bulk quantity. The general rules are that property in unascertained goods cannot be transferred until they have been ascertained and that once they have been ascertained the time when property passes depends on the intentions of the parties (ss.16 and 17 of the SGA).

Unless a contrary intention appears property will pass when the goods in a deliverable state have been unconditionally appropriated by the seller to the contract with the consent of the purchaser (s.18, rule 5).

In the case of manufactured goods this will normally be when the seller has completed all his obligations under the contract including those relating to delivery or the fixing of the goods in place. If the purchaser is obliged to collect the goods then it would be when the goods were in all respects identified and ready for collection.[14]

A particular point of interest is the position which applies when the purchaser has agreed to make stage payments during the course of manufacture. At the time when payment is made the goods will be part manufactured and, while arguably may be unconditionally appropriated to the contract, if suitably marked as the purchaser's property, they are clearly not in a 'deliverable state'. On the assumption that having made payment the purchaser wants the property in the goods to pass to him, then it is essential that the contract contains a clause dealing expressly with the passing of property and showing clearly a 'contrary intention' to that of rule 5.

Where the contract is for the sale of part of a bulk quantity then property will only pass when the part has been physically separated from the remainder in such a way that it can be positively identified.[15]

FRENCH LAW

When the contract only specifies goods of a particular type, without identifying the source from which they are to come (*les choses de genre*) then the property and risk will be transferred to the purchaser when they have been *individualisées*. If the purchaser is to come and collect the goods the transfer takes place when they are handed over to him. When the seller is obliged to deliver the goods, it would be when they have left the seller's factory or warehouse for handing over to the carrier.[16]

If, in an example given by Mazeaud, p.186, s.908, goods are sent in bulk, i.e. 300 sacks of wheat are sent together by train to three different purchasers, 100 sacks each, consigned to the same station, then the *individualisation* takes place at the time when the purchasers each take delivery at the station of 100 sacks. Accordingly the property and risk in this case pass on arrival. The example is in agreement with the facts of *Healey* v. *Howlett and Sons* referred to in note 15.

But although *individualisation* is often by delivery, this is not essential. It can take place before delivery by an act of the seller which clearly demonstrates that the goods have been *individualisées*, e.g. by their being placed on their own in a warehouse on the door of which is written the purchaser's name (example given by Mazeaud, p.184, s.905).

All the above rules share with those of English law, relating to unconditional appropriation, the common intention of physically identifying the goods which are the subject of the sale. There is however one important point of difference. English law requires that there should be an express or implicit assent by the purchaser to the appropriation. French law does not. The act of *individualisation* is the act of the seller which he may make without the participation or agreement, even implied, of the purchaser. However it is the responsibility of the seller to prove the act of *individualisation* and obviously where this is pre-delivery the easiest way of doing so is for the purchaser to be present when the goods are separated from the bulk and allocated to the contract.

GERMAN LAW

Since the transfer of property requires both an agreement that it should be transferred (*Einigung*) and the actual delivery of the goods into the control of the purchaser (see above, p. 241), the issues which arise in English and French law regarding the transfer of property in generic goods before delivery do not occur in German law. However, since the transfer of risk does not necessarily follow the transfer of property, which is in practice what generally causes the problems in English and French law, the question remains to be answered as to when risk is transferred in generic goods (see below, p. 247).

FUTURE GOODS

ENGLISH LAW

There are no specific rules under English law regarding the transfer of property in future goods which are to be manufactured. The same rules apply as for unascertained

243

goods. It is a question, subject to the express terms of the contract, as to whether the goods have been appropriated to the contract or not. Generally, in the absence of any express term to the contrary, appropriation will be considered to have taken place when the manufacture of the goods has been completed.

However, in practice the problem usually arises in connection with unfixed materials when the seller goes into liquidation and part payment has been made by the purchaser. Given the strict definition of the term 'appropriation' used by the Court of Appeal in *re Blyth Shipbuilding Co.*, that the goods must be positioned in relation to the hull of the uncompleted ship in such a way that to remove them would involve undoing work already done, it is important that the rights of the purchaser are spelt out clearly so as to leave no room for argument.[17]

FRENCH LAW

The preliminary question to be answered is whether a contract for the manufacture of goods is to be classified as a contract for sale or a contract for works. This distinction was discussed earlier (above, pp. 48–49). It will be recalled that the specificity of the work, and its being executed to meet the particular needs of the party placing the order, are regarded today as being the primary criteria by which a court will decide that a contract is one for works (*un contrat d'entreprise*) as opposed to a contract for sale (*contrat de vente*) in which the goods are manufactured for sale generally and to a specification determined by the vendor.

The distinction is of importance in relation to the time at which property passes. This section will deal with the position assuming that it is a contract for sale; the position for where it is a contract for works is covered below (p. 245).

In the absence of any provision to the contrary in the contract, the property in goods to be manufactured will pass at the time when 'effectively they are in a state to be delivered by the seller and received by the purchaser'.[18]

When however payments are to be made by the purchaser as the works progress then it would normally be provided in the contract that the property in the goods will also pass according to the progress of the works. An example given by Mazeaud of this is the construction of a ship. Having made payments as work progresses, the purchaser naturally wishes to be protected against the financial failure of the seller.[19]

In the case of natural products, however, the general practice seems to be that the property only passes at the time of the harvest or when the product has attained the state of development necessary to satisfy the *objet* of the contract.[20]

GERMAN LAW

The normal rule is as stated previously that property in the goods passes on delivery and agreement for the transfer of property. However, if the contract for the future goods is classified as a *Werklieferungsvertrag* (see above, p. 159) then ownership would pass when there is agreement for the transfer and the goods have been accepted by the purchaser, i.e. the *Abnahme* has been pronounced (see further on *Abnahme* above, p. 227) provided that the physical transfer of possession has taken place.

CONTRACTS FOR WORKS

ENGLISH LAW

The general rule is that materials delivered to site become the property of the employer when they are built into the works. However, most forms of contract for building or engineering works provide for the property passing at some earlier date. This may be on delivery or the entitlement of the contractor to have the value included in an interim certificate, whichever is the earlier (MF/1 Clause 37.1), or when their value has been included in an interim certificate and paid for by the employer (JCT 80 16.1).

FRENCH LAW

There has been a considerable debate among French legal writers as to whether in the civil law the property in the materials passes to the employer as the work progresses and incorporated into the works or only at the moment when the *réception* is pronounced.

However it now appears that the matter has been settled by decisions of the *Cour de cassation* in which the court approved the judgements of the lower court that the materials had ceased to be the property of the contractor 'as they became incorporated in the building during the progress of the works'.[21]

The same position seems to apply in public law.

GERMAN LAW

For works contracts for construction on land the general rule is that the property transfers to the client at the time when the work becomes an essential component of the land upon which the works are being built, i.e. it is affixed to the land (*BGB* para. 946). Additionally, assuming that progress payments are made, then under Art. 16 of the *VOB* there may be included in the value of such payments materials delivered to the site provided that the ownership in them is transferred to the client or, if he prefers, appropriate security is provided.

For a works contract not involving construction on land the same rules would apply as stated above for sales contracts of specific goods under Arts. 929–931, *BGB*.

THE PASSING OF RISK

ROMAN LAW

As referred to earlier (see above, p. 238) the Roman rule was that from the moment that the sale was perfect, i.e. there was agreement about the precise object to be sold and the price to be paid, and the sale was unconditional, then the risk passed to the purchaser even though the goods had not been delivered.[22] Risk here referred to loss caused by an event against which the vendor as custodian could not have guarded.[23] The rule is contrary to the principle *res perit domino* but, as Zimmermann has shown, is not unreasonable.[24] It remained part of the *ius commune* and was referred to by Pothier writing in 1768.[25]

For works contracts the risk of accidental loss or damage certainly became that of the employer after *adprobatio operis*. As to the position before *adprobatio*, it seems that the employer took the risk as regards matters within his scope of responsibility, e.g. suitability of the ground for building, but the contractor was responsible for anything which related to his own work.[26]

ENGLISH LAW

The modern rule is that the risk passes at the same time as the property in the goods unless the parties specify otherwise. In practice with specific goods this creates the same position as regards risk as applied under Roman law since the presumptions under ss.17 and 18 of the Sale of Goods Act, set out earlier (see above, p. 240), are effectively that property passes once the sale is 'perfected' without the need for delivery. With unascertained goods the time is when the goods have been unconditionally appropriated to the contract by the seller with the approval of the purchaser. There is no comparison possible here with Roman law which did not know of the sale of generic goods.

Under works contracts then, in the absence of any express provisions in the contract, the position is that the contractor will be liable to make good any damage to the works arising before completion unless this is due to the default of the employer, or the damage is such that the contract can be said to have been frustrated.[27]

FRENCH LAW

The French rules are very similar to the English. Unless the parties have stipulated otherwise, which they are free to do, the risk in the goods transfers from the seller to the purchaser at the same time as the property. In the case of specific goods this will be when the sale has been 'perfected' by agreement on the goods and the price, provided that the sale is not subject to any condition suspensive (see above, pp. 240–241), in which event the sale will be perfected when such condition has been satisfied. For generic goods the risk only passes when the goods have been *individualisées* (see above, pp. 242–243).

On contracts for works the risk passes to the employer under Art. 1788 of the *Code Civil* when the *réception* is pronounced. In fact the article refers to *livraison* (delivery) but it is generally taken to refer to *réception*. This has the consequence that if the *réception* has not been given, otherwise than due to the default of the *maître de l'ouvrage*, then the works remain at the risk of the contractor and if they are destroyed by, say, fire then this will be his responsibility. It also follows in such a case that the contractor cannot claim payment for the work destroyed and must refund any progress payments which he has received even though the contractor was not at fault.[28]

Normally in French standard conditions for building and engineering contracts the risk of loss or damage to the works under construction caused by *force majeure* due to natural events is the responsibility of the employer, while the loss or damage to materials, plant, tools and the contractor's site establishment would be the responsibility of the contractor.[29]

GERMAN LAW

Article 446.1 of the *BGB* provides for sales contracts that 'On delivery of the thing sold the risk of accidental destruction passes to the Purchaser'. Where the sale is of generic goods then the risk passes to the purchaser when the seller has done everything which is necessary for the delivery of the goods i.e. he has 'concretized' them (Art. 243(2), *BGB*). This provision is reinforced by Art. 300, *BGB*, under which the risk in generic goods passes to the purchaser from the time when he ought to have accepted them. Since unless the contract provides otherwise the place of delivery, i.e. of performance, is the seller's place of business (Art. 269, *BGB*), this means that if after generic goods have been packed ready for collection by the purchaser they are accidentally damaged or destroyed, and the purchaser is late in collecting them, then it is the purchaser who must bear the loss.

If under the contract the place of performance (*Erfüllungsort*) is the purchaser's place of business so that the seller is obliged to deliver the goods to the purchaser, then the risk passes on delivery being made to the purchaser (Art. 446(1), *BGB*). However, the mere fact that the purchase price includes the costs of delivery is not sufficient to establish that delivery is to be other than at the supplier's place of business; there must be an express obligation in the contract for delivery to the purchaser (Art. 269(3), *BGB*). If there is not, but on the puchaser's instructions the seller delivers the goods to a carrier, then Art. 447(1) applies and the risk passes when the goods are delivered to the carrier.

The principle that the risk passes with delivery applies in much the same way to contracts for works with the substitution of *Abnahme* for delivery. They are at the risk of the contractor until *Abnahme* (Art. 644 of the *BGB*) unless the client is in default in giving the *Abnahme* when the risk passes to him.

247

The *VOB*, clause 12.6, states that on *Abnahme* the risk passes to the client unless exceptionally it has passed already under clause 7. This clause provides that in cases of *force majeure* the contractor is entitled to claim payment for the parts of the works already executed but no other compensation.

NOTES

1. Dig. XVIII 1.17: 'The thing becomes the property of the Buyer by delivery only if either the price has been paid by the seller, or security for its payment has been given by him, or he has given credit to the Buyer without security' Trans. Zulueta p. 92. See also Institutes Book II, Tit. 1.40–45 and the comments and notes by Sandars pp. 191–4. Mere agreement did not transfer property. If the person to whom the goods were to be transferred already had possession, then property passed by the consent of the owner; cf. Art. 929(2) of the *BGB*: 'If the acquirer is in possession of the thing, the agreement of the transfer of ownership is sufficient'.
2. Digest XVIII 6.8: 'It is necessary to know when a sale is perfect, for then we know whose the risk is, because on the sale being perfected the risk passes to the Buyer. Sale is perfect if the identity, quality and quantity of the thing are ascertained, if the price is determined and the sale is unconditional'.
3. See the comments and notes by Zimmermann, p. 290 et seq.
4. Dig. XVIII 6.3. The seller was responsible for the higher degree of diligence *culpa levis in abstracto* which meant that he was only not liable if the goods perished from a cause entirely outside his control, or, if they were stolen, he could show that the theft occurred without fault on his part.
5. Seisin involved actual physical control over the thing. See Huebner, p. 404 and for transfer p. 436. However, in Roman law the agreement to sell was a *causa traditionis* of the transfer while in German law the conveyance is an abstract act separate from, and not dependent upon, the validity of the contract for sale.
6. Huebner, p. 551.
7. Bracton followed Glanville in maintaining that agreement on the price and delivery were necessary for the transfer of the risk from the seller to the buyer (61b-62) and see Scrutton *Influence of the Roman Law on the Law of England* Cambridge 1885 at p. 94 and Pollock and Maitland vol.2 p. 210. The modern law was stated in Anon YB 17 ED.IV f.1, pl.2 reprinted in Fifoot p.253 where it was stated by Chief Justice Brian: 'Further I say that the property is in the defendant by the bargain in the case at bar' and see the comments by Fifoot p. 229.
8. See Atiyah p. 288 and notes 22 and 24. In German law if the express terms of the parties are in conflict then the court will apply the terms of the *BGB* in lieu of the conflicting terms. In a French case where an express clause dealing with the transfer of property was in the middle of a set of conditions on the back of a purchase order, and the purchaser had only signed the front of the document, the clause was held ineffective (Cass. civ. 3 May 1979 Bull. civ. 1971.1.p. 103.
9. Section 61 of the SGA.
10. See Atiyah, p.292 et seq.
11. Cass. civ. 9 June 1971, Bull. civ. 1971.3, p. 257.
12. Cass.com. 4 December 1975, Bull. civ. 1957.3 p. 288.
13. See Cohn, vol. 1, p. 177.
14. *Carlos Federspiel & Co.* v. *Charles Twigg and Co. Ltd* where property was held not have passed because although the goods were packed ready for delivery the vendor had not arranged shipment. [1957] 1 Lloyds Rep. 240. Contrast *Hendy Lennox Ltd* v. *Grahame Puttick Ltd* where the goods identified by their serial numbers had been invoiced and were awaiting collection by the purchaser and it was held that property had passed, there being nothing left for the vendor to do ([1984] 2 All ER 152).

   Philip Head v. *Showfronts Ltd* where carpet for which the seller was responsible for laying had been delivered but not yet laid and was held still to be the property of the seller [1970] 1 Lloyds Rep. 140.
15. As one example see *Healey* v. *Howlett & Sons* [1917] 1 KB 337 where a number of boxes of mackerel were despatched by train but because of a delay to the train had deteriorated so as to be unsaleable before the boxes intended for the defendants had been earmarked. Accordingly the property and risk in the fish remained with the seller.

16. Ghestin op.cit. s.547 pp. 610 and 611.
17. [1926] Ch.494.
18. Cass. 1re civ. 1 August 1950 Bull.civ.1950 I no.184 p.141, quoted Ghestin *La Vente* p. 613.
19. The validity of such a clause has been accepted by the jurisprudence and it is effective against the general creditors if the ship-builder goes into liquidation – see Mazeaud, para. 925–1, p. 216.
20. Accordingly when the contract was for the purchaser of laying hens the property and risk did not pass to the purchaser until the hens had attained sufficient maturity. Cour d'Appel Rennes 25 June 1969 Gaz.Pal. 1969.2.201.
21. The case concerned a central heating installation (Cass.com. 24 October 1960 Bull.Cass. 332–302). See also Cass. civ. 3e 23 April 1974 when it was held that a building being constructed on the land of another was not the property of the contractor 'even before Reception'. See also Art. 1601–3 of the *Code Civil* regarding contracts for the sale of property to be constructed in the future but which transfer immediately to the purchaser ownership of the land and any existing works: *La vente en l'état de futur achèvement*. The future work becomes the property of the purchaser as construction progresses and the price is payable in accordance with the progress achieved.
22. Zimmermann, p. 281.
23. Zimmermann, p. 287.
24. Zimmermann, p. 290.
25. Pothier, *Traité du contrat de vente* p. 313: 'it is a principle established under the heading of the digest "de peric & comm.rei vend" that as soon as the contract of sale is perfect, the thing sold ought to be at the risk of the purchaser whether it has yet been delivered to him or not; such that if during this time it perishes without the fault of the seller, the seller ought to be relieved of his obligations, and the purchaser is not relieved of his own and is none the less obliged to pay the agreed price'.
26. Zimmermann, p. 401.
27. See Keating, pp. 62 and 134.
28. Cass.3e 27 January 1976 Bull.civ. III no. 34 and Cass.civ.3e 19 February 1986 Bull.civ.III no.10. It is to be noted that Art. 1788 is only concerned with risk and not with the passing of property – see note 21 above and the cases there cited. Note also that it is only material supplied by the contractor which is at his risk under Art. 1788. In the absence of an express bailment of the employer's material to the contractor the same position would apply under English law – see the discussion of *Colbart Ltd* v. *Kumar* (1992) (unreported) in *Building Law Monthly* vol.9, issue 8, August 1992.
29. For an example the following clause in the *Cahier des clauses et conditions générales applicable aux marchés de travaux SNCF*: 'in case of loss or damage caused on the work sites by a natural phenomenon which was not normally foreseeable or in case of force majeure:
    a) SNCF accepts the responsibility for loss or damage caused to the works or any part thereof in course of execution and materials as well as costs resulting from the necessary measures taken for their protection;
    b) the contractor for his part is responsible for the loss or damage caused to the storehouses, tools, equipment and site installations for the costs of which he is responsible under the contract also the costs necessary for their protection;
    c) SNCF and the contractor each bear their indirect damages which they may suffer resulting from the events due to force majeure in particular as to the consequence of the interruption of the works in the form of the costs of personnel, of equipment kept standing, other extra expenses and overheads.

18 Reservation of title and transfer of title to third parties

This chapter deals with two issues, common to all three legal systems under review and which are of much significance in commercial affairs.

The first issue is: under what circumstances and to what extent can a seller protect himself against the bankruptcy or liquidation of the purchaser occurring before the purchaser has paid for the goods the subject of the sale by means of retaining the title to the goods after delivery?

Second, under what conditions can a purchaser who has not obtained a good title to the goods, nevertheless pass a good title to a third party?

RESERVATION OF TITLE – ENGLISH LAW

Although s.19(1) of the Sale of Goods Act provides that the seller may retain the right of disposal of the goods until certain conditions have been satisfied, and that property in the goods does not pass to the purchaser until those conditions have been fulfilled, it is only comparatively recently that it has become normal commercial practice for sellers to include a clause in their conditions of sale providing that the property in the goods shall not pass to the purchaser until the seller has received payment in full.[1]

For convenience of analysis such clauses may be considered as falling into three categories:

1. A clause simply providing that the passing of the property in the goods to the purchaser is conditional upon payment to the seller in full of the purchase price.
2. A clause providing that the property in the goods shall not pass to the purchaser until all payments due from the purchaser to the seller have been made.
3. A clause extending the rights of the seller to the proceeds of sale of the goods and perhaps even to the proceeds of the sale of those goods mixed with others.

CATEGORY 1

There is no difficulty with this clause provided that the goods remain identifiable and in

250

the possession of the purchaser. Its effect is simply to defer the passing of the property in the goods until such time as payment has been made. The retention of title clause does not operate to create a charge in favour of the seller – which would be void against the liquidator or other creditor of the company unless registered under ss.395 and 396 of the Companies Act 1985 within twenty-one days of its being made – because the purchaser never acquires any right in the goods which could be made the subject of a security.[2]

Goods can remain identifiable even if incorporated into others as when diesel engines were incorporated into generating sets but were identifiable by their serial numbers as being those supplied by the seller and easily disconnected.[3]

However, if the goods have ceased to have a separate identity, because they have been mixed with other goods, then the simple clause would be ineffective since the seller would not retain the legal ownership of the goods, which is essential if the requirement for registration is to be avoided. One example is where resin was used in the manufacture of chipboard.[4]

While it is possible to draft the clause in such a way as to extend the ownership of the seller to the product resulting from such a mixture, it is difficult to do so in a way which avoids the clause being treated as a charge and therefore void unless registered under the Companies Act. The difficulty is that if the seller were to retake possession of the product, being a mixture of goods with others, and sell it, then one would normally expect that any excess in the proceeds of sale over the debt due to the seller should be repaid to the purchaser. But if that is the case then the transfer of the 'other goods' in the mixture to the seller must be by way of charge.[5]

Only if the clause provided that the seller was entitled to the whole of the proceeds could that conclusion be avoided, but that in turn raises other difficulties (see below, p. 252). There could be a further complication if, say, two sellers were involved and such a clause were to be included in both their contracts. So far this case has not come before the English courts.

CATEGORY 2

Again no problems are created at least so long as the goods are identifiable and in the possession of the purchaser. It is commonplace to use this clause where the seller is making regular deliveries to the purchaser and its effect is that so long as any sum is unpaid then title has not passed in respect of any of the goods delivered.[6]

CATEGORY 3

In any commercial sale other than to an end-user it is the intention of the seller that the purchaser should use the goods for the conduct of his business either by resale of those goods after they have been worked on in some way or after they have been mixed with other goods to produce another product. This must be so, otherwise the purchaser could never carry on his business and earn the money with which to pay the seller.

The purchaser in such cases can pass a good title to a sub-purchaser under s.25 of the Sale of Goods Act and s.9 of the Factors Act (see further the following section pp. 259–260) provided that the sub-purchaser buys in good faith and without notice of the reservation of title clause. Notice here means actual notice and not implied notice.[7]

For this reason the seller will often try to extend the reservation of title clause so that it covers not just the goods themselves but also the proceeds of sale whether those proceeds arise from the sale of those goods or from those goods mixed with others. Further, for his better protection the seller will usually stipulate that the proceeds are to be paid into a separate bank account and held in trust for him. It is here that the difficulties really start.

In order for such a clause to be effective it would appear necessary that the buyer should owe the seller a fiduciary duty in relation to the proceeds of any sub-sale. Such a duty must be expressly set out in the contract. It will not be implied since it is inconsistent with the normal relationship of buyer and seller. Nor will a mere reference to the buyer being a 'bailee' be sufficient.[8]

There is again no difficulty in drafting such a clause, although there could be in getting it accepted by a wide-awake purchaser, but the problem would still be of avoiding the requirement to register the agreement as a charge under the Companies Act. The only way appears to be if the clause not only refers to the purchaser as a bailee and under a fiduciary duty to the seller in respect of the goods and any proceeds of sale, but that this duty includes the obligation to account to the seller for the whole of the proceeds of sale. Again the commercial acceptability of any such clause must be in doubt although it was essentially the way in which the original Romalpa clause was drafted.[9]

It is also arguable in this latter case that the clause is so much a fiction, which is not intended by the parties to be operated in the way it is drafted, that the courts should disregard its fictional aspects and treat it for what it truly is, namely the establishment of a preferential charge over the buyer's assets in favour of the seller.

However, the general approach of English law seems to be based on a strictly contractual approach to the validity of retention of title clauses without taking into consideration the wider policy aspects of the operation of the clause in relation to the claims of other creditors. Atiyah p. 463 concurs with this view but appears to doubt its desirability. It is in marked contrast to French law (see below, p. 255).

The general rule of English law as stated earlier is that risk passes with property (s.20(1) of the Sale of Goods Act). If therefore the seller retains title in the goods then, unless the contract provides otherwise, the goods also continue at his risk.

Of course in practice any well drafted retention of title clause will provide that, after delivery, the risk passes to the purchaser. The purchaser must insure the goods against accidental loss or damage and hold the proceeds of any insurance claim as trustee for the unpaid seller, i.e. the insurance monies, in the same way as the proceeds of sale, must not be allowed to become part of the purchaser's general assets.

RESERVATION OF TITLE – FRENCH LAW

Traditionally French law has been hostile to the concept of reservation of title. As recently as 1980 an eminent French lawyer declared: 'the Reservation of Title is obnoxious in principle lethal in its effects'.[10]

There are no articles relating to reservation of title in the *Code Civil*. On the contrary one of the reasons for the antagonism towards the concept is that it contradicts Art. 1583 which states that 'It [the sale] is perfect between the parties and the ownership is acquired in law by the Purchaser in respect to the Seller from the moment when there is agreement on the thing and the price even although the thing has not yet been delivered nor the price paid'.

The main reason for antagonism, however, was the traditional view that other creditors in giving credit to the purchaser would do so on the strength of their belief that the goods in his possession were part of his *patrimoine*.[11] While therefore the courts were prepared to recognize the validity of a reservation of title clause as between the parties, they were not prepared to do so as against the general body of creditors or the liquidator/trustee in bankruptcy. As Houin and Pedamont put it the effect was that 'The Suppliers appeared as the privileged guarantors of their debtor'.[12]

It was not until the Law of 12 May 1980, now replaced by the Law of 25 January 1985, that there were any effective statutory provisions derogating from the *Code Civil*. These provisions are now contained in Arts. 115, 121 and 122 of the Law of 25 January 1985.

SCOPE AND APPLICATION OF THE LAW

Since the Law is a derogation from the *droit commun* its scope and application are strictly interpreted. The following is a summary of the main points:

1. The Law applies only to contracts for sale. This means that it does not apply to contracts for works (*contrats d'entreprise ou louage d'ouvrage*) nor importantly to sub-contracts.[13] This is in marked contrast with English law under which not only is a retention of title clause in a sub-contract for the supply and installation of goods valid, but because the sub-contract is not a 'contract for sale' the contractor will not be able to pass the title in the goods to the employer unless he has obtained title himself (see further below, p. 260).
2. The law refers to the goods which can be the subject of a reservation of title clause as *les marchandises*. At one time there was some doubt as to what kind of goods were covered by this term but is has now been settled that it includes both 'goods for consumption as well as items of equipment for professional use'.[14]
3. The reservation of title clause must have been agreed by the parties and in writing. These two requirements have been the subject of a number of cases before the French courts from which the following can be deduced:

   - The requirement for writing can be satisfied by any commercial document, e.g.

253

order, general conditions of sale, invoice or delivery note which makes reference to the reservation of title clause.

- Since as referred to above the clause is a derogation from the *droit commun* it must be established clearly that the purchaser was in a position easily to recognize the existence of the clause. Its inclusion therefore in small letters in the middle of a set of general conditions on the back of the document would not satisfy this requirement.[15] What would satisfy it must depend on the facts of the individual case and perhaps just as importantly the attitude of the court which has certainly in the past often been hostile to the seller and protective of the rights of the general creditors. However, ideally the clause should be at least referred to on the face of the document, if not actually set out there, and should be printed in such a way that it stands out from the rest of the text of the conditions. This protective attitude may not, however, be extended to a large organization which can be expected to have experts at its disposal to study the terms of contract.[16]
- The agreement may be express, as when the purchaser countersigns the seller's document plainly referring to the clause, but it may also be tacit. Provided that the clause is clearly expressed by the seller in documents issued to the purchaser, who makes no objection to the clause and proceeds with the contract, then the purchaser will be regarded as having given his tacit acceptance.[17]
- There must be no ambiguity as to the agreement by the purchaser. This requirement will not be satisfied if the general conditions of purchase refer to the property passing on receipt of delivery and there is no evidence that the purchaser ever agreed to change these.
- Where the seller is a foreign company then the clause will be valid if it is written in the language of that country.[18]

4. According to the Law of 25 January 1985 the writing which sets out the clause must have been agreed at the latest at the time of the delivery of the goods. So, if the invoices containing the clause are submitted and accepted at the time when the purchaser comes to collect the goods from the seller's warehouse according to the custom of the trade, this would satisfy the requirements of the Law, but not if the invoices were issued subsequent to the delivery. The burden of proof rests with the seller.

However the fact that the clause was not agreed upon at the time of the formation of the contract does not appear relevant provided that there is such agreement by or on delivery. This seems strange to an English lawyer for whom the clause would have had to be included within the contractual terms at the time when the contract was formed. Indeed Robine refers to this also having been held to be so in one case by the Tribunal de Commerce de Corbeil Esonnes but comments that having regard to the text of the law the decision 'is not understandable'.[19]

5. In order for the seller to be entitled to exercise his rights under the reservation of title clause it is necessary that the goods exist *en nature* and, assuming that the purchaser is not solvent, do so on the date of the decision instituting the procedure for *redressement judiciare de l'acquéreur*.[20]

In order for the goods to exist *en nature* they must be identifiable and retain their individuality. The requirement for the goods to exist *en nature* has given rise to numerous decisions, not all of them easily reconcilable, but from which the following general conclusions can be drawn:

- Equipment which, although installed in a building or caravan, is easily dismountable without causing damage is still *en nature*.[21]
- Materials which have been used in the process of manufacturing articles are no longer *en nature*, having lost their individuality.[22]
- If the operations performed on the goods do not however change their substance, then they will still be treated as being *en nature* although the seller must give credit to the purchaser for the money expended. Wood for joinery which had been artificially seasoned and cut up into two equal parts as the first stages of a long operation was still treated as being *en nature*.[23]

In general terms the results achieved in practice by the French courts are very close to those of the English courts (see above, pp. 251–252), even though the starting point may be different.[24] However there is an important distinction. In England the question of whether property may be retained by the seller in goods which have been mixed with others is treated as a matter of the contract between the parties subject only to the requirement for registration under the Companies Act. In French law it is the law of the *procédure collective* which governs the conditions under which the seller can recover goods sold with a reservation of title clause.

This point was established definitively in a case decided by the *Cour de cassation* on 8 January 1991.[25] Polyester fibres were sold by a German company to a French firm under a contract governed by German law with a reservation of title clause which reserved title in the fibres and in products manufactured from them to the German seller until such time as he had been paid in full. The clause was valid under German law (see below, p. 258). The French purchaser, having been put into *redressement judiciaire*, the German seller claimed the right to recover the goods manufactured from the fibres which no longer existed *en nature*.

However the *Cour de cassation*, in a judgement approving the decision of the Cour d'Appel de Besançon, distinguished between the law of the contract, which applied to the validity and effect in regard to third parties in general of a clause of reservation of title, and the law of the *procédure collective*, which governed the conditions under which goods sold with reservation of title may be recovered. Since the French law of the *procédure collective* requires that in order to put into effect the recovery of the goods they should be identifiable and above all exist *en nature*, the seller's claim was rejected.

PROCEDURAL PROVISIONS

The unpaid seller who wishes to take advantage of a reservation of title clause when the purchaser is no longer solvent must do so within strictly defined rules.

1. The right of recovery must be exercised within a period of three months from the date of the decision opening the procedure *de redressement judiciaire*.
2. The period of three months is an absolute fixed period which cannot be suspended, interrupted or extended.
3. The act of recovery may be initiated either by an ordinary letter or by re-taking the goods, but only if the liquidator or in the case of a *redressement judiciaire* the *administrateur* is in agreement. Otherwise the seller must initiate legal action before the court having jurisdiction over the proceedings within the three-month period. The accelerated procedure *en référé* may be used, at least provided that there is no serious dispute as to the seller's rights.
4. The *administrateur* or the legal representative of the creditors has the obligation to prepare an inventory of the goods in the possession of the company in financial default. The unpaid seller, wishing to exercise his right to recover goods under a clause of reservation of title, must for his part be able to identify in the inventory the goods which he claims are those he delivered and for which he has not been paid. The requirement for a precise identification of which goods are those for which payment has not been made is regarded as *ordre public*. It follows that not only is it strictly enforced but the parties cannot derogate from it in the terms of their contract.[26]

RECOVERY BY THE SELLER OF THE PRICE

Three situations can be distinguished:

1. The goods no longer exist *en nature* at the time of the opening of the *procédure de redressement judiciaire*. Here the same rule applies as in the case of the action for the recovery of ownership. If the goods no longer exist *en nature* because they have been used and transformed into other goods then the seller can no longer maintain an action to recover the price.[27]
2. The goods do exist *en nature* at the time of the opening of the *procédure de redressement judiciaire* but are sold by the administrator before the ending of the three-month period allowed to the seller in which to exercise his rights. If the goods are resold during the above period then the debtor is liable to pay the seller the price of the goods and the administrator is responsible for guaranteeing such payment. The debtor is allowed to work on the goods or transform them into other goods after the opening of the procedure but is then liable to the seller for the payment of the price.[28]
3. Before the opening of the procedure for *redressement judiciaire*, the goods have been resold by the purchaser but payment for the goods has not been received. The unpaid seller may have a direct action for the price against the sub-purchaser under Art. 122 of the Law of 25 January 1985 although in practice the possibility of exercising this right is limited. First, as for the other actions, the goods must still exist *en nature* at the time of the opening of the procedure. Second, payment may

have been made by the sub-purchaser not only by way of cash but also by other means, e.g. bills of exchange accepted by the sub-purchaser which have been discounted, by entry in a *compte courant* between the two parties[29] or by endorsement by the sub-purchaser of any negotiable instrument in favour of the purchaser.

CONCLUSION

In some ways the restrictions imposed by French law on the seller or contractor seeking to take advantage of a retention of title clause are more severe than those of English law. First, such a clause is only valid if it is strictly a contract for the sale of goods while there is no such restriction under English law. Second, it would appear that goods can only be recovered if the price for those goods remains unpaid so that an 'all sums' clause of the type used in *Armour* v. *Thyssen* (see note 2 above) would not constitute a valid retention of title clause under French law as against the creditors in a situation of *redressement judiciare*. Third, a Romalpa type clause which allowed the seller to recover the proceeds of the sale of mixed goods on the basis that the seller held these as fiduciary for the buyer would not be valid, since it is an essential condition that the goods exist *en nature* at the time of the opening of the *redressement judiciaire* procedure.

On the other hand, certain decisions would suggest that French law does allow for goods still existing *en nature* where they have been built into other products, or more particularly into buildings, which it is doubtful would be followed in English law. Finally, French law permits a restricted right for the seller to recover the unpaid original selling price of the goods from the sub-purchaser, which is not a right available under English law unless exceptionally the seller can establish that a right to the proceeds of the re-sale existed in equity as from the moment of the re-sale on the grounds that, when the buyer re-sold, he did so under a power of re-sale conferred on him by the seller which imposed on the buyer fiduciary duties (*Aluminium Industries* v. *Romalpa* [1976] 1 All ER at p. 512).

RESERVATION OF TITLE – GERMAN LAW

Of the three systems under review it is German law which provides to the seller the strongest possibility of ensuring eventual recovery of the purchase price through the use of retention of title (more correctly reservation of property – *Eigentumsvorbehalt*) clauses. Such clauses are based initially on Art. 455 of the *BGB* which states:

> If the seller of a movable has retained title until payment of the purchase price, it is to be presumed in cases of doubt, that the transfer of title takes place subject to the condition precedent of payment in full of the purchase price and that the seller is entitled to rescind the contract if the purchaser is in default with payment.

The use of retention of title clauses has become so commonplace in German commercial practice that at least so far as the simple clause which retains the seller's title to the goods while in the buyer's possession is concerned, this will usually survive the 'battle of the forms', i.e. it will be treated as part of the background law.[30]

However German law has proceeded far beyond the simple type of retention of title clause envisaged by Art. 455 and has recognized as valid the following extensive clauses at least so far as they have been agreed by the parties to have been incorporated in the contract. They will not however usually survive the 'battle of the forms'. These clauses can either be extended clauses (*erweiterter Eigentumsvorbehalt*) or extended property reservations (*verlängerter Eigentumsvorbehalt*). The former provide for reservation of title until all existing or future sums due from the purchaser to the seller have been paid. This is normally referred to as the 'current account' clause (*Kontokorrent-Vorbehalt*).

Reservation of title holds until all debts including those from other dealings are paid and such debts include those owed to other companies which are members of the same group as the seller. This is known as the 'multiple retention' or *Konzenvorbehalt*. It was this clause which was used by Thyssen Edelstahlwerke in the case brought against them by Armour as receivers of Carron Co. Ltd and held valid by the House of Lords under English law (see above, p. 251 and note 6).

Extended property reservations are reservation of title provisions which are intended to protect the seller against the consequences of the sale by the purchaser of the goods to a third party or the transformation of the goods or their intermingling with other goods.

The first type of clause is one under which the purchaser assigns to the seller all claims for payment which the purchaser will have against sub-purchasers of the goods, whether the goods have been processed or not. However the seller undertakes not to exercise his rights under such assignment unless the purchaser defaults in any payment, or insolvency proceedings are filed against him. In either event the purchaser must then give the seller all information necessary for him to enforce payment.

The clause is effective on the purchaser's going into liquidation unless a third party in ignorance of the assignment had already paid the purchaser.

The second type of clause is one under which:

- the reservation of title applies to the goods even after processing, and
- if the goods are mingled with other goods then the seller acquires title to the new goods arising out of the mingling in proportion to the value which the goods sold bears to the other goods at the time of the mingling and the purchaser holds the new goods on behalf of the seller. This provision will apply even if the goods sold become inseparably mixed or mingled with other goods not belonging to the seller and also even if the principal part of the new goods was provided by the purchaser (Art. 947 *BGB*). In the latter event the purchaser acquires sole ownership under Art. 947(2) of the *BGB* but the contract will normally provide that the purchaser transfers proportionate joint ownership (*Miteigentum*) to the seller.

It will be remembered that it was such a clause in a German seller's conditions of sale reserving title in processed goods that fell foul of the French rule that goods must exist *en nature* at the time of the opening of the *procédure collective* (see above, p. 255 and note 25).

RECOVERY OF THE GOODS

If the purchaser defaults in payment then the seller is entitled to recover the goods from him. Although under Art. 455 of the *BGB* the recovery of goods implies rescission of the contract, the seller can and usually does provide in his conditions of sale, that recovery does not imply rescission. It follows that although the seller has taken back the goods the purchaser is still responsible for payment of the purchase price. If the seller re-sells the goods then he can no longer claim that the purchaser performs his contract but is entitled to recover from him as damages (*vertrags-schaden*) the original contract price after giving credit for the proceeds of re-sale, less the reasonable costs incurred in such re-sale. This right not to rescind does not apply to consumer contracts which are subject to the Consumer Credit Act.

On the bankruptcy or liquidation of the purchaser the simple reservation of title clause allows the seller to recover the goods against the trustee in bankruptcy or the liquidator unless the latter exercises his right to maintain the contract and pay for the goods. If the contract contained an extended clause and if the goods had been processed or inter-mingled then the seller would no longer have the right of recovery but would have a preferential claim (*Absonderung*) for the unpaid value of the goods.

PASSING OF TITLE BY A NON-OWNER – ENGLISH LAW

The basic position from which English law starts is that no one can pass a better title to another than the one which he himself possesses, often expressed in Latin, *nemo dat quod non habet*. This is the old rule of English common law from which there were no really significant exceptions until Parliament in the nineteenth century passed a series of Factors Acts, the first in 1823, and a consolidating Act in 1889.

The purpose of these Acts was to facilitate commerce by providing in general for a *bona fide* purchaser to obtain title to the goods in three situations.

First, if the seller is a mercantile agent and is in possession of the goods with the consent of the owner then any sale of the goods by him in the ordinary course of business will be as valid as it would have been had he been expressly authorized by the owner to make the sale, provided that the purchaser is in good faith and has at the time no notice of the seller's lack of authority.[31]

In practice the most common application of this provision is the fraudulent sale of a vehicle where the dealer who has possession does not have the authority to sell.

Second, if the seller having sold the goods continues in possession of them and sells them again, then the second purchaser, providing he is acting *bona fide* and without

259

notice of the first sale, acquires a good title.[32] This rule can be justified on the grounds that the first buyer, in leaving the original seller in possession, was relying on the seller's honesty and he must accept the consequences if his reliance was misplaced.

Third, if B, having bought or agreed to buy goods from A, obtains with the consent of A possession of the goods and disposes of them to C who buys them *bona fide* and without notice of any rights of the original seller A, then C obtains a good title to the goods.[33]

Of the three provisions the third is in practice the most important since it has the effect that a sub-purchaser without notice of a reservation of title clause can obtain a good title to the goods even though title has not passed between the original seller and the purchaser.

However, four points must be noted:

1. The original contract between the seller and the purchaser must be a contract for sale. So if that contract is a contract for services, e.g. a sub-contract to supply and fix roof slates, s.9 of the Factors Act will not apply and the title in material delivered to the site by the sub-contractor will not pass to the building owner.[34]
2. Although the original contract may be a conditional contract of sale, in commercial transactions the buyer can still pass a good title. But a bailment even with an option to purchase is not a contract of sale, so that a sale by the bailee under a hire purchase agreement would not pass a good title unless it was a sale of a motor vehicle and came within the provisions of Part III of the Hire Purchase Act 1964 as re-enacted by the Consumer Credit Act 1974.
3. The second purchaser must not have had notice of the reservation of title clause. Notice here means actual notice. There is no obligation on the purchaser to make enquiries and he is better protected by not doing so. However it is considered that he would have notice if he required the first purchaser to supply him with copies of his sub-orders and those sub-orders clearly stated that the goods were being supplied subject to a reservation of title clause.
4. The seller must have been the owner of the goods or have had the consent of the owner to be in possession of them. The section does not apply if originally the goods have been stolen, no matter through how many hands the goods have passed.[35]

There are other exceptions to the *nemo dat* rule of lesser practical importance. These are listed here so as to show the complexity of English law but will not be discussed. For details see Atiyah, pp. 346–358 or Furmstone, pp. 74–80.

5. Estoppel by negligence.
6. Estoppel by representation.
7. Sale by an agent with ostensible authority.
8. Sale under a voidable title.
9. Sale in market overt.

PASSING OF TITLE BY A NON-OWNER – FRENCH LAW

By comparison with English law French law in this instance is not only simpler but starts from a totally opposite viewpoint; one which is moreover in most aspects different from Roman law. It is one of the few areas of the law relating to obligations in which the older customary law of France largely prevailed over Roman law.

The normal method of transfer of ownership in the Roman law of Justinian, *traditio*, operated on the basis that the seller was the owner. The seller could not transfer to the purchaser more than belonged to him. If he tried to do so then he transferred nothing. This, as we have seen earlier, is the same basic starting point as in English law with the *nemo dat* rule. But then as Zulueta has pointed out there is nothing in Roman law which resembles the exceptions in English law to that principle under the Factors Act and the Sale of Goods Act.[36]

The basic rule of French law which is expressed in Art. 2279 of the *Code Civil*: *En fait de meubles la possession vaut titre* (As far as movables are concerned possession is equivalent to title) is the direct opposite to *nemo dat*. It accordingly denies to the true owner the right of recovery of the goods against the third party in possession. The rule appears to have originated in the customary laws of France which followed Germanic practice and accepted the principle 'movables cannot be followed'. The only remedy of the person deprived of his property was against the person to whom he had entrusted it or who had stolen it from him. Although during the Middle Ages the Roman rules which did allow an action *rei vindicatio* by the true owner for the recovery of the goods themselves against the person who had possession were followed in parts of France, they lost out in general to the older custom because the latter was more suited to commercial practice. By half-way through the eighteenth century the maxim contained in Art. 2279 of the *Code Civil* had become quite widely established although Pothier in 1768 still maintained the Roman rule: *Nemo plus juris ad alium transferre potest quam ipse habet* but allowed for the purchaser to acquire title by prescription or usucapion and for the possessor who transferred the goods to be presumed to be the owner unless the contrary was proved.[37]

The rule in Art. 2279 para. 1 applies even if the true owner has been deprived of the goods by trickery or fraud. It is for the owner to choose carefully the person with whom he deals. However the third party who has possession must have acquired this in good faith, i.e. he must not have had reasons to be suspicious that the person with whom he was dealing was not the true owner. But it is for the deprived owner to prove the absence of good faith, which is presumed in the absence of evidence to the contrary. In one case where the purchaser of a considerable quantity of fertilizer had been warned by the true owner over the telephone and by a letter sent recorded delivery, it was held that the purchaser must have had a doubt as to the legitimacy of the ownership of the person from whom he was buying. Having therefore acted in bad faith the purchaser could not avail himself of the protection of Art. 2279 which had no application in such a case.[38]

Two points need noting in relation to Art. 2279. These are:

1. The rule only applies to corporeal movables capable of being transferred from hand to hand and therefore does not extend to patents, copyright etc. and in general to incorporeal movables or intangible assets. But it does extend to bearer securities.
2. The person having possession can only claim under Art. 2279 if he took possession as owner and not as a result of some agreement under which he is bound to return the goods in accordance with the terms of the agreement (*détention précaire*). However the holder of the goods as a security for a loan (*un créancier gagiste*) is entitled to invoke Art. 2270 until the time that the loan is repaid, since although he is only *un détenteur précaire* as regards the owner he is the true possessor as regards third parties by virtue of his title derived from the real right of pledge.[39]

EXCEPTIONS TO THE RULE

Despite the eclipse of Roman law by the principle that *possession vaut titre*, there was something retained in the *Code Civil* both of Roman law and also of other customary rules which had been developed in the Middle Ages. The exception which they establish to the rule in Art. 2279 deals with the cases where the true owner has parted with possession of his property against his will. It could be said they are cases in which he has not been at fault and where morally it would be unjustifiable to deprive him of his property.

In Roman law a person could acquire ownership through a period of use which for movables was three years (*usucapio*) if he acted in good faith but only if the goods had not been stolen in the first place. 'Stolen' here meant any sale or delivery of a movable belonging to another in the knowledge that it was not your own property.[40] Effectively therefore there was little possibility of acquiring ownership of a movable through *usucapio*.

But based on the concept of *usucapio* the introduction of a three-year prescription period which did apply even to goods stolen or lost was supported by some in France in the Middle Ages and eventually found its way into the *Code Civil* (Art. 2279 para. 2).[41]

It applies to cases in which the goods have been stolen from the true owner, in the strict sense of *vol* as defined in the Penal Code, or lost by him but not if the owner has been tricked or deceived into parting with the goods.[42] Within the three years the owner has the right to recover the goods from the person in possession of them. This is in contrast to English law under which if goods are stolen then no subsequent sale (other than in market overt) will result in the innocent purchaser obtaining a good title (see above, p. 260). The true owner does have to prove in this instance that the possessor acted in bad faith.

A further provision drawn from southern French customary law of the Middle Ages is to be found in Art. 2280. If the possessor of goods stolen or lost bought them at a fair, a market, a public sale or from a shop selling goods of a similar nature, then the true owner can only recover his property if he reimburses the possessor the price which he paid for them.

If the goods have been resold by a merchant who bought in good faith from the thief, then the owner must not only pay the possessor the price which the latter paid to the merchant but will be unable to recover anything from the merchant unless he can establish that the merchant committed some fault.[43]

COMPARATIVE CONCLUSIONS

Beginning from directly opposing principles both legal systems have in practice arrived at much the same position, the differences being ones of detailed application rather than principles. Both have recognized that in general terms the requirements of commerce are that the possessor in good faith should be protected in preference to the dispossessed owner. However because English law started with the *nemo dat* rule, it has only reached there by a series of complex exceptions, mainly statutory, whose interpretation has caused the courts great difficulties and given rise to distinctions which do the law little credit. French law by contrast has had far fewer problems due to the essential simplicity of the provisions of the code.[44]

PASSING OF TITLE BY A NON-OWNER – GERMAN LAW

In commenting on French law it has already been remarked that in this instance the *Code Civil* followed German rather than Roman practice. Early German law distinguished between two cases: first, that in which an owner parted voluntarily with possession of a thing, e.g. by bailment, and second, that in which the thing was lost by the owner or stolen from him so that this loss of possession was involuntary.

In the first case, having parted with the seisin of the thing to the bailee, the owner had no right of action otherwise than against the bailee. This applied whether the bailee lost the thing, had it stolen or wrongfully sold it to a third party. This principle was expressed in the old maxims *Hand muss Hand wahren* and *wo du deinen Glauben gelassen hast, musst du ihn suchen.*[45]

In the second case the dispossessed owner could pursue the recovery of the thing even into the hands of third parties no matter how innocent they may have been in acquiring the thing.

During the Middle Ages the rule *Hand muss Hand wahren* was in some areas abandoned and in others modified so there was no uniform rule across the various states and towns, each of which had their own particular law. Again the law relating to the pursuit of a thing lost or stolen was modified in many places to a claim for the value of the item if it had been sold in an open market.

With the reception of Roman law (see above, pp. 6–8), the action *rei vindicatio* which allowed for the recovery of movables, irrespective of the manner in which the true owner had been dispossessed, entered into the law of certain towns and states totally and others only in part. In some places a *bona fide* possessor for value was wholly protected; in others any claim against him was for compensation, only not for the return of the goods. In most places protection was given if the goods had been purchased in the open market or from a recognized dealer in such goods. But there was no overall German law on the matter. That only came into being with the issue of the *BGB* and the *HGB* which largely followed the Germanic as opposed to the Roman law.

PROVISIONS OF THE *BGB* AND THE *HGB*

If the seller is not the owner of the goods the purchaser nevertheless acquires a good title to them if the goods are delivered to him and there is agreement between the seller and the purchaser that ownership should be transferred to him, provided that the purchaser has acted in good faith (*BGB*, Art. 932 para. 1).

The only exception to this rule is if the goods have been stolen from the true owner, been lost or in any other way become missing (*BGB* 935(1)). In that event no subsequent sale is valid against the true owner no matter through how many hands the goods pass.

The expression 'become missing' refers to cases in which the owner has lost direct possession of the goods without intending to do so or against his will. It also extends to cases in which the owner is the indirect possessor but the goods have become missing from the direct possessor, e.g. when A lends a car to B (and so ceases to be the direct possessor) and the car is stolen from B (who is at that time the direct possessor). But if A hands over his car to a garage for repair, and the garage disposes of it to B from whom it is stolen by C who transfers it to D, then A cannot recover from D since the car did not become missing from the garage but was willingly disposed of by them.[46]

Exceptionally the rule in Art. 935 does not apply if the goods which have been stolen, lost or otherwise become missing are purchased in good faith at public auction (*BGB* 935(2)).

Good faith

The expression 'in good faith' is interpreted differently in commercial and non-commercial sales. According to *BGB* 932(2) the purchaser is not in good faith 'if he knows, or owing to gross negligence does not know, that the goods do not belong to the seller'. The wording shows that good faith is assumed and it is for the person claiming to be true owner to establish that the purchase was made in bad faith. Obviously if the circumstances of the sale or the price of the goods is such that any sensible person would believe that they must have 'fallen off the back of a lorry' and that the seller is not in consequence the rightful owner, then bad faith would be assumed.

It is to be noted that s.932(2) is only concerned with good faith in relation to the ownership of the seller and not for example as to whether someone's claim to have authority to sell on behalf of the true owner is correct or not. However, under the *HGB* s.366, if a merchant in the course of his business sells goods which do not belong to him, then not only do the provisions of the *BGB* protecting the purchaser apply, but the good faith of the purchaser extends to the authority of the seller to dispose of the goods on behalf of the owner. So if the merchant produces an apparent authority from the owner entrusting him with the right to sell the goods which is in fact forged, the purchaser is protected if he buys in reliance on such authority, at least unless on the face of it the authority was obviously fraudulent.

The section is very similar to, although not as restrictive as, s.2 of the Factors Act discussed earlier (see above, p. 259 and note 31).

TRANSFER OF TITLE AND ACQUISITIVE PRESCRIPTION

There is no doubt that a person who obtains title to the goods as a result of Art. 932 et seq. becomes the true owner and the title of the previous owner is extinguished. As regards the acquisition of title to goods by prescription this was not possible under the old German law. However, under Roman influence it became allowed, though with differing periods. In the *BGB* it is now provided under Art. 937 that if a person has a movable in his proprietary possession for ten years, which he obtained and retained in good faith, then he acquires ownership of it. This would be so even if the item had been originally stolen or lost provided of course that his own acquisition and retention was in good faith.

UNJUST ENRICHMENT

Since under Art. 932 et seq. the rights of the previous owner are extinguished, then in theory, under Art. 816 of the *BGB*, the person who made the sale without having title to the goods is bound to hand over the proceeds to the person whom he has deprived of ownership. In practice such a right against a person who has behaved fraudulently is usually of little value since he will have no assets with which to satisfy any judgement against him.

COMPARATIVE SUMMARY

The basic principle of German law is similar to that of French. Provided that the purchaser is in good faith, then he obtains ownership to the goods if he takes delivery of them under an agreement with the person then in possession. Such an agreement is intended to pass the title to the purchaser. The only significant difference is that if the goods have been stolen, lost or become missing then the true owner's title is protected subject only to the period of ten years' prescription under Art. 937, while under French law the true owner must recover the goods within three years of their theft or loss. The same critical comparison with English law therefore applies.

NOTES

1. Atiyah p.455. The first case relating to a reservation of title clause in a commercial contract for the sale of goods only came before the courts in 1976 and even then the seller imposing the clause was Dutch.
2. *Armour* v. *Thyssen* [1990] 3 WLR 181.

3. *Hendy Lennox* v. *Grahame Puttick Ltd*. [1984] 2 All ER 152.
4. *Borden (UK) Ltd* v. *Scottish Timber Products Ltd* [1981] Ch.25.
5. See further Atiyah p. 460.
6. This was the position in the Armour case referred to in note 2 above where the clause was held to be valid.
7. *Feuer Leather Corp*. v. *Frank Johnstone* (1981) Com LR 251: 'There is no general duty on a buyer of goods in an ordinary commercial transaction to make inquiries as to the right of the seller to dispose of the goods'. However, it is on this account considered that it is a dangerous practice for purchasers to require their main supplier to forward to them copies of their sub-orders, since if these clearly show that the seller has contracted with his suppliers subject to a reservation of title in their favour, this could constitute notice.
8. See the Lennox case referred to in note 3 above and *re Andrabell Ltd* [1984] 3 All ER 407.
9. In the second part of the clause which dealt with mixed foil, i.e. foil used by the buyers in their manufacturing process, the ownership of the seller extended from the foil to the finished product and further provided that until the monies owed by the seller to buyer were paid, the buyers would keep the finished products as 'fiduciary' for the sellers and that the buyers were authorized to sell the finished products on condition that the buyers would, if requested, transfer to the sellers the benefit of those sales. *Aluminium Industries Vaasen* v. *Romalpa Aluminium Ltd*. [1976] 1 WLR 676.
10. Quoted Robine s.129.
11. The term is barely translatable. In essence it means 'the totality of a person's goods and obligations, the latter being those both owed by and owing to the person concerned, appreciable in money terms'. See *Vocabulaire Juridique*, Cornu, Presses Universitaires de France and in English see Nicholas, p.29.
12. *Droit Commercial*, 9th ed., Dalloz, Paris, 1990 at s.582, p. 769.
13. See Robine, p. 10 for examples.
14. Cass. com. 13 March 1985.
15. Nancy, 20 February 1987.
16. Paris, 12 April 1983.
17. Cass. com. 15 July 1987 and other cases cited by Robine, pp. 34 and 35.
18. 3e Chambre de la cour de Paris, 28 January 1986.
19. Robine p. 44 and other cases cited there which confirm that the clause will be upheld provided that it was established in writing at the latest at the time of delivery – usually by being written on invoices.
20. This is the procedure established under the law of 25 January 1985 available to any business enterprise (merchant, craftsman or company) unable to pay its debts, which is intended to try to find a means to keep the business alive rather than going straight into bankruptcy or judicial administration. The procedure is under the supervision of the court and may lead either to the continuation of the business perhaps in a reconstructed form, its transfer to others or, if no means can be found for it to survive, then its *liquidation judiciaire*. See further Houin and Pedamont s.386.
21. Dismountable elements in a building (Versailles, 4 December 1985) and heaters and refrigerators in caravans (Orleans, 17 February 1988). Equally tyres mounted on wheels but still in the purchaser's factory yard still existed *en nature* (Cass. com. 18 July 1989, Bull. civ. IV no. 228 at p. 152). However, multi-bracket street lighting fittings, *candelabres*, which had been mounted and installed in place were as a result no longer *en nature*. Paris 3e chambre 26 July 1984.
22. Cass. com. 19 June 1985.
23. Cass. com. 17 May 1988.
24. There may be one difference which could be of some importance. In the decisions referred to above relating to material or equipment under a contract for the sale of goods which had been incorporated into a building but could be removed or dismounted without disturbing the fabric of the building, French law has generally accepted the validity of a reservation of title clause. Under English law, however, it is not clear that a court would allow a reservation of title clause to apply when goods had actually been incorporated into a building although it does not appear that the question has been answered in terms of a caravan – see Atiyah pp. 304 and 305.
25. Cass. civ. 8 January 1991, Bull.civ.I, no.9 and see Rev. trim. Droit com. 44(4) Oct.–Dec. 1991.
26. Cass. com. 9 January 1990 Bull. civ. IV, no.8 and see Rev. trim. Droit com. 43(3) July–Sept. 1990 at pp. 454 and 455.
27. Cass. com. 5 July 1988 quoted Robine p.113.
28. Cass. com. 23 October 1985 and other cases cited Robine pp. 116–119.

29. This is a form of running account between two enterprises in which debts and credits are set off against each other in a single account.
30. See the article by Von Mehren entitled 'The Battle of Forms' in the *American Journal of Comparative Law*, Vol.38 at p. 294.
31. Section 2 (1) of the Factors Act 1889.
32. Section 8 of the Factors Act 1889. There is some debate as to whether or not the second purchase must obtain actual delivery of the goods in order to obtain a good title – see for details Atiyah pp. 373 and 374.
33. Section 9 of the Factors Act 1889.
34. *Dawber Williamson Roofing Ltd* v. *Humberside CC* (1979) 14 Build. LR 70. The position is usually complicated by express contractual provisions but these are only likely to be effective as between the parties to a particular contract or sub-contract. See Keating pp. 526, 541 and 755 in relation to JCT 80 and form NSC/4.
35. *National Employers Mutual General Insurance Ltd* v. *Jones* [1988] 2 WLR 952.
36. At p. 39.
37. *La Vente* p. 340.
38. Cass. civ. 13 January 1965 Bull. civ. I no. 35.
39. Req. 2 March 1888 – see also Malaurie and Aynes *Droit civil*, Les Biens Éditions Cujas, Paris 1992 at p. 162.
40. *Institutes*, Book II, Title VI.
41. Brissaud *History of French Private Law*, Rothman, Reprints 1968, New York at p.246 et seq.
42. Cass. civ. 1 March 1988, Bull, civ. 1, no. 59.
43. Cass. civ. 11 February 1931, D.P.1931 1.129.
44. See the article by Harding and Rowell in the *ICLQ*, Vol.26, p. 354 and their conclusions on p. 380.
45. Huebner *History of Germanic Private Law*, Rothmans, Reprints, New York, 1968, p. 409 et seq.
46. Example given by Cohn, Vol.1, p. 183.

19 The contract and third parties: liabilities in contract and tort

This chapter deals with commercial situations in which there is a factual chain of contracts and the ultimate user of the works or product concerned suffers loss as a result of work carried out defectively by someone other than the person with whom he is in contract. While normally he will have a remedy against his co-contractant under the terms of their contract, either that remedy may be limited by those contract terms or his co-contractant may not have the financial resources with which to compensate for such loss. Examples of where this problem arises are between:

1. *Employer, main contractor and sub-contractor/supplier.* Work is carried out defectively by the sub-contractor or supplier but by the time such defect manifests itself the main contractor is in liquidation.
2. *Purchaser, seller and contractor/supplier.* Works or goods are constructed/ manufactured by the contractor/supplier for the seller who then resells or leases them to the purchaser. The works/goods are defective but the purchaser is unable to recover the loss which he suffers from the seller either because of his insolvency or the terms of the contract.
3. *Shipper/consignee, carrier and stevedores.* Goods are shipped and the bill of lading contains clauses limiting the carrier's and the stevedores' liability. Goods are damaged by the fault of the stevedores who were not a party to the bill of lading.

In each case the questions to be answered are:

(a) Are the rights and obligations of each party restricted to those which arise under their own contract?
(b) If they are not so restricted then under what circumstances can a party be held liable to, or entitled to enforce a claim against someone other than his co-contractant?
(c) Does any such liability or obligation arise in contract or tort and what consequences follow from this?
(d) Can an exemption clause in a contract provide a benefit to a person not a party to that contract? Alternatively can a third party to that contract set up against one of the parties an exemption clause contained in his own contract with another person?

ENGLISH LAW

The starting point for English law is the doctrine of privity of contract. According to that doctrine, as a general rule a contract cannot impose obligations on, or give rights to, anyone other than the contracting parties. In contract therefore the basic answer to the first question is 'Yes, with limited exceptions'.[1]

If in answer to questions (b) and (c) there is to be a right by the party who has suffered loss to claim against a third party to the contract, then that right can arise generally only in tort. In example 1 above the sub-contractor's liability, if any, to the employer could not be based upon the breach of his contract with the main contractor, but only upon the breach of a duty of care owed by him to the employer.

REQUIREMENTS FOR A RIGHT OF ACTION IN TORT

In order for a right of action to exist in tort the following conditions must be satisfied:

1. The third party, in the examples either the sub-contractor or the supplier, must be shown to have had a relationship of sufficient proximity to the employer or to the subsequent purchaser to show that he owed him a duty of care.
2. What is a sufficient degree of proximity is closely related to the nature of the loss which has been suffered. If the loss is pure economic loss, which is only exceptionally recoverable in tort, then there must have been a special relationship between those involved. The person suffering the loss must show that he was relying on the other to have exercised reasonable care in the making of statements/ giving of advice for which he possessed a particular skill, and the other must have known that such was the case and that the reliance was being placed on him. The relationship between the two must have been akin to that of contract.[2]
3. If the damages being claimed are for physical injury, or for damage to property other than that which is the product of the negligence, which are the normal damages recoverable in tort under the rule in *Donoghue* v. *Stevenson*, then it is sufficient if the person injured or whose other property suffered damage was someone whom the manufacturer, supplier or sub-contractor ought reasonably to have foreseen as being likely to suffer such damage, if there were a latent defect in his work.[3]

   Additionally, where it is a matter of physical damage to property, the person claiming such damage must have been the owner of the goods or works at the time when the damage occurred or at least had the possessory title to them.[4]
4. There must have been a breach of such duty of care which it was reasonable to foresee would result in damage, and the damages for which the claim is being made were themselves the reasonably foreseeable result of such breach.[5]

The most important distinction for our purposes in the above is between a defect in the work or product itself and damage to other property. If the work or product is simply defective then the loss which the person acquiring it suffers is normally only pure economic loss. The item is simply worth less and the acquirer must bear the costs of repair.[6] These damages are recoverable only from the other party to the contract. Only exceptionally will a latent defect in the works or product cause injury to persons or damage to other property of the acquirer which will justify a claim in tort.

In answer therefore to the third question (c), since the liability of a third party (sub-contractor or supplier) either to the employer or to the subsequent purchaser can arise, with limited exceptions only in tort, and since such liability is restricted in the manner set out above, the practical effect is that the third party has generally no liability to the employer or subsequent purchaser for defective work. The only way in which such liability can be created is for the third party to enter into a separate contract – a so-called 'collateral warranty' – for the benefit of the employer or for the rights of the employer against the contractor to be assigned to the subsequent purchaser.[7]

Essentially English law as regards defects in the execution of work or the supply of goods proceeds on the basis of the chain of contractual liability and assumes that each party in the chain not only has the potential right to sue his contractual partner but also the practical ability to recover from that partner the damages which are due to him. It is only very exceptionally that the possibility will exist for the remedy in tort to 'leap-frog' the chain and even then the 'contractual setting' may act either to prevent the tortious duty existing in the first place, or to bar the exercise of the tortious remedy.[8]

That brings us to the fourth question (d): can an exemption clause provide a benefit to a person not a party to the contract? There are two possible situations which need to be distinguished.

First, in the contract between the purchaser (A) and the main contractor (B) there is a clause which purports to provide any sub-contractor (C) with the same protection as is given to (B) against any claim made by (A) for damages arising out of defective work. For a typical example see the Standard Conditions MF/1 of the Electrical and Mechanical Engineers, clause 36.9.

Second, in the contract between the main contractor (B) and the sub-contractor (C) there is a clause which purports to provide sub-contractor (C) with exemption from liability for damages arising out of defective work and an equivalent clause is *not* contained in the main contract between (B) and the purchaser (A). This situation can easily arise if the main contract is on either of the standard building or civil engineering forms (JCT 80 or ICE) and the sub-contract for electrical or mechanical works is under MF/1.

For the purpose of this discussion it will be assumed that the clause in MF/1 would be held to be reasonable under the Unfair Contract Terms Act 1977 (see below, pp. 295–297). It will also be assumed that the damage is physical damage to other property of the purchaser and therefore the possibility exists of a claim by the purchaser in tort against the sub-contractor.

In the first example it has been held on several occasions that despite the privity of contract rule the sub-contractor is protected by a term in the main contract under which a particular risk is accepted by the purchaser.[9]

The view is that the purchaser, by reason of having agreed to the clause, has done so

270

for the benefit of all concerned in the project whether they are in contract with himself or not. It has been said that 'the contractual setting defines the area of risk which the [purchaser] chose to accept' and therefore the extent of the duty of care owed by the sub-contractor.[10] Although the decisions have been criticized academically, they seem to be justified commercially.[11] It is difficult to understand why a purchaser who has entered knowingly into a contract containing such a clause, which is known also to the sub-contractors and upon which they can assess their risks and insure accordingly, should later be allowed to act contrary to what any reasonable person would assume were his intentions those which he has publicly announced.

In the second example it would appear that an exclusion clause contained in the sub-contract could only bind the purchaser if he had expressly or implicitly consented to the clause.[12] So also, where under a contract of carriage of goods by sea the liability of the carrier is limited by the Hague-Visby rules, it has been held that such limitation cannot be set up by the carrier against the purchaser of the goods in an action brought against him in tort. However, that having been decided, rough justice was then done by denying the purchaser any right of action in tort at all on the grounds that he did not have any legal ownership or possessory title to the goods at the time when the damage occurred.[13] Had he in fact had title to the goods by reason of consignment or endorsement of the bill of lading, then he could have exercised in contract under s.1 of the Bills of Lading 1855 the same rights against the carrier as those which he would have possessed had the contract of carriage been made between the carrier and himself.

Situation 3 (above, p. 268) sets out a more typical case which arises under contracts for the carriage of goods by sea. The issue is whether or not the stevedores can set up against the consignee the limitation of liability provisions of the bill of lading. It has been considered by the courts on a number of occasions.

The general principle which has been established is that the stevedores will be entitled to set up such provisions if the terms of the contract of carriage are drawn sufficiently broadly so that they show clearly the intention to confer such benefit on the stevedores or other agents of the carrier. The legal basis for extending the protection given by the contract to the carrier has been doubted but its commercial expediency is obvious in an industry in which the use of such clauses is established practice.[14]

CONCLUSIONS

It is clear that the attempt of English law to maintain, and now even to strengthen, the contract/tort dichotomy is a failure. The chain of liability theory simply does not work in practice. It is agreed as unsatisfactory to allow it to be leap-frogged by actions in tort which pay little attention to the defaulting party's contractual rights and liabilities. It is equally unsatisfactory that the unfortunate purchaser, if he is to have any remedy other than against his co-contractant, must enter into a multitude of collateral warranties.

These problems are not peculiar to English law. Each legal system here under review has to face the situation of how to handle liabilities where there are triangular relationships. But it is agreed with Markesinis both that generally these are better handled in contract than in tort and that the rigid doctrine of privity of contract in English law has prevented the development of flexible contractual remedies.[15] The article by Markesinis was of course written before the decision in Murphy and the virtual extinction of Junior Books which have put the development of the law of tort in the area of economic loss into reverse but without any off-setting developments in contract. I suggest that it is now even more necessary to examine what lessons can be learned from the civil law systems of France and Germany.

FRENCH LAW

From a literal reading of Arts. 1165 and 1121 of the *Code Civil* it would appear that French law would be largely the same as English:

> Agreements only take effect as between the contracting parties; they do not impose any burdens on third parties and they only benefit them in the case foreseen by Art. 1121. (Art. 1165)
>
> One may also in the same way stipulate for the benefit of a third party when such is the condition of a stipulation that one makes for oneself or of a gift which one makes for another. The person who has made that stipulation may not revoke it if the third party has declared that he wishes to benefit from it. (Art. 1121)

Article 1165 establishes what is known as the principle of the 'relativity of agreements' –the nearest equivalent in French law to the English doctrine of privity of contract. However, unlike English law, the French courts since as long ago as 1820[16] have consistently maintained that a sub-purchaser of goods can exercise a right in contract against not only his own vendor but also against the original manufacturer and indeed any intermediate party, e.g. importer or wholesaler. Each party is liable *in solidum* (see above, p. 197) with all others provided that the defect in the goods existed at the time of the sale in question.

The right does not exist just in respect of *vices cachés* but also for a failure of the goods to comply with the purpose for which they were intended *according to the terms of the first sale*.[17]

The right has been clearly established by the *Cour de cassation* as being only contractual and therefore in accordance with the rule of *non-cumul*[18] there is no right to proceed in tort if an action in contract is not available because it is outwith the period of prescription.

> The action direct which the sub-purchaser has against the manufacturer or intermediate seller for breach of the guaranty against 'vice caché' affecting the thing sold from the time of its manufacture is necessarily contractual and it is therefore the responsibility of the 'juges de fond' (court of first instance) to investigate, as they were asked to do, if the proceedings had been commenced within the 'bref délai' [see above, p. 173] established by law.[19]

It will be remembered (see above, pp. 195–196) that the same reasoning has been applied to cases in which the *maître de l'ouvrage* has sought to bring an action direct against a supplier of materials whether for *vice caché* or non-conformity.

The basis of the action direct by the ultimate purchaser would appear to be that, as successor in title to his vendor (*l'ayant cause à titre particulier*) of the goods purchased he is entitled to the benefit of the rights of action which are accessory to the goods.[20] Although this explanation has been criticized no other seems to be possible following the decision of the Assemblée Plénière of the *Cour de cassation* on 12 July 1991 referred to earlier (see above, p. 196) that the action by the *maître de l'ouvrage* against a sub-contractor was delictual.

Considering the questions referred to on p. 268 it would seem therefore that a different answer must be given in the case of a vendor of goods and a sub-contractor who performs work.

Against a vendor of goods a subsequent purchaser may exercise *in contract* all the rights which belonged to the original purchaser. This applies not just to contracts for sale but also to *contrats d'entreprise*, so that such rights can be exercised by the *maître de l'ouvrage* or any subsequent purchaser of the property against the original manufacturer or any intermediate vendor again *in contract*.[21]

On the other hand, when it is a matter of defective work by a sub-contractor, it would follow from the latest decision of the Assemblée Plénière (see above, p. 196) that the *maître de l'ouvrage*, or it is assumed any subsequent purchaser, can only act against the sub-contractor in delict. This accords with earlier decisions of the Third Chamber of the *Cour de cassation*. Previously the first *chambre* had held that

> where a debtor had sub-contracted a contractual obligation to another the creditor could exercise against that other an action necessarily contractual within the double limits on his own rights and the extent of the obligations of the other under his contract with the debtor.[22]

There must now be serious doubt as to the validity of this line of reasoning.

The effect of the decision of the Assemblée Plénière is that while the *maître de l'ouvrage* or subsequent purchaser benefits from the longer period of prescription, ten years from the damage becoming apparent and not the period of the *garantie décennale* (ten years from *réception*), it also means that he, or the subsequent purchaser, must prove fault on the part of the sub-contractor. Obviously the longer the period between the execution of the work and the defect becoming apparent, the more likely it is that the 'defect' is due to mis-use or lack of maintenance and the more difficult therefore the proving of fault becomes.

The jurisprudence is too recent for us to be certain as to how it will develop but at the moment it seems that it is only the rights of the first purchaser of goods which are transmitted in contract. The wider doctrine of the transmission of contractual remedies within a 'group of contracts', developed by the First Chamber of the *Cour de cassation* has been condemned.

The position is also unclear as regards actions by the purchaser under the *droit commun* against either the architect or the contractor employed by the vendor. In principle it would appear that such an action should be contractual. However there is a ruling of the Third Chamber of the *Cour de cassation* which quashed a decision of the cour d'appel allowing an action in contract under the *droit commun* by the purchaser against the architect with whom his vendor had contracted, on the grounds that the cour d'appel had not established any contractual link between the two.[23]

The different approaches by the First and Third Chambers of the *Cour de cassation*, with the First Chamber favouring a contractual solution to the problem of third party relationships in the context of a series of contracts, and the Third Chamber a delictual one, is a continuing reproach to French law.

OTHER THIRD PARTIES

It is only the subsequent purchaser of the property who can ever exercise a direct contractual right against the architect, contractor or supplier. A lessee of the property is treated strictly as a third party to the contract and his rights are delictual. However since French law does not distinguish in a delictual action between economic loss and other losses, a lessee of a holiday village who was successful in establishing that the architect was at fault in the design of the buildings was entitled to recover all losses which he had suffered.[24]

The same principle applies to actions for *vice caché* or non-conformity in the sale of movables. A true third party to the contract can only sue in delict. So when a television set exploded causing a fire and resulting in injury to third parties to the contract who were present in the room at the time, it was held that their remedy against the supplier could only be delictual and depended on proof of fault.[25]

LIMITATION AND EXCLUSION CLAUSES

The answer to the question of the possible effectiveness of a clause limiting or excluding liability, contained within a contract to which the ultimate purchaser is not a party, depends upon whether the action is brought in contract or delict.

If the action must be brought in contract then in accordance with the decisions by the *Cour de cassation* and the Assemblée Plénière in 1986 (see above, pp. 195–196 and notes 53 and 54), it is open to the defendant to set up as a defence, any defences which would be available to the seller/contractor under the terms of the initial contract of purchase/construction. This would apply to an action brought by a subsequent purchaser either of movables or immovables or to an action by the *maître de l'ouvrage* against a supplier of materials to a sub-contractor for incorporation into the works.

Therefore in all these instances a clause limitative of the supplier's or contractor's responsibilities which was valid in the initial contract, or the failure by the ultimate purchaser to act within the *bref délai* under Art. 1648 of the code if the action is one for *vice caché*, could be set up by the supplier/contractor as a defence. Whether or not the defence would be successful would depend on the factors discussed earlier (see above, pp. 172–175 and Chapter 14).

However, following the latest decision of the Assemblée Plénière it would seem that an action by the *maître de l'ouvrage* or a subsequent purchaser against a sub-contractor must be delictual. So also it appears (see above, p. 274) must an action by a subsequent purchaser against the architect employed by the vendor if the action was brought under the *droit commun*.

If the action must be delictual then the party against whom the action is brought cannot take advantage of any clauses in his own contract limiting or excluding his liabilities or of any defence which would be open to the co-contractant of the creditor. Primarily this is because the terms of the contract apply only as between the parties. If, however, exceptionally the action is between the original parties to the contract, but arises in delict, then again the debtor cannot avail himself of any contractual terms limiting or excluding his responsibility, since Arts. 1382 and 1383 of the *Code Civil* are regarded as *ordre public* and cannot be derogated from by the terms of a contract where there is a proven fault.[26]

In summary, therefore, the suggested answers to the questions raised earlier are:

(a) No. A party can be held liable to a third party.
(b) The liability of a supplier in contract may extend up the chain from his immediate purchaser to subsequent purchasers. Similarly the liability of a contractor may extend in contract to subsequent purchasers of the property which he has constructed. In principle the extent of the rights of the subsequent purchaser to act against the original vendor/contractor will depend upon the extent of the rights possessed by the person with whom such vendor/contractor was originally in contract. The rights are accessory to the thing supplied or constructed.

The odd person out appears to be the sub-contractor who can only be sued in contract by the main contractor with whom he was in contract and by other parties only in delict. For that reason in an action brought by the *maître de l'ouvrage* or a subsequent purchaser, the sub-contractor cannot take advantage of any contractual clause limiting or excluding his responsibility whether in his own contract with the main contractor or in the latter's contract with the *maître de l'ouvrage*. Nor indeed can he benefit from any defence which would be open to him or the main contractor were the action in contract, e.g. expiry of the period of the *garantie décennale*.

(c) Other than that of the sub-contractor, the liability of the remainder of those involved, the original vendor/manufacturer or the main contractor to subsequent purchasers, or the original vendor/manufacturer to the *maître de l'ouvrage*, lies in contract. This means that such vendor or main contractor can avail himself of any defence which was open to him under the terms of his original contract. The sub-contractor, however, who can only be sued by a third party in delict, cannot avail himself of any defence based either upon the terms of his sub-contract or which would have been open to him had his liability been in contract.

(d) If the action is brought in contract then the party sued can set up against the third party the benefit of any exemption clause contained within his own contract and which would be valid against his co-contractant. If however the action must be brought in delict then the debtor cannot avail himself of any clause excluding or limiting his responsibility contained in his contract with the intermediate party, nor is the creditor restricted in his action by the terms of his contract with any intermediate party assuming that the action is brought on the basis of a proven fault.

CONCLUSION

The passing to the purchaser as an accessory to the thing sold of the rights which the vendor has as against his own vendor or anyone earlier in the chain is clearly from the purchaser's viewpoint a marked improvement to the rights which he possesses under English law. It would be a dramatic change for English law to adopt a similar rule but one which in the author's view is long overdue. Why English lawyers should apparently rejoice in there being no transmittable warranty in English law is difficult to understand.[27]

As to whether the warranty should be limited to goods sold or should extend to work performed by sub-contractors, it is suggested that the difference would, in English law, be wholly artificial and lead to fine distinctions of no merit. It should therefore apply to suppliers and sub-contractors alike.

La stipulation pour autrui

Having considered how the French courts have turned Art. 1165 virtually on its head through the limited way in which they have interpreted the expression *le tiers* (third party), it is time to look at Art. 1121, in which the departure from the probable intentions of the authors of the code has been no less dramatic.

The draftsmen of the *Code Civil* followed the Roman rules that the principles from which one starts are *alteri stipulari nemo potest* and *per extraneam personam nobis adquiri non posse*, so that even as between the parties the promise in favour of a third party was generally unenforceable.

Exceptions under Roman law

To these principles Roman law at the time of Justinian allowed certain limited exceptions. First, the stipulator could enforce the promise where exceptionally he had himself a pecuniary interest in its being performed. A well known example is that of a tutor who handed over the management of his ward to his co-tutor. He required from the latter a stipulation that he would properly administer the ward's property which was therefore a contract for the benefit of a third party. However, since the tutor had a pecuniary interest in the co-tutor carrying out the administration properly, as he still retained a liability for this towards the ward, it was considered that this interest validated the contract and would allow him to enforce the stipulation against the co-tutor.

If the stipulator had no pecuniary interest then it was possible to create one by adding to the stipulation a provision that should the promisor not carry out his promise towards the third party beneficiary, then the promisor would pay the stipulator a certain sum by way of penalty. This was again accepted as valid. But only the stipulator and not the third party beneficiary could enforce the contract.

The other exception allowed under Roman law was the *donato sub modo*. This was a donation under which there was imposed on the donee an obligation in favour of the third party beneficiary as a condition of the donation. In this instance the third party beneficiary could enforce the contract against the promisor.

Exceptions allowed under Art. 1121 – *Condition d'une donation l'on fait à un autre*

This is the *donato sub modo* of Roman law and the second possibility that French law allows under Art. 1121 as an exception to the principle of relative effect. It follows, with some expansion in detail, the Roman rule as stated above, but this has caused no difficulty, and the issue will not be discussed further.

Condition d'une stipulation que l'on fait pour soi-même

This, the first possible exception allowed under Art. 1121 to the principle of relative effect, raises difficulties of interpretation, but has provided French law with the basis on which to establish a wide right of action for third party beneficiaries.

It will be recalled that under Roman law the promise by P (*le promettant*) to S (*le stipulant*) to do something for the benefit of T (*le tiers*) was generally not enforceable. If, as we have seen above, S exceptionally had an interest in the performance of the stipulation, or had created one by the addition of a penalty clause, then the contract was enforceable only by S.

Further, neither Roman law nor the *ancien droit* in France differentiated as between the *stipulation pour autrui* and the obligation owed to S, as to which was principal and which was accessory. Even if the interest of S was accessory, provided that S did have a pecuniary interest, the contract was valid.

However the strict interpretation of Art. 1121 is that for the contract to be valid the obligation owed by P to S, which constitutes S's interest, must be the principal obligation and that of the third party beneficiary only accessory.

But this interpretation was not acceptable to the jurisprudence. As a result of a series of cases starting from the middle of the last century and primarily dealing initially with the problems of life assurance, the courts have not only reverted to the terms of Roman law and of the *ancien droit*, but have gone much further and in so doing have completely reversed the original meaning of Art. 1121 to the extent that what was once perceived as being the exception has become the rule.[28]

The present position may be summarized as follows:

1. The *stipulation pour autrui* is valid and enforceable provided only that S had an interest in the stipulation.
2. The interest does not have to be pecuniary but need only be moral.
3. There does not even have to be a *stipulation* for the benefit of S himself.
4. The *stipulation* is enforceable against P by the third party beneficiary as well as by S.
5. The *stipulation pour autrui* may be tacit or, as we would say in an English contract,

277

be 'implied', and this implicit presumption has been given a wide interpretation. So a traveller on a train who was killed in an accident has been held to have impliedly stipulated for the benefit of his widow and children so that they could recover damages directly in contract from the railway company who were under an *obligation de résultat* to carry the traveller safely to his destination.[29]

6. Since the *stipulation pour autrui* is established by the contract entered into between S and P, the third party beneficiary takes his benefit subject to any defence open to P as against S, in particular any clause limitative of P's responsibility.

7. The third party beneficiary must evidence the acceptance of the *stipulation* in order for it to become effective. He may do this simply by requiring it to be implemented.

   However, in two cases it has been decided that the close relatives of the victim could refuse to accept the benefit of a tacit *stipulation* and instead bring their action in delict under Art. 1384 para. 1 of the *Code Civil* and so avoid the application of a clause of non-responsibility which at that time would have been considered valid had the action been brought in contract.[30]

8. Until the third party beneficiary has evidenced his intention to accept the *stipulation* it may be revoked by S. Nevertheless from the time that it is made, the *stipulation* never forms part of the *patrimoine* of S and is a right enjoyed by the beneficiary against P. The *stipulation* passes directly from the *patrimoine* of P into that of the beneficiary and never through that of S. The effect is that the benefit is never available for the creditors of S except in the event of fraud.

Practical effects

The practical effect of the wide scope which has been given by the jurisprudence to the *stipulation pour autrui* is that in many instances an action which would have to be brought under English law in tort can be brought in French law in contract. For example in cases similar to those of *Smith* v. *Bush and Harris*, where the surveyor carried out a valuation for the mortgagee and was held, in the circumstances of a domestic sale at the lower end of the property market, to owe a duty of care in tort to the prospective purchaser to exercise reasonable skill and care, it is considered that a French court would find a *stipulation pour autrui* and hold that the purchaser could act directly against the surveyor in contract. This view is based on such decisions as that in which the contract between an expert in philately and the seller of a stamp was held to contain a *stipulation pour autrui* in favour of the purchaser.[31]

The benefit to the plaintiff of being able to proceed in contract is most obvious when the contractual rights of S, which the third party beneficiary can exercise, are *obligations de résultat* since there is then no need for T to prove any fault on the part of P and P can only escape liability by proving *cause étrangère*. The well known case in which a woman who contracted syphilis after a blood transfusion illustrates the point. The blood was supplied, at the request of the hospital treating the woman, by the National Blood Transfusion Centre who selected as a donor a girl whose blood was infected with the disease. No fault on the part of the Centre was ever established and the claim as originally formulated in delict must therefore have failed. However the

Cour de cassation reformulated the claim in contract and held that the contract between the hospital and the National Blood Transfusion Centre contained a *stipulation pour autrui* in favour of the sick woman guaranteeing the purity of the blood to be supplied by them and that no proof had been given by the National Centre, according to Art. 1147 of the *Code Civil*, of *cause étrangère*.[32]

GERMAN LAW

In German law the problem of the rights of third parties to a contract is solved partially in contract and partially in tort. The contract solution was developed primarily in order to deal with limitations in the law of tort relating to the recovery of pure economic loss and to the liability of the employer for the acts of his employees which are discussed below. However, there is no doubt that contract does provide a neater answer than tort in those cases where the third party is in effect stepping into the shoes of the contractual debtor. Because contract plays an important role in third party situations and must always be considered as providing a possible basis of action, it is with contract that we begin our review.

CONTRACTUAL REMEDIES – HISTORICAL BACKGROUND

The issue of contracts for the benefit of third parties provides another illustration of where contemporary German law has rejected the rules derived from Roman law and reverted with some additions to the older Germanic law.

Under that law a third party beneficiary of a contract had a direct right of action derived from the contract itself against the promisor. Then came the reception of Roman law and the replacement of the old rules by the very limited exceptions referred to earlier (see above, p. 15). But the Roman rules were incompatible with the already well established practices of merchants in respect of negotiable instruments across the whole of Western Europe and it was the needs of commerce which ultimately prevailed in commercial law.[33]

Of major importance in the development of the civil law was the rejection of the Roman rules by Grotius but only on the basis that the third party for whose benefit the promise had been made had signified his acceptance. It was in this form that the rule passed into the earlier codes of Bavaria, Prussia and Saxony, but their requirements of acceptance (the Saxon Code), or even of the joinder in the contract with the consent of the contracting parties (Prussian *Allgemeines Landrecht*), quickly proved too restrictive. Fictions had to be resorted to by the courts to do justice in particular cases.

Finally, when the *BGB* was formulated, the opportunity was taken of removing all such limitations and returning to the simplicity of the older law. Paragraph 1 of s.328 of the *BGB* simply states: 'A contract may stipulate performance for the benefit of a third party, so that the third party acquires the right directly to demand performance'.

The return here to the old Germanic law is clear; the right of the third party beneficiary is directly against the promisor as a result of the original contract. It is not necessary for the contract expressly to confer the right on the third party. Paragraph 2 of s.328 gives discretion to the court to deduce the existence of the right 'from the circumstances and especially the purpose of the contract'. This discretionary power has been used quite widely by the German courts but it must be noted that the right given by s.328 is a right to have the contract itself performed, for example a contract between a tour operator and an airport hotel in favour of the traveller and which he could therefore enforce.[34]

Although the beneficiary is enforcing his own right directly against the promisor, the latter can still set up against him any defence arising from the contract which it would have been open to him to use in an action brought by the other contracting party (s.334 of the *BGB*). But it is only a defence arising out of the contract, including those that the contract was voidable, which can be set up by the promisor and not one arising out of other relationships between himself and the stipulator, e.g. a right of set-off (BGH MDR 61,481).

THE CHOICE OF CONTRACTUAL RATHER THAN TORTIOUS REMEDIES

In handling cases which lie at the borderline between contract and tort the German courts have had to face up to two restrictions on the plaintiff's ability to succeed in a claim in tort. First a claim in tort does not lie for the recovery of 'pure' economic loss, that is economic loss which does not arise directly out of physical damage to the plaintiff's property or injury to his person or other absolute rights unless the damage is done wilfully (Arts. 823(1) and 826 of the *BGB*).

Second under Art. 831(1) of the *BGB* an employer is not strictly liable for the damage caused by an employee in the course of his employment. He can escape liability if he can show that he has been careful in the selection, instruction, training and supervision of his staff and supplied them with the correct equipment or that the damage would have arisen even if he had shown such care. While the German courts have done their best to mitigate the effects of this outdated early nineteenth century concept the risk nevertheless remains that the employer can discharge the burden of proof placed on him.[35]

In both these instances a claim which could be made in contract would have advantages. First, there is no restriction in contract on the right to recover damages for economic loss. Second, under Art. 278 of the *BGB* a debtor is responsible for the faults of persons he employs in performing his obligations to the same extent as he is responsible for his own faults, i.e. his liability is strict. There may of course be some disadvantages as we have seen already in relation to defects in goods sold where the limitation period under Art. 477(1) of the *BGB* is only six months whereas that for torts is three years from the time when the injured party had knowledge of the injury and of the identity of the person responsible (Art. 852(1), *BGB* – see above, pp. 213–214).

There are two doctrines which have been developed by the courts so as to bring within the scope of contract matters which in English law, because of the twin doctrines of consideration and privity of contract, could only be dealt with in tort. They are *Drittenschadensliquidation* (doctrine of transferred loss) and *der Vertrag mit Schutzwirkung für Dritte* (contract for protective effects for third parties).

Drittenschadensliquidation

The doctrine of 'transferred loss' deals with the issue which arises when the person who has the right to sue has no interest in doing so, while the person who is interested, because he is the one suffering the loss, has no right of action. The classic example of this is where the seller has parted with the goods to the carrier and been paid for them, the purchaser has the risk in the goods but not the title to them and the goods have been damaged by the negligence of the carrier. The seller, having been paid in full, has no interest in the matter, while the purchaser having no title to the goods, cannot sue under English law in negligence. Equally he cannot of course sue the carrier in contract because there is no privity of contract between them and no consideration has passed.[36]

The position is clearly unsatisfactory and yet as English law stands is logically in accordance with established doctrine.

Under German law, however, on the above facts there would be a right of action by the purchaser against the carrier in contract under the principle of 'transferred loss'. Since the right which the purchaser would be entitled to exercise would be that of the seller, the carrier would have open to him all defences or limitations of liability which he could exercise against the seller. There would therefore be no question of the carrier being under any greater liability than that which he bargained for at the time of entering into his contract.[37]

Vertrag mit Schutzwirkung für Dritte

Originally this concept was derived from Art. 328 but later became a separate remedy when the distinction was clearly recognized between the entitlement of a third party to demand fulfilment of the contract, and the right of a third party to be protected against the failure of a contracting party to perform his secondary obligations. This latter right is then not based directly on any provision of the *BGB* but is judge-made law under which 'the contract according to its purpose and the requirements of good faith demands the extension of the sphere of the duty of care and protection owed by one contracting party to another, to the third person plaintiff.[38]

Initially this remedy was applied only to cases where a person had suffered physical injury or damage to property, arising out of the defective performance of a contract to which they were not a party and with which they had no real relationship. There are numerous examples of this. In general under English law these cases would all be brought without difficulty in tort, at least since the passing of the Defective Premises Act 1972.

However in 1965 the remedy was applied to a case involving pure economic loss where a lawyer failed to make a will as he had been repeatedly instructed to do, as a result of which his client died intestate. This meant that the intended beneficiary under the will, his daughter, received only half his estate instead of the whole of it. She recovered the other half in an action against the dilatory lawyer on the grounds of breach of a contract (between her deceased father and the lawyer), with protective effect for third parties, i.e. herself.[39]

Subsequently the remedy has been utilized in a variety of cases involving economic loss such as the giving of negligent advice by a bank, supply of information by an expert valuer and a claim for loss of earnings. However the courts have been wary of extending too far the range of persons covered by the umbrella of the contractual remedy.

Limits on the application of contracts with protective effects for third parties

The courts, in defining the conditions for the establishment of such a contractual remedy, have sought to place limits on the circumstances in which a third party plaintiff can recover especially for economic loss. 'Liability', it has been said, 'is on principle bound up with the bonds which bind the debtor to the creditor otherwise the debtor can no longer assess the risks he is taking in undertaking the contract'.[40] Three conditions appear necessary to be satisfied although, as Markesinis points out, the case-law is not wholly consistent and the boundaries for the action appear to be continually widening.[41]

First, the third party plaintiff and the contractual debtor must share an interest in the performance of the contract so that any failure in performance by the debtor will affect the third party in the same sort of way as the contractual creditor.

Second, there must generally be a relationship between the contractual creditor and the third party such that the creditor shares in the responsibility for the welfare or protection of the third party. It is this which brings the third party within the scope of the bond which binds the contracting parties and makes it equitable for the debtor to be liable to the third party. As a general rule it has been said that such a relationship will not normally exist in a contract between the contractual creditor and the third party for the sale of goods or the performance of work.[42]

The debtor must have been aware of the above two considerations at the time of contract, or at least should have been aware had he thought about it, i.e. the test is objective. So a person effecting a repair in a house will be assumed to have known that the customer intended that his relatives living in the house would be protected against danger in the same manner as himself and would have the same rights as he had for compensation if they were injured through the work being performed defectively. It does not appear to matter that the third party beneficiary was not specifically identified at the time of the contract, provided that objectively he was ascertainable.

Application of the contract with protective effects for third parties in employer, main contractor and sub-contractor situations

In both English and German law it is now clear that the loss suffered by an employer in respect of remedying defective work carried out by a sub-contractor is economic loss

THE CONTRACT AND THIRD PARTIES

and therefore no claim for damages in respect of such loss can be made by the employer against the sub-contractor in tort.[43] Nor equally in English law can there be any claim by the employer against the sub-contractor in contract unless it is made under a separate collateral warranty (see above, pp. 146 and 270).

The question arises as to whether or not a German court would be prepared, in the event say of the main contractor having gone into liquidation, to find a contract with protective effects for third parties as between the main contractor and the sub-contractor, and therefore allow the employer (as the third party beneficiary), to claim against the sub-contractor for defective work. In other words, would a Junior Books type case be decided with the same result in Germany as in England, but in contract rather than tort?

There is no case directly in point, probably because first, as explained earlier (see above, p. 224) nominated sub-contracting is virtually unknown in Germany, and second, claims that a main contractor may have against his sub-contractor for breach of the warranties for performance are often assigned in advance to the employer.

In principle, while it is true that the main contractor may be said to share to some degree in the interests of the employer, it is difficult to see that the relationship between the two could be said to be such that the main contractor had any responsibility for the welfare or protection of the employer. Their relationship is an arms-length contractual one even if the main contractor must perform his contract in good faith (see note 42 above).

Further, in discussing the nature of sub-contracting, the *BGH* has held that the contracts between the main and the sub-contractor and between the employer and the main contractor are quite separate and that the sub-contractor owes his duties only to the main contractor.[44] If that is so, and it seems to be in accord with normal contracting practice, then there is no room for the existence of any implicit duty of care owed by the sub-contractor to the third party (employer).

The only exception to this could be in the kind of case in which an English court would find an implied collateral warranty by the sub-contractor in favour of the employer, e.g. the Shanklin pier case.[45] This is supported by a case in which an express warranty given by a manufacturer to a middleman who resold to the installation contractor, was held to constitute a contract with protective effects for the benefit of the ultimate purchaser who was the end-user of the product.[46]

Accordingly, although it is recognized that Schlechtreim has argued in the opposite way, it is considered that a German court would be unlikely to hold, other than in exceptional circumstances, that a sub-contract was a contract with protective effects for third parties so as to allow an employer to proceed directly in contract against the sub-contractor for defective work.[47]

The remedy in tort

If one party in the chain of transactions cannot establish the existence of a contract with protective effects for his benefit, he may nevertheless have a remedy in tort, e.g. a claim by the ultimate user against the original producer. In order for such a claim to succeed the user must establish that:

1. One of his rights as specified in Art. 823 of the *BGB* has been infringed. The most important of these rights for our purposes is that of 'property'.

It must be noted also that the list does not include economic rights which is why economic loss cannot in general be recovered in tort. There are two primary exceptions to this. The first is that economic loss will generally be recoverable where it follows directly from interference with a property right, e.g. the cost of hiring a substitute item when one's property has been damaged by negligence and more controversially may sometimes be recoverable for the direct violation of the absolute right of an established and operating business enterprise (*Recht am eingerichten und ausgeübten Gewerbetrieb*).

This latter right, which is judge-made law, has been applied restrictively by the courts. In the so-called 'cable cases' a claim for consequential loss of production based on the negligent severing of a power cable to the plaintiff's factory has been consistently refused, although a claim for physical damage has been allowed and with it the loss of profit on the damaged product (*BGH* 41,123 – in this case the loss of power spoilt the eggs in the farm's incubator and recovery was allowed for the value of the eggs and the profit which would have been likely to have been made on them).

It would appear that in order for it to succeed a claim for a breach of the *Recht am eingerichten und ausgebeüten Gewerbetrieb* must arise out of an act which is both closely connected with, and directly affects, the business enterprise as such in its essential characteristics. See *BGHZ* 9 December 1959 NJW 1959,479 and BGH 12 July 1977 NJW 1977, 2078. For English translations see Markesinis pp. 148 and 158.

It is clear from these judgements that they are based on the policy considerations of once having established a right of then keeping its application within strict limits so as to avoid the risk of a wholesale evasion of the limits of Art. 823(1) of the *BGB*.

There is a clear analogy with the English rule established in *Spartan Steel and Alloys Ltd* v. *Martin & Co.* [1973] 1 QB 27, where on essentially the same facts as the German cable cases recovery was allowed for the physical damage to the metal in the furnace caused by the break in electricity supply and the loss of profit on such metal, but not for the wider economic loss resulting from the loss of production. Moreover the reasoning of Lord Denning closely parallels that of the *BGH* even to the reference in the judgements in both countries to there being no contractual liability on the electricity supply authorities as constituting one reason for not allowing a tortious claim against the negligent contractor.

2. The property, the right in which is infringed, is distinct from the defective item itself which is responsible for the damage and which cannot be the subject of an action in tort since it was not damaged by the supplier but was simply always defective. As discussed earlier (see above, pp. 214–215) the German courts, in order to compensate in tort for the short prescription period in the law of sales of six months from delivery, have distinguished between a defective component and an entire piece of equipment of which the component forms part (see above, p. 214) so as to allow a claim in tort for damage to the equipment caused by the defect in the component.

This line of reasoning can however only be applied to a specific defective component where the harm caused to the whole piece of equipment is not substantially identical (*stoffgleich*) with the initial reduction in value of the equipment due to the defective part. The courts refer to the harm being 'an invasion of the purchaser's integrity interest in his property' as opposed to his interest in the equipment being worth what he paid for it, although the criterion for differentiating between them is somewhat elusive to discover.[48] As commented earlier, the distinction is clearly made only for policy reasons (see above, p. 214 and note 18). It is a further requirement, which is easier to understand, that the component must retain its separate identity so that the argument could not be applied to say construction materials.[49]

3. In respect of product liability the producer's conduct has been unlawful. He must have failed in his duties as prescribed by law, e.g. by placing on the market a product which is unsafe for ordinary use. This concept has a very wide definition so that the producer is obliged to seek out potential dangers and guard against them.[50] The producer and seller must also give warning instructions and again this duty is widely interpreted by the courts.

4. The party against whom the claim has been made was at fault. However, in product liability the normal rule as to burden of proof is partially reversed and once the end-user has established that the product is defective and claims that the defect originated during manufacture, i.e. within the sphere of influence of the producer, then the burden of proof shifts to the producer to establish that it was not due to his fault, a burden which is almost impossible to discharge.

Exemption and exclusion clauses

If the claim is brought in tort by an end-user, as a third party to the contract between the producer and the intermediate seller from whom he bought the goods, then no exclusion clause in a contract as between the producer and the seller can affect such a claim. However if the claim is brought in tort by the end-user against the seller (because for example the six-month prescription period in contract has expired), then the seller can set up against the purchaser an exemption clause contained in the conditions of contract, in the same way as he could were the claim to have been brought in contract, provided at least that the exemption clause was worded sufficiently explicitly to show that it covered claims in tort[51] (see further below, pp. 301–306) as to exemption clauses in standard conditions of contract.

ANSWERS TO QUESTIONS AT THE BEGINNING OF THIS CHAPTER (p. 268)

(a) No.

(b) In contract a third party may be able to enforce his rights against the contractual debtor under:

- Art. 328 of the *BGB*,

- the doctrine of contracts with protective effects for third parties.

Additionally, under the doctrine of *Drittenschadenliquidation* there is a right for the contractual creditor to recover damages in contract from the debtor which represent the loss suffered by the third party and under Art. 281 *BGB* the third party may require the assignment to him of this claim.

In product liability a third party may be able to claim against the original producer if one of his protected rights has been violated unlawfully by the producer.

(c) Liability may be in either contract or tort but normally the contractual remedy is not available to an end-user wishing to bring an action against the original contract debtor, i.e. the manufacturer. In general the contractual remedy is to be preferred since it enables the third party to recover damages for pure economic loss, which are not recoverable in tort. Also the contractual debtor is strictly responsible for the faults of persons employed by him, while in tort it is possible for the debtor to escape such liability.

(d) In contract the third party is bound by any clause exempting or limiting liability in the same manner as the contractual debtor. In actions brought in tort the third party is not bound by an exemption clause. However, if the contractual creditor brings the action in tort then he would be bound by the exemption clause assuming it extended to such actions.

COMPARATIVE CONCLUSIONS

Of the three systems examined English law is the least favourable to the rights of third parties. English law, alone of the three systems, denies a third party to a contract the right to an action in contract even when it is clear that the contract was intended to benefit the third party. It is accepted that once one departs from the rigidity of this position then difficult questions will arise as to where to draw the contractual line. When the intention to benefit is to be implied then there may be issues as to who is included within the definition of a beneficiary and the extent of the damages to which he is entitled. But the handling of these problems is a great deal easier in contract than in tort.

Further, English law by its general refusal to breach the privity of contract rule, having closed the tortious gate for economic loss by the decision in *Murphy*, except for the somewhat uncertain loophole provided by *Hedley Byrne*, and its present rigid separation of contract from tort, has raised formidable barriers against any judicial inventiveness to provide rights to third parties. Only it seems can Parliament now rectify the matter, as was recommended provisionally by the Law Commission in their consultative paper issued on 23 October 1991 and it is interesting to note that their provisional recommendations follow closely the provisions of Art. 328 of the *BGB*.

In contrast both French and German law systems continue to experiment with the expansion of remedies for the benefit of third parties whether in contract or tort. Sometimes these experiments have run into judicial or academic criticism, as happened with the theory of a 'chain of contracts' in French law or the widening of the application of the doctrine of a contract with protective effects for third parties in German law. However, what is important in these instances is the vitality of the legal system in responding to the perceived demands of society and providing remedies in favour of the person whose interests have been harmed. This is shown also in the development in German law of tortious liability for damage to the product, being classified as damage to 'other property', so as to defeat the short limitation period for defects and allow in tort what is in effect a claim for economic loss, despite Art. 823(1) of the *BGB*.

While this vitality, it may be objected, causes uncertainty in the law and means that business people and their insurance companies are left unclear as to their legal liabilities, certainty can be purchased only at the price of a rigidity which pays no regard to the changes in the common perception of what the law ought to be as opposed to what it has been in the past.

NOTES

1. In the Linden Gardens and St Martins Property Corporation cases (see *The Times* 23 July 1993) the House of Lords allowed the original employer to recover damages under his contract with the contractor in respect of the losses suffered by the subsequent purchaser of the property because of the contractor's defective performance. The argument appears to be that such damages were the foreseeable result of such defective performance and the contractor, knowing at the time of contract that the properties were for the occupation of a third party, must be regarded as having entered into the contract on the basis that the employer would be entitled to enforce his contractual rights for the benefit of that third party.
2. *Hedley Byrne* [1964] AC 443.
3. See the famous judgement of Lord Atkin in *Donoghue* v. *Stevenson* [1932] AC 562.
4. *Leigh and Sullivan* v. *Aliakmon Shipping* [1986] AC 785.
5. *The Wagon Mound* [1961] AC 388.
6. *Murphy* v. *Brentwood District Council* [1990] 3 WLR 414.
7. But see now the Linden Gardens case referred to in note 1 above in which the purported assignment was not effective since the employer had not obtained the contractor's consent as was required under the contract, but nevertheless the employer could recover in contract the losses suffered by the subsequent purchaser for the defects to the building.
8. *Southern Water Authority* v. *Carey* [1985] 2 All ER 1077 and *Norwich City Council* v. *Harvey* [1989] 1 WLR 828.
9. E.g. in the cases cited in note 8 above.
10. See *Southern Water Authority* v. *Lewis & Duvivier* 1 Con. LR 40 at p. 48.
11. Markesinis in *LQR*, Vol. 103, p. 354 in the article 'An Expanding Tort Law – the Price for a Rigid Contract Law' at p. 395.
12. *Twins Transport Ltd* v. *Patrick & Brocklehurst* 4 Con. LR 117 at p. 133.
13. The Aliakmon case cited in note 4 above.
14. See the commentary on the Satherwaite case [1975] AC 154 in *Standard Business Contracts Exclusions and Related Devices*, Yates and Hawkins, Sweet and Maxwell, London, 1986 at p. 251.
15. See the article by Markesinis referred to in note 11 above.
16. Cass. civ. 25 January 1820 and see also Cass. civ. 7 March 1990, Bull. III, no. 72.
17. See the note to Cass. Ass. Plen. 7.2. 1986 D.S. 1986 293.

18. 'The Articles 1382 and following of the *Code Civil* (which deal with delictual responsibility), do not apply when it is a matter of a fault committed in the performance of a contract', statement of principle contained in the judgement of the *Cour de cassation* Cass. civ. 1 January 1922 D.P. 1922, 1.16 and see the judgement and commentary in *Les Grands Arrêts de la Jurisprudence Civile*, 9th edition, Dalloz, Paris, at p.450 et seq. See also commentary on Art. 1147 of the *Code Civil*, Dalloz 1992/93 on pp. 761 and 762 for more recent decisions.

19. Cass. civ. 9 October 1979 Bull. I, no. 241.

20. See Ghestin *La Vente* s.1051.

21. Although the European Court of Justice in their decision of 17 June 1992 decided that for the purposes of determining whether or not a French court had jurisdiction under Art. 5.1 of the Brussels Convention in a dispute between a French sub-purchaser and a German manufacturer the relationship between the two was not contractual, it is not considered that this will affect the position under French domestic law – see the commentary by Larroumet in *La Semaine Juridique*, Ed.G.no.43, Jurisprudence (1992) p. 340 no. 21927.

22. Bull. civ. I, no. 69, p. 46.

23. Cass. civ. 7 May 1986 Bull. III, no. 62.

24. Cass. civ. 26 October 1988 G.P. 21 January 1989 som. p. 131 and see Caston pp. 499 and 500.

25. Cass. civ. 30 November 1988 Bull. II, no. 240 and see also Rev. trim. Droit com. 43(1) January–March 1990 p. 90.

26. Cass. civ. 17 February 1955 J.C.P.1955 II 8951 and see also commentary in *Les Grands Arrêts de la Jurisprudence Civile* p. 455 et seq.

27. The principle of not allowing in English law 'something in the nature of a transmissible warranty of quality' was stated by Lord Keith with evident approval in *Murphy* v. *Brentwood Council* at p. 430 of the report in the *Weekly Law Reports*.

28. Mazeaud and Chabas p. 907.

29. Cass. civ. 6 December 1932 G.P.1933.1.269.

30. Cass. civ. 23 January 1959 D.1950.281.

31. Paris, 18 June 1957 J.C.P.57.II.10134.

32. Cass. civ. 17 December 1954 D.1955.269.

33. Huebner, op.cit, pp. 520 and 572.

34. *BGH* 93,273 NJW 86,1615 and see Jauernig Vollkommer para.3, p. 354.

35. For an example where the employer defendant did successfully discharge the burden of proof see *BGH* 25 January 1966 quoted Markesinis p. 560.

36. This was the situation in the Aliakmon case referred to in note 4 above.

37. Markesinis *An Expanding Tort Law – the price of a rigid Contract Law*, LQR, Vol.103, July 1987, at p. 389 and *The German Law of Torts* p. 49.

38. *BGHZ* NJW 1965,1757 quoted Zweigert and Kotz, Vol.2, p. 147.

39. *BGH* 6 July 1965 NJW 1965, 1955 and see discussion and commentary on the case by Professor Lorenz in *Essays in Memory of Professor Lawson*, Butterworths, London, 1986 at pp. 87–89.

40. *BGH* 26 November 1968 *BGHZ* 51,91 quoted Markesinis p. 355.

41. Markesinis p. 46.

42. See comment in *European Product Liability*, Kelley and Attree (Eds.), Butterworths, London, 1992, at p. 138.

43. The English case of *Junior Books* v. *Veitchi* [1983] AC 520 can no longer be regarded as good law following the decision in *Murphy* v. *Brentwood District Council* – see above p. 270. As regards German law see *BGHZ* 39, 366 referred to in the judgement of the *BGH* 24 November 1976 *BGHZ* 67,359 given in Markesinis p. 368 at p. 371 and the commentary on p. 397.

44. *BGH* 23 April 1981 NJW 1981, 1779 given in Markesinis p. 179. However, see also the commentary in Markesinis on p. 45 and the comments by Lorenz, op.cit., pp. 96 and 97.

45. *Shanklin Pier* v. *Detel Products Ltd* [1951] 2 KB 854.

46. *BGH* 15 December 1978 NJW 1979, 2036 reproduced in Markesinis p. 379.

47. Schlechtreim *Deliktshaftung des Subunternehmers Geschäftsbedingungen dem Bauherrn wegen Minderwerts seines Werks 25 Jahre Karlsruher Forum (1983)* at p. 65 referred to by Lorenz, op.cit., at p. 92.

48. The essential criterion appears to be that the defective part is insignificant in value to the whole and that the damage caused was different in nature and of a higher value than the original defect. So an accident caused to a car by a blow-out in a defective tyre was different from the tyre having been fitted illegally to

the car in the first place. Had the defect been discovered before the blow-out occurred then there would have been no damage upon which a tort action could have been founded. *BGH* 5 July 1978 NJW 1978, 2241. For a comment on the concept of Stoffgleich see *An Introduction to German Civil and Commercial Law*, Gerhard Dannemann, BIICL, 1993.

49. *BGH* NJW 1978, 1051.
50. A useful list is given in Kelley and Attree, op.cit. at p. 141.
51. This requirement, that the exclusion clause should be explicit, was referred to in the tyre blow-out case – see the translation of the judgement in Markesinis at p.379. It could not, however, protect the seller against gross negligence.

20 The control of unfair terms

Although they are to a degree interrelated the two issues with which this chapter is concerned need to be distinguished.

First there is the broad, general issue of whether or not there is a legal requirement for the terms of a contract to be fair, so that if they are not, then they will be unenforceable by legal action.

Second there is the narrower issue of the extent to which terms of a contract should be enforced which limit or exclude the liabilities, to which a party to that contract would otherwise be subject, by operation of the general principles of law applicable to the type of contract in question.

THE BROAD ISSUE OF UNFAIRNESS

The problem raised by the broad issue is not a new one. The issue of the fairness or otherwise of a contract was a matter which concerned the Greeks and Romans. A provision in Justinian's code to the effect that on the sale of land the vendor was entitled to rescind if he had sold for less than half the true value but the purchaser was entitled to make up the price to the true value was developed by the medieval jurists so that it applied both to land and movables and even to the purchaser as well as the seller.[1] This doctrine of *laesio enormis* fitted in well with the attempted regulation of economic activity through the religious and moral concepts of usury and the just price which were a prominent feature of medieval life both in England and on the continent of Europe.[2]

The same theme was taken up by the natural lawyers. For example, Grotius maintained that there should be equality in contracts as regards knowledge of the facts, in the exchange itself and in the subject matter of the contract, although he also appears to have recognized that to maintain actions based on inequality after the contract had been concluded would lead to innumerable disputes which it would be difficult to decide.[3] Pothier seems to have been of much the same mind. If the contract was unequal then it was defective in equity, which affected the man's conscience, but at the same time unless the *lésion* was enormous then it would not affect the validity of the contract since otherwise stability and freedom of commerce would be undermined. However he also refers to the obligation to sell at a 'just price' with only limited exceptions, 'the nature of the contract being that each receives the just equivalent of that which he transfers'.[4]

As Atiyah has shown the concept of law in England as paternalistic and its concern with the fairness of an exchange remained in existence until well into the eighteenth century.[5]

In the latter half of the eighteenth and more especially during the nineteenth century these ideas, and in particular that of the 'just price', gave way to the new economic liberalism and to the idea that it was the responsibility of each person to act with prudence and to take the decision for himself as to the price at which he was prepared to purchase. It was the agreement, conceived of as being reached by parties each entering into the contract with a proper understanding of the bargain they were making, which determined the price and nothing else.

That was the basis of the French civil code with one exception. The concept of *lésion* was retained only in three general cases of which the only one that need be mentioned is that relating to sales of land:

> If the seller has suffered harm by more than seven twelfths in the sale of immovable property then he has the right to demand the rescission of the sale even if he expressly renounced in the contract the right to such rescission and declared that he gave the plus-value. (Art. 1674 of the *Code Civil*)

The right to require rescission is independent of the circumstances of the sale.

The responsibility for this exception to the general principle, that *lésion* does not affect a contract, being included within the *Code Civil* appears to belong to Napoleon himself and to have little to do with either the doctrine of the just price or of equality of exchange. It was included as part of his concern for the maintenance of a strong family which would uphold the stability of the state. The sale of movables such as diamonds and paintings did not concern the state, but the disposal of land did, and it was the obligation of the owner not to dispose of it contrary to the interests of the family: 'Can it be within the principles of civil justice to allow an act by which a person sacrifices the heritage of his ancestors and the patrimoine of his children in a moment of folly?'[6]

Although the Roman doctrine of *laesio enormis* formed part of the *Gemeines Recht*, it had fallen into disuse by the time of the drafting of the *BGB* and as a specific provision was excluded from the *Code Civil*. However it still retains some life in Art. 138(2) of the *BGB* which provides that contracts are void if a person exploits the need, experience, lack of judgement or significant weakness of will of another to obtain a benefit for himself which is clearly disproportionate to the performance provided.

This provision is usually applied today in conjunction with Art. 138(1) which simply states that a legal transaction which is against common decency is void. A recent example is that of a contract binding up-and-coming artists to specific promotion companies where the long-term gain to the company far outstripped any reasonable result from the contract for the artists and where the company exploited the inexperience and youth of new talent to lure them into disadvantageous contracts (BGH (I ZR 190/87) 1 December 1988, [1989] GRWR 198).

An interesting comparison can be made between this case and that of *A. Schroeder Music Publishing Co. Ltd* v. *Macaulay* [1974] 1 WLR 1308, which was similarly concerned with a contract between an experienced music publisher and an unknown artist. The House of Lords held that the agreement was void as being contrary to public policy since the party having the stronger bargaining power had imposed on the weaker a bargain in terms of restraint of trade which was unconscionable. However the English decision was peculiar to contracts in restraint of trade in which the fairness of the bargain appears as a necessary condition of the validity of the contract and it does not establish a general principle of the necessity for the bargain to be fair – see below.

In the eighteenth century in England the Court of Chancery did at times act to set aside contracts which had been entered into by those who were either foolish or ignorant and had been taken advantage of by their co-contractant. Even today such equitable relief will continue to be given in those cases unless the other party can establish that the bargain is fair and reasonable. Mere undervalue on its own, however, will not be sufficient to establish fraud unless it is so gross that no person of commonsense could accept it without proper explanation. Nor will the unfair use of an inequality of bargaining power itself be regarded as justification for invalidating a contract despite the attempts by Lord Denning to establish such a general principle.[7]

Even though fraud is not established, so allowing the contract to be rescinded, equity has always been prepared to refuse to enforce a bargain when the court considers that to do so would be contrary to the substantial justice of the case.[8] However, in these instances, the contract being valid, the plaintiff may be entitled to recover damages at common law.

The willingness of the French courts to hold that a party to negotiations must not act abusively (see above, pp. 62–63) and the wide definition which they have given to *dol*, including the obligation to inform (see above, pp. 124–128) may be considered as examples of the application of good faith in the formation of contracts. So also one may consider the extent to which the courts have gone in developing the liability of the professional in his dealings with non-professionals as based on considerations of good faith (see above, pp. 172–173).

Although Art. 1134 of the *Code Civil* requires that 'contracts should be executed in good faith', the general position of the *Cour de cassation* as regards the interpretation of contracts has been that if the meaning of a clause is clear then it must be applied and the judge has no power to relieve one party of his clearly expressed obligations.[9] Of course in practice a French court which wishes to avoid the enforcement of a clause it regards as inequitable can sometimes find ways in which to do it which will not result in their judgement being quashed.

Additionally it appears that the position is changing and that even the *Cour de cassation* is now prepared to allow in certain instances that the exercise by one party of his rights under the contract is dependent on his acting in good faith.[10]

But there is nothing like the power which the German courts have felt themselves free to exercise based on Arts. 138, 157 and 242 of the *BGB*. These will be examined in more detail in the next section. It is sufficient to note here that the principle of good faith is fundamental in German law. It may be expressed in general terms by saying that it is the obligation of one party to the contract to act in such a way as to take into account the legitimate interests of the other. Its application has led to the development in German law of a large number of secondary duties on a contracting party such as the

292

requirement to supply information regarding the use and maintenance of goods supplied, and on a principle not to interfere with or obstruct a commercial agent but to support him in the performance of his work (equally on the agent not to act for the principal's competitors).

Again to illustrate the width of the application of the rule, it was held to be a breach of good faith when a bank only granted credit to a businessman on terms that would require his wife to be personally liable for repayments in the event of default, if the funds were provided only for business purposes and the bank had no other rights in relation to the wife which required such protection (BGH (XI ZR 111/90) 22 January 1991 DB 542).

CLAUSES EXCLUDING OR LIMITING LIABILITY

ENGLAND – THE COMMON LAW

So long as the doctrine of *caveat emptor* held sway English law had no need of such clauses. The converse was true. The vendor was liable to the purchaser in terms of the quality of that which he had sold only if he had given an express warranty to that effect. Such warranties as to quality did not become implied generally into contracts of sale until the second half of the nineteenth century and then were subsequently codified in the original Sale of Goods Act 1893. But such implied terms were specifically stated by the Act in s.55 to be capable of being negatived or varied by express agreement between the parties. Then, perhaps because the remedy against the vendor was the normal one of damages for breach of contract, which could include the consequential losses suffered by the purchaser, it began to become the fashion to limit the vendor's liability.

In parallel, and with the increase in the mass sale of manufactured goods, there developed the practice of manufacturers and sellers contracting on standard terms of business. This was still further encouraged by the trade associations of manufacturers and suppliers now being formed, one of the early tasks of which was to establish the standard forms of contract upon which their members agreed between themselves to conduct their business with purchasers. Many sections of industry were dominated by such associations right up until the passing of the Restrictive Trade Practices Act 1956.

The overall effect therefore was that manufacturers and sellers sought through their terms of contract to avoid the implied conditions and warranties of the Sale of Goods Act and to offer the purchaser in lieu limited rights to have defective goods repaired. Often, as in the case of cars, these rights were restricted to the provision of replacement parts, labour costs being for the account of the purchaser; in other instances the goods had to be returned to the seller's work carriage paid and the seller's obligations were limited to the repair and replacement of the parts agreed by them to be defective and did not extend to the costs for dismantling and reassembly.

Even these rights were limited to a period of six months or sometimes less.

Invariably fitness for purpose was excluded as were any liabilities for consequential damages. Where performance figures were quoted these were usually stated to be estimates and not guaranteed.

Similarly any responsibility for delay in delivery was avoided by providing that any times given were estimates only and the supplier was under no liability if these times were exceeded.

Finally, suppliers and others sought to avoid any liability even for the consequences of their own negligence.

This situation prevailed well into the period post World War II when, because of the seller's market then prevailing, and the strength of the hold of trade associations on their members, it was extremely difficult for purchasers to contract on terms which were more favourable.

The judicial attitude towards such clauses was generally hostile, especially in cases involving a consumer, but the approach was indirect through the use of the favourite method of construing the contract strictly and in the event of any ambiguity against the party imposing the restriction. So when a clause referred only to an exclusion of 'warranties' this was held not to include 'conditions'; when a clause only referred to 'conditions or warranties' that were 'implied' this was held not to include express terms; an exclusion of liability for 'latent defects' did not include the implied condition under the Sale of Goods Act that the goods would be reasonably fit for purpose. Liability for negligence could only be excluded either expressly or by wording which was wide enough in its ordinary meaning to include negligence and there was no other source of liability against which the party drafting the clause could reasonably be supposed to be protecting himself.

There was a kind of running battle between the courts and the draftsmen acting for the superior party. As particular clauses were found by the courts to be ineffective so the drafting of standard forms was tightened. It was at one time thought that there were indeed certain clauses so fundamental to the contract that liability for their breach could not be excluded – the so-called doctrine of 'fundamental breach' – but that has now been discarded in a case which represents the high-water mark of judicial willingness to accept that where there are two business parties of equal bargaining power then it is up to them to make their own arrangements. If, therefore, they agree on the one party not being liable at all or only under very limited liability, no matter how serious the breach he commits and that agreement is expressed in terms which permit of only that interpretation, then the courts will give effect to the clause.[11] Even then there are limits, although it cannot be said that they are very clearly defined. There seems little doubt that a deliberate breach of contract would not be regarded as covered by an exclusion or limitation of liability clause however widely drafted.

Under the civil law this would be because such a provision would be contrary to public policy (see Art. 276 of the *BGB*: 'a debtor may not be released beforehand from responsibility for wilful conduct' and Art. 1134 of the *Code Civil*: 'contracts must be executed in good faith' from which has been derived the rule that clauses exonerating a debtor from responsibility are invalid in cases of *dol* (which includes a deliberate intent not to execute the contract) or *faute lourde*.[12]

In English law it is a matter of construction of the contract and as to whether or not the deliberate breach was of trivial or major importance.[13] It would seem probable that under French law the *Photo Production* case would have been decided differently since the negligence of the watchman who deliberately started the fire which accidentally burnt down the factory, would have been characterized as *faute lourde* and the clause exonerating Securicor would therefore not have been applied.[14]

THE UNFAIR CONTRACT TERMS ACT 1977

The title of this Act is a well-known misnomer. It does not deal with unfair contract terms as such at all. Its scope is restricted to controlling terms which seek to limit or exclude liability. Only a brief review of the complex provisions of the Act will be given so far as they relate to contracts between business organizations.

By s.2(1) of the Act a person cannot exclude or restrict his liability for death or personal injury resulting from negligence. By s.2(2) a contract term or notice by which a person seeks to exclude or restrict his liability for negligence giving rise to loss or damage other than death or personal injury is only valid if it satisfies the test of reasonableness. By s.3 a person who deals with another on his standard terms of business cannot, unless the term satisfies the test of reasonableness:

- exclude or restrict liability in respect of his own breach;
- claim to be entitled to render contractual performance substantially different from that which was reasonably expected of him;
- claim in respect of the whole or any part of the contract to render no performance at all.

By ss.6 and 7 the test of reasonableness is applied to any terms in contracts, under which the ownership of goods passes, which purport to exclude or restrict liability for breach of the statutorily implied terms as to correspondence of the goods with any description or sample or as to their quality or fitness for any purpose. In every instance it is for the party imposing the term to satisfy the burden of proving it to be reasonable.

As between two business concerns which are of approximately equal bargaining power the test of whether a particular exclusion or limitation or liability term is reasonable or not is always going to be difficult. The most common type of provision in which this difficulty will arise is where the vendor has offered in his contract an undertaking to make good any defects in the goods during a limited period – say twelve months – in lieu of any rights which the buyer would otherwise have either because of a breach of an express term in the contract or a breach of the implied conditions as to merchantability or fitness for purpose under the Sale of Goods Act. In particular such a guarantee clause would normally exclude any rights of the buyer to claim damages for loss of use or of profit.

Two cases in which this question has come before the courts may be contrasted.

The first, *White Cross Equipment* v. *Farrell*[15] concerned the sale of a compactor which the judge held should have been fit for certain purposes and clearly was not. The buyer by his conduct had lost the right to reject but could have claimed damages except that the contract which was on the sellers' conditions contained a clause in which the sellers undertook to repair or at their option to replace all goods or parts required because of faulty work and materials but otherwise all warranties, conditions and so on were excluded and the sellers were not liable for any loss or damage whatsoever, consequential or otherwise.

The judge based his judgement on the parties being of equal bargaining power, the buyer knew what he was doing and could have bargained away the clause if he had tried, and a six-month warranty was given which included complete replacement. He therefore held that the clause was reasonable and defeated the buyer's claim for damages.

In a case decided on 7 April 1992 *Edmund Murray Ltd* v. *BSP International Foundations Ltd*[16] the subject matter of the sale was a drilling rig which failed to meet the specific performance requirements contained in the contract.

Again there was no doubt the sellers were responsible for fitness for purpose. Their conditions of sale to which the contract was subject contained a clause stating that they would replace or repair at their option any goods 'defective by reason solely of faulty materials or workmanship'. There were then similar clauses as before, providing that this guarantee was in lieu of all warranties, conditions, etc. and excluding the right to claim damages.

The Court of Appeal concluded that, although the parties were of roughly equal bargaining strength and the buyer knew of the exclusion clause, the terms were unreasonable on the grounds that the rig was specially ordered and the specification contained complete details of the required technical standards. In these circumstances it could not be reasonable to take away the buyer's rights to sue for breach of the express term or of the implied condition of fitness for purpose under the Sale of Goods Act.

The two cases are difficult to reconcile, and it is even more difficult to accept the conclusion, which appears to follow from the latter case, that if there is an express or even implied condition as to fitness for purpose, that a clause removing the buyer's right to sue for damages is unreasonable. It is considered that in contracts between business concerns of equal bargaining power it should be left to the parties to decide on how they wish to apportion the risks between them. Further, if the one is so careless, foolish or misguided as to contract on terms which in the event he later regrets, or finds that he has contracted on the seller's terms without having bothered to appreciate the significance of his acts, then why should the law come to his assistance? Consumers can be excused their ignorance or stupidity, but not surely major business concerns.

It would be different if the seller were in a quasi-monopolistic position and the buyer had no choice but to contract on his terms, but then the parties would not be of equal bargaining strength.

This seems to be exactly what Lord Wilberforce had in mind in his comments in the case of *Photo Production Ltd*. He referred to commercial matters when the parties are not of unequal bargaining power and said, 'not only is the case for judicial intervention undemonstrated but there is everything to be said and this seems to have been Parliament's intention, for leaving the parties free to apportion risks as they think fit and respecting their decisions'.

FRANCE – *DROIT COMMUN*

At the time of the drafting of the *Code Civil* the typical contract was thought of as one being entered into between two individuals who were on a more or less level footing. The distribution of economic power between them was never overwhelmingly in favour of one party.[17] It seemed reasonable to assume that in general the parties in the formation of their contracts would follow at least the principles of the *dispositions supplétives* in the *Code Civil* in determining their respective rights and responsibilities. The contract was then an expression of the free wills of the parties.

However, as industrialization and mass marketing spread to France, it became the norm that contracts were in fact entered into, not between individuals negotiating on reasonably level terms but between professionals and laymen, between associations of firms and individuals, and between major enterprises often possessing quasi-monopoly powers and consumers. In these circumstances the balance of economic power had shifted totally in favour of the seller or supplier of the service and as Weill and Terré have expressed it, 'Legal equality became a sham'.[18]

It was in this situation that in 1909 the French civil jurist Raymond Saleilles developed the theory of the *contrat d'adhésion* which has been identified as having four characteristics:

1. A deep-seated economic inequality between the parties.
2. The offer is made generally, and not to an individual.
3. The contract is prepared by the party having the economic power in a standard form which is applied to all concerned without negotiation.
4. The contract is expressed in a highly technical form which makes it difficult for the layman to understand its meaning, and its terms are such as to be solely in the interests of the organization which prepared the contract.[19]

Saleilles maintained that a *contrat d'adhésion* was not a true contract since it did not represent a genuine agreement between the wills of the parties. The 'contract' was the result of the unilateral will of the party who created it and the adhesion to it of the other party. The contract is not therefore the 'law for the parties' under Art. 1134 of the *Code Civil*, and there is no 'common intention of the parties' to be sought for under Art. 1156 when interpreting the contract. There is only the law and intentions of the party who prepared the contract.

This analysis leads to the conclusion that the judge would have wide powers to modify those terms of the 'contract' which he considered to be unjust.

However the analysis was rejected by most of the 'doctrine' and by the jurisprudence. The courts have been required by the *Cour de cassation* to apply the same rules to *contrats d'adhésion* as they have applied to contracts the result of negotiations freely conducted by the parties. If the clause is clear and legal then it is the responsibility of the judge to apply it even if the result is extremely harsh on the defendant.

An early case in 1866 which confirmed this rule concerned a female worker at a carpet factory. Attached to the door by which one entered the factory was a notice forbidding workers to enter the factory wearing clogs and making them liable to a penalty of 10 francs if they did so. A worker, Mrs Juillard, broke the rule and 10 francs was duly deducted from her wages. She appealed to the 'conseil des prud'hommes' (industrial disputes tribunal) at Aubusson who reduced her fine to 0.50fr. on the grounds that

> the law ought to protect those whose situation or circumstances puts them at the mercy of others; that in this case the factory-owner cannot be opposed because she can always find workers who will accept her terms; the fine is obviously excessive since it represents nearly half a month's wages of Mrs Juillard; for these reasons reduce to 0F.50 cent.

One can only applaud the decision of the conseil des prud'hommes for their enlightened judgement and view it perhaps with some astonishment, seeing that it was decided around the middle of the last century, and despite the fact that the conseils des prud'hommes are composed of equal representatives of workers and management. However it did not find favour with the *Cour de cassation* who quashed the decision on the grounds that

> In terms of Art 1134 of the Code civil agreements legally formed take the place of the law for those who make them and that when the agreement requires that the party who fails to execute it pays a fixed sum as damages then the other party is not to be granted a sum which is greater or less.[20]

(Of course the rule in Art. 1134 only applies to *lois* which are *lois supplétives* and not to *lois impératives* which the parties cannot derogate from by the terms of their agreement – see above, p. 8.)

The rule that the court cannot increase or decrease the amount of a penalty was changed by the Laws of 9 July 1975 and 11 October 1985 (see below, pp. 330) but the principle that the contract 'takes the place of the law for the parties' regardless of however inequitable the effect of this may be is still valid (see further below, pp. 332–333).

Nevertheless the jurisprudence, as we have already seen, have refused to apply clauses which limit or exonerate the debtor from liability when the default is the result of *dol* or *faute lourde*. Although the parties are in principle free to settle the terms of their contracts, they must execute their obligations in good faith and *faute lourde* is generally assimilated to *dol* according to the maxim *culpa lata dolo aequiparatur*.

This rule has been applied (see Chapter 13) to contracts of sale between professional sellers, who as a matter of law are treated as having knowledge of the defects in the goods which they are selling, and purchaser not of the same speciality in order to render invalid clauses on non-responsibility in relation to *vice caché*. Further as noted in Chapter 13, when the action is brought under the *droit commun* for *inexécution* as opposed to *vice caché* the clause exonerating the seller, although in principle valid, will be held invalid if the *juges de fait* characterize the default of the seller as *faute lourde* (see above, pp. 175–176).

There is still in all this no distinction made between clauses contained in standard conditions and those in contracts negotiated freely between the parties. On the one hand this can be considered as giving less protection to purchasers, especially consumers, whilst on the other hand it can operate to defeat the expressed intentions of the parties on an individually negotiated contract.

FRANCE – LEGISLATION

There is nothing in France equivalent to the Unfair Contract Terms Act. Nor is there any legislation relating to standard term contracts. What does exist by way of general legislation is the Law No. 78–23 of 10 January 1978, the Loi Scrivener, and the Law 92–60 of 18 January 1992.[21] The former set up a commission of *clauses abusives* to examine the terms of contract customarily imposed by professionals on non-professionals and consumers and recommend those which ought to be suppressed or modified because of their abusive nature. The commission was also to recommend to the government the issuing of decrees specifying abusive clauses which would then be invalidated.

In fact only one decree has so far been issued: no. 78–464 of 24 March 1978. This provides in general terms that in contracts between professionals and non-professionals or consumers:

- in contracts of sale it is forbidden to include a clause which denies the consumer or non-professional the right to have defective goods repaired;
- in any such contract it is forbidden to include a clause allowing the professional unilaterally to modify the goods or services to be provided;
- in any such contract the professional may not provide a guarantee for the goods to be supplied or the service rendered without stating that this is without prejudice to the legal guaranty which requires the professional to guaranty the purchaser against the defaults or *vices cachés* in the goods supplied or services provided.

The impact of the above provisions has been limited even although the Commission has made some progress in negotiations with trade associations for the voluntary amendment of their standard conditions of sale and has issued some 33 recommendations inviting professionals no longer to include in their contracts certain clauses which may be abusive.

Very recently the role of the Commission has been increased by the Decree no. 93–314 of 10 March 1993. This provides that if the issue of a contractual clause being abusive is raised before a court then the court may request the Commission for its advice as to the abusive nature of the clause as defined under Art. 35 of the Law of 10 January 1978. The court is not bound by the advice, which must be given within three months of its being requested, but must stay the proceedings until it is received or the expiry of the three-month period, although it can make any necessary interim orders of an urgent nature. It is far too soon to comment on how effective this change will be or how much it will be utilized by the courts. The hope is that it will be used and that if a clause is held consistently to be abusive then it will be made the subject of a decree forbidding its use.

In the meantime in the absence of other legislation the courts appear to have taken a fairly broad view of the provisions of the degree. In the first instance they have not limited the term 'non-professional' to persons buying goods other than for a professional use. So they have included within the definition of a 'non-professional' a firm of estate agents who contracted with a company supplying alarm systems. As the *Cour de cassation* said 'the appeal court had found that the work of a firm of estate agents had no relationship with the very special techniques of an alarm system and that relative to the content of the contract the firm was in the same state of ignorance as any other consumer, from which they were legally entitled to deduce that the law of 10 January 1978 was applicable' (Cass. civ. 1, 28 April 1987, D.1987).

Second, the courts have given a wide definition to a contract for sale. So when a person bought a film the price of which included the cost of development, this was considered, even if only partially, as a contract of sale since the transaction could not be divided into two and was entered into at the time of the purchase of the film. Art. 2 of the decree of 24 March therefore applied and the clause limiting the responsibility of Kodak to replacing lost films by new ones was invalid (Cass. civ. 1re, 25 January 1989 D.1989.253).

Of even more interest is the question whether or not the courts, without any decree, will take the initiative to declare as abusive and therefore void a clause falling within the scope of Art.35 of the Law of 10 January 1978 as abusive.[22] Case-law and doctrine suggest that they will do so.

A recent decision of a 'tribunal d'instance' approved by the *Cour de cassation* on 14 May 1991 supports this view. The case concerned the development of paper prints from slides but in this instance was certainly not a contract of sale. The slide had been left with a developer whose terms of contract included a clause which exonerated him from all liability if the slides were lost, which they were for an unknown reason.

The tribunal held that the developer was under an *obligation de résultat* and responsible therefore for the loss in the absence of being able to prove *cause étrangère*, and further that the clause exonerating the developer from responsibility included in the ticket for the slides should be struck out as abusive.

Basing its decision on Art. 1789 of the *Code Civil* the *Cour de cassation* first held that the developer was liable for the loss unless he could prove that it was not due to his fault. Since the cause was unknown he could not do this and the decision of the tribunal was therefore legally justified. However, they did not characterize the obligation of the developer as being one of *résultat*.[23]

300

The *Cour de cassation* also agreed with the tribunal that the clause exonerating the developer from liability obtained for him an excessive benefit which he was able to impose on his client by reason of his economic position. It was therefore abusive and should be deleted from the contract. No basis was given for this part of the judgement, but the language used is that of Art. 35 of the *Loi Scrivener* itself: 'In contracts between professionals and non-professionals or consumers may be prohibited . . . by the decrees of the *Conseil d'Etât* after advice from the Commission . . . clauses relating to . . . the extent of responsibilities and guarantees . . . when such clauses appear **imposed on non-professionals or consumers by an abuse of economic power of the other party and confer on the latter an excessive advantage**'.

While strictly the right to strike out a clause as being abusive can only follow from a decree issued by the *Conseil d'Etât*, and not from the *Loi* itself, the *Cour de cassation* appears to have wished to give a signal both to the courts below and to the legislature itself as to the direction in which they shoould follow.[24]

GERMANY – THE CIVIL CODE

The philosophy underlying the German civil code, the *BGB*, is that a person who enters into a contract does so of his own free will with a proper understanding of his rights and obligations and is capable of looking after his own interests. It follows that freedom of contract, in the sense that the parties were free to decide on their own terms, the provisions of the *BGB* being mainly dispositive, was the legal norm.

However it soon became apparent that business organizations of all types, suppliers of goods, insurance companies and the banks had taken advantage of their economic power to develop standard conditions of contract which seriously disadvantaged the customer and which he was powerless to resist.

It was not long before the German courts decided to draw a distinction between contracts which had been genuinely the subject of freely conducted negotiations in which the stronger party had been willing to modify his proposed terms and those which had been placed on standard conditions. At first they relied on Art. 138 of the *BGB* under which a contract is void if it offends against common decency, or if one party has taken advantage of the other's need, carelessness or inexperience, to obtain for himself a grossly disproportionate economic advantage (see above, pp. 291–292). So in a decision in 1921 the Reichsgericht held that a provision in the standard conditions of all Mannheim carriers and forwarders that limited their liability for their own negligence to 60 Marks for each shipment was an exploitation of their monopoly and a gross violation of the moral standards of those people whose thinking is just and equitable, and therefore void under Art. 138. The court added that such a clause exempting the carrier from his own negligence could only be valid if it resulted from a freely negotiated agreement.[25]

Subsequently the courts, after some hesitation, decided that they would intervene more actively using as a base Art. 242 of the *BGB* which provides that every debtor must perform his obligations in good faith and according to common usage, still retaining the fundamental distinction between the contract freely and individually negotiated and one placed on standard conditions. In the case of the latter the courts struck down as void those clauses in standard conditions of contract which deviated from the legal norm to an extent which could not be justified either by reference to the general nature of the transaction in question or by the substitution of other rights which provide adequate alternative protection. For the German courts the provisions of the *BGB* provide a balanced set of legal norms which apply in a typical situation. In a contract placed on standard terms there must therefore be some specific justification if there is to be a departure from those norms and the stronger the term departed from, the stricter the application of the principle of good faith and the more compelling must be the justification if the term is to be upheld. The courts were in agreement with academic writers that in a standard form contract imposed by one party on the other there is no true freedom of contract. The contract terms gain their effectiveness not from the private autonomy of the parties but only from the submission by one party. It follows that the terms of standard form contract which apply to an indefinite number of instances must be denied effectiveness if they contradict the principles of good faith.[26]

The distinction between the German approach and that of England and France is striking. The German courts have been prepared to go where those of England and France have feared to tread. It can be argued that the German approach creates some uncertainty as to the validity of specific contract terms but there can be no denying that it established the basis from which the Standard Contract Terms Act (*Gesetz zur Regelung des Rechts der Allgemeinen Geschäftsbedingungen*) was derived and that the two together have been an important force for change in improving standard terms of contract for those in need, whilst leaving those genuinely able to negotiate freely to look after their own interests.

GERMAN LAW – LEGISLATION

Despite the best efforts of the courts, by the early 1970s it had become apparent that legislative action was necessary to combat the abuse of standard terms. Judicial control is always a matter of chance as to which cases are brought before the courts. Many consumers faced with the standard terms of a powerful and wealthy concern will hesitate to spend the time and money to pursue a claim that such terms are invalid if the amount at stake is not all that significant.

The Standard Contract Terms Act (AGBG) came into force on 1 April 1977 and applies although in differing degrees to both consumer and business contracts. The Act has been the subject of numerous decisions of the courts and thousands of pages of commentary. Within the scope of the present book only an outline of the most important points concerning the AGBG can be given.

The AGBG starts off by defining what is meant by standard contract conditions. They are those which one party ('the user') has prepared for use in a number of instances and which are presented to the other party at the conclusion of a contract. Conditions are not considered as 'general' if they have been individually negotiated between the parties. In order to establish that conditions have been individually negotiated there must be evidence that the other party had a genuine opportunity to influence the drafting of those conditions which are contrary to the legal norms foreseen by the *BGB* for the type of contract in question – for example that he was invited to submit alternative wording in circumstances in which the user indicated his willingness to accept or at least negotiate upon such alternative proposals. In general unless there has been some substantive amendment to such terms in the standard conditions it is unlikely that a court will accept the contract has been individually negotiated. A contract can, of course, contain in part standard conditions and in part those individually negotiated. Provided that the clauses which are standard do not offend against the AGBG then the contract will be considered as valid.

Individually agreed terms

Terms peculiar to the transaction may be agreed by the parties such as the delivery date or that the goods forming the subject matter of the contract possess particular characteristics. Such individually agreed terms will take precedence over printed standard terms. If the two cannot be reconciled then the standard term will be ignored. In particular one cannot include in the standard conditions a term which effectively negatives an express provision of the contract. So an undertaking to deliver goods by a specific date cannot be negated by a term in the standard conditions which states that the seller will not be liable if he fails to deliver the goods on time.

A clause commonly found in a seller's standard conditions which provides that nothing is binding which has not been agreed upon in writing will not be regarded as valid if there is clear evidence to the effect that both parties had intended that effect should be given to their oral agreement (BGH (VIII ZR 226/83) 31 October 1984, [1985] DB1014).

Surprise clauses

Standard contract conditions which are so unusual that in the circumstances the other party need not expect them are deemed not to have been incorporated into the contract. Obviously in commercial transactions a businessman is expected to be alert and to read the 'small print' and the provision is less likely to apply than in consumer transactions. An example of a clause which was held to be so unusual that it contravened the AGBG and therefore did not form a valid part of the agreement, was one which was contained in a contract for the sale of a property under which interest on the purchase price was to accrue from a date several months before the signing of the contract (BGH (VII ZR 195/84) 6 March [1986] DB 1519).

On the other hand even in business transactions a clause contained in the standard conditions must be capable of being read in order for it to be validly incorporated. So where a clause relating to the choice of law was in such small print that it could hardly be read with a magnifying glass it did not become part of the agreement (BGH (II ZR 135/82) 30 May 1983, [1983] RIW 872).

Principle of good faith

Article 9 of the AGBG provides that standard terms are void if they place the other party at an undue disadvantage to such an extent as to be inconsistent with the requirements of good faith. This is supplemented by two presumptions as to undue disadvantage:

- if the provision is incompatible with the fundamentals of a legal norm, or
- restricts fundamental rights or duties inherent in the contract to such an extent as to jeopardize its object.

An example of a clause which was held void under Art. 9 as contrary to good faith was a clause in standard conditions under which a client was charged at the same rate for the travelling time of a mechanic who was called out to service a machine at the client's premises as for the time spent by the mechanic in doing the work (BGH (X ZR 75/83) 5 June [1984] DB 1719).

Different rules in business and consumer contracts

In consumer contracts the Act distinguishes between the terms which are always void, those listed in Art. 11, and those which are listed in Art. 10 which require a value judgement of the court to decide in the particular circumstances whether as a matter of law the clause is reasonable or not.

According to Art. 24 of the Act the provisions of Arts. 10 and 11 do not apply directly to business contracts but they do apply indirectly through the application of Art. 9. So a clause which under the Act is automatically void in a consumer contract may be held to be void under Art. 9 in a business transaction although the control which is exercised will be more flexible. Effectively a clause which is void under Art. 11 of the Act in a consumer transaction will be held void also in a business transaction unless the user can establish to the court's satisfaction some very good reasons why it should be held valid.

Clauses which may be void according to the value judgement of the court

The most important provisions of Art. 10 of the Act which the court may in the exercise of its value judgement find to be void are as follows:

- S.2   This is a clause allowing the user an unreasonably long period for the performance of an obligation after it has become due. As noted already (see above, pp. 216–219) German law requires that generally a party is only in default, say in terms of an obligation to deliver, if he is first given notice to deliver by a fixed date unless the contract provides specifically for a fixed delivery date. A clause in the general conditions of contract of a manufacturer of prefabricated houses which gave the manufacturer the right to delay delivery for six weeks after the agreed delivery date was held to be void (BGH (VII ZR 276/83) 28 June 1984, [1984] DB 2341).
- S.3   A right for the user to rescind the contract unilaterally without good and sufficient cause. There must accordingly be reasons which justify termination. Even

though Art. 321 of the *BGB* allows termination of an obligation which a party must perform first, if after the conclusion of the contract a serious deterioration occurs in the financial situation of the other party, it has been held that a clause in the standard conditions of a lessor of medical equipment which gave the lessor the right to terminate without notice, if there was a deterioration in the financial position of the lessee, was invalid, as it unfairly disadvantaged the lessee (BGH (VIII ZR 247/89) 8 October [1990] DB 2367).

- S.4   A right for the user to deviate from his performance obligations unless the other party having regard to the interests of the user can reasonably be expected to agree to such a provision. The burden of proof that it is reasonable rests as always on the user. There has been disallowed a reservation that delivery could be made of a follow-on model from that which has been ordered (OLG Koblenz ZIP 81,509).

- S.7   A provision entitling the user on early termination of a contract to unduly high compensation. So on the early cancellation of a contract for the hire of equipment the user was entitled to recover his loss of profits actually incurred. A clause in his standard condition providing that he was entitled to recover his full calculated profits was invalid as it released him from any obligation to minimize his losses by reselling or rehiring the equipment (BGH (VIII ZR 296/89) 10 October [1990] DB 2463).

Article 11   Clauses in a contract which are absolutely void

Article 11 provides that in consumer contracts certain terms are absolutely void. As regards business contracts some of these will in practice be held void by the courts according to Art. 9 of the Act. There will only be mentioned here those which appear from court decisions to be generally considered void in business transactions:

- S.3   Exclusion of a right of set-off in respect of a claim not disputed or in respect of which a final judgement against the user has been obtained. So a clause in standard conditions allowing no right of set-off under any circumstances would be void (BGH (X ZR 97/83) 16 October 1984 [1985] DB 222).[27]

- S.5   A clause entitling the user to liquidated damages which exceed the amount normally to be expected in such cases as those to which the agreement relates or which prevent the other party from showing that no damages were suffered by the user or only substantially less than the liquidated amount.

    The principle of German law relating to liquidated damages, that they should be a genuine pre-estimate of the loss likely to be suffered, is the same as English law. But unlike English law it is open to the other party to show that either no loss or a loss substantially less than that due under the liquidated damages clause has been suffered and that the damages due should be reduced accordingly (see above, pp. 232–233).

- S.7   The exclusion or limitation of liability for gross negligence. This clause will generally be applied to business transactions and it would be wise in drafting standard conditions not to attempt to exclude it.

- S.10a   The exclusion or limitation of the supplier's liability for defects in new goods. But these rights may be suspended while the supplier reserves the right either to rectify the defects, replace the defective goods or assign to the purchaser the rights which the seller has against his own suppliers.

- **S.10e** A clause stipulating that the other party must notify the user of latent defects within a period shorter than the statutory period for elimination of defects. This is not in itself invalid in business contracts but a limitation to an unreasonably short period would be a violation of Art. 9. So a clause in standard conditions for use between businessmen which limited the purchaser's rights to complain of defects to the time of delivery, and so excluded any rights in respect of defects not immediately obvious, was held void (BGH (VII ZR 152/84) 3 July [1985] DB 2556).

- **S.10f** This provides that the statutory limitation period cannot be reduced. Here again this is not necessarily applicable as such to business transactions but the reduction must not be excessive otherwise the clause will be void under Art. 9. Again in practice in drafting a defects liability clause for defects in business contracts it would be wise to retain the statutory period which is short enough anyway.

    An unusual case concerned the standard conditions of a purchaser which provided that the period for defects was to be three years and not the statutory six months, and this was held void as contravening the AGBG (BGH (VIII ZR 292/88) 17 January [1990] DB 578).

- **S.11** A clause in contracts of sale or work and labour which excludes or restricts liability for damages for breach of an express warranty that the thing sold or the subject of the work has specific qualities or characteristics. This provision applies generally to business transactions. It follows that although the seller may exclude consequential damages, e.g. loss of profit or other economic loss for defects he will not be permitted to do so for breach of the express warranties under Arts. 463, 480(2) and 635 of the *BGB*.

- **S.15a** A clause reversing the burden of proof contrary to the rules on evidence especially if the facts are within 'the sphere of responsibility of the user'.

Effect of a clause being held void

The effect of a clause being held void is that the invalid clause will be deleted and replaced by the relevant provision of the civil code, i.e. the courts will not redraft the clause so as to make it valid and serve its original purpose so far as possible (BGH (VI ZR 4/84) 24 September 1985, [1986] DB 480).

According to Art. 6 of the Act the only exception is that if the enforcement of the contract without the void term would impose 'intolerable hardship', but this has little application.

CONCLUSION

Because of the serious impact which the finding by the court that a term of the standard conditions was void would have on the extent of the seller's or contractor's obligations, the drafting of standard conditions is an exercise only to be undertaken by experts and with great care, erring if anything on the side of caution.[28]

COMPARATIVE SUMMARY

Leaving aside the particular problem of consumer protection, there is a significant difference of approach as between the two civil law systems and that of the English common law. The English law of contract has been profoundly influenced by the practice of merchants and by the opinion that in commercial transactions it is for the parties themselves to decide upon the allocation of risks between them. It is the general view that the certainty which comes from the courts upholding a bargain upon the terms into which it is entered, is to be preferred to the uncertainty which would prevail if the courts were to upset the parties' expectations and the basis therefore upon which the contract had been priced.

The Unfair Contract Terms Act 1977 has changed the common law position by the requirement, applicable to most business contracts, for the party seeking to rely on an exclusion or limitation of liability clause to satisfy the test of reasonableness. However, as between businessmen who can be expected to seek legal advice as to the meaning of such clauses and to negotiate with the other party accordingly, if necessary insuring themselves against the risks to which they remain exposed, the approach of the courts has been generally cautious towards finding the clauses unreasonable other than in the most extreme cases.

In contrast, the extent to which a professional seller, even if dealing with another business entity, can exclude or limit his obligations which constitute the legal norm under either the *Code Civil* or the *BGB*, has been limited in France primarily by the courts and in Germany by a combination of the courts and the Standard Contract Terms Act. True the two civil law systems do differ in their approach and in the detail of the rules which they apply. In French law only if he is dealing with a professional of the same speciality can a professional seller limit his liability for damages for *vices cachés*. Further, although in principle if the goods are not in conformity with the contract, a limitation of liability clause would be valid, in practice the courts get round this by characterizing the failure as due to *faute lourde*. All this is quite regardless of whether the contract is on standard terms or not. In German law the problem for the seller or contractor usually arises only under standard form contracts but these in practice form the vast majority of transactions. There, although the professional seller/contractor can limit his liability for latent defects to repair, replacement or a reduction in the price, he cannot avoid his liability in damages for breach of an express warranty.

Considering a case such as *Edmund Murray Ltd* v. *BSP International Foundations Ltd* (see above, p. 296), and accepting the defects were as the buyer claimed, it is clear that under French law the defects would have been characterized as a failure to deliver conforming goods due to *faute lourde*, and under German law as a breach of express warranty *Fehlen zugesichterte Eigenschaft*. In either event there could have been no argument about the non-applicability of the seller's standard clause limiting his liabilities and denying the purchaser the right to claim damages. Although the Court of Appeal, over-ruling the trial judge, did find the exemption clauses unreasonable, it was not an outcome which could have been easily foreseen, nor is the court's reasoning wholly convincing.

NOTES

1. See the discussion in Zimmermann, p. 259 et seq.
2. See Atiyah *The Rise and Fall of the Freedom of Contract*, p. 62 et seq.
3. Grotius *De Jure Belli et Pacis*, Vol. 2, Clarendon Press, Oxford, 1925, at p. 348 et seq.
4. Pothier *Traité du Contrat de Vente*, Part II, Ch. II, p. 251 et seq.
5. Atiyah, op.cit., p. 167 et seq. 'The Fair Exchange'.
6. Napoleon quoted by Von Mehren, p. 825.
7. See his judgement in *Lloyds Bank* v. *Bundy* [1975] QB 326, and the comments in Cheshire on p. 315 on the decision of the House of Lords in *National Westminster Bank plc* v. *Morgan* [1985] AC 686.
8. See for example *Conlon* v. *Murray* [1958] NI 17.
9. Cass. civ. 6 June 1921 D.P.1921 1,73.
10. Cass. civ. 20 May 1985 a case in which the *Cour de cassation* allowed an appeal by a road haulage company against the refusal of an insurance company to pay out for a loss by stealing because they had not approved the haulier's anti-theft system, ruling that the Cour d'Appel should have investigated whether or not the insurers having taken the premiums covering theft had acted in good faith.
11. *Photo Production Limited* v. *Securicor Transport Ltd* [1980] AC 827.
12. Cass. com., 15 June 1959 D.1960,97 reproduced with commentary in *Les Grands Arrêts de la Jurisprudence Civile*, p.415.
13. If the deliberate breach is of trivial importance then the court may well construe the exemption clause as covering the breach in question, but if the breach is of major importance then it appears to be a rebuttable presumption that the parties did not intend the clause to apply. Contrast the statement in the *Suisse Atlantic* case [1967] 1 AC 361 that a deliberate delay of 1 day in unloading could be covered by an exemption clause with that in the *Sze Hai Tong Bank* v. *Rambler Cycle Co.* [1959] AC 576, that a clause in general terms could not exclude the liability of a bailee who threw away the goods entrusted to him.
14. French law makes the same distinction as exists in English law between clauses which restrict the scope of a party's normal obligations under that type of contract and those which limit his responsibilities for default. However, in practice the distinction is not of great practical importance. If either the act is a breach of an obligation which is essential to the performance of the contract, or is one which is very probably to result in damage, then the courts are likely to characterize the act as being *faute lourde* so that the clause limitative or exonerative of responsibility would be void. Cass. civ. 1 18 January 1984 aff. du Loto B.I. no. 29, and see Malaurie and Aynes 472–474.
15. (1983) 2 TLR 21.
16. Unreported, but see articles in *The Buyer*, Vol.14, Issue no.7, July 1992, p.1 and *Building Law Monthly*, June 1992, Vol.9, Issue 6, at p. 4, both journals published by Monitor Press, Sudbury.
17. Ghestin, s.54, p. 37.
18. S.94 at p. 90.
19. See Weill and Terré, s.95.
20. Cass. civ. 14 February 1866 and *Les Grands Arrêts de la Jurisprudence Civile*, p. 480.
21. In addition there is the Ordinance of 1st December 1986 relating to the freedom of prices and competition and the decrees and arrêts which have been made under the provisions of the Ordinance which relate in general to consumer protection and in particular to the need to provide the consumer with information relating to the price of goods and services and any limitation of the seller's contractual liabilities. As such the details are outside the scope of the present work. For the Ordinance see *Code de Commerce*, Dalloz, p. 577.

22. In the proposals for the Law of 18 January 1992 there was included Art. 9 which would have given the court the power expressly to decide that certain clauses were void if they were imposed on a consumer or non-professional by reason of the abuse of economic power by the other party. However, in the proceedings before Parliament in November and December 1991 the Article was withdrawn. For a comment on this and consumer protection generally in France see 'Les hauts et les bas de la protection contre les clauses abusives' by Jerome Huet in *La Semaine Juridique*, Ed.G, No.25, p. 271, Doctrine 3592.

23. In fact, they seem to have decided on an intermediate position, *un obligation de moyens renforcée*. The fault of the debtor is presumed unless he can prove the absence of fault or *cause étrangère*. This solution had been adopted previously in relation to the liability of a dry-cleaner – see Cass. civ. 24 March 1987, B.I. no. 106.

24. See the commentary in *La Semaine Juridiqiue*, Ed.G., no.48, Jurisprudence (1991), no.21673, p. 418. It would appear that the courts may have been influenced by the Loi of 5 January 1988 which has allowed recognized consumer associations to ask the courts to order the removal of abusive clauses from standard conditions of contract used by firms in their dealings with consumers. See on this point Mazeaud and Chabas, p. 772, and for an example of the application of the law Grenoble 13 June 1991 J.C.P. 92, II, 21819.

25. 26 October 1921 RGZ 108,82 judgement given in English translation, Schlesinger et al., p. 715.

26. See the judgement of the Bundesgerichtshof 7 February 1964 BGHZ 51,151 given in English translation in Schlesinger et al., pp. 719 and 720.

27. This may be compared with the decision of the Court of Appeal in *Stewart Gill Ltd* v. *Horatio Myer & Co. Ltd* [1992] 2 All ER 257, in which a clause purporting to exclude any right of set-off whatsoever was held unreasonable under the Unfair Contract Terms Act.

28. See Dannemann, op.cit., p. 45, and the example he gives of a standard sales contract on p. 123.

21 Remedies and excuses for non-performance

ENGLISH LAW

SPECIFIC PERFORMANCE

The normal remedy for breach of contract at common law was an award of damages. The only exception was an order for the payment of a sum of money. The remedy of specific performance in regard to all other contractual obligations was available only in equity. Even now specific performance is regarded as an 'equitable remedy'. It follows from this that the granting of the remedy is at the discretion of the court and that discretion is only likely to be exercised according to the modern view of the matter if in all the circumstances the granting of specific performance would be the most appropriate remedy for the breach of contract concerned. The burden of establishing that the remedy of damages would not be the appropriate remedy rests on the plaintiff.

Instances in which it has been established that damages would not be an appropriate remedy and specific performance has been ordered have usually been where there is no available substitute for the subject matter of the contract in question, e.g. houses and goods which are unique.

Recently the courts have been prepared to extend the category of goods which are unique from family heirlooms and the like to those which have become 'unique' because of commercial circumstances. So where steel belonging to the manufacturer was in the possession of British Railways who refused to delivery it because of their fear of strike action, the court ordered specific performance of the contract. The steel had in effect become 'unique' because of the severe shortage of the material at the time. Treitel argues that in similar circumstances the remedy of specific performance should also be available to a buyer even if the goods in question are not specific. While s.52 of the Sale of Goods Act gives the court discretion to order specific performance in respect of specific or ascertained goods it does not exclude the possibility of the court applying the remedy according to the general principles of law. The author agrees with Treitel's views.[1]

As noted above the remedy of specific performance is discretionary and the essential principles upon which the court will decide whether to exercise its discretion or not are generally those which one would expect to find given that the remedy has its origins in equity. The reasons why the court will be unlikely to grant the remedy are:

- the decree would operate harshly, e.g. the costs of performance are wholly out of proportion to the benefit which the plaintiff would obtain;
- a lack of fairness in the terms of the contract;
- the conduct of the plaintiff in behaving unfairly during the pre-contractual negotiations.

In addition a court will not generally order specific performance of a contract for personal services and in the past specific performance has been refused on the grounds that its enforcement would require constant supervision by the court. However specific performance has been ordered, even of a building contract, where the works were described in detail, damages would not in the particular circumstances have been an adequate remedy and the land had already been transferred to the defendant.[2]

In practice it seems that the rule owes more to the lack of precision in regard to the obligation to be enforced than it does to any general principle that specific performance will be refused because of the need for supervision.

However, even when due allowance is made for the circumstances in which a court may be persuaded to exercise its discretion, it nevertheless remains the case that English law thinks first and foremost that the general remedy for a breach of contract lies in damages and that specific performance is very much an exception to the rule.

RESCISSION

Under certain circumstances an innocent party may have the right to bring the contract to an end in addition to his right to claim damages. Apart from any express rights to do so under a termination clause set out in the contract, such a right may arise where there is a breach of a term of the contract which is a condition, or where the breach is fundamental in the sense that the innocent party is substantially deprived of the whole of the benefit which it was the intention of the parties that he should receive.

A term in the contract may be classified as a 'condition' if:

- it has been expressly made so by the parties in the contract, or
- it is implied as such by statute, or
- it is decided to be such by the courts.

Term expressly made so by the parties

The parties may actually use the express 'condition', e.g. in stating in the contract 'It is a condition that . . .' or they may use words which indicate it was their intention that the term should be read as a condition, e.g. the use of the expression 'Time is of the essence'. Normally if the parties to a formal contract use such language then the courts will give effect to it without regard to the actual impact that the breach had on the innocent party. They would only do otherwise if the contract read as a whole showed that this was not the intention of the parties. As an example, in a contract for a four-year distributorship the distributor as a 'condition' had to visit six named customers once a week. In fact he failed to make one visit out of some 1400 visits. It was held by the House of Lords that the parties could not have intended that any minor breach of such a clause which called for a total of 1400 visits should result in the right to terminate.[3]

Term implied by statute

Prime examples of this are the implied 'conditions' under s.14 of the Sale of Goods Act as to the merchantability or fitness for purpose of the goods. Usually these raise no problems, but the implied condition under s.13 that on a sale of goods by description there is an implied condition that the goods correspond with the description may do so, if there is only a technical breach and the buyer's real reason for wishing to rescind is that the market has turned against him. It has been suggested by Lord Wilberforce in one such case in the House of Lords that only words which constitute a substantial ingredient of the description of the thing sold should be considered as part of the description for the purpose of deciding whether or not there has been a breach of the implied condition. Mere words of identity which only served to point out the goods were not sufficient.[4]

Term decided to be so by the courts

The court will look at the contract as a whole to decide whether or not the intention of the parties was that the term which has been breached should be treated as a 'condition' and therefore carry with it the right to rescind. Where in the type of contract in question the term is usually regarded as of major commercial importance to the innocent party then this will be strong evidence that it should be so treated. In mercantile contracts, for example, stipulations as to the time when obligations are to be performed will usually be treated as conditions (per Lord Ackner in *CCSD* v. *Czarnikow*).[5]

Breach which is fundamental

Whether or not a breach is fundamental depends on whether it goes to the root of the contract. For example in a contract for delivery of goods by instalments, defects in one delivery would not be regarded as fundamental unless the seller's intentions showed that he was unwilling to comply with his contract. Similarly failure by the employer to pay one instalment will not normally justify rescission unless other factors show he no longer intends to be bound by the contract. It follows therefore that, in the absence of any express clause in the contract entitling the contractor to suspend work, he has no right to decline performance of his own obligations because of non-payment by the employer unless the default by the employer amounts to repudiation. English law, it seems, knows nothing of the defence of *exceptio non adimpleti contractus* which is to be found in French and German law and may entitle the innocent party to suspend performance until the other party has performed his own related obligation (see below, pp. 324 and 339).

The same principle as to the need for the default to be fundamental applies in construction contracts where there are defects in the work or delays in performance.

In the absence of any express clauses for determination it is only if the defects or delays are such as to show that the contractor either cannot or will not comply with his contract, so as to bring the works to completion in the manner provided for by the contract, that the employer would be justified in rescinding (*Sutcliffe* v. *Chippendale and Edmondson* [1971] 18 BLR 157).

THE CLAIM FOR DAMAGES

The general principle of English law is that the purpose of the award of damages is to compensate the plaintiff. They are not to punish the defendant for his breach of contract.

Categories of damages

Damages are normally divided into three categories:

- reliance
- restitution
- loss of expectation.

In practice it is the last of these which is the most commonly encountered and the most important so the other two categories will be dealt with only briefly.

Reliance   This occurs when the plaintiff incurs expense in performing the contract, or perhaps even in preparing for its performance, in reliance on the defendant also performing his part of the bargain.

Restitution   The typical situation in which a claim will be made for restitution is that in which an advance payment has been made for goods; the goods are defective on delivery but at that time the market value of the goods has fallen more than the decrease in value due to the defects.

Loss of expectation   The general rule is that the creditor is entitled to be put into the same position as he would have been had the debtor complied with the terms of his contract. We find the same rule expressed in French law. Article 1149 of the *Code Civil* states

> the damages due to the creditor are in general the loss which he has suffered and the profit of which he has been deprived subject to the following exceptions and modifications [these are discussed later, see below, pp. 326–329] and this has been expressed by the Cour de cassation in terms that 'the nature of the obligation is to re-establish, as accurately as possible, the equilibrium destroyed by the damage and to restore the victim to the position in which he would have found himself if the act causing the damage had not taken place'.[6]

The distinction between the 'loss suffered' and the 'profit deprived' is usually expressed as the difference between *damnum emergens* and *lucrum cessans*. In fact *damnum emergens* does not refer only to an expectation loss but may also be a reliance loss. It can cover therefore either the difference in price between that which the purchaser was due to pay under the contract and that which he had to pay to buy replacement goods due to the seller's default, or expenses incurred by one party in anticipation of the execution of the contract. English law has never used the distinction in these terms but in commercial practice *lucrum cessans* would often coincide with what is referred to commercially as 'consequential damages'.[7]

Remoteness

All three legal systems under consideration use some test as to whether or not a particular loss is in the circumstances of the case to be judged too remote to allow it to be recovered.

In English law the rules on remoteness were first developed in the celebrated case of *Hadley* v. *Baxendale* (1854) 9 Exch. 341. It was at one time thought that the case should be understood as establishing two rules, namely 'that the damages should be such as may fairly and reasonably be considered as arising either:

a) naturally, i.e. according to the usual course of things from such breach of contract itself, or
b) as may reasonably be supposed to have been in the contemplation of both parties at the time they made the contract as the probable result of the breach.'

The first rule applied to that which any reasonable person would have realized would flow from the breach. This second rule applied where there were particular circumstances known to *both* parties at the time of the contract which increased the consequences of the breach and therefore the defendants' liability. As was pointed out in the case, it would be unjust to impose such an additional liability without giving the defendants the opportunity to limit their liability or, it might be added, to adjust their price for the extra risk.

The remoteness test established in *Hadley* v. *Baxendale* was reformulated in *Victoria Laundries* v. *Newman* in what has been referred to as a classic statement of the law:[8]

> The aggrieved party is only entitled to recover such part of the loss actually resulting as was at the time reasonably foreseeable as liable to result from the breach. What was at the time so foreseeable depends on the knowledge then possessed by the parties, or at all events by the party who commits the breach.

The two rules of *Hadley* v *Baxendale* become one. There is the imputed knowledge which every reasonable person is taken to know in the ordinary course of things and the actual knowledge of special circumstances of which the contract-breaker was aware at the time of entering into the contract.

From the latest formulation of the test of remoteness by the House of Lords in the *Heron II*[9] it now appears that the correct test should be the probability of the loss occurring. A consequence could be foreseeable but most unlikely to occur and that should not give rise to a claim in damages in contract. But the difficulty their Lordships then had was in trying to formulate a test of the degree of probability which would justify liability.

They were not happy with the test of Lord Asquith of 'liable to result' and even less with his colloquialism of 'on the cards'. That seemed to them to be too low a degree of probability and to equate the test in tort to that in contract. They therefore sought to find words to express the requirement for a higher degree of probability. As Lord Reid said:

> The crucial question is whether or not on the information available to the defendant when the contract was made he should, or as a reasonable man in his position would, have realised that such a loss was sufficiently likely to result from the breach of contract to make it proper to hold that the loss flowed naturally from the breach or that a loss of that kind should have been within his contemplation (p. 385).

Others of their Lordships used slightly different expressions to describe the degree of probability required: 'would have appeared to the defendant as not unlikely to occur'; 'a very substantial degree of probability'; 'may be an even chance of its happening'.

However it is easier in these circumstances to criticize than to be constructive and it is not clear that any of the tests referred to in the Heron II case clarified the matter any further other than to confirm that the degree of foresight or contemplation required in contract is higher than it is in tort.

In a more recent decision, *Balfour Beattie Construction (Scotland)* v. *Scottish Power*,[10] a construction company contracted with the Electricity Board for the supply of power to a concrete batching plant which it was operating for various works including the construction of an aqueduct which required continuous power. There was an interruption in the supply of power which constituted a breach of contract by the Electricity Board and made necessary the demolition and reconstruction of a major part of the structures. The contractor brought an action claiming damages for the demolition and reconstruction work but it was held that damage of that type could not have been in the reasonable contemplation of the board at the time when the contract was made and that accordingly the loss claimed was too remote. There was no evidence that the board had been warned of the likely consequences if there was an interruption in the power supply and the court was not prepared to hold that damages of the kind that were suffered were such as should have been in the reasonable contemplation of the board in the ordinary course of events. For anyone with even a layman's knowledge of how concrete is made, poured and laid, the decision seems unusually favourable to the defendants but could perhaps be justified on the grounds that it is only knowledge which a person in the electricity supply could be expected to have as a member of that industry which is to be taken into account.

Directness

There seems to be no separate test in English law of directness once the issue of foreseeability has been resolved. We shall see that French law does have a requirement that the loss should be the immediate and direct consequence of the default of the other party but it seems doubtful whether or not in practice this produces any significantly different results from those which an English court would reach using only the contemplation test.

Of course the default must be at least partially the cause of the loss. If there are, however, two causes both concurring in the loss and of equal efficacy then this is sufficient to find the defendant liable. So where in 1939 a ship was delayed for unseaworthiness and as a result of the delay in sailing was placed under an embargo because of the outbreak of war, it was held that the charterers could recover their loss in chartering a neutral ship to carry their cargo to its Swedish destination. The outbreak of war and the embargo were considered to be foreseeable events. However where the two events are not connected, as would be the case if the ship, having been delayed, were caught in a typhoon, then the shipowner would not be liable as the unseaworthiness would only have a 'fortuitous connection' with the loss of the ship.[11]

A particular case of concurrent causes is where the defendant is himself partially responsible for the loss. The situation here is unsatisfactory under English law as it stands and has been the subject of the Law Commission Working Paper no. 114 on the issue of whether or not contributory negligence should be available as a defence in an action in contract. Such a defence was not open to the defendant sued in contract at common law. Either his conduct was causally irrelevant, in which case he recovered the whole of the loss, or it was the predominant cause, in which event he recovered nothing at all.

The question then arose as to the effect in contract of the Law Reform (Contributory Negligence) Act 1945 which provided for the apportionment of damages where both parties were at fault. It is thought that the Act only applies where the defendant's liability in contract to use reasonable skill and care coexists with his liability in tort and proof of the existence of a contract is not necessary to establish liability in tort (*Vesta* v. *Butcher* [1988] 3 WLR 565), although as the Law Commission pointed out the Court of Appeal's remarks on the subject were strictly *obiter*.

The preferable solution seems to be that the defence should be allowed generally in contract cases regardless of whether the breach complained of is of a duty to exercise reasonable skill and care or of a strict liability.

Mitigation

It is a general rule of English law that the plaintiff is under a duty to mitigate his loss. For example if the seller has failed to deliver the goods then the buyer must act reasonably by purchasing substitute goods as near to the time of the breach as is reasonable. If he delays beyond then and the market price rises he cannot claim for the additional loss.

LIQUIDATED DAMAGES AND PENALTIES

Damages for delay in completion of a construction or engineering contract or for failure of a process plant to reach the required contractual level of performance are frequently stated in the contract in advance. There are usually advantages in this arrangement to both sides. From the employer's viewpoint it avoids him having to go to the trouble of quantifying his loss and proving that it was in the reasonable contemplation of the parties at the time of their entering into the contract. As a liquidated sum he can deduct it from the payments otherwise due to the contractor on completion.

From the contractor's viewpoint it establishes the limit of his liability and prevents him from facing claims for damages for loss of profit which may be substantially in excess of the contract price, since once an employer has stipulated for the payment of liquidated damages then he cannot recover more than those damages regardless of the extent of his actual loss. By corollary the employer does not have to establish that he has suffered any actual loss in order to recover the liquidated damages. The matter is viewed as having been settled at the time when the parties entered into the contract.[12]

However, all the above is based on the presumption that the sum stated in the contract is regarded by the courts as being liquidated damages and not a penalty. We have met penalties before in Chapter 1 in the discussion on penal bonds. The essence of a penalty is that it is a sum included in the contract in order to compel performance by placing the party *in terrorem* if he fails to comply with his obligations. The courts base their decisions on equitable principles and so will not enforce payment of a penalty. It is therefore important to distinguish between the two possibilities.

Essentially the difference lies in the amount which is specified. If this is 'so extravagant in comparison with the greatest loss that could conceivably be proved to have followed from the breach' then it will be a penalty (per Lord Dunedin in *Dunlop Pneumatic Tyre Co. Ltd* v. *New Garage & Motor Co. Ltd* [1915] AC 79).

It may also be held to be a penalty if the same sum is payable on the occurrence of two or more events, and one event is bound to cause a much greater loss than another. This can be so even if the amount is reasonable in respect of the breach which actually happened but would have been totally unreasonable if the breach had been some hypothetical minor event. But in considering such a clause regard is to be had only to the range of possible losses which are reasonably likely to occur. A clause will not be regarded as a penalty if the stipulated amount would only be extravagant in relation to the damages which the plaintiff could otherwise recover in the absence of the clause, in a hypothetical situation which was wholly fanciful and improbable (*Philip Hong Kong Ltd* v. *Attorney General of Hong Kong, The Times* 15 February 1992).

It is for this reason that where a part of a process plant, or a part delivery of the total quantity of goods, can be used independently of the remainder, then the damages must be calculated only on the portion which is in default.

Assuming the sum is held to be a penalty this does not alter the fact that the defendant is in breach of contract. It only means that the plaintiff must now prove his claim for damages at large.

THE DOCTRINE OF FRUSTRATION

The original rule of the common law was that, if at the time of its conclusion a contract was legally valid, then it remained enforceable unless its performance subsequently became illegal. The reasoning was simple. If a party wished to be excused in particular circumstances from further performance then it was for him to say so within the terms of his contract.[13] The only exception seems to have been a contract for personal services where the party concerned was unable to carry out the promised performance because of death or serious incapacity, or if performance became illegal.

The modern doctrine of frustration only began with the decision in *Taylor* v. *Caldwell* in 1863. There the plaintiffs had hired the defendant's music hall for the purpose of giving a series of concerts, and six days before they were due to begin the music hall was burnt down accidentally. The defendants were held not liable for the plaintiff's wasted expenses on advertising etc. on the grounds that the contract was subject to an implied condition that the parties were to be excused from performance if, before any breach, performance became impossible because of the perishing of something, i.e. the music hall, upon the continued existence of which the possibility of performance depended.[14]

In recent years the doctrine of frustration has been increasingly interpreted by the courts in a restrictive manner. The general principle upon which frustration will be allowed was probably best expressed by Lord Radcliffe in 1956 when he said that frustration occurs when

> without the default of either party a contractual obligation had become incapable of being performed because the circumstances in which performance is called for would render it a thing radically different from that which was undertaken by the contract. It was not this that I promised to do.[15]

From this statement the limitations on the operation of the doctrine may be expressed as:

1. The obligation must be incapable of being performed. Mere difficulty, inconvenience, extra expense have repeatedly been held not to justify a finding that the contract has been frustrated. It is for the parties to make appropriate provisions in their contracts to cover such eventualities.
2. If the purpose for which the contract has been concluded can still be performed, if only in part or under great difficulty or would only provide to the other party a fraction of the benefits intended, the contract still remains binding. It is only if the frustrating event is such that the whole purpose of the contract is defeated that the contract will be treated as frustrated. In deciding what is the purpose of the contract a court will only take into account the means by which the contract was to be performed if such means were an essential term of the contract.[16]
3. A contract will not be treated as frustrated if the alleged frustrating event is due to the act or default of the party claiming the contract is frustrated. This will include any election made by the party seeking to rely on the frustrating event as to which contract he will perform in circumstances in which he cannot perform all the contracts which he has undertaken. So if he elects to perform contract A, and cannot as a result perform contract B, since as a result of the alleged frustrating event, he lacks the means to perform more than one of the two contracts, he cannot claim

contract B is frustrated unless the means were an essential term of contract B.[17]

The effect of frustration is that the contract is automatically brought to an end at the time of the frustrating event. Therefore at common law rights which had accrued at the time of the frustrating event remained but otherwise rights were unenforceable. A part payment made, therefore, before a contract was frustrated could only be recovered if no benefit had been received, i.e. there had been a total failure of consideration. But this could be unfair if the partial payment had already been expended on preliminary work in the performance of the contract and was now wasted.[18] Equally where there had been part performance of an entire contract, the contractor could recover nothing in respect of work partially performed when, for example, a contract for the erection of machinery was frustrated because of the destruction by fire of the factory into which it was being installed.[19]

The position was changed by the Law Reform (Frustrated Contracts) Act 1943 which allows the recovery of expenses incurred provided that under the contract there were stipulations for pre-payment. Also the Act provides for the court to award a just sum if one party has received a benefit from the efforts of the other before the frustrating event providing, it would seem, that the benefit survives the frustrating event. The wording of the Act and its interpretation by the courts cannot, however, be considered satisfactory in solving the injustices of the common law rules.[20]

The Act also does not apply to certain contracts, in particular those to which s.7 of the Sale of Goods Act applies, i.e. contracts for the sale of specific goods, where the goods perish without the fault of either party before the risk passes to the purchaser. These therefore continue to be subject to the old common law rule so that if, for example, the goods perish while the seller is putting them into a deliverable state, the purchaser can recover any advance payment he has made but the seller cannot offset any expenses he has incurred. If the goods, say machinery, were not specific, then the seller at common law again could not recover any expenses incurred before the frustrating event but could do so under the Act if there had been an advance payment. The author agrees with Atiyah's comment that 'the Act still leaves much to be desired'.[21]

FRENCH LAW

EXÉCUTION EN NATURE

In contrast to English law the basic right of the creditor is to have the contract performed by the debtor. In principle in the same way as under Art. 1243 the creditor may not be required to accept any other than the thing which is due to him under the contract, he may also refuse to accept damages instead of the performance by the creditor of his obligations. According to Art. 1184 of the *Code Civil*, in the case of a synallagmatic contract, 'the party in whose favour an obligation has not been executed has the right either to compel the other to execute the contract, if that is possible, or to request the rescission of the contract with damages' (see further below, pp. 327 and 328). However in practice, since a creditor may not exercise physical compulsion over the debtor, this principle is subject to exceptions where it is a matter of personal performance.

It is convenient to distinguish between obligations to transfer property (*de donner*) and obligations to perform or not perform some act (*de faire ou de ne pas faire*).

Obligations de donner

Where the goods are specific there is no problem provided that they have not been destroyed. The property has passed to the purchaser as a result of the agreement for sale (see above, p. 240). The creditor has the right to apply to the court for the goods to be seized by the *huissier* (bailiff) and handed over to him (*saisie revendication*) – see Art. 156 Annexe 32 of the Code of Civil Procedure (Law of 31 July 1992).

Where the goods are unascertained (*choses de genre*) and the debtor refuses to deliver, then the creditor can obtain from the court the right to obtain substitute goods at the expense of the debtor and the debtor may be required by the court to provide an advance of the sums needed by the creditor for this purpose (Art. 1144 of the *Code Civil* as amended by the Law of 9 July 1991 which came into force on 1 January 1993). The authorization of the court is not required if the contract is subject to the commercial law. It is then only necessary for the creditor to give the debtor prior notice in writing (*une mise en demeure*) of his intention to purchase replacement goods. The replacement goods in any event must be of the same quality and quantity as those which were to be supplied under the contract (see also above, pp. 179–180).

Obligation de faire ou de ne pas faire

If one were to take literally Art. 1142 of the *Code Civil* then an action *en nature* would not be allowed for a breach of such an obligation. The Article reads: 'Any obligation to do or not to do resolves itself into damages in case of non-performance on the part of the debtor'. This follows the old maxim *nemo praecise cogi ad factum*.

However in practice Art. 1142 is treated by the jurisprudence as an exception and is only applied in two circumstances. The first is when the performance of the obligation is no longer either physically or legally possible. The actor who is engaged to perform on a certain day and fails to appear can only be penalized in damages. The courts apply strictly Art. 1184 of the code referred to above so that the party who is entitled to the benefit of the non-performed obligation may, if it is still possible, compel performance. So in a case in which a building owner demanded that the contractor provided the correct number of four steps leading to a swimming pool as referred to in the contract instead of the three which he had constructed it was held that his demand could not be rejected unless it had been established that it was impossible to correct the work so that it was in accordance with the contract.[22] The *Cour de cassation* rejected the argument which had prevailed in the cour d'appel that no evidence had been given that the modification to three steps was such as to render access to the swimming pool difficult. This right of the creditor is wider than that foreseen under English law in which under such circumstances it is considered that a court would only award damages to the building owner (see above, p. 313). If then these were to be assessed on the basis of diminution in value of the property, which on the brief facts given seems quite probable, then such damages could well be nominal.

The second exception is that of contracts which require personal performance: 'How can you compel a strip tease artiste who has regained her feelings of modesty to exhibit herself in the nude against her will?'[23]

As referred to earlier in relation to a failure by the seller to delivery *choses de genre*, the creditor has the right, if there is a failure by the debtor to do that which he has undertaken to do, to ask the court to be permitted to execute the obligation himself at the expense of the debtor (Art. 1144 of the *Code Civil*). But, other than for the exception of the purchase of replacement goods under a contract governed by the commercial law, it must be noted that in all cases the creditor must obtain the authority of the court before be can proceed to perform the obligation himself at the debtor's cost, and the remedy is at the discretion of the court.

As regards the obligation not to do, modern jurisprudence considers that the creditor has a right to demand the destruction or termination of that which has been done in contravention of the contract and that it is only open to the court to substitute an award in damages if the destruction or termination would be impossible. So in a decision of the Third Division of the *Cour de cassation* in May 1981 it was stated

> In accordance with Art. 1143 of the *Code Civil* the owner of a plot in a housing development had the right to require that what had been built in contravention of the obligations arising from the specification should be demolished, independently of the existence or importance of the damage suffered, from the moment that the contravention of the specification had been established and it had not been put forward that the demolition was impossible. (Cass. civ. 3e 10 May 1981 Bull. civ. 111 no. 101)

Another case decided in the same way related to an employee having been made redundant starting up a business in contravention of a non-competition clause in his contract of employment. The cour d'appel had merely awarded damages of 6000 francs but the *Cour de cassation* quashed the decision as being in contravention of Art. 1143, since the previous employers had demanded that the competitor's business should be closed. While in the latter case an English court might have awarded an injunction, provided that they were satisfied that the clause in restraint of trade was reasonable, it is doubtful if in the former case they would have ordered the demolition of work built in contravention of the specification. The remedy, if any, would have been in damages and it would have been necessary for the creditor to establish the damage which he was entitled to recover. Under French law, however, it is clear from that and other similar cases that the creditor who demands *exécution en nature* does not have to establish that he has suffered any loss at all. It is sufficient if the debtor has failed to fulfil his contractual obligation.

RÉSOLUTION

The basis of the right to rescind a contract is Art. 1184 of the *Code Civil* to which reference was made earlier. The text of paragraph one reads: 'A condition for rescission is always implied in synallagmatic contracts for the case in which one of the parties does not comply with his obligation'.

In this case the contract is not rescinded as a matter of law. The party for whose benefit the obligation has not been performed has the choice either to compel the other to perform the contract when that is possible, or to claim its rescission with damages.

The rescission must be claimed by action at law and the defendant may be granted a period of grace in which to perform his obligation according to the circumstances. The essential condition which must be satisfied in order for the contract to be rescinded is that there must have been a failure by the defendant to perform his contractual obligation. It is not however necessary that this should have been due to any default on his part. Even in a case where his failure has been due to *force majeure* or *cause étrangère* the other party may still claim rescission. Nor need the failure be a total failure; it may be a partial or late failure. It is for the court to decide if the extent of the failure is sufficient to justify rescission of the contract. Goods may have been delivered which are defective or late. It has been repeatedly stated by the *Cour de cassation* that

> Art. 1184 does not distinguish between the causes of the non-performance of contracts and does not allow *force majeure* to be an obstacle to the rescission of the contract in the case where one of the parties does not fulfill his obligations; in effect in a synallagmatic contract the obligations of one of the parties are the cause of the obligations of the other and reciprocally in such a way that if the obligations of one are not fulfilled, for whatever reason, the obligations of the other are deprived of cause; . . . and in the case of a partial failure to execute the contract it is for the court below to assess according to the circumstances of the facts if such partial failure has been of sufficient importance that the rescission of the contract should be pronounced immediately or if it would not be sufficiently remedied by an award of damages; that power of assessment is within the absolute control of the court below.[24]

In practice the court will take into account the importance of the failure (*inexécution*). Are the goods delivered so late or so defective that they no longer possess any real interest for the purchaser? Would the purchaser have entered into the contract had he foreseen the extent of the seller's defective execution? The principle behind these questions has been said to be to determine whether or not the obligation which has not been complied with constituted the *cause* of the obligation of the purchaser (see above, pp. 96–97). However it is not clear how the breach of a subsidiary obligation (*obligation accessoire*) could ever constitute a lack of *cause* and yet it is admitted that rescission can be granted by the court not just for the breach of the *obligation principale* but also for an *obligation accessoire*.

In addition the court will take into account the conduct of the parties. Have they behaved in good faith? Is the failure due to a fault of the debtor? Although as stated above fault is not a necessary condition for the exercise of the remedy of rescission, nor is the bad faith of the debtor, the court will have regard to the parties' moral behaviour. Is it a reason for rejecting the creditor's demand for rescission that he is

322

acting in bad faith by using the *inexécution* of the debtor as an excuse to rid himself of an unfavourable bargain?[25] This attitude is a consequence of the remedy of *résolution* being derived in large part from canon law and the teaching of the natural lawyers, in particular Domat, in which the concept of *résolution* was a sanction, which was followed in the *pays de coutumes* and is not derived from Roman law.[26] It is summed up in the maxim *Frangenti fidem, non est fides servanda* (When one breaks faith, faith is not obliged to be kept by the other).

It is for the court to decide whether in the circumstances to reject the request for rescission entirely, allow the contract to be rescinded totally, grant partial rescission and reduce the non-defaulting party's rights to a claim in damages. In contracts subject to the commercial law the court may decide, if the default is not sufficiently serious to justify rescission, and the goods are still of use to the purchaser, to adjust the contract by a reduction in the price.[27] Again in contracts for the delivery of goods by instalments, only if the contract is non-divisible will the court rescind the contract in its entirety for a default in the delivery of one instalment. In other instances the court will grant partial rescission with a corresponding reduction in price.[28]

Rescission and the award of damages

Damages may be awarded in addition to rescission or instead of rescission at the discretion of the court. However, once the contract has been rescinded the injured party's only remedy for the future is in damages; he can no longer require the performance of the contract.

Rescission under the express terms of the contract   The parties may include express provisions in the contract which entitle the injured party to rescind without reference to the court and even without the prior issue of a notice (*mise en demeure*) – see the discussion above, pp. 178–179. In general such provisions are not looked upon with favour by the courts and they will be given a restrictive meaning. Despite their apparent width, therefore, such clauses will only be upheld by the court if their drafting is absolutely clear. For example if the clause refers only to the right to terminate for *inexécution*, then this will not avoid the need to go to court but only restrict the right of the court to allow the defaulting party time to remedy the breach. For some suggested drafting which would allow rescission without reference to the court and even without the need to give a *mise en demeure*, see above, p. 179.

The injured party must also act in good faith when implementing such a clause.[29]

English law comparison

The comparison with English law is striking. First, based largely on mercantile matters, such as charter-parties or the purchase of goods for resale, English law will tend to construe as conditions the terms of a contract relating to performance and therefore automatically allow rescission for breach of that term irrespective of the damage suffered by the purchaser. The objective of the law has been said to 'promote certainty without regard to the magnitude of the breach'. French law has no such classification of the terms of a contract as 'conditions' and will look both at the nature of the breach and its effect on the innocent party together with the conduct of both parties in order to decide if rescission is justified. The moral basis of French law has no counterpart in English law.

Second, while English law allows the injured party to rescind on his own initiative French law insists that, in the absence of an express termination clause in the contract giving that right, the rescission can only be ordered by the court other than in circumstances where there is an urgent need to take immediate action.[30] If therefore a purchaser himself terminated a contract because the seller was in breach of his contractual obligation to deliver within a certain period, without an express provision in the contract entitling him to do so, and the delivery was not urgent, then he would be liable in damages to the seller.[31]

Third, a French court when asked to rescind a contract has a wide area of discretion as to the award which it makes including that of granting the party in default time to remedy the breach and of allowing partial rescission in a way which effectively adjusts the respective obligations of the parties. An English court which decided that the action of the injured party in rescinding was not justified would be limited to awarding damages for the breach.

EXCEPTIO NON ADIMPLETI CONTRACTUS

The use of the Latin expression is still common, the French term being *l'exception d'inexécution*. It refers to the defence which may be invoked by one party to a contract of suspending performance of his obligations because the other party has defaulted in the performance of his own.

There is no article in the *Code Civil* referring to the *exceptio*, which is a product of the jurisprudence. Although its basis is sometimes said to be that the *cause* of one party's obligations is in the performance by the other party of his, and in the absence of such performance, there is an absence of *cause*, it seems preferable to base it on the requirement to execute a contract in good faith and to assert that it would be contrary to good faith to claim to receive without performing oneself.

In order for the *exceptio* to be invoked legitimately the following conditions must be satisfied:

1. The obligation, the non-performance of which is claimed to give rise to the *exceptio*, must be co-relative with that of the *exceptio*. There has to be an interdependence between the two obligations which must originate in the same legal relationship. So one cannot withhold payment for goods because the seller has failed to fulfil his obligations under a separate contract for repair.
2. The obligations must be due at the same time. So where credit has been given for the balance of a price the *exceptio* may only be claimed in respect of the amount currently due.
3. If the failure is only partial then the right to the *exceptio* depends on a reasonable balance between the obligation unperformed and that of the *exceptio*. So the mere

fact of the landlord not having maintained as he ought to have done the premises let would not entitle the tenant to withhold the rent. When however the tenant was forced out of the premises during the winter because of carbon monoxide poisoning from the defective construction of the chimneys, then he was not surprisingly held to be entitled to withhold payment since he was deprived of his right to the normal usage of the premises.[32]

4. The *exceptio* must be invoked in good faith. Not only does this mean that the *inexécution* must not be due to the default of the party invoking it, but also it means that the *inexécution* must not be minimal.

5. The *exceptio* cannot be applied when to do so would be contrary to the express terms of the contract. As an example, a construction contract has provided that the contractor shall continue to work until an issue which it alleges to be a breach of the contract by the employer has been resolved by arbitration. The contractor could not in that instance suspend performance and invoke the *exceptio* as a defence to a claim by the employer for breach of contract for non-performance. He would be held by reason of the express terms of the contract to have waived any such right.

The important point about the *exceptio* is that it can be invoked by the party concerned without the necessity of going to court and without even the need to issue a *mise en demeure*, even though in practice the giving of notice is advisable. Of course the other party has the right to go to court and claim that the *exceptio* has been incorrectly invoked and, if successful, to recover damages for the loss he has suffered.

COMPARISON WITH ENGLISH LAW

There is no direct equivalent between the remedy of the *exceptio* and the provisions of English law. The difficulty in seeking to make a comparison is that the English rules are generally discussed under the heading of termination.

English law draws a distinction first between obligations which are independent of each other and those which are related. If the obligations are independent, as in the case of those of the tenant to pay rent and the landlord to effect repairs, then the fact of the tenant being in arrears does not alter the landlord's obligation to repair (*Taylor* v. *Webb* [1937] 2 KB 283). While French law requires that the obligations should arise out the same contractual relationship this will of itself generally satisfy the requirement for interdependence provided that the test of proportionality has been satisfied and the action has been taken in good faith.

So a case on the same facts as *Taylor* v. *Webb* was decided in the opposite way since the payment of rent was considered to be the essential obligation of the tenant breach of which allowed the landlord to refuse to perform his obligations of maintenance.[33]

The English cases where the obligations are interdependent can be classified as either cases in which the one obligation is a condition precedent to the performance of the other or both are concurrent. In these instances if the default is temporary this may justify the innocent party in withholding his own performance whilst the default continues although it would not give him the right to terminate.

The most obvious circumstance in which this arises is non-payment by the buyer when the seller still retains possession of the goods. The contract could not normally be terminated by the seller because of the buyer's breach, since under s.10 of the Sale of Goods Act time of payment is not of the essence of the contract, unless otherwise specifically provided. The seller would, however, be entitled to retain possession of the goods until he receives payment.

However, it has been stated several times in the courts that there is no general right of a contractor to suspend work on a building contract if interim payments are wrongly withheld. Such a right can only exist if it is expressly provided for in the contract.[34]

This contrasts with the position under French law where it is considered that the defence of the *exceptio* could be invoked if the contractor declined to proceed with the work under a *contrat d'entreprise* because of failure by the employer to pay sums due, until such time as he had been paid, unless its application was negated by the express terms of the contract.[35]

DAMAGES

There are three articles of the *Code Civil* which deal in general terms with the damages which are recoverable:

1. The damages which are recoverable by the creditor are in general the loss which he has suffered and the profit of which he has been deprived, subject to the exceptions which follow. (Art. 1149)
2. The debtor is only liable for the damages which were foreseen or could have been foreseen at the time of the contract when it was not due to his *dol* that the obligation was not performed. (Art 1150)
3. Even in the case where the non-performance of the contract is the result of the *dol* of the debtor the damages only cover the loss suffered by the creditor and the profit of which he has been deprived which are the immediate and direct result of the non-performance of the contract. (Art. 1151)

Article 1149 expresses the general obligation that the debtor is responsible for the totality of the damage, both the loss suffered (*damnum emergens*) and the profit of which the creditor has been deprived (*lucrum cessans*). This is then subject to the limitation imposed by Art. 1151 which requires that both types of damage must be the immediate and direct consequence of the breach.

Directness of the damage (Art. 1151)

This Article is applied both to contractual and delictual liability and the majority of the cases which are reported on this issue arise in delict. The classic and often quoted example given to explain the difference between damages which are the direct result of a contractual fault, and therefore recoverable, and those which are the indirect consequences and not recoverable was given by Pothier.[36]

The example concerned the sale of a mythical cow to a farmer with the seller knowing it was infected by a disease. The sick cow transmitted the disease to the farmer's other animals which died. The seller was clearly guilty of *dol* in knowingly selling a diseased animal and as such would be responsible for the loss of the cow and of the other beasts. However, assume now that as a result of the loss of the other beasts the farmer was not able to cultivate his land and so lost his income. In consequence the farmer could not pay his debts and his creditors seized his land and goods which were sold for a low price.

Pothier is clear that the loss incurred by the farmer in not being able to pay his debts and so losing his assets is too far distant to be the responsibility of the seller of the cow. He is less certain however about the loss of income itself by not being able to cultivate the land. This seems to him not necessarily to be due to the loss of the animals because the farmer could have cultivated the land with the use of other animals. But this would have earned him less profit than he would have earned using his own animals so the seller should be liable for at least part of the farmer's loss of income.

Although Pothier's example was based on the seller being guilty of *dol*, which made him liable for damages, in fact Art. 1151 applies whatever the degree of fault or negligence involved. Today, as a result of the assimilation of the professional seller to one who is aware of the existence of hidden defects, the liability of the professional seller under Art. 1645 to pay damages is not restricted to cases of *dol* or even *faute lourde* (see above, pp. 172 and 173). However there still has to be a lien of causality between the defect and the damage suffered. So in a case where the contractor had installed an alarm system, but the purchaser had been burgled, the *Cour de cassation* insisted that it was the responsibility of *les juges de fond* to establish whether or not there was a sufficient causal link between the default in the functioning of the system and the burglary.[37]

An example of damage being considered as direct given by Malaurie and Aynes is that of the recovery of the loss and expense caused to an owner of a vehicle or an aeroplane, which is recalled by the manufacturer for modifications because of the discovery of defects in that particular model, by reason of its non-availability to him during the time it is being modified.[38]

Another example quoted by Starck is that of a hotel fire which could have been restricted to the ground floor but spread to the upper floors where the bedrooms were situated due to the inflammable nature of the materials which had been used for interior fittings and decoration. The fault of the hotel in having utilized such materials was therefore the direct cause of the damage suffered by the guests.[39] However where the loss of a parcel of clothes by a dry-cleaner was claimed to have caused a loss of custom, this was held to be uncertain and indirect.

The question whether the damages are direct and therefore recoverable is essentially a matter for *les juges de fond* and, provided they have formulated their judgement correctly, escapes the control of the *Cour de cassation*. But if the court has found that there is an insufficient link between the fault and the damage and the damage is too remote, then they must explain their reasons for having done so, otherwise their judgement will be quashed. So if a store suffers loss by theft because of the failure of a burglar alarm system, then the court must say why they found the loss to be too indirect to be recoverable from the installer of the system.[40]

In theory the court should not take into account the degree of fault involved in deciding the question but in practice it seems that it is used as a means of moderating the damages they wish to allow. Provided however that this does not appear in the judgement it is outwith the *Cour de cassation*'s control.

In marked contrast with English law (see above, p. 316) where the damage has been due partially to the fault of the debtor and partially to the fault of the creditor, then the damages recoverable by the creditor will be reduced in proportion to his degree of responsibility. French law does not in this respect distinguish between contractual and delictual responsibility under the *droit commun*. See below pp. 335–336.

Foreseeability (Art. 1150)

In practice the test of foreseeability is often confused with that of directness and tends to be the more important in contractual disputes.

There are five important points to be made as regards the application in practice of the text of Art. 1150:

1. The unforeseeability may relate to any fact which is unknown to the debtor at the time of contract and which in some way increases the significance to the creditor of the performance of the contract. A contractor could not be expected to foresee that a warehouse which would normally be used as a shelter for materials was intended to be used by the purchaser for the breeding of race-horses. If a person suffers injury to his health because he has an allergy to damp, and the house which has been built for him has a defective ventilation system, the court must investigate whether or not that injury was foreseeable by the builder at the time of the contract, before awarding damages against him.[41]
2. What is to be foreseen is not just the type of damage but also the extent. This has been established in numerous cases as regards objects deposited, handed into dry-cleaners or given to carriers. If these are stolen or lost then it is only the value which they could normally be expected to have in the circumstances of the case which the court will take into account. Such circumstances may include the nature of the packing or, if garments are stolen in a hotel, the status of the hotel. Guests at a one-star hotel would not be expected to possess luxury garments. If items are of special value then this must be declared at the time of the contract to the person to whom they are entrusted.[42]
3. The appreciation of the foreseeability is to be made objectively or *in abstractio*. It is sometimes stated that this means that the degree of foreseeability is that of the reasonable man (*bon père de famille*). However one must be careful in stating it in this way since it is not the degree of foreseeability of the ordinary person which is to

be taken into account but that of the group of persons of the same degree of speciality as that of the debtor. A medical specialist may be expected to foresee more than a country doctor.

4. Although the extent of the damage is that which was foreseeable at the time of the contract, the evaluation of the damage is to be made at the time when the court gives its decision: 'the dispositions of Art. 1150 of the *Code Civil* which limit the responsibility of the debtor relate only to the estimate and the foreseeability of the elements comprising the damage and not the monetary equivalent intended to repair it'.[43] In practice this means that an expert in the field in question will be called upon to assess the increase, or exceptionally the decrease, in cost since the time of the contract. The purpose is to 're-establish as closely as possible the balance destroyed by the damage and to restore the victim to the position in which he would have been if the act causing the damage had never taken place'.

The changes in cost may be the result of a general increase in the level of prices or simply the market price for the goods concerned. There is no equivalent in French law to the requirements in English law for the debtor to mitigate his loss.

5. The requirement as to foreseeability does not apply in the case of *dol* to which the courts have assimilated *faute lourde*. As regards professionals the courts have gone further and the position would appear to be today that a professional seller does not benefit from Art. 1150 and would therefore be liable for any damage resulting from a hidden defect in the goods sold. If the action was brought under the *droit commun* rather than for *vice caché* the same result would probably arise in practice since the courts, in the case of a professional dealing with a non-professional, will tend to characterize the default as *faute lourde* (see above, pp. 175–176).

LIQUIDATED DAMAGES AND PENALTIES

French law makes no distinction of the kind made in English law between liquidated damages and penalties. It is recognized that a *clause pénale* may have two objectives: first, that of establishing the sum of money which is recoverable by the creditor in the event that the debtor fails to perform his obligations; second, that of a means of pressurizing the debtor to fulfil his obligations by a due date.

There are two characteristics which are common to both English and French law. First, once a *clause pénale* is included in the contract, the creditor does not have the right to demand more or less than the amount of the penalty. Article 1152 of the *Code Civil* states: 'When a contract provides that the party who fails to perform it shall pay to the other a sum by way of damages then the other may not be awarded a greater or lesser amount'. As we shall see later this was subject to the power of the court to intervene if the debtor was guilty of *dol* and is now subject to the right of the court to moderate or even increase the penalty (see below, pp. 330–331).

The second similarity is that the creditor does not have to prove that he has suffered any loss in order to invoke the *clause pénale*. The real distinction between the two legal systems is that French law does not have the requirement that, in order to be valid, the amount of the penalty should be a genuine pre-estimate of the damages. Indeed by expressly recognizing that it is a legitimate object of the *clause pénale* that it should operate to pressurize the debtor into performing his contract, it is clear that in many instances the amount of the penalty will exceed the foreseeable damages.

To be liable to pay the penalty the debtor must of course be in default of his contractual obligations so if the obligation is only one of *moyens* then the creditor must prove that he was at fault (see above, p. 155). If the obligation is one of *résultat* then the debtor will be liable simply by reason of not having achieved the promised performance, unless he can establish this was due to *cause étrangère* (see above, pp. 155–157).

Relationship between the penalty and other rights of the creditor

The creditor, instead of demanding the penalty, can request the court to order the execution of the contract by the debtor *en nature* (Art. 1228, *Code Civil*). If this is granted by the court then the creditor loses the right to demand the penalty for the failure by the debtor to perform the principal obligation of the contract, but he can still demand a penalty for delay in performance (Art. 1229, *Code Civil*).

Equally, even if the contract contains a penalty clause for failure to perform the creditor still has the right to demand rescission of the contract. He ought under those circumstances still to be able to claim damages as foreseen by Art. 1184 of the *Code Civil* but it is not clear whether or not he can recover as damages the amount of the penalty.[44]

Revision of the penalty

Unlike English law the power was recognized by the *droit commun* of the right of the court to increase the amount of the penalty where the debtor was guilty of *dol*, and the amount of the penalty was substantially less than the loss suffered by the creditor. The case concerned an actor in the Comédie française who accepted a part in a film in contravention of a clause in his service contract in which was included a penalty of 2500 francs for such an infringement. He was willing to pay the penalty no doubt because it was significantly less than the amount he would earn from the film. However the Comédie française obtained an award in excess of the penalty on the grounds that the penalty clause did not apply in the case of *dol*. The award was upheld by the *Cour de cassation* who agreed that the actor committed *une faute dolosive* by acting deliberately in breaching his contract even though he had no intention of damaging his co-contractant.[45]

However, there was no power to reduce the amount of the penalty where this was grossly superior to any loss that the debtor might suffer and there were many instances of this in contracts for leasing or hire purchase. As a result a law was passed in 1975, amended in 1985 and amends Art. 1152 by providing that 'Nevertheless the court can of its volition increase or decrease the amount of the penalty which has been agreed if it is manifestly excessive or derisory. Any stipulation to the contrary shall be deemed not to apply'. Further, Art. 1231 was also amended to provide that where a contract was partially executed the court could reduce the penalty in proportion to the interest which the partial execution had for the creditor and again this provision could not be written out of the contract.

In exercising their power the courts must state not only that they find the penalty excessive but also the reason why this is so. In determining their reasons the court may take into account everything that has arisen up to the time of their decision, such as the circumstances and conduct of the parties, and the object of the clause which may have been to pressurize the debtor. If the court does find the penalty manifestly excessive, they can freely fix the amount to be paid provided, however, that the amount of the penalty is not reduced below that of the damage actually suffered.[46] In the absence of any loss resulting from the breach then the amount may be reduced to the nominal sum of 1 franc.[47]

ASTREINTE

A particular provision of French law is that of the *astreinte*. This is defined as

> a monetary fine generally fixed at a rate of so much per day of delay which is accessory to and added by the court to the principal judgement in a case in which the party against whom judgement has been obtained, has not complied with the terms of that judgement, so as to persuade him to comply under the pressure of a continually increasing debt.[48]

The *astreinte* is fixed by the court at their discretion and at a rate which is considered to be appropriate to force the debtor to fulfil his obligation usually to do or not to do some act. The only circumstance in which an *astreinte* will not be applied is where performance is no longer possible, e.g. where an artiste was due to appear on a particular night and did not do so. The only remedy can then be in damages.

One issue which was for long controversial has now been settled. The *astreinte* is independent of any damages to which the creditor may be entitled (Art. 6 of the Law of 5 July 1972 now replaced by the Law of 9 July 1991, Art. 34, which confirmed an earlier judgement of the *Cour de cassation* on 20 October 1959).[49] It is the seriousness of the default and the need to fix the *astreinte* at a level which, in relation to the assets of the debtor, is likely to be effective in forcing him to comply with the judgement, which in practice are the relevant factors, although these do not need to be stated by the court.[50]

The *astreinte*, although it is in reality a fine for having failed to remedy a court order, is nevertheless payable to the creditor and not to the state. It may take one of two forms, either definitive or provisional. If it is provisional, which is the normal form, the *astreinte* is liquidated, i.e. turned into a fixed amount by the court at the end of the period which it has set (or when the debtor has made good his default). If at the end of the fixed period the debtor has still not complied then the court can set a further *astreinte*.[51]

In liquidating the *astreinte* the rules under which the court operates have been changed by the law of 9 July 1991, which came into force on 1 January 1993. Previously the court had total discretion in the matter and was not bound to state any reasons for its decision other than the failure by the debtor to comply with the court's order. It was not necessary for the court to take into account the debtor's degree of fault, except if he raised the issue of *force majeure* or *cause étrangère*, which if established would be a defence, nor the extent of his resources.[52] Nor, since the *astreinte* was independent of damages, was the court entitled to take into account the prejudice suffered by the debtor. This latter rule still applies but under the new law the court is to take into account the behaviour of the debtor (Art. 36 para. 1) and it is considered therefore that in practice the court will have to state its reasons for the rate at which it liquidates the *astreinte*.[53]

Only if the court states so when making the order will the *astreinte* be definitive (Law of 9 July 1991, Art. 34) and an *astreinte définitive* can only now be pronounced after an *astreinte provisoire* (Art. 34, para. 3) with which the debtor has not complied. In that event the court no longer has any discretion in amending the amount and it becomes only a matter of arithmetic to establish the amount of the *astreinte* according to the rate and the period of time in which the debtor is in default. He will only be excused if he can establish *cause étrangère* (Art. 36, para. 3 of the Law of 9 July 1991).

According to Art. 3 of the Law of 16 July 1980 the same distinction is made between the two types of *astreinte* in the administrative law.

The *astreinte* has been and continues to be used by the courts in a wide number of cases in order to compel the performance of their judgements. Once it may have been to restore an electricity supply abusively disconnected, or the demolition of a wall improperly constructed; today it may be the delivery of a computer programme. Whatever the circumstances the failure to do or refrain from doing that which the court has ordered may lead to the application of what, if the debtor has means, is the most effective of sanctions: to punish him in the pocket until he complies. It is the natural counterpart of the judgement *en nature* without which the recalcitrant debtor could escape just retribution.

In English law, since the remedy of specific performance is only rarely applied, the fact that the only means of enforcement of such a judgement is that of contempt of court which is totally discretionary, is not a handicap. The creditor in such an action does not, of course, benefit from the enforcement; any financial penalty would be for the benefit of the state. The remedy of the *astreinte* appears the more effective and if the purist argues that the fine should be for the benefit of the state and not the creditor, is it not the creditor who has suffered from the contumacious attitude of the debtor? Who better to be compensated?

EXCUSES FOR NON-PERFORMANCE – *IMPRÉVISION, FORCE MAJEURE ET CAUSE ÉTRANGÈRE*

Adjustment of the contract

It is a basic principle of French law that

in no case do the courts have the right, however equitable may appear to be their decision, to take into account the time and the circumstances, to modify existing contracts and substitute new provisions for those which have been freely accepted by the contracting parties.[54]

These words state the legal principle of judgement of the *Cour de cassation* in the famous Canal de Craponne case decided in 1876. Agreements had been entered into between 1560 and 1567 under which the original contractors and operators of the canal undertook to supply water for irrigation canals on the plain of Arles *in perpetuity* at a rate of 15 centimes per 190 sq. metres. In the nineteenth century the successors of the original operators sought an increase to a rate of 60 centimes based on a four-fold increase in labour costs since the sixteenth century.

The cour d'appel had allowed the increase on the grounds that the original contracts were successive and that contracts which provided for periodic payments could be modified by the court when there was no longer an equitable co-relation between the sums to be paid periodically and the charges incurred by the other party, i.e. the costs of maintenance. However the *Cour de cassation*, basing its judgement on Art. 1134, 'Agreements legally formed have the force of law for those who make them', which they said applied to contracts of any nature, would have none of this and quashed the judgement on the grounds that it violated Art. 1134.

The decision, although criticized, has been maintained consistently by the jurisprudence. In a case decided in December 1979 the storage company under a warehousing contract which ran for an indeterminate period sought, and were allowed by the cour d'appel, a revision to the price because the original price was no longer just under the changed economic circumstances. Again the *Cour de cassation* quashed the decision and stated, referring to Art. 1134, that 'In application of that text the court may not under the pretext of equity or for any other reason, modify agreements entered into between the parties'. Since the contract contained no clause foreseeing a change in price the decision was a violation of Art. 1134.[55]

These decisions and others like them may be compared with that of the Court of Appeal in *Staffordshire Area Health Authority* v. *South Staffordshire Waterworks Company* in 1978. There the waterworks company had contracted in 1919 to supply the hospital with water at a fixed price. By 1975 the cost of so doing had risen by eighteen times and the company gave seven months' notice of termination of the contract. The majority of the court considered that on its true construction the contract was for an indefinite period and therefore was prepared to apply the general principle that in commercial contracts of an indefinite duration, a term could be implied that the contract was terminable on reasonable notice.[56]

No such general doctrine exists under French law which, as stated earlier (see above, p. 87), does not accept the concept of 'implied terms'.[57] While the same result is often reached by the application of the principles of equity and good faith under Art. 1134 para. 3 and Art. 1135 of the *Code Civil* their application in this case has been expressly ruled out by the *Cour de cassation*.

In the administrative law, however, the doctrine of *imprévision* has been accepted as a counterpart to the obligation of the contractor to go on providing a public service. In the famous case of Gaz de Bordeaux in 1916[58] the company holding the concession to supply gas were successful in their application before the Conseil d'Etat for an increase in the price because of the increase in the price of coal which was in excess of anything which could have been foreseen at the time of the granting of the concession and which was the consequence of World War I. The price had gone up from 23 francs a ton to 116 francs.

The conditions for the exercise of the doctrine are:

1. The contract must be classified as an 'administrative contract'. The doctrine does not apply if the contract, although placed by the administration, is subject to the *ordre judiciaire* (see above, pp. 29 and 30).
2. The event giving rise to the increase in the costs of providing the service must have been unforeseeable and external to the parties.
3. There must have been a *bouleversement* (total upset) of the economy of the contract. This entails first, that the increase in cost must be beyond the limits which the parties could have foreseen at the time of the contract, and second, that the contractor/concessionary must be suffering a real loss in continuing to perform the contract/concession and not just a loss of the profit which he had hoped to make.

The consequences of *imprévision* are that the contractor/concessionary must continue to perform his contract but he is compensated by the administration for that part of the increase in costs which is due to the unforeseeable event. Either the parties, as in the Bordeaux gas case, may be invited to renegotiate the contract or the amount may be settled by the court. Although the contract/concession has come to an end an award can still be made since this is the means by which the contractor/concessionary is encouraged to continue to provide the service.

Even if the contract contains a clause providing for a revision in price for increases in labour and material costs, the doctrine of *imprévision* may still apply if the factors causing the increase in costs, which has resulted in the *bouleversement* in the economy of the contract, could not have been foreseen and have not been corrected by the application of the price revision clause (CE 11 June 1947 *Ministre de la guerre* v. *Nadaud Rec.* 255 and 2 February 1951 Secrétaire d'Etat à la défense, Rec. 67). In the latter case it was the deliberate lack of productivity of the labour which was the factor responsible.

Force majeure et cause étrangère

The concepts of *force majeure* and *cause étrangère* were discussed earlier (see above, pp. 191 and 199). It is sufficient here to recall briefly the characteristics of each and then to note their effects.

Force majeure   The characteristics of an event of *force majeure* are that it must:

* have been unforeseeable at the time of contract to any well-advised person placed under the same circumstances as the debtor. Although this test is objective there have been cases in which the subjective knowledge of the party seeking to invoke *force majeure* as to, e.g. local conditions, has been held to exclude the remedy.

Again foreseeability is given a wide meaning as when the derailment of a train due to sabotage by workers during a strike was held to be foreseeable (Cass. civ. 30 June 1953 JCP 1953 II 7764);

- be irresistible, i.e. the execution of the contract must have become impossible for anyone, not just more difficult or more expensive;
- be external to the debtor so that a strike affecting only the vendor's factory would generally be held not to constitute *force majeure*.

It follows that if the event is one which could have been foreseen by the debtor at the time of the contract, then even though it subsequently prevents the debtor from carrying out the contract it will not count as *force majeure*. As has been stated by the *Cour de cassation*:

> Whereas if the irresistibility of an event is in itself alone constitutive of *force majeure* when its prediction does not permit one to avoid its effects, this is not so when the debtor may normally foresee such an event at the time of entering into the contract (Cass. civ. 1re 7 March 1966 JCP 1966 II 14878).

Alongside irresistibility is also the notion of being unsurmountable; if there is a way of avoiding the difficulty then it must be followed, e.g. by chartering an aircraft to avoid the consequences of a strike affecting shipping (Cass. com. 12 Nov. 1969 JCP 1971 II 16791).

The effects of *force majeure* are to exonerate the debtor totally from the performance of his contractual obligations. The party invoking *force majeure* will then, unless there are specific provisions in the contract regulating the matter, apply to the court for the contract to be annulled (Art. 1184 of the *Code Civil*). The court then has a discretion depending on the facts to suspend performance if the event is only likely to be temporary, annul the contract retroactively or terminate it. If the contract is annulled the parties must return any benefits received. If the contract is terminated (*résiliation*) then each party retains the benefits already received.

Cause étrangère This term covers *force majeure* but in addition the act of a third party or an act of the creditor himself.

However, in cases of contract the following situations need to be distinguished if it is an act of a third party or the creditor:

1. An act of the third party (or parties). The debtor is entirely discharged of liability if the act was unforeseeable and irresistible. In any other case the debtor is liable but may have a right against the third party.
2. An act of the creditor – unforeseeable and irresistible. The debtor is entirely discharged of liability.
3. An act of the creditor not unforeseeable and irresistible. If the act constitutes a fault then the debtor will be relieved wholly or partially of his responsibility depending on the degree of fault of the creditor. If the act does not constitute a fault then the debtor is wholly liable.

The requirement that the act of the third party should be both unforeseeable and irresistible has limited significantly the cases in which the debtor can establish the defence of *cause étrangère*. So SNCF has been held on a number of occasions to be responsible for acts such as injury to a traveller caused by the fall of third party's luggage from the rack and even from an act of sabotage when a warning had been sent in advance. One case in which SNCF was exonerated was where entirely unforeseeably a person suddenly ran on to the track out in the open countryside causing the driver to brake sharply, so injuring a passenger.

The requirements for establishing *force majeure* or *cause étrangère* according to the *droit commun* are therefore extremely strict. As a result contracts frequently contain clauses defining *force majeure* in terms which extend the acts to be considered as such. In principle such clauses are valid but they are likely to be construed strictly by the courts and therefore need careful drafting.

COMPARISON WITH ENGLISH LAW

Clearly many of the principles which apply to frustration apply equally to *force majeure*. Both doctrines are restrictive in their scope. The event must not have been self-induced and it must have made the contract impossible of performance, not merely more onerous or more expensive. However there is one major difference: that of foreseeability. As illustrated above it is an essential requirement of *force majeure* that the event was unforeseeable. But this is not so in frustration. There the question is put round the other way. A contract is not frustrated if the event either was actually foreseen, or it must have been highly probable that it would occur, so it can be assumed that the parties contracted with the risk of that particular event in mind both in its occurrence and in its scope.[59]

In the English case of *W.J. Tatem Ltd* v. *Gamboa* a ship was chartered during the Spanish civil war for the evacuation of civilians from North Spain for 30 days from 1 July. She was seized by the nationalists on 14 July and not returned until 11 September and hire was sought to be recovered for the whole period. It was held that the contract was frustrated.

It is considered that, on the facts relating to the war and the nationalist naval power as known at the time, the ship's seizure must have been foreseeable at the date of contract, although in the case it was said that it was not foreseeable for such a long period. It also seems that the decision would have been the same even if the risk had been foreseen on the grounds that the basis of the contract had come to an end on the seizure.[60] However that may be, it seems clear that a French court on similar facts would not have held that the act of seizure was one of *force majeure* since it was *prévisible* by anyone *avisé*.

GERMAN LAW

SPECIFIC PERFORMANCE

In theory the primary remedy in German law for the creditor is to have the obligation performed by the debtor. So s.241 of the *BGB* provides that: 'The effect of an obligation is that the creditor is entitled to claim performance from the debtor. The performance may consist in forbearance.'

The same rule has already been met (see above, p. 160) in relation to contracts for works where under Art. 633(2) of the *BGB* the employer is entitled to demand the removal of defective work.

If of course performance has become impossible, as when specific goods have been destroyed, then the only remedy can be in damages.

German law also provides in detail specific remedies if the debtor fails to perform the obligation after having been ordered by the court to do so. These are set out in ss.883–90 of the Code of Civil Procedure. Movables can be taken away from the debtor by the court bailiff and handed over to the creditor while the bailiff can eject the debtor from immovables and put the creditor into possession.

When it is a matter of performing some act then a distinction is drawn between an act which can be performed by anyone skilled in the trade in question (*vertretbar*) and one which can only be performed by the debtor himself (*unvertretbar*).

In the former case the court can authorize the creditor to have the act performed by another at the debtor's expense and if so requested by the creditor order the debtor to pay a sum in advance to cover the costs with the right of the creditor to demand an additional payment if the actual costs exceed those advanced.

If, however, the act is *unvertretbar*, then there is a further distinction made between an act the performance of which depends 'exclusively on the will of the debtor' and one which does not do so. With an act dependent wholly on the will of the debtor, then in the event of his refusal he can be compelled by fines, which are in principle unlimited, or by imprisonment up to six months. The fines, unlike those levied against the debtor under the French remedy of *astreinte* (see above, pp. 331 and 332), go to the Treasury, not the creditor.

With an act not wholly dependent on the will of the debtor, i.e. one which requires the cooperation of others over whom the debtor does not exercise control or which depends on artistic inspiration, then there is no such remedy. Nor is the remedy of compulsion applicable to work to be performed under a contract of employment (Art. 888 of the Code of Civil Procedure). Here the only remedy would be in damages.

However despite these detailed and extensive provisions both of the *BGB* and the Code of Civil Procedure (ZPO), they are little used in practice especially in commercial matters where damages are generally considered by the creditor to be a more effective remedy. There is nevertheless, as a kind of half-way house between damages and specific performance, the right for the creditor to require the debtor to make what amounts to substitute performance in order to restore the situation to what it would have been had the debtor not defaulted (ss. 249 and 250, *BGB*). As Zweigert and Kotz point out, these provisions were of particular value in the early postwar period when money was valueless. For example, in order to restore the position, the debtor in default by not supplying specific goods was ordered to supply similar goods of an equivalent value.[61] Even now one can imagine particular circumstances where the creditor could prefer the immediate delivery of substitute goods to monetary compensation.

RESCISSION (*RÜCKTRITT*)

Distinction between rescission and refusing performance

German law draws an important distinction between the remedy of rescission (*Rücktritt*) and that of refusing to accept further performance of the contract (*Ablehnung der Leistung*).

The exercise of the right of *Rücktritt* under German law is an alternative to the claim of damages for non-performance of the contract so that the exercise of the right cannot generally be coupled with the right to claim such damages. For example Art. 325 of the *BGB* provides that

> If the performance due from one party under a mutual contract becomes impossible because of a circumstance for which he is responsible the other party may demand compensation for non performance *or withdraw from the contract ('von dem Vertrage zurücktreten')* which is referred to later in Art. 325 as 'Rücktrittsrecht'.

By contrast Art. 286 of the *BGB*, referring to delay in performance, provides in s.1 that the debtor must compensate the creditor for the delay and in s.2 that 'if the creditor does not desire performance because of the (debtor's) default, he may, *by refusing performance demand compensation* for the non-performance ('*unter Ablehnung der Leistung Schadensersatz wegen Nichterfüllung verlangen*').

It follows that since certainly the claim for compensatory damages for non-performance and possibly the moratory damages for delay, cannot be claimed in conjunction with *Rücktritt*, the remedy in practice is seldom exercised. The debtor in case of delay will act under Art. 326 of the *BGB* or Arts. 635 and 636 in the case of a contract for works, give the supplier/contractor a time in which to perform and after that time claim damages for non-performance; future performance of the contract is then barred. The debtor will also in these cases be entitled to moratory damages and damages for breach of any secondary obligations of the debtor or for positive breach of contract. For the requirements as to the giving of notice in order to put the debtor into default (*Mahnung*) and to exercise the power to terminate or claim damages for non-performance, see above, pp. 217–218.

The consequences of termination

The consequences of the exercise of *Rücktritt* are that the contract is brought to an end and the parties can claim back their own performance, e.g. return of goods delivered or of payments already made. As has been referred to earlier (see above, pp. 216 and 217 in relation to contracts for constructional works) this is often quite impractical and the courts prefer to act on the basis of termination which applies only to the future.

Conditions for the exercise of termination or a refusal to accept performance

In contrast to French law there is no requirement under German law for the creditor to obtain a court judgement in order to terminate a contract. However the debtor is protected to some degree by the requirements under German law for the giving of notice first in order to put the debtor into default and second before the creditor can exercise either the right to rescind or refuse to accept performance. For the rules on these see above, pp. 215–218.

Generally the debtor must have been at fault, although if the issue of fault is disputed the burden is on the debtor to prove that he was not at fault (Art. 282, *BGB*). The debtor is however liable without proof of fault if the contract is for the supply of generic goods (see above, p. 206).

There is a further exception of the fault rule in works contracts. If the works are defective the employer may give the contractor notice with a declaration that if the defect is not removed within a specified period he may terminate the contract (*Wandlung*) (Art. 634(1), *BGB*).

THE *EXCEPTIO* IN GERMAN LAW

It will be recalled that the *exceptio non adimpleti contractus* in French law is not based on any article of the *Code Civil*. In German law however there is a statutory basis in Art. 320 of the *BGB*:

1. Whoever is bound by a mutual contract may refuse to perform his part until the other party has performed his part, unless the former party is bound to perform his part first.
2. If one side has performed in part, the counter-performance may not be refused to the extent that the refusal would be in the circumstances contrary to good faith, especially in view of the disproportionate triviality of the remaining part.

In comparison with the five requirements which were listed as being necessary in French law for the debtor to be able to exercise the defence of the *exceptio* (see above, pp. 324–325), German law provides:

1. Interdependence of obligations. The German rule is stricter than that of French law. The obligation which the debtor claims the right not to perform must be related synallagmatically with that which has not been performed by the creditor. The performance of one must be in exchange for the other.
2. The obligations must be due at the same time. The German rule is the same as that of French law. If the debtor is required under the terms of the contract to perform first then he cannot set up the *exceptio* against the creditor.

339

3. The failure is only partial. The German rule here in para. 2, Art. 320, *BGB* is that the parties must exercise good faith. So to refuse to pay for building work which was subject to a slight defect, the cost of curing which was minute in relation to the contract price, would not be in accordance with good faith although the client would be entitled to delay payment of the cost of remedying the defect and to withhold the issue of the *Abnahme* until it had been remedied (*BGHZ* 54,249).
4. It is possible in individually negotiated contracts to provide that Art. 320 *BGB* is modified so that the failure by one party to fulfill his obligations does not entitle the other to withhold his own performance. However, in standard form contracts with consumers this right is now forbidden under para. 11 2(a) of the *AGBG*. As regards contracts between businessmen, para.11 2(a) does not apply directly but may be applied by the courts if they consider the conduct of the businessman imposing the standard form to be contrary to good faith under Art. 9 of the *AGBG* – see Wolf/Horn/Ludacher AGB-Gesetz Kommentar 2nd ed. Beck München 1989 pp. 926 and 927. The right is not included in the Standard Conditions of Sale drafted by Friederich Graf von Westphalen and included in Dannemann p. 119 with English translation.

Right of retention

The strictness of the German rule as to the two obligations being connected synallagmatically is to a degree mitigated by the provisions of Art. 273(1) of the *BGB* relating to retention. According to that Article, where the debtor has a claim which is due against the creditor arising out of the same legal relationship, he may, unless a contrary intention appears in his obligation, refuse performance until what is due to him is effected by the creditor. Although not expressly stated in Art. 273 this right, like the *exceptio*, must be exercised in good faith.

The right of retention (*Zurückbehaltungsrecht*) is wider that the *exceptio* since it is only necessary for the right to arise out of the 'same legal relationship' (*demselben rechtlichen Verhältnis*). There must be a *Konnexität* but this can exist even if there are two different contracts provided that they have a sufficient business connection (BGH 54,250).[62] However, unlike the *exceptio*,the debtor has to prove his entire claim and not as with the *exceptio* assert the conditions for its applicability and the failure of the creditor, leaving it to him to prove his entitlement.

THE CLAIM FOR DAMAGES

The circumstances in which an action in damages can be brought have already been discussed (see above, pp. 211 and 229).

Summarizing these in principle the German law of damages distinguishes between:

- impossibility of performance,
- delay in performance, and
- positive breach of contract.

Assuming that the impossibility arises after the commencement of the contract then the question to be determined is who is responsible for the default. If it is the debtor who is at fault then he is liable to pay damages (Art. 280 *BGB* and Art. 325 *BGB* for reciprocal contracts). If it is the creditor then the debtor is under no liability and indeed may even under a reciprocal contract have a claim in respect of his counter-performance after deduction of what he has saved (Art. 324 *BGB*). If neither are at fault then no liability arises (Art. 323 *BGB*).

If it is a question of delay then provided that the debtor has been put in default or the contract is a *Fixegeschäft* (see above, p. 218), and the delay is not due to a circumstance for which he is not responsible, then the creditor can claim damages for delay (Arts. 284, 285 and 286 *BGB*). The creditor may couple a claim for delay with one for performance or, if the period of the delay is such that the creditor is no longer interested in performance, then he may claim damages both for the delay and for the non-performance (Art. 326 *BGB*).

Where there is no delay, but the performance is rendered defectively, then the creditor may have a claim for positive breach of contract which is not governed by any article of the *BGB* – see above pp. 162 and 213.

This section will therefore deal only with the provisions in German law which relate to the extent of the damages which the creditor is entitled to recover assuming that, under the circumstances and rules referred to above, he has an entitlement to claim. The first issue that then arises is whether or not the damages claimed are too remote.

Remoteness

We have already seen that in principle both English law and French law use the test of 'foreseeability' at the time of entering into contract as the primary test for determining this question. True English law now formulates the test by the use of such expressions as 'could have been contemplated' rather than the expression 'foreseeability' and French law does not apply it in cases of *dol* but the guiding principle in both systems is the same.

German law, however, is very different and does not use the test of foreseeability. Its starting point is Art. 286 of the *BGB* under which the debtor is required to compensate the creditor for any damage resulting from his default.

Obviously a literal application of this provision would lead to ridiculous results. One theoretical example given is that of a taxi driver required to come at a particular time to take the traveller to the station. He is late so that the traveller misses the train. He takes the next one which has an accident as a result of which he is injured. In hospital his wallet is stolen. Is the taxi driver to be liable for all the damages which the traveller has suffered?

The answer must be clearly not and German law applies generally the test of 'adequacy of causation'. According to this theory damage may only be recovered if it arose from an act which in the ordinary course of events objectively and significantly increased the probability of the damage occurring. This assessment is to be made on the basis of that which would have been made at the time the damage occurred by an expert observer, based on a knowledge of all the relevant circumstances including the particular knowledge of the debtor.

In the above example there would be no causal link between the taxi driver and the accident and the loss of the wallet. But there could have been such a link between his late arrival and the fact that missing the train led the traveller to fail to keep an important appointment which in turn caused him to suffer a loss, especially if the traveller had made it clear to the taxi driver how important it was that he caught the train. However it is not thought that he would have had to tell the driver the particular purpose he had in mind or the loss he would suffer.

One may compare this example with the French case where the railway company was held not liable to compensate a businessman for the loss of profit he suffered because the late arrival of his train caused him to fail to conclude a profitable deal because at the time of entering into the contract the company did not know the purpose of the businessman's journey and so could not have foreseen the particular risks involved.[63]

In German law, provided there is an adequate causal link between the type of loss which will be suffered, e.g. loss of profit, and delay, then it would seem that the actual loss of profit suffered is recoverable. So the *Victoria Laundries* v. *Newman* case would have been decided differently under German law. Since there was an adequate causal link between the delay in delivery of the boiler and the loss of income, then the whole loss including the excessive profits would have been recoverable and it would have made no difference that these were not foreseeable at the time of the contract.

Indeed it is to be noted on this last point that the assumed knowledge of the 'expert observer' is assessed under German law not at the time when the contract was made but at the time when the default occurred. It is a retrospective view which again increases the risk for the defendant.

However, recognizing that the 'adequacy of causation' rule may at times be inequitable the German courts will also apply the 'scope of the rule' theory in order to limit the cases in which damages can be recovered to those related to the scope and object of the contract. It has been commented that in the case of a delay in the supply of the goods it is the financial interests of the creditor which are to be protected, so that if he suffers a nervous breakdown from the delay, damages for that would not be recoverable. However, damages for mental distress have been allowed under English law for delay by a builder in completing work to a private house. Under German law – such damages could not be claimed in contract (Art. 253 *BGB*).

Assessment of damages

In contracts for the sale of goods there are two bases of assessment: the 'abstract' and the 'concrete'. The 'abstract' method is that normally followed in English law so that damages are assessed generally as the difference between the contract price for the goods and the market price at the time when the breach of contract was discoverable by the purchaser, unless the circumstances show that some other date should be chosen.

In German law the 'concrete' method is the general rule which takes into account the actual loss and expense suffered by the creditor. So if the creditor has resold the goods to a third party but is unable to complete the purchase due to the seller's delay, he can recover the difference between the price he would have paid the seller and the price he would have obtained on the resale. If alternatively he effects a cover purchase then he can claim the difference again between the price he would have had to pay under the delayed contract and the price he has actually had to pay.

An exception to the 'concrete' method is provided for under Art. 376 of the *HGB* according to which if a contract between merchants provides a fixed time for performance, and if the purchaser demands damages for failure by the seller to perform by that time, and the goods have a market price, then the damages are assessed as the difference between the contract price and the market price. This rule applies even if the purchaser could in fact have bought at a lesser price than the market price.

Time for assessment

Where the assessment is made on the 'abstract' basis then the time is that of default or the expiry of the *Nachfrist* and not as in French law at the time of judgement.

Differenztheorie

The general rule of the assessment of damages is that the creditor is entitled to be put in the same situation as would have existed had the debtor not defaulted. In a reciprocal contract in which either the debtor's performance has become impossible due to his default (Art. 325 *BGB*), or he has defaulted in performing on time after notice from the creditor (Art. 326 *BGB*), this means that the performance owed by both parties must be taken into account in settling the damages due from the debtor. According to the *Differenztheorie*, which is generally applied by the courts in these circumstances, this is achieved by releasing the creditor from his own performance and allowing him to recover the difference in value between the benefit he would have received from the debtor's performance and what it would have cost him to perform his own obligations.

ENGLISH LAW COMPARISON

The German law of damages is unnecessarily complicated in its requirements as to fault, the giving of warning notices, which is a particular trap for those from common law countries, the rule that rescission (*Rücktritt*) cannot be combined with an award for damages for non-performance and the three different types of breach, delay, impossibility of performance and positive breach of contract, each with their own rules.

As regards the assessment of damages the German rules will often lead to the same result in practice as those under English law and where this is not so, will generally tend to favour the creditor because of the absence of a requirement for foreseeability. All three systems have here faced the same problem: that of restricting the debtor's liability, and while differing in theory their outcomes in general are similar.

Penalties and liquidated damages

Both these are known in German law. The distinctions between them and the rules applicable to each have already been dealt with in Chapter 16 under pp. 232 and 233 and the subject will not therefore be dealt with further here.

Frustration

Two opposing principles existed in medieval law. First there was *pacta sunt servanda*, which by then had become the principle that contracts must be honoured, and that of *clausula rebus sic stantibus*: contracts are binding only so long as and to the extent that matters remain the same as they were at the time of the contract coming into force.

Both principles were developed by the canon lawyers, the second, which was implied as a condition of the contract, setting the limits within which the first was to be complied.

While the concept of the *clausula* flourished in the seventeenth century and the early part of the eighteenth century, it disappeared with the rise in importance of the 'classical' doctrine of contract. According to this, while the parties were free to enter into contracts or not, and as to the terms upon which they did so, once the contract had been concluded they were bound strictly by its terms.

However, at least in German law the concept's disappearance was only temporary, and its return under another name was due to the same circumstances of devastating economic disruption consequent upon the loss of each of the two World Wars. A similar situation had encouraged its use in the seventeenth century. The rigidity of nineteenth century contract doctrine was itself, at least in part, based upon the perceived greater degree of certainty with which trade could be conducted than had applied previously and on the concept to which Atiyah has referred of the contract being an instrument of private planning.[64]

This rigidity was reflected in the drafting of the *BGB* which contained only provisions covering the impossibility of the performance of the contract.

As regards delay in performance there is only the one brief article in the *BGB*, 285, which states that the debtor is not in default if the performance does not take place because of a circumstance for which he is not responsible. The proof of non-responsibility rests on the debtor and it must be shown that the performance was objectively impossible. No definition of *force majeure* as such is given in the *BGB* but one based on court decisions has been suggested as follows: '*force majeure* is an extraordinary event which could not be foreseen, arises out of the ambit of the affected party, could not be prevented by using the greatest care possible and cannot be remedied by using the means at the disposal of the business'. The highly restrictive nature of the definition is obvious and the defence only rarely appears to have been successful other than in cases where performance was prevented by war (Jurgen Einmahl, Dr Axel Epe and Manfred Finken in Kurkela ed. *Comparative Report on force majeure in Western Europe*, Union of the Finnish Lawyers Publishing Company Ltd, Helsinki 1982).

The draftsmen of the *BGB* rejected specifically the inclusion of any provision for the doctrine of *clausula rebus sic stantibus*. However, events were to destroy the confident optimism of the nineteenth century and compel the German courts to handle an unprecedented number of cases arising out of the economic collapse following World War I, in particular those concerning the revalorization of debts.

In the beginning the courts had been hostile to the termination or revision of contracts due to changed economic circumstances. However, by 1921 the Reichsgericht was prepared openly to acknowledge that in bilateral contracts the use of the *clausula rebus sic stantibus* doctrine was justified by their reciprocal nature since

> in such a contract it must be assumed that the parties entering into such a contract intended to enter into a fair contract of exchange. . . . It is true that in general each party must look after his own interests and that the contract remains effective even though one or both of the parties are mistaken in relation to past or future events. But the case is otherwise if the events so change values, especially the value of money, that the obligee would receive for his performance a counterperformance that no longer comes anywhere near to containing the equivalent contemplated by the contract. The obligor is in breach of the requirement of good faith if he insists on performance under such circumstances.[65]

Finally, in the famous decision of 28 November 1923 the Reichsgericht decided that the revalorization of debts was permissible even though it was contrary to the principle of the then currency legislation that 'mark equals mark'. The grounds given were that

> the principal provision of Art. 242 of the *BGB* (performance is required in accordance with good faith) which rules all legal relationships must be given precedence because at the time the currency legislation was passed the possibility that the currency inflation would cause such legislation to conflict with that principle was not taken into consideration.[66]

In conjunction with the principle of good faith the courts have also utilized the doctrine of *Geschäftsgrundlage* (contractual basis) developed by Professor Oertmann in 1921 to justify the revision or termination of the contract. According to this doctrine the 'contractual basis' of the contract is the common assumption made by the parties as to the circumstances which form the basis of their contractual intentions. Combining the two concepts, the decisions of the courts have established the general principle that if these circumstances change in an unexpected manner, and the change affects the value relationship between the respective performances required of the parties to the contract to such an extent that it would be contrary to good faith to hold the parties to their original bargain, then the contract can be revised. However, application of the doctrine requires that performance on the original contract terms would be to go beyond what has been termed the *Opfergrenze*, the 'limit of sacrifice' which can be expected of a contractor in the circumstances of the particular case; see further Professor Hermann Korbion in *Selected Problems of Construction Law*, pp. 202 et seq.

An important proviso to the operation of the doctrine is that it does not apply where the circumstances in question fall into the area of risk which in the transaction concerned belong to one of the parties (BGHZ 74,373). So the normal risks of the performance of the contract being disturbed fall upon each of the parties concerned according to their function. The risk of obtaining supplies for the purpose of carrying out a sales or works contract is therefore on the seller/contractor and that of the possibility to make use of the work or market the goods that of the purchaser (BGH NJW 72,1702; BGH NJW 74,1747). The purchaser of development land runs the risk of its suitability for building purposes (BGHZ 74,374). This position will also be the case where one party has himself assumed the risk of a disruptive event, e.g. assumption by the seller of the planning risk (BGHZ 76,25).

Unlike English law where the consequences of the contract being held to be frustrated are that it is brought to an end, German courts have arrogated to themselves wide powers as to the remedy which they will apply, if they decide that there has been a gross disturbance of the equilibrium of the contract which justifies relief. The contract may be terminated but is more likely, especially if it is a change of economic circumstances, to be revised on terms which the court considers are equitable to both parties, taking into account their respective obligations.

There is no equivalent in German law to the Law Reform (Frustrated Contracts) Act, but there is no need for one, given the much wider and more flexible revising powers of the German courts in comparison with the limited powers in this respect of the English courts.

COMPARATIVE CONCLUSIONS

All three legal systems have recognized the existence of the problem but their solutions differ widely. French civil law has consistently denied any doctrine of *imprévision* or *clausula rebus sic stantibus*. English law within very strict limits has allowed for a contract to be frustrated when the changed circumstances would make its performance radically different from that which was undertaken. German law has gone furthest in allowing for the revision of contracts when, because of the change in circumstances, it would be contrary to good faith to require performance according to their original terms, taking into account the obligations which the parties have assumed.

There is no doubt that the attitude of the German courts has been strongly influenced by the enormous economic upheavals after the end of the two World Wars. Equally, as Zweigert and Kotz have suggested, English law has reacted to the perceived need of commerce, especially in matters of charter-parties, that parties should fulfil their bargains.[67] Just why the French civil courts have rejected the doctrine of *imprévision* remains unclear. It has been suggested that they have preferred the moral injustice which may be inflicted on one of the parties to economic instability which may lead to inflation, and certainly the control of indexation (price rise and fall) clauses in French contracts have been the subject of much greater control in France than in England.[68]

In these circumstances it is not surprising that the parties themselves have sought to provide in their long-term contracts, in addition to price revision, for adjustment in the event of serious economic dislocation ('hardship' clauses), and that this tendency seems to be increasing. Legislators, courts and commentators may believe that for the sake of assisting with achieving economic stability businessmen should take the greatest risks, associated especially in international contracts with inflation, exchange fluctuations and political change. However those actually involved in long-term contracts have as one of their primary objectives the avoidance or at least the minimizing of risk. In this context the inclusion of a 'hardship' clause, drafted in such a way as to be effective under the applicable law, should be a necessary provision in any such contract as supplementing the clauses on price revision and *force majeure*.[69]

NOTES

1. See Treitel *Contract*, pp. 906 and 907.
2. *Wolverhampton Corporation* v. *Emmons* [1901] 1 QB 515.
3. *Wickman Ltd* v. *Schular AG* [1974] AC 235.
4. *Reardon Smith Lines* v. *Hansen Tangen* [1976] 1 WLR 989.
5. *Financial Times Law Report* 17 October 1990 and see also report in the *Buyer Monitor Press*, 1991, Issue 3.
6. Cass. civ. 28 October 1954 JCP 1955.8765 quoted Mazeaud and Chabas s.623 at p.737.
7. In speaking of 'consequential damages' businessmen are normally referring to economic loss or loss of profits which result from delay in delivery or from goods or work being defective. However, in legal terminology if losses of that type are the direct and natural result of the breach then they are direct and not 'consequential'. Damages are only classified as consequential if they are due to some special circumstance or some supervening event. *Millar's Machinery Co. Ltd* v. *David Way and Son* (1934) quoted with approval in *Saint Line Ltd* v. *Richardson Westgarth* [1940] 2 KB 99 and *Croudace Construction Ltd* v. *Cawoods Concrete Products Ltd.* (1978) 8 BLR 20.
8. [1949] 2 KB 528 at 539. So stated by Cheshire, p. 599.
9. [1969] 1 AC 350.
10. Reported in *The Buyer* for November 1992, Vol.14, No.11.
11. *Monarch SS Co.* v. *A/B Karlshamns Oliefabriker* [1949] AC 196.
12. *Clydebank Engineering Co.* v. *Don Jose Ramos y Castaneda* [1905] AC 6 where warships were delivered late to the Spanish Navy, but had they in fact been delivered on time would almost certainly have been sunk by the Americans. The mere fact of the late delivery was sufficient to justify the application of the liquidated damages clause.
13. *Paradine* v. *Jane* (1647) Aleyn at p. 27.
14. (1863) 3 B & S 826.
15. Extract from his judgement in *Davis Contractors* v. *Fareham UDC* [1956] AC at 728, 729.
16. This is clear from the various cases which arose from the closing of the Suez canal. Although the journey time via the Cape was significantly greater this was held not to amount to frustration even if the use of the Suez canal was referred to in the contract. The view was taken that the use of the canal was not a fundamental term of the contract which would justify frustration. *Palmco Shipping Corporation* v. *Continental Ore Corp.*[1970] 2 Lloyds Report 21.
17. This is based on the reasoning of the Court of Appeal in the *Super Servant Two* [1990] 1 Lloyds Report 1. The contract for the transport of the plaintiff's drilling rig provided that it was to be performed by either the Super Servant One or the Super Servant Two which were self-propelling barges specially designed for this purpose. The defendants allocated Super Servant Two to the performance of the contract but before it could be performed the barge sank without the defendant's negligence. At that time the defendants had already entered into other contracts for the use of the Super Servant One which precluded its use for the performance of the plaintiff's contract. The defendants claimed that the contract was frustrated but this claim was not upheld by the Court of Appeal as the defendants had at least in theory a choice of means by which the contract could be carried out and had taken on the risk of the number of contracts into which they had entered. Frustration would only have applied it was suggested if the contract had provided for it to be performed only by Super Servant Two.

The reasoning appears harsh and has been criticized as unrealistic and difficult to justify – see Treitel, pp. 805 and 806.

18. *Fibrosa Spolka Akcyjna* v. *Fairbairn Lawson Combe Barbour Ltd* [1943] AC 32. An advance payment having been made by a Polish company to an English supplier for the manufacture of machinery, the contract was frustrated by the outbreak of war. It was held that the Polish firm could recover the advance payment as there had been a total failure of consideration, although the English supplier had in fact expended the money on preliminary work.

19. *Appleby* v. *Myers* (1867) LR 2 CP 651.

20. See the commentary by Atiyah, pp. 333 to 341.

21. Atiyah, p. 341.

22. Cass. civ. 17 January 1984 JCP 84, IV, 93 and see Schmidt-Szalewski for the report of the judgement.

23. Paris, 8 November 1973 D.1975,401 quoted Starck s.1352 at p. 474.

24. This was established as long ago as 1891 in a famous decision of the *Cour de cassation* Cass. Civ. 14 April 1891 DP 91, 1, 329 and reported in *Les grands arrêts de la jurisprudence civile* p. 445. It has been repeatedly confirmed e.g. Cass. Civ. 2 June 1982 Bull. Civ. I, no. 205. The concept that Art. 1184 applies equally to the case in which the non-performance by the debtor is due to *cause étrangère,* as it does to the case in which it is due his default, has been criticized by part of the doctrine on the grounds that rescission (*résolution*) ought only to be applied where the debtor is responsible for the non-performance – see Mazeaud and Chabas s. 1097 and Starck s.1595.

    However, Weill and Terré s.486 consider that the jurisprudence is justified. It does not contradict the text of paragraph 1 of Art. 1184 which makes no reference to the need for the debtor to be in default. Further, the requirement under Art. 1184 for the intervention of the court allows the court to take into account all the circumstances in deciding upon whether the contract should be rescinded or not. This could, as Weill and Terré have noted, extend to the question as to whether or not there had indeed been an act of *force majeure* or *cas fortuit.*

25. Paris, 1 December 1956 D.1957 somm.62 quoted with approval Starck s.1603 at p. 555.

26. For the history of the development of the remedy of *résolution* see Weill and Terré, pp. 499 and 500; Ghestin *Les Effets du Contrat* s.386 p. 397 and Malaurie and Aynes *Les Obligations* s.738 p. 396.

27. Cass.com. 23 March 1971 B.IV, No.89; sale of crayfish tails which were second-rate; price reduced by a half.

28. Cass. civ. 3 November 1983 B.I. No. 252.

29. Cass. civ. 6 June 1984 Bull. civ. III, No. 111.

30. Cases of urgency normally only arise in commercial contracts especially for the purchase of perishable goods.

31. When the purchaser of a car which was not delivered on the contractual date terminated the contract without there being any particular requirement of urgency in the matter he was liable to the seller. Cass. com. 24 June 1980 B.IV, No. 273.

32. Soc. 10 April 1959 D. 1960–61 quoted Starck s.1648.

33. Cass. civ. 26 November 1951 G.P.52.I.72. The inconsistency between the position of the landlord and that of the tenant is explained by the obligation of the tenant to pay rent being fundamental to a lease while that of the landlord to maintain the premises in good repair is only incidental unless it deprives the tenant of the ability to occupy the premises.

34. See for example *Supermarl Ltd* v. *Federated Homes Ltd* 9 CLR at p. 28, and *Lubenham Fidelities Investment Co.* v. *South Pembrokeshire District Council and Wigley Fox Partnership* 6 CLR at p. 110 where it was stated by the Court of Appeal in a case involving defective payment on an architect's certificate and in which it was argued that there was a general rule that a contractor in such circumstances was entitled to suspend work 'we are quite satisfied that there was no legal basis on which the suspension of work could be justified in this case'.

35. Malaurie and Aynes *Les Obligations* p. 394 referring to Cass.co, 15 January 1973 B.IV, No.24, a case in which it was decided that, on a breach by the concessionaire of his obligations the concedant although entitled as a result of the breach to sell itself in the territory granted by it exclusively to the concessionaire until the concessionaire had paid the sums due by him, and to apply for this purpose the *exceptio* as a defence, was not entitled to appoint another exclusive agent without having first obtained through the court termination of the contract for the concession.

36. Pothier *Obligations* ss 166 f. quoted at length in Malaurie and Aynes *Les Obligations,* p. 454.

37. Cass. Civ. 18 March 1986 Bull. Civ. I, No. 75.

38. At p. 454, note 106.
39. At page 494, s.1412, Cass. Civ. 29 January 1985 JCP 85 IV.139.
40. Cass. Com. 14 Dec.1981.Bull Civ. IV, 34.
41. Cass. Civ. 27 June 1984, unpublished but quoted in Schmidt-Szalewski, p. 591.
42. Cass. Civ. 7 July 1924 D.1927,I,119. Owner of goods lost in transit only able to recover value declared at the time of contract for customs purposes 475 FF and not the value claimed of 16,685 FF which was alleged to be the true value.
43. Cass. Civ. 27 January 1987 unreported quoted in Schmidt-Szalewski at p. 591.
44. It seems that a penalty clause for delay in execution will not survive the rescission of the contract and the creditor can only claim for damages according to the general law – Cass. req 8 July 1873 D.1874,1,56 and *Chambre des Requetes* 29 June 1925 D.H.1925, p. 594. However, if the penalty clause relates to the non-execution of the contract then it would appear that it survives the rescission and remains applicable, Ghestin, *Les Effets du contrat* s.469, p. 466.
45. Cass. civ. 4 February 1969 JCP 1969 II 6030.
46. Cass. civ. 24 July 1978 Bull. civ.I,no.280.
47. Cass.com. 13 March 1979 Gaz.Pal.1979 2,243.
48. *Vocabulaire Juridique*, Cornu University Press of France.
49. 'The provisional Astreinte, is a means of constraint entirely distinct from damages, and which is only a means of overcoming the resistance to the execution of the judgement, and does not have as its purpose to compensate for the damages for delay and is usually liquidated on the basis of the seriousness of the default of the debtor and of the extent of his resources' D.1959.537.

    The text of the Law of 5 July 1972 as modified by the Law of 9 July 1975 is to be found under Art. 501 in the New Code of civil procedure Litec Codes Paris 1993, at p. 1948.
50. Starck s.2250 p. 811.
51. Soc. 24 February 1960 Bull. civ. IV, No.21. p. 166.
52. Cass. civ. 9 March 1977. Bull. civ.I, 98 and Cass. Civ. 19 October 1976 Bull. Civ. III, 269.
53. Starck, vol. 3, *Régime général* s.502–2.
54. Cass. civ. 6 March 1876 set out with commentary in *Les grands arrets de la jurisprudence civile* at p. 405.
55. Cass. com. 18 December 1979 B.IV no. 339.
56. [1978] 1 WLR 137.
57. Under Art. 1134 of the *Code Civil* if a contract is for an indefinite period then it may be terminated by either party unilaterally provided that such termination is not an abuse of law. It would be an abuse if a concession were terminated with only a few days' notice before the presentation by the concessionaire of the summer fashion collection.
58. C.E. 30 March 1916 – see for report and commentary *Les Grands arrets administratifs*, Sirey, Paris p. 182.
59. See the views expressed by Treitel at p. 800.
60. [1939] 1 KB 132.
61. At p. 160.
62. In contracts between merchants s.369 (1) *HGB* creates what is known as a *commercial lien in personam (kaufmannisches Zurückbehaltungsrecht)*. This allows a merchant to retain possession of goods and commercial documents belonging to another merchant because of due claims which he has against him, 'arising out of mutual commercial contracts'. There is not therefore the same requirement of *Konnexitat* as under s.320 of the *BGB*.
63. Cass. civ. 23.12.1913 D.1915.1.35, *Source Book* p. 494 and Malaurie and Aynes *Les Obligations* p. 456, note 122.
64. Atiyah *The Rise and Fall of the Freedom of Contract*, pp. 420–421.
65. *Reichsgericht* 29 November 1921, 103 ERGZ 177 extract from the judgement translated in Von Mehren, pp. 1080 and 1081.
66. *Reichsgericht* 28 November 1923 107 ERGZ 78 reproduced in translation in Von Mehren, pp. 1084 – 1087.
67. At p. 227.
68. See Isabelle de Lamberterie's report in *Contract Law Today* at p. 222 et seq. By contrast, English law has never subjected price escalation clauses in sales and construction contracts to legal control (other than for wartime price controls).

69. See the study on *Les Clauses de Hardship* in *Droit des Contrats Internationaux*, Fontaine, Forum Européen de la Communication, Paris, 1989 and the conclusion on page 285 that 'The Hardship clause plays a crucial part in contracts of long duration in order to avoid the position that an inflexible application of the principle *pacta sunt servanda* does not result in intolerable consequences'.

Index